Linguistics at School

Linguistics is a subject that has remained largely confined to the academy, rather than being integrated into school curricula. This is unfortunate but not surprising as, although some teacher education programs include courses on linguistics, it is not comprehensively integrated into teacher education, so it is largely absent from the curriculum.

This volume brings together a team of leaders in the field of linguistics and education, to provide an overview of the current state of research and practice. It demonstrates changes which can be made to teaching, such as revising teachers' preparation, developing and implementing practical applications of linguistics in both primary and secondary classrooms, partnering linguists with classroom teachers, and working to improve state and national education standards. The contributors emphasize the importance of collaboration between professional linguists and educators in order to meet a common goal: to raise awareness of the workings of language.

The editors

KRISTIN DENHAM is Associate Professor of English and Linguistics at Western Washington University. Her work includes articles on theoretical syntax and linguistics in education and she is co-editor with Anne Lobeck of *Language in Schools: Integrating Linguistic Knowledge into K-12 Education* (2005). Denham and Lobeck are also co-authors of *Linguistics for Everyone: An Introduction* (2009).

ANNE LOBECK is Professor of English and Linguistics at Western Washington University. Her work includes articles on theoretical syntax and linguistics in education, and in addition to her two books with Kristin Denham she is author of *Ellipsis: Functional Heads, Licensing and Identification* (1995) and *Discovering Grammar: An Introduction to English Sentence Structure* (2000).

Linguistics at School

Language Awareness in Primary and Secondary Education

Edited by

Kristin Denham

and

Anne Lobeck

CAMBRIDGE
UNIVERSITY PRESS

CAMBRIDGE UNIVERSITY PRESS
Cambridge, New York, Melbourne, Madrid, Cape Town, Singapore,
São Paulo, Delhi, Dubai, Tokyo

Cambridge University Press
The Edinburgh Building, Cambridge CB2 8RU, UK

Published in the United States of America by Cambridge University Press, New York

www.cambridge.org
Information on this title: www.cambridge.org/9780521887014

© Cambridge University Press 2010

First published 2010

Printed in the United Kingdom at the University Press, Cambridge

A catalogue record for this publication is available from the British Library

ISBN 978-0-521-88701-4 Hardback

Contents

Notes on contributors   *page* viii
Foreword: The challenge for education
RAY JACKENDOFF   xiii

Introduction
KRISTIN DENHAM AND ANNE LOBECK   1

**Part I Linguistics from the top down: encouraging
institutional change**   7

Introduction to Part I
KRISTIN DENHAM AND ANNE LOBECK   9

1 Ideologies of language, art, and science
EDWIN BATTISTELLA   13

2 Bringing linguistics into the school curriculum: not one less
WAYNE O'NEIL   24

3 How linguistics has influenced schools in England
RICHARD HUDSON   35

4 Supporting the teaching of knowledge about language in
Scottish schools
GRAEME TROUSDALE   49

5 Envisioning linguistics in secondary education: an Australian
exemplar
JEAN MULDER   62

6 Linguistics and educational standards: the California experience
CAROL LORD AND SHARON KLEIN   76

7   Developing sociolinguistic curricula that help teachers meet standards
    JEFFREY REASER   91

8   Linguistic development in children's writing: changing classroom
    pedagogies
    DEBRA MYHILL   106

    **Part II   Linguistics from the bottom up: encouraging
             classroom change**   123

    Introduction to Part II
    KRISTIN DENHAM AND ANNE LOBECK   125

9   From cold shoulder to funded welcome: lessons from the
    trenches of dialectally diverse classrooms
    REBECCA S. WHEELER   129

10 Positioning linguists as learners in K-12 schools
    LONG PENG AND JEAN ANN   149

11 Fostering teacher change: effective professional development for
    sociolinguistic diversity
    JULIE SWEETLAND   161

12 On promoting linguistics literacy: bringing language science
    to the English classroom
    MAYA HONDA, WAYNE O'NEIL, AND DAVID PIPPIN   175

13 Linguistics in a primary school
    KRISTIN DENHAM   189

14 Educating linguists: how partner teaching enriches linguistics
    ANNE LOBECK   204

15 The Linguistic Olympiads: academic competitions in linguistics
    for secondary school students
    IVAN DERZHANSKI AND THOMAS PAYNE   213

    Part III   Vignettes: voices from the classroom   227

    Introduction to Part III
    KRISTIN DENHAM AND ANNE LOBECK   229

16 And you can all say *haboo*: enriching the standard language arts
    curriculum with linguistic analysis
    ANGELA ROH   234

17 Code switching: connecting written and spoken language patterns
    KARREN MAYER AND KIRSTIN NEW   240

18 A primary teacher's linguistic journey
    DEIDRE CARLSON   244

19 Why do VCE English Language?
    CAROLINE THOMAS AND SARA WAWER   251

20 Language lessons in an American middle school
    ATHENA McNULTY   257

21 The diary of Opal Whiteley: a literary and linguistic mystery
    DAVID PIPPIN   264

22 Using the Voices of North Carolina curriculum
    LEATHA FIELDS-CAREY AND SUZANNE SWEAT   272

23 A-level English Language teaching in London
    DAN CLAYTON   277

    References   282
    Index   303

Notes on contributors

JEAN ANN is an associate professor of Linguistics at the State University of New York, Oswego. Her research concerns the relationship between linguistics and K-12 teaching, L2 sound systems, TESOL in urban schools, and the structure and use of sign languages. She conducts professional development with ESL/bilingual teachers. Her recent publications include a book about Taiwan Sign Language handshapes and an article about urban education.

EDWIN BATTISTELLA is Professor of English and Writing at Southern Oregon University in Ashland, where he served as Dean of the School of Arts and Letters and as Interim Provost. His publications include four books: *Markedness: The Evaluative Superstructure of Language* (1990), *The Logic of Markedness* (1996), *Bad Language: Are Some Words Better Than Others?* (2005), and *Do You Make These Mistakes in English? The Story of Sherwin Cody's Famous Language School* (2008). Battistella's work has also appeared in the *Chronicle of Higher Education*, *Academe*, and the *Vocabula Review*, and he is currently the co-editor-in-chief of Wiley-Blackwell's *Language and Linguistic Compass*.

DEIDRE CARLSON taught in a public elementary school setting for eighteen years before becoming a private school teacher. She holds degrees in English and Education. She is currently working on the curriculum for Fairhaven Girls' School in Bellingham, Washington, and is excited about developing a strong linguistics program within that curriculum.

DAN CLAYTON teaches English Language A-level to 16–18-year-olds at St. Francis Xavier Sixth Form College in south London and is an A-level examiner. He runs a Language blog aimed at students and teachers of English Language (http://englishlangsfx.blogspot.com/) and has been involved in forging links between university linguists and A-level teachers with a series of conferences and workshops.

KRISTIN DENHAM is Associate Professor of Linguistics in the English Department at Western Washington University. Her current research focus is on the integration of linguistics into K-12 education. She and Anne Lobeck received a National Science Foundation grant for the integration of linguistics in education, and they are also co-editors of *Language in the Schools: Integrating Linguistic Knowledge into K-12 Teaching* (2005). They are co-authors of *Linguistics for Everyone* (2009), an introductory linguistics textbook, as well as other textbooks for teachers.

IVAN DERZHANSKI has been the principal person in charge of the extracurricular activities in linguistics for secondary school students in Bulgaria since 1998. He is one of the founders of the International Olympiad in Linguistics and a key member of its organizing committee, problem committee, and jury. He has authored over fifty linguistic problems.

LEATHA FIELDS-CAREY teaches English at Johnston County Middle College High School in Smithfield, North Carolina. She has taught for sixteen years with the Johnston County school system and is certified by the National Board for Professional Teaching Standards.

MAYA HONDA is an associate professor of Human Development at Wheelock College in Boston. Her work in linguistics education focuses on making linguistic inquiry conceptually accessible to all students. She is co-author with Wayne O'Neil of *Understanding First and Second Language Acquisition* (2004) and *Thinking Linguistically: A Scientific Approach to Language* (2008).

RICHARD HUDSON's interest in educational linguistics started in the 1960s while working with Michael Halliday and continued as a sideline through a career at University College London in descriptive and theoretical linguistics. He continues to build bridges between linguistics and schools, such as downloadable material on grammar for teachers at www.phon.ucl.ac.uk/home/dick/education.htm.

RAY JACKENDOFF is Seth Merrin Professor of Philosophy and Co-Director of the Center for Cognitive Studies at Tufts University. His primary research is on the semantics of human languages and its connections to the conceptual system and to linguistic expression. He was 2003 President of the Linguistic Society of America and also the 2003 recipient of the Jean Nicod Prize in Cognitive Philosophy. His books include *Foundations of Language* and *Language, Consciousness, Culture*.

SHARON KLEIN is a professor of Linguistics in the English Department and Linguistics/TESL Program at California State University, Northridge. She has worked and taught in several areas of educational linguistics, with a commitment to raising preparing teachers' awareness both of aspects of language itself and of the nature of linguistics as a critical field of inquiry.

ANNE LOBECK is Professor of English at Western Washington University. Her publications include *Discovering Grammar: An Introduction to English Sentence Structure* (2000), and as co-editor with Kristin Denham, of *Language in the Schools: Integrating Linguistic Knowledge into K-12 Teaching* (2005). Lobeck and Denham are also co-principal investigators on a National Science Foundation grant to improve linguistics education in elementary and secondary schools.

CAROL LORD has a joint appointment at California State University Long Beach as Associate Professor in the Department of Teacher Education and the Department of Linguistics. Her research interests include literacy development, language issues in content area assessment, grammaticalization, and African languages. A former public school teacher, she is currently investigating the efficacy of electronic books in after-school programs for struggling readers.

KARREN MAYER has worked twenty-six years as a kindergarten, 1st-, and 2nd-grade teacher, and currently serves as a communication skills specialist for Norfolk Public Schools, working with K-5 students. She also does ongoing staff development with teachers. She is currently working at Larchmont Elementary in Norfolk, Virginia. She received a bachelor's degree in Early Childhood Education and a master of science degree in Education, specializing in reading.

ATHENA McNULTY is an 8th-grade English teacher at Cascade Middle School in Sedro-Woolley, Washington. She has a BA in English, and an MA in Teaching, both from Western Washington University, where, as part of her BA degree, Athena took linguistics courses from Anne Lobeck. McNulty and Lobeck worked together as partner teachers at Cascade Middle School in 2007.

JEAN MULDER is a senior lecturer in the School of Languages and Linguistics at the University of Melbourne. Her research ranges over educational linguistics, language documentation, and grammatical and discourse analysis, covering a variety of languages including Australian English, Sm'algyax (Canada), Ganalbingu (Australia), siSwati (Swaziland), Cree (Canada), and the Philippine languages.

DEBRA MYHILL is Professor of Education at the University of Exeter, and Head of the School of Education. Her research interests focus principally on aspects of language and literacy teaching, including underachievement, equality issues, children's writing, and talk in the classroom. She is the author of *Better Writers* (2001), *Talking, Listening, Learning: Effective Talk in the Primary Classroom* (2006), and the *Handbook of Writing Development* (forthcoming).

KIRSTIN NEW has worked as a 1st- and 2nd-grade teacher and as a communication skills specialist for Norfolk Public Schools. She is currently working as a literacy teacher at Larchmont Elementary School in Norfolk, Virginia. She received a bachelor's degree in Early Childhood Education and a master of science degree in Education, specializing in reading.

WAYNE O'NEIL is Professor of Linguistics at MIT and an instructor in human development at Wheelock College, working on linguistics in the school curriculum and second-language acquisition. With Maya Honda, he is co-author of *Understanding First and Second Language Acquisition* (2004) and *Thinking Linguistically* (2007). O'Neil has long been connected with educational practice: at Oregon Curriculum Study Project (1962–1966), at Harvard University (1965–1973; 1977–1986), and at Wheelock College (1991–).

THOMAS PAYNE is a linguistics consultant with SIL International, and general co-chair of the North American Computational Linguistics Olympiad. He has done major linguistic fieldwork on North American, South American, and Austronesian languages. He is the founder of the US Linguistics Olympiad and an advisory board member of the International Linguistics Olympiad.

LONG PENG is an associate professor of Linguistics at the State University of New York, Oswego. His research focuses on phonology and education. The phenomena he has studied span languages from Kikuyu, Warao, and Taiwan Sign Language to Hong Kong and Singapore English, Nigerian English, and English of Spanish speakers. His work in education concentrates on linguistics in K-12 schools, urban education, and education research.

DAVID PIPPIN teaches English and boatbuilding at Billings Middle School in Seattle, Washington and has taught for eighteen years in both public and private schools at the elementary and middle school levels. It was a need to bring a constructivist pedagogy to the English curriculum that led him to the field nine years ago. Formal training came at the 2005 Linguistics Society of America's summer institute.

JEFFREY REASER is an assistant professor in the teacher education and linguistics programs at NC State University. His primary research involves developing, implementing, and measuring the effects of dialect awareness programs in the public schools. He is co-author of the Do You Speak American? and Voices of North Carolina curricula.

ANGELA ROH has been an educator in the public school system for the past eight years, and currently teaches language arts at Oliver M. Hazen High School in Renton, Washington. She holds bachelor's degrees in Linguistics and Secondary English Education, both earned at Western Washington University. She has also earned a master's degree from Lesley University in Educational Curriculum and Instruction.

SUZANNE SWEAT currently teaches Freshmen English at Clayton High School. She received her undergraduate degree in Journalism from the University of North Carolina at Chapel Hill and her teaching certificate from East Carolina University.

JULIE SWEETLAND is a senior research associate at the Center for Inspired Teaching, where her current research projects focus on the nature of teaching and learning in District of Columbia public schools and the process of teacher change. Julie has several years of experience as a classroom teacher in a variety of urban contexts and a background in curriculum design. She is a graduate of Georgetown University, where she first got interested in educational linguistics, and holds an MS and Ph.D. in Linguistics from Stanford University.

CAROLINE THOMAS has been teaching English and ESL for over thirty years. A keen interest and studies in Linguistics at the University of Melbourne inspired her involvement in English Language. She has participated in its development as a teacher, examiner, co-author of a textbook, and provider of professional development and tutor.

GRAEME TROUSDALE is a senior lecturer in English Language at the University of Edinburgh. In addition to research interests in grammaticalization, Construction Grammar, and non-standard varieties of English, he is committed to work in educational linguistics, particularly that which involves collaboration with high school teachers and students across the United Kingdom.

SARA WAWER has been a teacher of English, French, and Hebrew in Government and Private Schools in Victoria for over thirty years. She majored in Linguistics in her Arts degree at Monash University and has gained a Masters of Educational Studies. Sara currently teaches English Language and mentors beginning teachers in this subject.

REBECCA WHEELER works with K-14 urban schools to bring linguistic insights and strategies to the dialectally diverse classroom. She is an associate professor of English Language and Literacy at Christopher Newport University in Virginia. Recent publications include *Code-switching: Teaching Standard English in Urban Classrooms* (2006) and "Becoming Adept at Code-switching," in *Educational Leadership: The Journal of the Association for Supervision and Curriculum Development* (ASCD) (2008).

Foreword: The challenge for education

Ray Jackendoff

A few years ago, my daughter received a Master's degree in Education from a prestigious and progressive program, and the school district in which she had interned hired her immediately to teach third grade. My pride in her notwithstanding, I was astonished to learn that her training had included nothing at all about the contemporary understanding of language: the structure of English, the systematicity of dialects, the cognitive challenges faced by beginning readers and English language learners, and the sociology of language prejudice – issues that from a linguist's point of view are central to all levels of K-12 education.

By virtue of having grown up with a linguist in the house, my daughter did indeed have some exposure to these issues. But typically, classroom teachers do not. The teaching of the structure of language as part of language arts was largely abandoned in the US twenty-five years ago, so many teachers do not even have a background from their own primary and secondary education, as they do in science and math. Rather, they are simply left to deal with language problems in their classrooms in terms of what they – and their administrators and their students' parents – take to be common sense.

As linguists constantly stress in their introductory courses, people's "common sense" about language is far from accurate. Moreover, it often stands in the way of effective education in speaking, understanding, reading, and writing mainstream English. In turn, command of mainstream English is essential not only for its own sake, but also for success in every other subject, from history to science and mathematics, as well as for success in later professional settings.

For many years, a few linguists here and there have concerned themselves with these issues, collaborating with classroom teachers to try to inject some of the science of language – and the joy of exploring language – into K-12 curricula. Most of these efforts have been rather isolated and small-scale. But in the last decade, a community of researchers has begun to coalesce around the Linguistics in the School Curriculum Committee of the Linguistic Society of America. Many of the same people are also active in the National Council of

Teachers of English, and for some years the two societies have sponsored successful joint symposia.

I am delighted to see in the present volume a cross-section of the exciting work being done in this community, as seen by linguists and also by the teacher educators and classroom teachers with whom they have collaborated.

Several important themes recur throughout the volume. Perhaps the most crucial is how essential it is to validate students' own languages and/or dialects. Many of the contributors stress that teaching mainstream English proves far more effective if the language can be viewed as a tool rather than a threat, intended to supplement rather than supplant students' customary linguistic practices. This change alone makes a major difference to students' growth in competence in the mainstream language, not to mention to their test scores.

Another striking theme is the value of learning about language by playing with it. Students love observing their language, experimenting with it, and comparing it systematically to other accents, other dialects, other languages, to language at home, in the street, in school, and in the media. Encouraging and capitalizing on such creative metalinguistic activity has benefits all across the spectrum, from reading and writing to critical thinking and problem solving.

Which leads to a third theme: The most natural application of linguistics is of course to language arts, where it helps underpin learning in speaking, reading, and writing. But it also can play a valuable role in social studies, where for instance the study of dialects can serve as a springboard for studying social stratification and the history of migration and settlement. Furthermore, the science of linguistics can serve as a low-tech example of empirical investigation and scientific theory-formation, in which students can find the data all around them, free for the picking.

Many of the projects discussed here are collaborations among a small group of linguists and teachers. The challenge they pose is how to extend their benefits to a larger cohort of students. There obviously can't be a linguist in every classroom. At least three tasks have to be addressed in tandem: winning broader public acceptance of these approaches to language teaching; creating self-standing classroom materials that teachers can use without the intervention of a partnering linguist; and finding ways to train teachers in the use of such materials, whether through schools of education, inservice workshops, or the internet. None of these three can really succeed without the others. Yet it can be done, as shown by the large-scale integrated language curricula in Great Britain and Australia, also presented in this volume.

An important key to these goals is getting teachers on board. On their own, linguists cannot develop K-12 curricula in language arts, social studies, and science. Teachers and teacher educators must be collaborators throughout the process. It will not be easy. Teachers often find they must overcome their own linguistic prejudices and insecurities. In addition, they face enormous pressures, from parents, administrators, and even from state assessment requirements, to maintain the traditional approach to language study. But, as the chapters in this book show, with teachers and linguists working together, it is possible to shift language study to an approach informed by the science of natural language. Teachers who have learned to deal with language from this new perspective love it, and their students thrive.

All these issues came to the fore in a 2006 workshop on Linguistics in Education at Tufts University, co-hosted by the Center for Cognitive Studies and by Maryanne Wolf's Center for Reading and Language Research. The participants included many of the contributors to the present volume. The excitement generated by the workshop led to new collaborations and to a series of follow-up workshops organized by Anne Lobeck and Kristin Denham, some of whose fruits appear here.

The overall goal of these efforts, of course, is to benefit our children and our society through the better teaching of language. The publication of this book is an important step toward this goal. I hope readers will be inspired to join the effort.

Introduction

Kristin Denham and Anne Lobeck

Over the past thirty years, research in linguistics has led to a deeper under-standing of language, and linguists have developed better analytic tools for describing the structure of words, phrases, and discourses – better theories of grammar. The scientific study of language, linguistics, has provided us with greater understanding of how languages are acquired, how they develop over time and space, what it means to be bilingual, how languages are similar to each other, and what accounts for their differences, among many other aspects of this uniquely human phenomenon. Nevertheless, the advances of linguistic science have remained largely confined to the academy, and many of us who teach linguistics still find that our students know very little about language. This lack of knowledge of language is unfortunate but not surprising; though some teacher education programs include courses on linguistics, linguistics is not comprehensively integrated into teacher education, and is thus largely absent in the K-12 curriculum. The chapters in the book show, however, that this tide is starting to turn; linguists are becoming more and more active in K-12 education in a variety of productive ways. You will also see from the chapters in this book that there is no "right" way to integrate linguistics into K-12 education. If we do have one message, it is that we linguists can't do this alone; we need to collaborate with practicing teachers and work in partnership toward the common goal of improving language education.

The need to bridge theory and practice

Much research has been conducted to identify ways in which raising aware-ness of language can be of use to K-12 teachers, and thus of benefit to their students. For example, the study of sentence structure (syntax), word for-mation (morphology), sound patterns (phonetics and phonology), and mean-ing (semantics) can aid in understanding and analyzing oral and written language (and sign language). Knowledge of syntax, phonology, and mor-phology deepens understanding of and provides tools to analyze distinctions among literary genres, stylistic choices, and cultural literacies, spelling pat-terns and irregularities, accent and pronunciation, etymology and vocabulary.

1

Knowledge of these fundamental areas of linguistics can be an important tool in analyzing reading and writing development and patterns of error. Knowledge of semantics, pragmatics, and discourse helps teachers identify and understand different conversational patterns and narrative structures (in oral, written, and signed language). Knowledge of differences in cross-cultural conversational practices can be of use in mitigating miscommunication that impedes learning. Knowledge of language acquisition can be applied in analyzing developmental patterns in writing and literacy in both first- and second-language readers and writers, and can help teachers distinguish between actual language disorders and what are perceived to be disorders that can in reality be attributed to second-language learning or dialect difference. Knowledge of language change and variation helps teachers respond in informed ways to differences between academic and home speech varieties in reading, writing, and speaking. Understanding that language varies and changes systematically helps situate "standard" and "non-standard" varieties of English in the classroom in reasoned rather than discriminatory ways. Studying language change and variation deepens our understanding of language as a dynamic system, expressed by shifts in word meaning, syntax, and pronunciation (the latter reflected in the English spelling system). Studying language as a social tool helps dispel myths and stereotypes based on language and fosters linguistic equality in an increasingly multicultural society. (See research compiled in Denham and Lobeck 2005; as well as in Adger, Snow, and Christian 2002; Baugh 1999; Wheeler 1999a, 1999b; Andrews 1998, Mufwene *et al.* 1998; Smitherman 2000; Delpit 1988; among others)

Educators are also acutely aware of the need for language study, though the goals for its integration and implementation in the classroom are typically different from those of linguists. These goals include accountability requirements that demand that students demonstrate high level literacy skills (Abedi 2004), an increased focus on writing which calls for expert control of text and sentence structure, as well as vocabulary, and state assessments that demand expert reading skills. Further, although some of the unique linguistic demands associated with the content areas have been identified (e.g., Lee and Fradd 1996; Abedi and Lord 2001), educators' lack of understanding of language leads to inaccurate assessments of and responses to English language learners and other students whose academic language skills lag behind their social language skills (Genesee, Lindholm-Leary, Saunders, and Christian 2004; Heath 1983; Short 1994). Improving teaching and learning for these students often involves revising linguistic practices, texts, and knowledge about second language learning (Echevarria, Vogt, and Short 2004). In addition, the possible role of dialect differences in the persistent achievement gap between Black and White students is often mentioned but not well understood. Indeed, there is a high degree of politicization with respect to language use in school about which the public, including teachers, is often naive, as witness conversations during the Oakland Ebonics controversy that referenced myths about dialects more often than scientific information (Vaughn-Cooke 1999). Teachers therefore need a broad understanding about the structure of language and its use to help their students understand how language works so that they can use it well for reading, writing, and speaking in the increasingly multicultural and multilingual classroom (Fillmore and Snow 2002). Nevertheless, though widely used English Education textbooks in the US (Christenbury 2000; Atwell 1998) include chapters on dialect diversity and discuss the value of home language, it appears that primary and secondary teachers continue to rely on traditional approaches to language, approaches that are inconsistent with what we now know about language structure, variation, change, acquisition, and use as a social tool.

Some roadblocks

Given linguists' and educators' joint commitment to the importance of the study of language in the K-12 curriculum it is perhaps surprising that research in linguistics has had only a minimal impact on school teaching. The reasons for this state of affairs are complex. Linguistics is a donor discipline to English language arts. In addition to supplying knowledge about the subsystems of language, it has helped to shape the knowledge base on reading, writing, speaking, and listening (e.g., Farr and Daniel 1986; Labov 1970; Wolfram, Adger, and Christian 1999). But the connection between linguistics and English language arts has not been as strong as it should be, particularly with regard to grammar, a language process that underlies language production and comprehension. Linguistics' decades-long focus on generative syntax (e.g., Chomsky 1965, 1981, 1995) has had little impact on grammar study in colleges of education and in schools. Linguistics and English language arts have had different views of what grammar is and should be, and different goals for its use. Linguists have sought to build a grammar that would be adequate for describing the language, and English language arts has sought to apply a grammar that is already constructed. It is perhaps not surprising that there continues to be longstanding debate over the efficacy of teaching grammar in primary and secondary school, based on early controversial studies that claimed that grammar teaching was ineffective in teaching writing (see discussion cited in Hartwell 1985 and, for updates, Weaver 1996). Connections between linguistics and other curricular areas (history, social studies, science) are virtually non-existent, largely because of the public resistance to identifying linguistics as a science, and because, with a few notable exceptions (publication in 1995 of Steven Pinker's popular *The Language Instinct* and the weekly commentary by linguist Geoffrey Nunberg on National Public Radio), linguistics remains largely confined to the academy (Battistella 2005).

The importance of an eclectic approach

It is our belief that in order to truly integrate linguistically informed instruction into education, we must approach the task from all angles: targeting teacher preparation, developing and implementing practical applications of linguistics in both primary and secondary classrooms, partnering with classroom teachers, working to change state and national standards with respect to language education, writing textbooks (at all levels), pursuing funding, among other approaches. In short, we will advocate for both a top-down and a bottom-up approach to integration of linguistics into the school curriculum, an approach illustrated by the contributions in this volume.

Variation in local and/or national educational standards with respect to language education makes it especially important to approach the task from every possible direction. So, for example, in the states/districts/provinces in which at least one linguistics course is required for prospective teachers, linguists can develop course curricula and materials that help teachers productively apply linguistics in their classrooms. However, in places in which there is no linguistics education for teachers, the task must be approached in other ways – by developing materials that are easily accessible for non-specialists, by sitting on regional/national standards boards, by developing materials and course modules that can be used as continuing education credits, by becoming involved in textbook and other materials development, by pursuing grants that bring together linguists and educators. At the same time, working from the bottom up (locally) can also effect broad-reaching change by exposing teachers to the benefits of linguistic knowledge, by developing assessment tools that demonstrate how important linguistic knowledge is, and by developing materials and lesson plans that can lead to linguistically informed teaching and learning.

The chapters in this volume also highlight the importance of teaching linguistics "in and of itself" in the classroom. Too often, linguistics is seen within the field of education as relevant only to teaching writing or reading (as part of the "language arts"), even though the applications of linguistic knowledge reach far beyond these borders. Several contributions in the volume will address the benefits of engaging students in the scientific study of language in and of itself, an area of study that enriches the curriculum in ways unavailable to more narrow approaches.

A call to action

The target audience for this volume is linguists, whom we hope to inspire to participate in this important work. We hope this volume with also be of use to teachers, teacher educators, and others interested in the integration of linguistic knowledge into primary and secondary education. Although the volume does include some ideas for implementation of linguistics into K-12 education it does not focus on educational/pedagogical theory (other than as it arises in the vignettes by teachers, in Part III). Rather, the focus is on successful ways to improve education about language, and how linguists can make a difference in this regard. We focus primarily on the projects in the US, simply because that is the system we are most familiar with. However, there are important examples from the UK and from Australia as well.

There are some common themes in each chapter, some threads that weave the chapters in this volume together. We mention them here, so that each author can get right to the substance of each chapter's topic and avoid redundancy. Those shared themes are the following:

- There are many reasons why linguistics is valuable in education as a topic in and of itself, as well as integrated into other disciplines.
- There are known barriers to curricular change: teacher preparation and the structure of educational programs, assessment pressure, prescribed curricula, lack of materials.
- Collaboration between linguists and teachers is crucial in order to reach curricular goals. Linguists need to really work *with* teachers, as many of the contributors to this volume are doing.
- Linguists need to get more involved in the integration of linguistics into primary and secondary education; let the chapters in this book serve as a call to action.

Regardless of the differences between the two fields, linguists and educators share a common goal, namely to integrate the science of language into K-12 pedagogy in ways that raise awareness of the workings of language. Successful collaboration between linguists and educators has begun to emerge. It is these successful collaborations, both from the bottom up and the top down, that you will read about in this book.

Acknowledgments

The theme of this book is collaboration; as each chapter makes clear, it is only with the cooperation, support, and expertise of practicing teachers that linguistics can gain any kind of foothold in the schools. We therefore thank, above all, the many teachers who have taken the time out of their already demanding days to work with us on the projects chronicled here. We also thank their students, whose ingenuity, enthusiasm, and linguistic intuitions inform the projects highlighted here in invaluable ways. And a special thank you to our colleagues in linguistics for persevering in this sometimes difficult but always ultimately rewarding work. It is through all of these efforts that we collectively extend the reach of linguistics beyond the borders of academia into "real life."

We were very fortunate to have had the opportunity to work with the fine editors and staff at Cambridge University Press in preparing this book for publication. We are forever grateful to our very patient editor Helen Barton, whose support for this project never waned, even when we were far past our original deadline. We thank Christopher Hills, Jodie Barnes, and Penny Wheeler for excellent copy-editing and other help, and the reviewers for their insights and excellent commentary. Some of this material is based upon work supported by the National Science Foundation under Grant No. 0536821.

Part I

Linguistics from the top down: encouraging
institutional change

Introduction to Part I

Kristin Denham and Anne Lobeck

The chapters in Part I provide historical background on linguistics in education, in the form of discussion of successful (and not so successful) projects that have resulted by working mainly from the "top down." The contributors discuss diverse ways to integrate linguistic knowledge at the institutional level, through national or regional curricula, standards and assessment, and teacher training and collaboration, and by working to change ideologies about language and its place in education. Authors also address challenges they've encountered in their work, which may help others avoid such stumbling blocks in the future. Below we outline each chapter, and highlight recurring themes among them.

Edwin Battistella's chapter addresses the public misperceptions about linguistics and the role those misperceptions play in shaping language education; linguistics is irrelevant and academic, descriptivism promotes the elevation of non-standard dialects, and so on. He draws parallels with public perceptions of biology and visual art, both of which have faced resistance for similar reasons. Battistella highlights what we can learn from the challenges faced by other fields and how we can use those lessons to change perceptions of linguistics and encourage institutional change.

Wayne O'Neil's chapter discusses the failure of a "top-down" approach to institutional change in the 1960s (Project English in Oregon State). The rise and fall of this project provides us with important insights into what it takes for large-scale, top-down curricular change to succeed, and what stumbling blocks can arise along the way to derail such projects. O'Neil outlines a project that began as a successful, university–K-12 collaborative project, the core of which was teacher training and materials development, and which involved piloting and experimentation. For a number of reasons, this project devolved into turning out textbooks that were intended to "run on their own." Gone was the university–schools connection, and all that was left were "inert" textbooks. O'Neil continued his work on creating and piloting educational materials that promote the science of language, and recounts the story of his and Maya Honda's ongoing and very successful collaboration with Seattle school teacher David Pippin (see Chapter 12 in this volume by Honda, O'Neil, and Pippin). He reminds us of the importance of nurturing queries from teachers, because what begins as a simple exchange can lead to the kind of university–school collaboration that he believes is essential to curricular change.

Richard Hudson's chapter outlines a successful model of "top-down" curricular change in England, emphasizing that such comprehensive change takes the collaboration not only of linguists and teachers, but also of government officials. Also important to the integration of linguistics was the implementation of a National Curriculum. Hudson discusses how linguistics found a curricular niche in the National Curriculum with the demise of "drill and kill" grammar teaching, which was unsuccessful in meeting teachers' goals. Linguistics, under the umbrella of "knowledge about language" or KAL, was integrated into the curriculum through applications to the study of literature and creative writing, building on the interests and skills of teachers. Linguistics was also linked to improving the teaching of foreign language, which had also been identified as a curricular need. Strong leadership by linguists dedicated to reforming education, such as Randolph Quirk, Michael Halliday, David Crystal, Hudson himself, and others, was instrumental in this process, as were teachers themselves, who were enthusiastic about and committed to these changes. One result of this curricular change is the linguistically informed A-level course in English Language (see also Clayton, Chapter 23 in this volume on "A-level English Language teaching in London"), and a wealth of resource materials, including websites, teacher training materials, and email discussion lists. As a result of these changes, dialect diversity is now more tolerated, and prescriptivism is in decline. Language is viewed as an object of study in and of itself. Hudson notes that teacher training, though not an insurmountable problem, is still a challenge that remains to be overcome.

Graeme Trousdale's chapter on integrating linguistics into the curriculum in Scotland echoes many of the themes in Hudson's chapter, with some important differences. While KAL is part of the Scottish curriculum, guidelines are unclear, and participation in courses on language is rather low. To boost interest in KAL and to encourage more interest in this area of study, a number of different organizations have been formed to promote KAL in the curriculum. Trousdale discusses these organizations, among them the Committee for Language Awareness in Scottish Schools (CLASS), a group of university linguists, educationalists (those involved in teaching and research on educational policy and teacher training), primary and secondary teachers, and writers who have a particular interest in raising language awareness in the curriculum. By connecting KAL to Scottish language and culture, the study of English and of foreign languages, these committees and organizations have made progress in not only changing the curriculum, but in fostering the kinds of essential collaborations needed for such work to succeed and continue. The collaborative groups Trousdale discusses host workshops and conferences, create Google groups and blogs, offer professional development for teachers, create materials for English and foreign language teaching, and offer a variety of opportunities for exchange between universities and primary and secondary schools.

Jean Mulder's chapter traces the development and implementation of a national linguistics curriculum in Australia, called VCE (Victorian Certificate of Education) English Language, developed by a group of academic linguists and secondary English teachers. This "top-down" work was supported by a call for institutional change and, as we've seen before, for an approach to language to fill the void created by the abandonment of traditional grammar instruction (a factor in the projects undertaken by both O'Neil and Hudson, described in this section). Mulder focuses primarily on the curriculum itself – what is taught and why, and how linguistics is connected to the study of text in a variety of ways. She elaborates on the role of linguist as learner rather than expert when it comes to designing materials for secondary schools, and the importance of collaboration with teachers. Mulder provides important insights into the challenge and process of writing a linguistically informed textbook that will meet teachers' needs, and offers useful commentary on the kinds of judgment calls linguists must make in developing lessons and assessments.

Carol Lord and Sharon Klein's chapter explores how educational standards have developed over the years, to help us better understand why linguistics has been largely excluded from such standards. Understanding the forces that drive standards (currently, to measure school success and to enforce accountability) helps us understand how to respond in constructive ways. Lord and Klein discuss how to bring the advances of linguistic science into education standards by linking that research with pressing educational needs (in California, the academic success of English language learners, for example). Effective standards must also be aligned with teacher preparation, curriculum development, and assessment. Such alignment offers linguists many opportunities to become involved in shaping education. Lord and Klein, like Mulder, discuss the importance of working not only on curriculum but on textbooks. The success of their work also relies, as we have seen with the other examples of top-down change in this section, on "bottom-up" collaboration with teachers.

Jeffrey Reaser's chapter describes two curriculum projects he and his colleagues have developed for high schools. One is a companion to the Public Broadcasting System's series *Do You Speak American?*, created by Robert MacNeil *et al.* (1986). The curriculum is explicitly tied to the educational standards of both the National Council of Teachers of English and the National Council for the Social Studies, and is designed for use by teachers who have no training in linguistics. Reaser also discusses Voices of North Carolina, a regionally based dialect awareness curriculum which is also tied explicitly to North Carolina educational standards and teacher identified topics of interest. A multitude of materials is available for both curricula; DVDs, websites, teachers' manuals, and workbooks, all of which are tied to Social

Studies rather than English/Language Arts standards. This situation is advantageous for several reasons, one of which is that it avoids the potential tension (outlined by Wheeler and Sweetland among others in the volume) that arises between appreciating linguistic diversity and teaching Standard English.

Debra Myhill's chapter shows the importance of linguistic research in order to link linguistics to teachers' needs and goals. Myhill assesses the impact of grammar teaching on children's writing development, which methods and approaches work, which do not, and why. She argues (as does Wheeler in Chapter 9) that successful strategies for teaching and evaluating writing have the most impact in the schools, and that research in this area has much to offer. Her research shows that through linguistically informed methods of teaching writing, learners gain the necessary metalinguistic understanding to become confident crafters of written texts. Teachers can also use linguistics as a tool to assess the development of students' writing. She provides insights into when and how writers make the transition from oral to written grammatical patterns, and when and how to teach certain structures and concepts (coordination and subordination, for example), based on assessments of students' lexical choice, sentence complexity, coherence, thematic variety, use of passive voice, and so on. She offers ways to reconceptualize the pedagogical approach to grammar and writing and discusses how linguists can help in this endeavor not only by doing research on the linguistics of writing, but also by incorporating such research into teacher training.

1 Ideologies of language, art, and science

Edwin Battistella

On the bookshelf in my living room is a copy of Franklin Folsom's *The Language Book*, a 1963 book for pre-teenagers. Richly illustrated, the book covers topics as varied as animal communication, language origins, language families, the development of writing, Indo-European, sign language, spooner-isms, and communication by machine. It serves as a reminder that linguistics has much to offer teachers and young students – perspectives on grammar and writing instruction, history, multiculturalism and diversity, critical thinking, and science instruction. Yet linguists have not had much success in institutionalizing our field in the K-12 curriculum. The chapters in this volume are a way to build our field into the curriculum from the top down and the bottom up, and my aim in this chapter is twofold. First, I explore one of the reasons linguists have not had much success in the past: our failure to manage the misperceptions about linguistics and how our field relates to culture and to the goals of education. Next, I compare public perceptions of linguistics with those of two other fields: biology and visual art. This entails looking at the social and cultural controversies about evolution on the one hand and about artists and art on the other. In looking outside our field, I hope to highlight some common issues and to suggest some approaches for enhancing public understanding of the value of linguistics.

Linguists: permissive enablers and science fetishists

One indication of the general public's view about linguistics comes from the treatment of the field in the opinion-maker press. Professional writers are heavily invested in consistency of style, so we should expect that commentators will be sympathetic to prescriptive approaches. What is especially interesting is the negative attitude toward linguistics as the science of language. Textbook and classroom discussions by linguists often begin by pointing out that the term grammar itself is ambiguous, referring both to the scientific account of a language and to the rules that educated speakers supposedly follow when writing and speaking formally. Descriptive linguistics aims at the former. Its modern origins were in the traditions of European historical linguistics,

13

structuralism, and descriptive anthropology, and typically the scientific investigation of language involves study of sounds, words, grammar, and meaning – phonetics, phonology, morphology, syntax, and semantics – and the facts of language use, variation, and change.

The study of variation and change entails a critical examination of the notion of correctness and puts descriptive linguistics at odds with the view of many traditionalist commentators. John Simon, in his 1981 collection *Paradigms Lost*, portrays linguistics as a "statistical, populist, sociological approach, whose adherents claimed to be merely recording and describing the language as it was used by anyone and everyone, without imposing elitist judgments on it" (1981: xiv). The theme of traditionalists of course is that civility and civic cohesion requires prescriptive norms of language, and that populism is both morally and politically suspect. John Updike, reviewing Robert Burchfield's *The New Fowler's Modern English Usage*, talks about linguistics as "a slippery field for the exercise of moral indignation" and sees its editors as "lenient." Discussing one entry, Updike suggests that Burchfield "takes cover behind another permissive, precedent-rich authority, *Webster's Dictionary of American Usage*." And concerning the perennial shibboleth *ain't*, Updike sees him as "pleading the outcast's case like a left-wing lawyer." The tone of Updike's review is emphasized by a sketch of Fowler captioned "Henry Watson Fowler: cataloguer of grammatical sins." For Updike, moral indignation and civility come together in adherence to traditional grammar; lenience, permissiveness, and moral relativism characterize scientific linguistics.

The tension between scientific description of usage and grammatical discipline is sometimes framed as the irrelevance of science to usage. Mark Halpern, writing in *The Atlantic Monthly*, asserts that "What linguistic scientists have been doing ... has absolutely no relevance to the constellation of literary–philosophical–social–moral issues that we are talking about when we discuss usage" (Halpern 1997: 19–22). In a later essay in *The American Scholar*, Halpern argues that linguistics is both too broad and too specialized. He predicts that it will lose its status both as an autonomous discipline and as a source of judgment about usage:

Questions of usage – judgments as to how we should write and speak today – will be recognized as lying within the purview of the general educated public, with philosophers, literary critics, and poets perhaps seen as leaders. We, the new usage arbiters, may occasionally turn for assistance to the findings of what is now called linguistics, if we judge such information to be relevant to our own objectives, but if we do we will be looking not for judicial rulings but for expert testimony on technical points, whose values we will assess by our own lights. (Halpern 2001: 13–26)

For Halpern, usage questions are to be decided by the educated general public, relying on common sense rather than a scientific method.

Novelist David Foster Wallace, in a long, interesting review article of Bryan Garner's *A Dictionary of Modern American Usage*, also targets descriptive linguistics as irrelevant, though in a broader way. Wallace sees linguistics as reflecting an outdated faith in science, writing that "Structural linguists like [Phillip] Gove and [Charles Carpenter] Fries are not, finally, scientists but census-takers who happen to misconstrue the importance of 'observed facts'." In his view, the value-free descriptivism attributed to Gove and Fries undercuts semantically useful distinctions (such as the difference between *imply* and *infer*) and the norms which, Wallace argues, are important because they "help us evaluate our actions (including utterances) according to what we as a community have decided our real interests and purposes are."[1]

The attitudes of the opinion-makers and the public become most apparent at periodic flashpoint debates over usage. The publication of the National Council of Teachers of English report on *The English Language Arts* in 1952 was one such flashpoint. That report endorsed the idea that language change was both ongoing and expected. It also stressed the idea that correctness is based on spoken usage and that usage is relative to context. The publication of *Webster's Third New International Dictionary* in 1961 was also a call-to-arms for traditional-minded editorialists who responded with such critiques as "Permissiveness Gone Mad" and "Sabotage in Springfield," among others. Other flashpoints have involved dialect. The National Council of Teachers of English "Student's Right to Their Own Language" resolution in 1974, the Ann Arbor Black English court case of the late 1970s, and the Oakland Ebonics controversy of the 1990s all provided opportunities for opinion-makers to comment on language and linguistics. While space precludes a detailed survey, readers are invited to browse the news coverage surrounding these events for images and descriptions of linguistics.[2]

Survival of the fittest

Linguistics is not the only place where reliance on science is perceived as misguided. Political and social pressures from religious fundamentalists and

---

[1] Wallace criticizes structural linguistics for a faith in science as neutral and unbiased observation, a view that he suggests has been displaced by poststructuralist views of science. At the same time he sees linguistics as promoting a relativism that serves as a source for the "language in which today's socialist, feminist, minority, gay and environmentalist movements frame their sides of the political debate" (Wallace 2001: 45). He tries to eat his cake and have it too.

[2] See for example Finegan 1980, Morton 1994, and Rickford and Rickford 2000. Charles Fries and Phillip Gove have been particular targets of traditionalists, and each was compared to sex researcher Alfred Kinsey. A more humorous reaction was Alan Dunn's *New Yorker* cartoon of 1962, reprinted in Morton 1994. The cartoon reflected the public's sense that descriptivism is impractical by showing a receptionist at the Merriam Webster Company greeting a visitor with a cheery, "Dr. Gove ain't in."

creationists have made biology a hotly contested element of the US science curriculum. A recent well-publicized example was the 1999 action by the Kansas Board of Education, which voted to drop the teaching of evolution from the state's science curriculum standards and from the standardized tests taken by Kansas students, leaving the specific science curriculum to local school boards and teachers. The head of the conservative American Vision group lauded the decision, saying: "You can't apply the scientific method to evolution. It's never been observed. You can't repeat the experiment. And so what's being sold as science, in terms of evolution, really isn't science in terms of the way they define it."[3] In the eight years from 1999 to 2007, Kansas had five sets of science standards as the state board was alternatively dominated by conservatives and moderates. Mainstream science guidelines were most recently reinstated in 2007, treating science as involving natural explanations for observed phenomena.

The Kansas experience is just one of many, and such attacks on the teaching of evolution in schools have been part of the American cultural landscape for quite some time. Textbooks today in Alabama carry a state-mandated disclaimer (in the form of a sticker) that says evolution is a theory believed by some scientists, not fact. In 2001, the Arkansas legislature's House Committee on State Agencies and Governmental Affairs recommended banning evolution from state-funded textbooks used in schools, museums, and libraries. In Michigan in 2002, lawmakers debated a bill requiring that public school students be taught "intelligent design" alternatives to the theory of evolution. And the school board in Dover, Pennsylvania, voted in 2004 to require that a disclaimer be read to 9th-grade biology students noting gaps in the theory of evolution. The board was replaced by challengers in 2005.

The contest between evolution and various forms of creationism has also been tested in the court system. In 1981 Arkansas enacted a law requiring public school teachers to give equal time to evolution and Biblical creation and that law was overturned in federal court the following year. In 1987 the Supreme Court ruled that it was unconstitutional for Louisiana to require that creation science be cotaught with evolution because teaching creationism meant the state was endorsing religion. In 2004 the Dover, Pennsylvania, School Board mentioned above was sued over its policy, with the result that a federal judge ruled that intelligent design was a mere relabeling of creationism. And in 2007 a federal court in Georgia also ruled against the use of stickers like those in Alabama schools, though at this time Alabama schools continue to use disclaimer stickers.

---

[3] The quote is from "Kansas School Board's Evolution Ruling Angers Science Community," CNN, August 12, 1999, by correspondent Brian Cabell (Cabell 1999). In February of 2001 a new higher education board reversed the decision, after protests from the scientific and educational communities.

The most famous legal challenge to the teaching of evolution was of course the Scopes trial of 1925, which arose after a number of states barred teaching evolution in public schools. John Scopes, a Tennessee high school teacher, volunteered to be charged with violating the ban to provide a test case. After a trial that included Clarence Darrow and William Jennings Bryan, among others, Scopes was convicted and fined $100. The Tennessee Supreme Court later voided his conviction on a technicality, but upheld the law, which was finally struck down by the Supreme Court in 1968.

The Scopes trial provides insight into the way in which attitudes have been shaped, since it is in many ways the defining event in the cultural battle between evolution and creationism. Edward Larson, in his Pulitzer-Prize winning *Summer for the Gods: The Scopes Trial and America's Continuing Debate of Science and Religion*, describes how Bryan and others saw the theological liberalism of mainstream Protestantism as a danger to American culture. In particular the Biblical historicism of so-called modernists sparked a reaction by conservative Christians to battle for what they perceived as fundamentals. Larson writes that:

Modernists viewed their creed as a means to save Christianity from irrelevancy in the face of recent developments in higher literary criticism and evolutionary thinking in the social sciences. Higher criticism, especially as applied by German theologians, subjected the bible to the same sort of literary analysis as any other religious text, interpreting its 'truths' in light of historical and cultural context. The new social sciences, particularly psychology and anthropology, assumed that Judaism and Christianity were natural developments in the social evolution of the Hebrew people. (1997: 42)

In addition, some anti-evolutionists focused on the idea of "social Darwinism" – the view that people struggle to survive in society with only the fittest surviving. Bryan, for example, saw both war and greed as related to the social applications of Darwinism. In addition, the infatuation with eugenics of some evolutionary biologists (such as George Hunter, whose *Civic Biology* was the text used by Scopes) provided further grounds for objections.

Larson emphasizes that the Scopes trial was not just a simple contest between science and religion, but also incorporated themes of academic and intellectual freedom and state control of the curriculum. However, the dramatic climax of the trial – Darrow's calling Bryan to testify and Bryan's death a few days after the trial – has given the Scopes trial an enduring role as a symbol of progress versus reaction. This symbolism has become established in literary culture through such works as Frederick Lewis Allen's *Only Yesterday* and the stage and movie productions of the play *Inherit the Wind*.

During the Scopes trial, opposition to the teaching of evolution was grounded in the belief that human evolution did not occur and that biologists were misguided. As Molleen Matsumura of the National Center for Science Education notes, today there are a number of strategies commonly used in attempts to force creation science into public schools.[4] Of nine strategies she discusses, three are especially worth highlighting. The first is the anti-evolutionists' focus on the 'theory' versus 'scientific fact' distinction, equating a theory with a guess and claiming that evolution is "only" a theory. Matsumura suggests engaging the public in a discussion of what constitutes a scientific theory – a model based on observation and reasoning that has good predictive power for explaining natural phenomena.

A second key anti-evolution theme is fairness – anti-evolutionists ask whether it is fair for students to be taught only evolution and not creationism. Here Matsumura suggests emphasizing that a fair science curriculum is one that is both current and accepted in the scientific community, where content is not determined by pressure groups. Matsumura notes too that fairness does not require educators to balance valid ideas with invalid ones. Rather it entails focusing on genuine disagreements within the scientific community (such as disagreements about pace of evolution). A third anti-evolutionist theme is the claim that teaching creation science and evolution together fosters critical thinking skills. But Matsumura stresses that a good science curriculum relies on scientific standards of evidence and inference and that "Teaching critical thinking doesn't mean presenting irrelevant and ill-founded 'alternatives' to basic knowledge that we want all students to understand." Matsumura's key observations apply to linguistics as well as biology. Linguists should emphasize that the best curriculum is one that is current and accepted in the research community and that relies on expert standards of evidence and inference rather than unsupported opinions and the influence of

---

[4] Matsumura's full list, available on the National Center for Science Education website, is as follows:

(1) Proposals to teach "creation science" may be disguised by euphemisms such as "arguments against evolution" or "alternative theories," "balanced treatment," "intelligent design theory," "abrupt appearance theory," "irreducible complexity."

(2) Legislation or curriculum proposals that call for teaching evolution as "theory, not fact."

(3) A very effective argument is that fairness requires teaching "both sides of the issue," meaning both evolution and some form of "creation science."

(4) Claims that critical thinking skills are enhanced by teaching both evolution and "creation science" (or one of its synonyms).

(5) Proposals to use disclaimers, and other approaches treating evolution as a "controversial issue."

(6) Claims that evolution education violates children's religious beliefs, or parents' right to raise children according to those beliefs, accompanied by demands for alternate assignments or release from the classroom ("opting out").

(7) Claims that evolution is "religious," and that requiring teachers to teach evolution violates the First Amendment.

(8) Suggestions to change specific "sensitive" terms in curriculum standards: For example "adaptation," "natural selection," and "evolution," terms which have specific scientific meanings, are sometimes targeted as "controversial."

(9) Questionable "alternate" or "supplementary" books are donated to school districts or proposed for classroom use.

pressure groups. This is as important in the language curriculum as it is in the science curriculum.

Portrait of the artist

In his 1986 essay "What Are Mistakes and Why," historian Jacques Barzun writes that "Two of the causes of decline of *all* modern European languages have been: the doctrines of linguistic 'science' and the example of 'experimental' art. They come together on the principle of Anything Goes – not in so many words, usually, but in unmistakable effect" (Barzun 1986: 4). Barzun's comment reflects the prevailing attitude that descriptive linguistics is a relativistic and permissive discipline, but his invocation of art suggests another avenue of comparison. How are attitudes about art and artists like those about language and linguists?

The visual arts can seem to lack utilitarian purpose, especially when distinguished from craft or design. Neil Harris, in *The Artist in American Society*, suggests that Americans have always had a distrust of high art, beginning with the founding generation's view of it as reflecting European decadence and corruption. Today the attitude is not so much directed at European decadence as at modernism, conceptualism, postmodernism, and minimalism. Philosopher Larry Shiner, in *The Invention of Art*, argues that the present-day concept of art as the autonomous and original expression of genius evolved relatively recently from an earlier view of art as production for hire, and Shiner claims that we have arrived at a point where almost anything can be called art. Or as Barzun would say, "Anything goes."

Today's art *is* less representational – less concerned with subject matter derived from and representing the natural world – and more concerned with experimentation with media, design, and composition. How has the transformation of art played out in the public consciousness? One result is suspicion of the meaning and value of works of art. Another is a shift in focus from art to artist. These changes are reflected in the stereotypes associated with visual artists and with appreciation of art. Critic Robert Knafo notes that advertising portrays both art and artists as objects of scorn. In one television credit card ad, a painter "fatuously discourses on the deep meanings of the all-white canvas standing before him while his girlfriend looks on, giving it – and him – the skeptical once-over before prompting him to confess that he's actually run out of money for paint." In another ad, this one for beer, a young man is taken to a gallery by his girlfriend. He is perplexed and bored, finds a drink, and sits down to enjoy it in "a Rodin Thinker-like pose on a pin-spotlighted, minimalist white cube." When his girlfriend comes to get him, a security guard "warns her not to touch the 'art.'"

Such advertisements rely on the gulf between the tastes of the general public and those of the patrons of serious art. This gulf is apparent in other ways as well. The *Chronicle of Higher Education*, noting the popularity of landscape painter Thomas Kinkade, asked several art historians to explain his appeal. One academic characterized the work as mere kitsch: "Kinkade is reinventing the wheel: His work is like Currier and Ives. It presents no particular challenge; it's just a nice, nostalgic look at the little stone cottage." Another added that Kinkade "fulfills a need for people to surround themselves with what we used to call craft, which provides for escape and is lovely, and is something that doesn't really ask questions" ("Despite Elitist Gripes, He's America's Most Popular Artist," 2002: B4). Such work as Kinkade's stands in contrast to experimental art on the other end of the spectrum. Here we find art which directly confronts conventional symbols and which may offend even its defenders. Recent examples include such works as Chris Ofilii's *The Holy Virgin Mary*, Tom Sach's *Prada Deathcamp*, or Andres Serrano's *Piss Christ*. Good artists of course do more than just shock and offend the public – they create insight in unexpected places, and they are able to show the beauty in what we dismiss as offensive or the ugliness in what we take for granted. However it is also easy for weak art to lose its way by relying too much on shock value and too little on artistic merit.

In controversies over art, several themes emerge – whether the role of art is to force society to confront issues, whether the public has a right not to be offended, and whether public funding should be used for discomforting art. As is the case with biology, discomforting ideas are challenged by opponents on the grounds that the public ought to be able to determine what is exhibited (or taught) with its money. The debate about art also underscores the tension between public opinion and expert opinion. As John Frohnmayer notes in his memoir of his short tenure as chairman of the National Endowment for the Arts, the criterion for support of public art is artistic merit. Merit is determined by the NEA's panel of reviewers, who do not reflect the tastes of the most easily offended segments of society. And while some art will inevitably offend even its defenders, Frohnmayer sees support for controversy as a sign of the courage of a government.[5]

The lesson that art offers to linguistics is twofold. The evaluation of art is about the judgments of experts – artists and informed critics – who place work

---

[5] Responding to critics like Irving Kristol, who argue that public funding has given artists too much freedom to ignore public taste by removing the marketplace from art patronage, Frohnmayer notes that organizations like the NEA are "never intended to subsidize marketplace tastes. It has been a countermarket strategy to make the very best available, to educate, and ultimately to raise the level and appreciation of American culture. It exists to enable those with genius to make lasting contributions to the wealth of our civilization and the breadth of our experience as citizens" (Frohnmayer 1993: 145). Frohnmayer also emphasizes that art has always been controversial and he notes that Michelangelo's *David* was stoned, that the genitals of the figures in his *Last Judgment* were covered by another artist after his death, and that the statue of the Venus de Milo was tried and convicted of nudity in Germany in 1853.

in context and analyze technique and intent. Similarly, understanding language involves the exercise of expert knowledge and judgment about language history, change, variation, form, and function. Art reminds us too of the necessity for a dialogue with the sensibilities of the general public. There is a component of public education to good art museum exhibitions that engages the public with experts by opening up the thinking behind it. Looking at art reminds us that both the question "What is good art?" and the question "What is good usage?" require more than simple, prescriptive answers. The comparison reminds us also that the answers must be more convincing than Barzun's impression of "Anything goes." Artists and linguists have the responsibility of public education if our fields are to be perceived in their full depth.

Language, art, and science

If we think of bringing linguistics into the schools from the top down, there is no bigger top than the cross-disciplinary perspective. By looking at the public perceptions that other disciplines face we may arrive at a better sense of the social, cultural, and public policy context for our efforts. So, we see that biology (specifically evolution) faces resistance from a segment of the public that disputes the validity of its results and that is wary of its social consequences. The resistance takes the form of alternatives such as creationism, creation science, and intelligent design and in political action resulting in laws and policies affecting classroom science teachers. Visual art faces a different set of problems. Stereotypes of impracticality, disconnection, obtuseness, charlatanism, and degeneracy result in a widespread disinterest in contemporary art with episodes of active resistance to socially controversial works and exhibitions.

Linguistics shares many of these challenges with art and science. Many people see academic linguistics as irrelevant to the everyday problems of language (as irrelevant to writing, speaking, testing, language pathology, and second language education). There is also opposition to the imagined social consequences of descriptivism (the elevation of non-standard speech, the breakdown of standards, etc.). Linguistics has weathered the publication of *The English Language Arts* and *Webster's Third International Dictionary*, and the King School decision and the Oakland Ebonics controversy. But it has never quite faced the organized, sustained opposition that evolution has seen or the Congressional reaction that was directed at the visual arts during John Frohnmayer's tenure at the NEA. There has not yet been a John Scopes or Robert Mapplethorpe of descriptive linguistics.[6] Such controversies have a cost,

---

[6] Noam Chomsky has been a controversial figure of course, but his notoriety among the general public seems more due to his political writing rather than his linguistic work.

both for individuals and for the disciplines involved, but controversies also indicate that the public is paying attention to a field and provide opportunities to focus attention on central questions.

Being more attuned to the cultural conflicts in other disciplines may help us to forge some natural alliances with specialists in other fields. And it should remind us to take the long view and not be too worried about immediate results. Moreover, exploring such similarities should help us to think about the role of the specialist (the artist, biologist, linguist) in defining curricula and in having a voice in public debates. We may get new ideas about how to be more effective at communicating our relevance to the curriculum and to society. We may be able to anticipate some of the social and practical obstacles to integrating linguistics into the school curriculum. Several things come to mind:

- K-12 schools are prone to tension between more conventional ideas and more cosmopolitan ones as students make the transition between lower grades and higher ones. And K-12 teachers are much more likely to feel the pressure of local control than university professors. As linguists develop materials and approaches that introduce scientific ideas about languages we should also acknowledge the perspectives and interests of parents and the constraints on teachers and schools.

- Linguists should learn about and be involved in the development of K-12 state standards, curricula, and assessment models in order to identify the places where linguistics can connect to state curricula such as supporting state goals for writing, science and critical thinking, diversity, and state history. (See Chapter 6 in this volume, by Carol Lord and Sharon Klein for discussion of their experiences in this area.)

- Linguists should take into account what teachers are already doing in the language arts curriculum and what they are likely to have been exposed to both in their professional training and by the opinion-makers. Thus our efforts should emphasize how linguistics is useful in writing, in discussing contemporary usage and in understanding the multicultural world, rather than reiterating that traditional grammar is hopelessly muddled and asserting that all usage is equally good. As we unpack the concepts of modern linguistics we need to decide what to unpack first.

- Linguists need to convince university colleagues and school administrators of the importance of linguistics in teacher training, teaching English as a second language, and other language-related fields. Here interdisciplinary perspectives can be especially helpful in building bridges with curriculum committees, administrators, and decision-makers who may see language acquisition as a matter of correctness, prescription, and discipline.

- Linguists should develop some strategies like those of the National Center for Science Education or the Arts Education Partnership for promoting the role of linguistics into the schools and for helping teachers respond to local issues related to grammar and dialect.[7]

Parallels with other disciplines also help us to understand how the situation of linguistics is unique. The general public is often unaware that linguistics is a unique discipline – it may just be "the new grammar." As a consequence, students and parents do not come to the discussion understanding its value. They do have positive preconceptions about the value of biology (fostering the scientific method; understanding the body, the environment, and life; and opening paths to careers ranging from medicine to forestry). They even understand the value of art (fostering creativity; understanding the use of design elements, the artistic traditions, and the role of visual imagery in society; and opening career paths in graphic design, publishing, and the fine arts). Understanding the value of something is likely to promote listening to experts in those fields more seriously, and so we need to be able to articulate the value of linguistics more clearly. We need to show how linguistics trains students in the use, history, and psychology of language and communication and how it prepares students for careers ranging from writing and editing to medicine, law, and technology and public policy.

Linguistics faces another challenge in terms of the apparent familiarity of our subject matter. Since everyone uses language, everyone has an opinion. The strength of non-expert opinion combined with the unfamiliarity of our discipline undercuts our role as useful experts. We have a barrier to overcome as well in terms of dialect prejudice, which remains both socially acceptable and widespread. One avenue to pursue here might be to study the history of the civil rights and women's movements to search for strategies to educate people about accent discrimination and dialect prejudice. As we move forward, there will be many fields from which to draw connections.

The next steps are up to us, and the models of biology and visual art offer valuable lessons in how to make our field part of the broadest possible conversations. Like the sciences, we need to establish the reality of "theory." Like the arts, we need to show how things that are seemingly ordinary have great depth and impact beyond their apparent immediate function. The study of language can introduce the scientific method and the science of language acquisition, pathology, and technology. Linguistics can promote a practical understanding of the aesthetic and social use of symbols and a broader understanding of human and mass communication and literacy. And linguistics can open a range of career and life paths that build on skills in language, critical analysis, and thinking across disciplines.

---

[7] The Arts Education Partnership (AEP) is a coalition of over 140 national, state, and local organizations that promote arts education. Its focus is making the arts the center of learning by emphasizing their role in imagination and creativity. The AEP website includes a state-policy database, state profiles, and a series of advocacy reports and resources for educators.

2 Bringing linguistics into the school curriculum: not one less[1]

Wayne O'Neil

Many: *A dozen school districts and a hundred teachers in Oregon and the State of Washington*

Few: *Three school districts and a handful of teachers in Massachusetts*

One: *A peripatetic middle-school teacher in Seattle*

1   Introduction

What follows is an account of my attempts to introduce modern linguistics into the school curriculum. This account is quite personal; yet I believe it fairly represents the general development, or lack thereof, of this sort of work in the United States: from work in headier days on large projects directed toward bringing about fundamental changes in the language component of the English-language curriculum to working one-on-one with a teacher here and another there. My relationship to this effort is perhaps different from that of other people who have put their mind and hand to it because of its longevity: forty-five years and counting.

There was another approach, a publisher-promoted one, that I'll not discuss. This is best illustrated by *The Roberts English Series*, an attempt to bring a very rigid, programmatic approach to transformational grammar into the K-12 language arts curriculum (Roberts 1967). For a critique of that failed attempt, see O'Neil (1968a).

And there are other ways in which linguistics has tried to connect with education: informing the teaching of reading and of foreign languages, dealing with language prejudice, and so on. The important work of Walt Wolfram is a model of how and why to bring sociolinguistics into the schools in order to

---

[1] *Not One Less* (*Yīge dou bu neng shao*), a film directed by Zhang Yimou (1999): "In a remote mountain village, the teacher must leave for a month, and the mayor can find only a 13-year-old girl, Wei Minzhi, to substitute. The teacher leaves one stick of chalk for each day and promises her an extra 10 yuan if there's not one less student when he returns." www.imdb.com/title/tt0209189/plotsummary.

instill both an understanding of and respect for language variation and to combat language prejudice (Wolfram and Reaser 2005).

I've also been part of these sorts of applications of linguistics (see, e.g., O'Neil 1968b; 1972; 1978; 1990; 1998a; 1998b), but the focus of this chapter is on introducing *formal* linguistics into the English-language curriculum, specifically generative grammar, the goal of which is a general educational one: developing critical inquiry into and a tentative explanation of natural phenomena, in this case linguistic phenomena.

This story begins in the immediately post-Sputnik (October 1957), post-Gagarin (April 1961) world, when public education in the United States was held responsible for this country's ostensibly falling behind the USSR in the race to dominate the planet and outer space. What better way to win the race, reach the moon, and thwart the Russians than to pump public (through, *inter alia*, the 1958 National Defense Education Act) and private moneys into curriculum development: a New Physics, a New Math, a New Biology, etc. to replace the Old, thereby producing a New Generation of Americans, armed with its New Education, to take command? Little matter that the US reaching the moon in July 1969, well before the Newly Educated finished their high school calculus and physics, belies the existence of a national educational emergency new or different from the forever on-going one.

Last into this game were the humanities and the social sciences – a New English arriving in 1962 with Project English, funded through the US Office of Education after intense lobbying by the National Council of Teachers of English. Through Project English and Albert Kitzhaber, one of the Project's chief authors, the Office of Education initially scattered twelve curriculum centers about the country. One of the centers was in the Department of English at the University of Oregon, where I was then the department's kept linguist.

Project English at Oregon is the first of the three major stopping points in this story, each of which is captured in the lines at the beginning of the chapter. Among the three, there were other relevant linguistic adventures, some of which I will mention only in passing, others not at all.

2   Many

2.1   *The Oregon Curriculum Study Center (1962–1966)*

In winter 1961–1962, while teaching a University of Oregon extension course on English grammar to public school teachers, I had this idea: that linguistics could and should be part of the English-language curriculum, serious linguistics, scientific linguistics, like they did at MIT, which at that time in my own linguistics education, having been raised in structural linguistics, I had very little understanding of. People should not have to come to linguistics, this remarkable window on the workings of the human mind, in graduate school, as I did, or not at all.

Shortly after this epiphany, Kitzhaber's branch of Project English arrived at the University of Oregon, and the Oregon Curriculum Study Center was established; its goal: to reform the secondary school English curriculum (Grades 7 through 12 – ages 11 through 17, roughly speaking). I was asked to direct the grammar/language piece of the tripartite (language/literature/rhetoric) English curriculum. My Oregon Plan, its conception, its rise, and its fall, can be briefly summarized as follows:

- the basic idea: growing in the minds of students, during their secondary school years, a generative grammar and a dictionary of English, a way of understanding language, based in linguistic theory;
- the initial success, based on extensive teacher education and on the central role teachers played in the development, implementation, and critique of the curriculum and its materials and activities;
- the ultimate failure as the project devolved into textbook production divorced from the teachers who would make and use the materials.

This was a full dress effort: School systems in the area were recruited (Eugene and Portland, Oregon; Seattle, Washington; and places in between); classrooms visited; teachers selected; summer-school classes scheduled; and after the first year of planning, materials produced and piloted. Beginning with the seventh and eighth grades, the idea was to rebuild the curriculum in three years, two years at a time.

The pedagogy of the linguistics part of curriculum was to be Socratic as influenced by Jerome Bruner's spiral of learning based on "the hypothesis that any subject can be taught effectively in some intellectually honest form to any child at any stage of development," that a "curriculum as it develops should revisit [its] basic ideas repeatedly, building upon them until the student has grasped the full formal apparatus that goes with them" (Bruner 1960: 33, 13).

With respect to language, the idea was to have students, in interaction with their instructors and with one another, move beyond their intuitions about the structure of English. Students would construct the grammar and lexicon of a substantial piece of the language, at ever higher levels of sophistication in the course of their secondary education. Although there would be some attention to sociolinguistics and historical linguistics as well, the central goal was the development of a way of understanding linguistic phenomena that was based in transformational grammar – not so much specific knowledge, rather a sense of how to go about acquiring an understanding and a tentative explanation of one's unconscious knowledge of language, of mental grammar.

In the summer of 1963, the first set of teachers took a course in linguistics at the University of Oregon. On the basis of their work in the summer session, a few of the teachers were selected to work on the curriculum materials, materials that would be piloted by the rest of the teachers. Another set of teachers was introduced to linguistics in summer 1964. So it was to proceed, summer-by-summer. Over the six-year course of the Oregon project, 150 teachers were trained "to pilot test the experimental materials on some 50,000 students, located in seven school districts in Oregon and Washington" (Donlan 1972: 132).

Also during summer 1964, as part of broadcasting the news, the Center made a series of movies for Oregon educational television: *Kernels and Transformations: A Modern Grammar of English*, distributed in 1965 accompanied by a text of the same title, with exercises by Annabel Kitzhaber (O'Neil and Kitzhaber 1965).

The 7th- and 8th-grade materials were published as the language part of Kitzhaber (1968). The linguistics in these volumes followed along the lines of Chomsky (1957): Phrase structure was "abducted"[2] and after it was found to be adequate for the description of only a small set of "kernel" sentence types, transformations that tidied-up kernel structures (to get tense morphemes properly connected, for example) were introduced. And in order to capture the intuitively felt grammatical relationship between, for example, such pairs of sentence types as the following, structure-changing transformations were motivated:

(1) The FBI captured Emma. → Emma was captured by the FBI.
(2) Alex gave a book to Emma. → Alex gave Emma a book.
(3) Emma looked up the number. → Emma looked the number up.

Rather than have the sentences on the right-hand side of the arrows generated separately by phrase structure rules, thereby proliferating rules of this type and ignoring the obvious kinship between structures, the relationships would be captured by formal operations on phrase structures, transformations (as shown quite crudely above):

- one that, loosely speaking, derives a passive sentence from an active kernel one by switching the positions of subject and object, inserting a passive form of *be* and an agentive *by*;

- another that moves an indirect object to the left of a direct object and deletes *to*;

- a third that moves a verb particle like *up* beyond a direct object.

A second kind of transformation (generalized transformations) was introduced in order to capture the intuitive relationship between pairs of sentences and embedded structures such as the following, with (8) deriving from (7) by relative clause reduction:

---

[2] From *abduction*: "[S]elfdesign, i.e., learning, seems pretty much like what [Charles Sanders] Peirce called 'abduction,' a process in which the mind forms hypotheses according to some rule and selects among them with reference to evidence and, presumably, other factors" (Chomsky 1980: 136).

(4) The FBI captured the anarchist. The anarchist lived in Seattle. →
(5) The FBI captured the anarchist who lived in Seattle.
(6) Emma gave a book to Alex. The book was entitled *Living my life*. →
(7) Emma gave a book that was entitled *Living my life* to Alex. →
(8) Emma gave a book entitled *Living my life* to Alex.

The only review of these materials that I have seen is Stordahl (1969). The last sentence of his review, though perhaps too polite, is pretty much on the mark: "For my tastes, the structure is a bit too rigid, and the fun factor is a bit too slow" (Stordahl 1969: 463). What Stordahl detected was the sea change that the Oregon linguistics curriculum had undergone as it went into textbook form. Because teacher training was no longer thought feasible to support the material or add to it, the books had to be teacher-proofed so that they could run on their own. A long-term process of teacher education and of material development and revision, a university–schools partnership, moved beyond reach. Gone was the interaction that underlay the development and use of the material; all that remained was the inert product of that interaction.

I left Oregon for MIT in Fall 1964, but kept in close contact with the project through 1966, my relationship with the project ending late in that year, by which time the open-ended curriculum that I had envisioned was lost, enshrined in textbooks that looked very little different from the old textbooks. So I distanced myself from the project, announcing my disappointment with how it had turned out in O'Neil (1968a) and elsewhere.

It is my view that Project English (1962–1968) brought an end to what may have been the last, best attempt to bring formal linguistics into general education in the United States. With hindsight, one might have predicted the NCTE-based overthrow of the New Grammar, in part because of the promise by some linguists that this newness would solve all the old ills of the English curriculum: that an understanding of grammar would lead to better users of language, better writers, better readers – a promise that could hardly be realized, as demonstrated by the perversion of the formal analysis of complex sentences into sentence-combining exercises designed to make students write more complex sentences though not necessarily more interesting, nor more carefully analytic papers (see Mellon 1969).

For further discussion of Project English at Oregon, see O'Neil (2007). For too early a report on Project English, see Slack (1964); for a discussion at some distance but not enough, see Shugrue (1968); at somewhat more distance, see Donlan (1972).

2.2   *Interlude: from Eugene, Oregon to Cambridge, Massachusetts*

After a year at MIT but because of my work in Oregon, I ended up at Harvard as Professor of Linguistics and Education. There I was able to continue developing my Oregon ideas and to write about them (see O'Neil 1968a and 1969, for example) but with little to no chance of working in schools. See O'Neil (1968b), however.

After my return to MIT in 1968, there was even less chance. Language prejudice did, however, became a focus of my extracurricular attention as I worked and taught in a world now changed by the urban riots of the 1960s and by the war in Vietnam. Any urgency to change the English language curriculum was put on hold.

3   Few

3.1   The Educational Technology Center (1983–1988)

A grant from the US Department of Education established Harvard's Educational Technology Center (ETC): "Its mission was to study ways of using new technologies to improve education in science, mathematics, and computing" (Perkins *et al.* 1995: v). Hidden away in ETC was the Nature of Science/Scientific Theory and Method Project, and within that project there was linguistics, and Susan Carey, Carol Chomsky, Maya Honda, and me. Rather than being embedded as a major part in the English language curriculum, linguistics was now to be a major part of a very small piece of a technology project experiment.

In three Massachusetts school systems (Cambridge, Newton, and Watertown), we built an argument for and a model of a linguistics niche in the junior- and senior-high school science curriculum. Clearly, the ETC project was quite different from the Oregon curriculum project, for though the schools were still secondary schools, the teachers were science teachers and the classes were science classes. The goal was to incorporate two weeks of linguistics into a four-week unit on the nature of scientific inquiry, replacing the standard introduction to scientific method. Linguistics was now part of triggering the science-forming faculty of the mind, "to wonder about what seem, superficially, to be obvious phenomena, and to ask why they are the way they are, and to come up with answers" (Chomsky 1984: 166).

In this high-tech center, our very low-tech linguistics was largely based on English-language problem sets, more Socrates, and on the principle that cooperative work on problem sets pays off. Students worked together in small groups and as a class; this principle has since become the hallmark of our work at every educational level. Importantly, the problem sets are "staged" or incremental and somewhat idealized. These are not the problem sets of my linguistics youth: Here are sixty noun forms; figure out Turkish vowel harmony!

The problem sets are the vehicle for engaging students in rational inquiry and for drawing out their explanations of the phenomena of language, of, for example, the distribution of the forms of the suffix for the plural forms of regular nouns in English: *dog*/z/, *cat*/s/, and *dish*/ɪz/, and for the parallel distribution of the endings for the past-tense forms of regular verbs in English: *fan*/d/, *drop*/t/, and *wait*/ɪd/. Or formulating the constraint on *wanna*-contraction that prevents contraction in (1) but not in (2), and deals with the ambiguous (3) ambiguously (an asterisk indicating an ill-formed contraction):

(1) Who do you want to go?   →   Who do you *wanna go?
(2) Where do you want to go?   →   Where do you wanna go?
(3) Who do you want to visit?   →   a) Who do you *wanna visit?
                                     →   b) Who do you wanna visit?

And then turning to explaining why the contraction of *is* (as an example of a contractible auxiliary verb) is grammatical in (4) but not in (5):

(4) I wonder when Emma is at home.   →   I wonder when Emma's at home.
(5) I wonder where Emma is today.   →   I wonder where *Emma's today.

Solving the problem sets on plural and past-tense forms required coming to some understanding of how the sounds of language are constructed of distinct gestures of the speech articulators and how these gesture-based sounds interact one with another: the final voiced sound /g/ of *dog*, for example, attracting the voiced suffix /z/; the final voiceless sound /p/ of *drop*, for example, attracting the voiceless suffix /t/; and the final sibilant sound of *dish* distancing itself from a voiced /z/ with the unmarked vowel /ɪ/ (subsequently reduced to schwa or barred /i/).

The constraints on *wanna*-contraction and the contraction of *is* required figuring out the structural point in the sentence, distinct from its accidental location, at which *wh*-words (*who, when, where*, etc.) are interpreted in each case (where they essentially "belong") and the relationship between where they are interpreted and whether *want to* can be contracted to *wanna* or not, or *is* to *'s*. For example, if the essential location of *who* falls between *want* and *to* – as in (1) and (3a), contraction is not possible. Elsewhere, as in (2) and (3b), contraction is possible but not necessary. The solution to the contraction of *is* and its ilk (*have, will*, etc.) is both similar to and different from that of *wanna*-contraction, but interestingly different.

For a discussion of the early stages of this project, see Honda and O'Neil (1993); O'Neil (1998c). For the complete story, see Honda (1994), at the end of which she properly concluded:

I believe that this study clearly shows that knowledge of language should have a prominent place in young people's science education. The domain of inquiry is captivating, and the phenomena are accessible to investigation and explanation of some depth. Through the process of making explicit their implicit knowledge of language, students came to understand something about the constructive nature of scientific inquiry, and indeed, something about themselves – a compelling reason for beginning science education with linguistic inquiry. (Honda 1994: 182)

The project ended without, as far we know, "the compelling reason" taking root anywhere. Nor was it meant to. However, within ETC, we were able to carry out a more or less controlled experiment on how doing linguistics could play a role in triggering students' science-forming faculty of mind, and the results of that experiment were very encouraging.

3.2 Interlude: between Cambridge, Massachusetts and Seattle, Washington

But other roots were planted, for between ETC and the next stage our work in schools – notice that there is now a "we" at work – Honda and I honed our problem-set approach to making conscious the knowledge of language that one has when one can be said to know a language:

- Since spring 1991 in an introductory linguistics course at Wheelock College;
- At meetings of the Linguistic Society of America;
- In colloquiums, conferences, short courses, etc. – here and abroad: with American Indian teachers in the Southwest at the American Indian Language Development Institute; with language teachers in Brazil, Iceland, Japan, and Nicaragua; with Boston-area teachers in Teachers as Scholars seminars; etc.

We were well prepared for opportunity to knock on our linguistics door. We were even willing to make house calls.

4 One

4.1 Seattle, Washington (1999 to date)

On 26 October 1999, opportunity knocked, as befitted the late twentieth century, in an e-mail message:

My name is David Pippin, and I am an English teacher at Seattle Country Day School. Last night I went to a book talk by Steven Pinker. While he was signing his verbish book [*Words and Rules*] I asked him if he could direct me to any linguistics teaching resources. He said that you and [Maya Honda] had developed a linguistics course for the schools. My goal is to bring a fresh perspective to the study of grammar in my fifth grade classroom. Of course I don't want to overwhelm my students with too many x-bars, but our population is a highly capable group of kids … It seems to me that they would appreciate a bit of linguistics because patterns appeal to them. I taught them about SVO vs. SOV languages, and that sunk in more than any subject-predicate underlining exercise ever did. I'm very interested in any work you have done with schools, even if it is with teachers of older students than mine.

I replied:

How free are you to try out new things in your classroom? I ask because Maya Honda has suggested that she (or we) could work with you in setting up a mini-course on scientific grammar inside of whatever it is that you are constrained to teach more traditionally. Would it be possible to visit your school and classes? And if so, when would be a good time to do that – after the first of the year in any case.

Pippin replied:

As I sat down to write a thank you note for the list of linguistics references that you sent yesterday, I received your invitation to set up a course in scientific grammar. I'm ecstatic. This sounds like a wonderful opportunity for me, the kids and you (I hope)... I am not bound by any curriculum so I could start this program whenever you like.

Thus began our most fruitful and longest foray into the schools, back to the English classroom, but from a linguistics-as-science point of view, and with 10- and 11-year-olds, students younger than we had ever worked with.

Now each spring we visit Pippin's school for a week or so, teach his students, and observe his teaching. The problem-set approach that we developed at ETC and have continued to develop in our introductory linguistics course at Wheelock College had by now settled on telling a connected story about the structure of language on the basis of two kinds of thoughts that people can express through their unconscious knowledge of language: how to talk about more than one of something (noun phrase pluralization) and how to ask and answer questions (question formation). The problem sets examine these two phenomena cross-linguistically. The constantly growing list of languages on which the problem sets are based now includes African American English, Armenian, Brazilian Portuguese, Cherokee, English, Indonesian, Kiowa, Mandarin Chinese, Nicaraguan English, Spanish, and Tohono O'odham. The set of languages continues to grow beyond the limits of those represented in Honda and O'Neil (2007).

Expanding the set of languages beyond English strikes out in an interesting new direction. In the past, we have argued that inquiry into their own languages is the best way to introduce students to formal linguistics, for working with the language that one has knowledge of allows a student to move freely beyond the data presented in order to trigger an explanation of the phenomenon, to find examples in support of hypotheses and counter-examples in disconfirmation of them, leading to reformulating a hypothesis. But even though this advantage is lost when working with a language that students do not know, they soon bring to other languages, from their understanding of their own language, a growing sense of how language works, thus of what might be possible or impossible in the next language. The variables at play in the structure of language, its phonology, morphology, and syntax, begin to emerge as a small set, a small universal set. Moreover, in the United States, there is now often a great number of languages represented in nearly every classroom and/or at home for which data can readily be generated and further problems formulated and explained. Thus Pippin's students go home with an idea about how to think about question formation, noun phrase pluralization, and more for Farsi, German, Greek, and so on.

For discussion of our work and the success in reaching our goals that we believe we have achieved at the middle-school level, see *Papers on Linguistics in Education* 2005 (specifically, Honda, O'Neil, and Pippin: "Linguistics in the English Classroom: The View from Room 202" and "When Jell-O Meets Generative Grammar: Linguistics in the Fifth-grade English Classroom") and Chapter 12 in this volume, "On promoting linguistics literacy," by Honda, O'Neil, and Pippin.

4.2   *Beyond problem sets and Pippin beyond his classroom*

Throughout the year, the three of us are in constant e-mail contact. As we develop new material and problem sets for our Wheelock College class, we pass them on to Pippin and he passes back to us his experience with them as well as his other ideas and linguistics-related classroom activities. In Seattle, in addition to doing problem-set-based linguistics, looking at a number of languages, we have also introduced work on language change, language acquisition, and language prejudice – the last, through problem sets on the constraints on New England /r/-retention and /r/-intrusion (as in *Inman Square is not squaah* and *The law/r/ of the sea is not yet the law*, respectively), and on Appalachian /a/-prefixation (as in *he's a-drinking the water but not *a-eating the food*). The New England /r/ problem set also feeds back into a discussion of language change and the way in which the phenomenon plays out as language prejudice in the United States.

And now ten years on, our collaboration has moved well beyond Pippin's classroom: We have now presented eight conference papers together and separately (see, for example, *Papers* 2005). Pippin also attended the 2005 Harvard/MIT LSA Summer Institute, a heady supplement to his largely self-taught work and at-a-distance tutoring in linguistics. So he really doesn't need us any longer, but we need him. Moreover, the three of us are having such a good time that we don't plan to end this collaboration any time soon.

Seattle in the spring still beckons, and the threat of "not one less" lies far beyond the horizon.

5   Conclusion

Finally, there is this nagging question: Why is linguistics such a hard sell in the schools of the United States? I believe it is because linguistics does not fit well with the utilitarian burden under which much of American education labors, nor with the rationale of the English curriculum, which – after a brief flirtation with the field – rejected linguistics in the late 1960s in favor of anglophilia, the notion that the English classroom should be restricted to "an intimate study of the complexities, potentialities, and essential conditions of human nature" (the position of F. R. Leavis, see Day 1996: 160; also see O'Neil 2007).

Linguists do not deal in the cosmic, essentially unanswerable questions of philosophy, nor do they offer anything of utilitarian value: They don't make soap and they don't plumb the depths of the human condition. So, especially now in the currently test-driven state of US education, where's the value?

There is also the intuition that linguistics ought to be applied to improving the use of language, that it ought to do something for you besides open your mind to a partial explanation of how the mind works. This is part of a general problem in US education: that students should study this or that subject in school for some secondary effect that it has rather than for the thing itself.

Finally, I believe that linguistics has failed to find its place in education but has succeeded in Seattle with Pippin because he is the one teacher who in my experience actually initiated a relationship with the field and then cultivated that relationship in a serious way. On the others, regardless of how they came to regard or value it, it was forced.

For linguistics of the kind we have in mind, where does or can a future lie? I believe that the bottom-up type of relationship that we have forged with Pippin, working with a teacher or teachers who have chosen to do linguistics in the schools, is a viable way to go. Thus linguists who wish to see their field enter the schools must nurture each and every query from someone in the schools that comes their way. Much of this correspondence comes to a dead end, but there is now and then a Pippin, and that makes it all worthwhile.

3   How linguistics has influenced schools in England

Richard Hudson

Introduction

Can linguistics influence school-level education? Indeed, should it do so? Linguists are divided on the second question, but I believe that education needs us (Hudson 2004). But even if it is desirable for our research to influence education, is this possible in the real world, and especially in the real world of English-speaking countries? After all, there is a history in these countries of silly ideas about language teaching which any linguist could refute – most obviously prescriptive ideas about good and bad grammar. Could there be some inherent and deep-seated incompatibility between research-based ideas from linguistics and school-level policy on language education?

This chapter is a description of a number of fairly recent changes in the education system of England – Wales and Scotland are somewhat different, though both have undergone similar changes. All these changes can be traced directly to the influence of linguistics, and they are all supported both by bottom-up grassroots enthusiasm among teachers and also by top-down official legislation. The most strikingly successful example is the A-level course in English Language, which I describe in the following section, but there are others which I also outline. The intervening section sketches the historical background to these changes, so this is where I provide most of my evidence for the influence of linguistics. In a nutshell, I argue that an extreme reaction against arid grammar-teaching in the 1960s and 1970s produced a language-teaching vacuum which linguistics has filled. I finish with some thoughts about how these changes might generalise to other countries and education systems.

The new elements that have been imported from linguistics all share one or more of the following characteristics with the teaching and research that can be found in any university linguistics department:

- Students learn to study language rather than to change their language.
- Students acquire knowledge about language rather than just knowledge of it.
- Students learn to apply general ideas about language in investigation and observation.

- Students learn a metalanguage for talking about language structure and use.
- Students learn to compare languages.
- Students study all kinds of spoken and written language, and not just the language of literature.

The innovations described below mean that every child in our schools should have experienced at least some of these elements during their school life, subject to obvious reservations about teacher competence.

The A-level in English Language

Advanced-Level (or **A-level**) courses are taken by students in the last two years of secondary school. In our rather odd education system, as soon as education becomes optional (at age 16, i.e. after Year 11), it also becomes specialised, so students at Advanced Level who are aiming at university typically study just four subjects in Year 12, reducing to just three in Year 13 (their last year at school). This means that a full A-level course has about a third of the total available time through two years – a significant allocation of time. This generous time-scale is clearly important when an A-level subject is a totally new subject for the students taking it, as in the case of the A-level course in English Language (**ALEL**); further details about the examining bodies and their course specifications are available on the internet.[1]

The present form of ALEL reveals a complex history dating back to the early 1980s with roots not only in linguistics but also in both literature and 'creative writing'. The key figures in its history were all teachers or teacher-trainers who were well informed and enthusiastic about linguistics: George Keith, Denis Freeborn and Tony Tinkel (Keith 1990; Keith 1994; Keith and Shuttleworth 2000, Freeborn 1987; Freeborn *et al.* 1993; Freeborn 1998; Tinkel 1988). The role of linguistics was explicit; for example, an early coursebook starts as follows:

The purpose of this book is to demonstrate how the formal study of language – linguistics – can be applied to written and spoken English in order to describe styles and varieties of language use precisely and accurately ... how a linguistic study can help to identify those features of a text which make it distinctive. (Freeborn *et al.* 1993: xi)

However, these enthusiasts faced the same fundamental challenge as all the others who have seen the relevance of linguistics: how to tailor the course to the needs of existing teachers who have no formal qualifications in linguistics. Clearly there was no point in aiming at a course grounded in a solid grasp of the technicalities of linguistics which very few teachers could teach.

The solution was to compromise by building on the interests and skills that English teachers do have: the close study of texts, an interest in style and genre

---

[1]   www.phon.ucl.ac.uk/home/dick/ec/gce.htm

variation, and enthusiasm for original and creative writing. The modern ALEL exam developed out of three different courses that evolved independently in the 1980s, each of which had its own characteristics; but by far the most successful of these owed at least some of its success to the concessions it made to English teachers. The most striking of these survives into the modern exam in the form of a test of the students' own writing skills, which, at least in the eyes of most linguists, have little or nothing to do with the analytical skills of linguistics. However, even this surprising element has an analytical component thanks to a linguistic self-commentary on the writing, and in any case the original writing element is only one-third of the total course. There can be little doubt that this writing exercise is part of the reason why ALEL has been so popular with both students and teachers.

A tangible measure of this popularity is the number of candidates taking the exam.[2] After the first full ALEL course was launched in 1983, as an 'experimental' A-level with just 210 candidates in 1985 (Bleiman and Webster 2006), the number of candidates doubled every year for a decade (John Shuttleworth, personal correspondence), and twenty years later it is still rising – see Figure 3.1. (This graph only shows candidates for one examining board, albeit the most successful one. Unfortunately exact figures are not

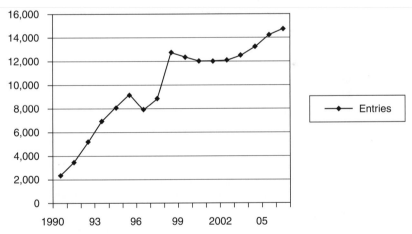

Figure 3.1 Entries for AQA[3] A-level English Language, 1990–2006 (source: AQA)

---

[2] www.phon.ucl.ac.uk/home/dick/ec/gce.htm#howmany
[3] The modern examining board called AQA (the Assessment and Qualifications Alliance – www. aqa.org.uk/) is the result of a series of exam-board mergers, so some of these candidates were examined by its predecessors.

available for the early years.) In 2005, ALEL was the eleventh most popular A-level subject (out of a list of eighty subjects), with about 16,000 candidates, rising to 28,000 if we include those who took a related exam in which language and literature are combined. To put this number into perspective, about 1,200 new undergraduates register each year in UK universities for degrees which include linguistics as at least a minor element.

Another reason for ALEL's popularity is its focus on texts, which both students and teachers can relate to, in contrast with the language system which is the focus for most linguists. Texts are what we read all the time, but systems (such as verb paradigms or vowel systems) are much more abstract and totally unfamiliar to most students. If presented with two texts for comparison, any student can say at least something about them, even if it is trivial (e.g. one is longer) or intuitive (e.g. one is more interesting or harder to read). However the aim of ALEL is for students to be able to analyse texts using what the official definition of ALEL[4] calls 'frameworks for the systematic study of language, including phonology and phonetics, lexis, morphology, grammar and semantics'. In theory, at least, this is pure linguistics, though the practice may fall short of the analytical skills we would expect in a linguistics undergraduate. But in spite of the focus on texts, the analytical requirement means that courses must also devote significant amounts of time to the underlying language system, and when well taught there can be the same productive interaction between texts and systems as we find in linguistics research.

The best way to describe ALEL is through a fairly typical lesson. The following description was written for me by Dan Clayton, who teaches English (including ALEL) at a college in South London.[5]

The plan for this lesson was to look at youth slang in south London, processes of change and how young people feel about their language. Equipped with a slang dictionary from 2005, an article from *The Guardian* on slang on the screen behind me and slang bouncing off every wall every day, we started …

'*Nang?*' I said. 'Is that word still used round here?'

'No that's from East,' comes a reply.

'They don't even say that anymore. It's "*peng*" now,' says another.

Slowly the whiteboard starts to fill up with new definitions.

'*Buff*' is now '*choong*', '*merked*' is just '*moist*' now everyone's using it, while '*losers*' are now '*wastemans*'. '*Bling*' just gets a derisory laugh.

'My nan says bling,' scoffs one.

Soon we had the whiteboard covered and it was time to draw the linguistic strands together.

With discussion of semantic change, in-group and out-group language and some reference to code-switching, soon we'd looked at slang as the counter-language – the opposition to whatever standard has been imposed at a given time – we'd discussed how

---

[4] www.qca.org.uk/3063_2395.html   [5] http://englishlangsfx.blogspot.com/

slang gives power to those traditionally seen as powerless and I've set a homework that doesn't need to be marked because it gets posted onto a blog where students can record new slang terms as they hear them.

This lesson illustrates several of the key features of ALEL:

- Students are actively involved rather than passive recipients.
- All varieties of English are accepted as objects of study.
- Generalisations are drawn in terms of theoretically motivated frameworks.
- The aim is to deepen the students' understanding of language.

With teaching like this, the popularity of ALEL is hardly surprising.

However, teaching like this does require a teacher with more understanding of linguistics than most teachers of literature and creative writing have. The main constraint on the course's growth has been the availability of suitable teachers rather than of students, so one reason why English Literature candidates still outnumber ALEL candidates is simply that every school or college that offers A-level courses offers English Literature, but not all offer ALEL. Where both are available, ALEL often outnumbers Literature. ALEL is often taught by experts in literature who depend on various support systems for their linguistic expertise and teaching ideas. There is a certain amount of in-service training for teachers,[6] a great deal of training and teaching material available online on specialised websites, especially Teachit[7] and Universalteacher[8] (a site freely developed by an extraordinarily talented and energetic teacher, the late Andrew Moore), and a dedicated email list called Englang[9] which has no fewer than 900 members and every day generates ten or twenty messages requesting and offering help. Looking into the future, we may expect existing teachers to gradually become more expert in linguistics, and new recruits will increasingly come from linguistics degrees.

ALEL is a particularly clear example of how linguistics has influenced schools in England. It is an exercise in linguistics in all but name and shows how popular the study of language can be when suitably packaged.

Historical background

The history of A-level English Language is part of a much more general development in our schools in which linguistics has played an important part. Perhaps the most important historical fact in this narrative is the demise of grammar teaching in most English classes during the 1960s, producing 'the first grammarless generation' (Keith 1990: 83). The reasons for this change are complex and certainly include the very poor quality of most grammar-teaching

---

[6] www.phon.ucl.ac.uk/home/dick/ec/courses.htm   [7] www.teachit.co.uk/
[8] www.universalteacher.org.uk/default.htm
[9] http://markboardman.com/englang/englangfront.php

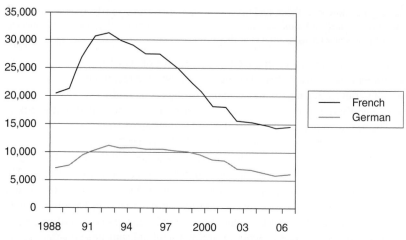

Figure 3.2 Entries for A-level French and German

at the time (Hudson and Walmsley 2005; Crystal 2006: 199–207), so in many ways it is a cause for celebration; but it left a vacuum in the English class which tended to be filled either by literature or by creative writing in the hope that inspiring models or unguided practice would be enough to improve language skills – a hope which turned out, of course, to be ill-founded.

About a generation later, a similar crisis developed in foreign-language teaching, the other main kind of language teaching, but in this case the problem was how to persuade students to study the subject once they had the chance to drop it. The best indicator of the problem is the number of entries for French and German (the main foreign languages offered in our schools) at Advanced Level, which has declined steadily since 1992 – see Figure 3.2[10] (Moys 1998: 39; Kelly and Jones 2003: 8; Mitchell 2002). Foreign languages are officially recognised to be in crisis (Moys 1998; The Nuffield Languages Inquiry 2000; Anon. 2002).

In both first-language English and foreign languages, therefore, the education system has been in deep trouble for some time and public concern has produced strong 'top-down' pressures from the government to find solutions. The Crowther Report of 1959 (Central Advisory Council for Education 1959) concluded:

We are all agreed that 'mastery of language' is one of the most important elements of a general education and one where there is little ground for complacency about the effectiveness of present teaching methods …

---

[10] Thanks to the Centre for Information on Language Teaching (www.cilt.org.uk/) for the figures for 1988 and 1989. For more recent figures, see www.phon.ucl.ac.uk/home/dick/ec/stats.htm.

Crowther suggested that part of the problem might be the end of Latin teaching, and called for 'a rethinking of the whole basis for linguistics in the schools' (Central Advisory Council for Education 1959, quoted in Hawkins 1994: 1935). It is hard to know what Crowther meant by 'linguistics', but it is clearly different from 'grammarless' teaching.

Meanwhile, of course, linguistics has been growing, and by a happy coincidence the demise of traditional grammar coincided with the rise of modern linguistics (Hudson and Walmsley 2005). The impact of linguistics on English schools started with a collection of essays co-edited by Randolph Quirk (Quirk and Smith 1959) which explored the ways in which linguistics might contribute to the teaching of English, followed by a popular book showing how interesting a language can be (Quirk 1962). These ideas coincided with the Crowther report cited above and presumably inspired first the Nuffield Foundation (a charity which often funds innovative educational projects) and then the Government to fund a very large-scale 'Programme in Linguistics and English Teaching' directed by the linguist Michael Halliday at University College London from 1964 till its end in 1971 (Pearce 1994; James 1999; Hudson and Walmsley 2005); I myself was a member of his team from 1967 to 1970, along with two other linguists and ten teachers. Quirk's later descriptive work on English grammar (Quirk et al. 1972; 1985) countered the argument that '[it is] impossible at the present juncture to teach English grammar in the schools for the simple reason that no-one knows exactly what it is' (Board of Education 1921: 289) – and of course Quirk's grammars have now been joined by a shelf-full of massive grammars and dictionaries. This solid descriptive work supported the pedagogic ideas which came out of Halliday's project and which spread rapidly through a large network of teachers and teacher-trainers. Since 1971, when Halliday left England, the baton has been picked up by other linguists, with David Crystal in the lead not only in terms of publications for teachers and pupils (Crystal 1987; 1988; 1991; 1995; 1997; Crystal and Barton 1996) but also in terms of face-to-face contact through lectures and workshops.[11]

One of the main changes in our schools which is at least partly due to the influence of linguistics is a remarkable reduction in prescriptivism both among teachers and among those who draft official documents. Indeed, prescriptivism came to such a complete end that many English teachers were reluctant even to teach standard English (e.g. Christensen 1990 and the continuing uncertainties expressed in Bex and Watts 1999). Even the official curriculum described previously 'has totally rejected the prescriptive mentality. Standard English continues to be seen as a major educational goal, but it is viewed in an inclusive

---

[11] David Crystal calculates (p.c.) that he has given about a thousand live presentations to teachers or pupils.

way, with all varieties – spoken and written, formal and informal, professional and everyday – taken into account' (Crystal 2006: 206). No doubt our class-rooms still contain some unreconstructed prescriptivists, but they are a small minority whose voice is rarely heard. It is hard to know how much this change is the result of rational argument by linguists, and how much is simply part of the general rebellion of the Beatles generation.

However, two other new ideas can definitely be attributed directly to linguistics: language awareness and knowledge about language. Language awareness, the idea that children should become consciously aware of language as a phenomenon worth studying in its own right (Hawkins 1987; 1994; 1999; 2005; Carter 1994b), can be traced directly to Halliday's project.[12] The term 'language awareness' was adopted as the name for a strong grassroots movement among teachers who are united by two main tenets:

- that school children in the middle years (Years 6 to 9) should be made aware of language as an object of wonder and exploration by considering topics such as language acquisition and animal languages;
- that language is basically the same whether it is first-language English or a foreign language, so these subjects should be taught collaboratively (in contrast with the traditional indifference or even antagonism between these subject departments in most schools).

During the 1980s, schools and individual teachers had a great deal of autonomy to innovate in this way, and language awareness spread fast through our schools so that by 1988 10 per cent of schools claimed to have courses inspired by it (Hawkins 1994). These ideas have now been integrated into official policy, and the movement has grown an international following, supported by an international association (the Association for Language Awareness[13]) and a scholarly journal (*Language Awareness*[14]).

The other big pedagogical idea from linguistics is 'knowledge about language', often abbreviated to KAL. This is the name for the idea that language teaching should be explicit and should therefore impart some knowledge about the structure of language and a metalanguage for talking about it – precisely the kind of knowledge that linguistics can provide. This idea contrasts with the optimistic belief that children's language will automatically grow, without any explicit teaching, simply by exposure to good models, which dominated teaching until recently and which claimed support from the educational

---

[12] 'There should be some place for language in the working life of the secondary school pupil … The development of awareness has a marked effect upon a pupil's ability to cope with the whole range of his work …' (Doughty *et al.* 1971: 10).
[13] www.languageawareness.org
[14] www.multilingual-matters.com/multi/journals/journals_la.asp

research showing that grammar teaching is a waste of time (Braddock *et al.* 1963; Cawley 1957; Elley *et al.* 1975; Harris 1962; Hillocks and Mavrognes 1986; Macauley 1947). Explicit teaching is also at odds with the claim in mainstream linguistic theory that children neither need explicit teaching nor benefit from it when learning their first language. Arguments based on these premises have been very influential in the teaching both of first-language English (Weaver 1996) and of foreign languages (Krashen 1982). Those who advocate KAL reject both of these arguments, though it has to be admitted that the debate about KAL has been muted (Anon. 1998; see also my officially commissioned website defending the role of grammar teaching in the official teaching strategy[15]). The argument for KAL rests on two premises: that children's 'natural' language learning does not provide them with the full range of language skills needed in adulthood, which include written language and more formal and academic registers; and that some children can only learn these extra varieties of language with the help of explicit instruction.

The history of KAL was first expressed in public, not by linguists, but by 'Anon.', the drafter of a government discussion document (Anon. 1984) which suggested 'that pupils should be taught more directly about the forms and structures of the English language' (Carter 1994a: 1138). Whoever Anon. was (and he or she almost certainly knew about the linguistics of the time), the idea received strong support from the linguists who served on a series of committees that were later set up to consider and develop this and other ideas: Gillian Brown, Henry Widdowson and Mike Stubbs. Like language awareness, KAL is now a core element of the official view of how both English and foreign languages should be taught; and of course it is accepted that the content of KAL, the specific facts and ideas that should be taught explicitly, ultimately rest on research-based linguistics.

The main obstacle to implementing these ideas, especially KAL, is that they require teachers to teach things that they themselves did not learn either at school or (in most cases) at university. Both language awareness and KAL have in fact been embedded in the official documents that define curriculum content, but not all of the innovations that exist on paper have been applied to classroom practice. Primary teachers often struggle with grammar (which they also teach) but are happy to learn from the available training material (especially Anon. 2000). In contrast, secondary English teachers are bound to feel to some extent 'de-skilled' by the changes because the expertise in literature which brought them into teaching is no longer enough. The challenge, therefore, is to provide not only technical knowledge of grammar, but also evidence that it is worth teaching. A particularly important response to this challenge was a project

---

[15] www.phon.ucl.ac.uk/home/dick/kal/top.htm

called LINC (Language in the Curriculum), a nationwide training project to spread KAL among teachers. This was directed by another linguist, Ron Carter, who had strong links with the teaching profession (Carter 1990). This project only ran for three years (1989 to 1992) but had an enormous impact through its policy of involving classroom teachers: 'Enormous energy was invested in classroom studies of language at work, and many pupils were drawn into exciting research capable of increasing dramatically their linguistic understanding. Many classroom teachers' perspectives of grammar and its potential in their work were completely transformed by the sorts of activity sponsored and encouraged by the project' (Dean 2003: 25). Many of the teachers who were involved in LINC are now teaching A-level English Language. Carter later applied the same principle of involving teachers in research on grammar to produce a very useful booklet on the grammar of spoken English (Anon. 2004). Nevertheless, the in-service training of practising teachers continues to be a worrying problem.

On the other hand, initial teacher-training gives some cause for optimism, thanks to a clear increase in the willingness of teacher-training institutions to accept a degree in Linguistics or English Language as a relevant preparation for training as a secondary English teacher. Whereas a survey in 1994 found that all but about four of these institutions insisted on a degree in English (i.e. English Literature), a survey in 2006[16] found twenty-six that were willing to consider Language or Linguistics graduates. This change may be taken as an encouraging measure of the increasing acceptance of linguistics in our schools.

This historical sketch is important for understanding the changes in first-language and foreign-language teaching that I outline on pages 36–39.

Other recent developments

The intellectual climate described above not only gave rise to the highly successful A-level course in English Language, but also influenced a number of other innovations which central government has driven through our schools during the last decade or so. The main change was a great increase in the amount of central control over what is taught through the introduction in 1989 of our first ever National Curriculum (brought in by Mrs Thatcher's Conservative government but continued by Tony Blair's Labour government). By and large, this change has benefited linguistics because many of our ideas have been adopted as official policy. Top-down change can work well when expert and competent civil servants can offer politicians good ideas, and in this case we

---

[16] www.phon.ucl.ac.uk/home/dick/ec/pgce-clie.htm

have benefited from some very good civil servants who happen to have been heavily influenced by linguistics.[17]

English and literacy

By the time the National Curriculum came into effect, the debate about KAL had been resolved. An influential committee called the Kingman Committee (chaired by a mathematician) concluded in favour of KAL (Anon. 1988), and a later one developed the ideas further (Anon. 1989; Cox 1991). The outcome of these debates was a curriculum for English which included a great deal of KAL (Perera 1994b); one of the main authors of the curriculum was a linguist, Catherine Perera, whose area of expertise was the development of language in school-age children (Perera 1984; 1990; 1994a). The English curriculum has since been revised twice (in 1995 and again in 1999), but the strong focus on KAL remains. For example, a draft 'Program of study' for Years 7 to 9 published in 2007[18] gives the following as one of the reasons why English is an important subject: 'Looking at the patterns, structures, origins and conventions of English helps pupils understand how language works.' Later in the same document we find a major statement about KAL:

Language structure and variation

The study of English should include, across speaking and listening, reading and writing:
- the principles of sentence grammar and whole-text cohesion, and the use of this knowledge in their writing
- variations in written standard English and how it differs from spoken language
- the significance of standard English as the main language of public communication nationally and globally
- influences on spoken and written language, including the impact of technology.

---

[17] Civil servants tend to remain anonymous, but there is no doubt that the following have been responsible for spreading the influence of linguistics:
- Peter Gannon and Ron Arnold (HMIs, i.e. school inspectors, with close links to Halliday's project and enthusiasm for language awareness and KAL)
- Sue Hackman (Director of the Secondary National Strategy; she once gave the most convincing talk about grammar teaching that I have ever heard)
- Janet White (a senior member of the English team at the Qualifications and Curriculum Authority, and a linguist who studied with Halliday)
- Gerry Swain (Director of the English strand of the Secondary National Strategy, who has a BA in English and Linguistics)
- Stephen Anwyll (previously Director of the National Literacy Strategy; as a young foreign-language teacher he taught language awareness)
- Lid King (National Director for Languages with a degree that included Linguistics).

[18] www.qca.org.uk/secondarycurriculumreview/subject/ks3/english/index.htm

A note explains 'the principles of sentence grammar and whole-text cohesion':

This should include:
• word classes, parts of speech and their grammatical functions
• the structure of phrases and clauses and how they can be combined to make complex sentences (e.g. through coordination and subordination)
• paragraph structure and how to form different paragraphs
• the structure of whole texts, including cohesion, openings and conclusions in different types of writing (e.g. through the use of verb tenses and reference chains)
• the use of appropriate grammatical terminology to reflect on the meaning and clarity of individual sentences (e.g. nouns, verbs, adjectives, prepositions, conjunctions and articles).

The influence of linguistics on the National Curriculum for English is very clear, though it is too early to expect these changes to have had their full effects in actual teaching practice.

Foreign languages

As I explained in the first section, foreign-language teaching in our schools is generally perceived to be in the crisis which is documented so clearly in Figure 3.2. In this graph, the crisis can be dated quite precisely to 1993, with a cohort of students who started to study foreign languages eight years earlier, in 1985. Until then, the popularity of foreign languages had been growing, but with this cohort the growth turned into a long and steady decline which affected both French and German in the same way and at the same time. Why? One plausible explanation is that this was the time when the official syllabus for foreign languages espoused purely communicative teaching, in which 'traditional precepts of translation, comprehension and accuracy were replaced by the four skills [listening, speaking, reading and writing], authenticity of source materials and error tolerance ... Grammar teaching was often pushed to the sidelines in an attempt "to get pupils talking"' (Grenfell 2000: 24[19]).

It is true that communicative syllabuses have roots in linguistics, with Dell Hymes's notion of 'communicative competence' (Hymes 1972) as one of their main intellectual justifications, but in our schools Hymes's ideas have been misinterpreted as a justification for abandoning grammar teaching altogether. In an over-reaction against the old-fashioned grammar-translation method, communicative teaching rejected both grammar and translation, leaving the syllabus with virtually no intellectual challenge. A foreign language was presented as little more than a collection of useful phrases without any attempt at

---

[19] www.ittmfl.org.uk/modules/policy/4d/paper4d2.PDF

explaining their structure or how to generalise beyond them. No wonder that 16-year-olds were pleased to abandon languages.

However, the crisis may already be over thanks to a major change in teaching dating from 1999. In this year a revised National Curriculum was introduced which brought both language awareness and KAL into foreign languages.[20] This trend is continued in a revised Programme of Study for Foreign Languages[21] published in 2007 which includes the following passage which recommends language awareness in all but name:

[Pupils] explore the similarities and differences between other languages and English and learn how language can be manipulated and applied in different ways. The development of communication skills, together with understanding of the structure of language, lay the foundations for future study of other languages and support the development of literacy skills in a pupil's own language.

It also includes 'knowledge about language' as one of the 'key concepts that underpin the study of languages', and glosses it as:

• Understanding how a language works and how to manipulate it.
• Recognising that languages differ but may share common grammatical, syntactical or lexical features.

Since both of these ideas originated in linguistics, we linguists can take some credit for the new approach to foreign-language teaching.

Will the new National Curriculum and its implementations help to reverse the decline in languages? The omens so far look good. For the first time, the number of entries for foreign languages in 2006 showed a modest increase, 5 per cent for German and 1 per cent for French. Encouragingly, the students concerned belong to the first cohort which was affected by the 1999 curriculum throughout their secondary career.

Some general principles for influencing education

There can be no doubt that linguistics has had an impact on English schools, and I believe that this influence has on balance been positive. It is true that this impact is most easily seen in official documents, and that there are still a great many teachers who know too little linguistics to 'deliver' the new sylla-buses properly. Nevertheless, official documents do have some influence and things are gradually getting better both in first-language English and in foreign languages.

How has this come about and are there any general principles that might be applied in other places? I finish with five lessons that might be drawn:

---

[20] www.nc.uk.net/webdav/harmonise?Page/@id=6004&Subject/@id=3959
[21] www.qca.org.uk/secondarycurriculumreview/subject/ks3/modern-foreign-languages/index.htm

- Change takes time. Quirk and Halliday sowed seeds in the 1960s which germinated in the 1980s (A-level English Language, language awareness) and finally bore major fruit in the 1990s (the National Curriculum), more than a generation later.
- Some linguists must be willing and able to communicate with teachers. Here the prime examples are Halliday and Crystal, but there are many others who have played a smaller part. This communication must include listening as well as talking.
- Individuals mould official policy. It only takes half a dozen influential individuals in official positions to change policy, and the impact of linguistics is certainly at least in part due to the individuals listed in footnote 17 as well as a number of influential linguists.
- Teacher-training is a challenge, but not an insuperable problem.
- Linguistics can be taught successfully at school.

Acknowledgements

I should like to thank the following for help with this paper: Richard Aplin, Ron Carter, Dan Clayton, David Crystal, Keith Davidson, Eric Hawkins, Maya Honda, John Shuttleworth, John Williams and two anonymous referees.

4 Supporting the teaching of knowledge about language in Scottish schools

Graeme Trousdale

1 Introduction

This chapter discusses the current situation in Scotland regarding the provision of teaching of knowledge about language (KAL) in schools, and the increasing collaboration between linguists working at universities, and teachers in schools, in order to produce resources which are functional and relevant to the needs of Scotland's children as they learn about language. The discussion is preceded by a synopsis of the educational system in Scotland, including the Scottish Government's 'A Curriculum for Excellence'[1] (ACfE) initiative, which has reassessed the Scottish school system for children and young adults from the ages of 3 to 18. In order to facilitate further discussion of issues relating to the teaching of KAL in Scotland's schools, a recent initiative spearheaded by academics at the University of Edinburgh has sought to bring together academic linguists, educationalists, writers and (most importantly) teachers to form the Committee for Language Awareness in Scottish Schools (CLASS). CLASS seeks to raise awareness of issues surrounding KAL in the Scottish education system, seeking to develop links between the teaching of English and Foreign Languages (both modern and classical), which is also a feature of the ACfE project. Members of CLASS are also engaged in Continuing Professional Development (CPD) work on KAL for existing teachers, as well as offering elective modules on KAL for those currently training as teachers, and visiting schools to speak to groups of teachers and students about relevant KAL issues. Instances of such activities are discussed in this chapter. In conjunction with the Language Committee of the Association for Scottish Literary Studies (ASLS), members of CLASS are also working on the development of resources for teachers, particularly those working on language issues relevant to the Scottish communities in which their students operate.

---

[1] For further information on languages in 'A Curriculum for Excellence', see: www.ltscotland.org.uk/curriculumforexcellence/languages/index.asp

Thus the educational context and the on-going collaboration between teachers and academics in Scotland is relevant to a wider audience of researchers working on educational linguistics. The initiatives which are described below are not exhaustive of recent activities in Scotland designed to enhance the teaching and learning of KAL in schools, but they do provide an illustration of the kinds of events, courses and bonds that are being established in that country.

The chapter is organized as follows: it begins (in section 2) with a discussion of the general educational context in Scotland, considering the range of positions taken on the place of KAL in the current school curriculum, at the 5–14 level and in the curricula leading to the Standard, Intermediary, Higher and Advanced Higher[2] qualifications, before considering some of the issues raised by the new Scottish curriculum, ACfE; section 3 is concerned with various recent and current initiatives to promote the study of linguistics in schools, including the work of CLASS (section 3.1), ASLS (section 3.2), the Language into Languages Teaching, or LILT, project (section 3.3), and some Continuing Professional Development (CPD) opportunities relating to KAL which are offered by some universities (section 3.4).[3] Some examples of work that has been carried out with individual teachers, or groups of teachers from a specific region, are discussed in section 4.1, and a review of other ways in which resources are being developed is provided in section 4.2. Section 5 is the conclusion.

2   The Scottish context

The education system in Scotland is distinct from that of England, so many of the developments in the 1990s regarding KAL in the National Curriculum in England (see Hudson, Chapter 3 in this volume, and Hudson and Walmsley 2005) have not figured directly in the Scottish system. The Scottish educational system as a whole has undergone substantial review in light of the Scottish Government's decision to implement a series of reforms under the umbrella of

---

[2] Standard Grade examinations typically mark the end of the compulsory four-year period of secondary education in Scotland; students take these exams usually when they are aged 16, though they may take some Standard Grades earlier than this. Higher examinations are taken when candidates are usually aged between 16 and 18, while Advanced Higher examinations are typically taken in the final year of school (often along with additional Higher examinations), when the candidates are aged 17 or 18. Breadth of knowledge (especially compared to the A-level system in England) is valued highly in Scotland, with students on average continuing to take a wider range of subjects after the end of compulsory education than is the case in England. The system of public examinations in Scotland is currently under review, with a new system expected to be in place in 2012.

[3] As already stated, this list is not intended to be exhaustive of the KAL-based initiatives in Scotland; I have discussed only those initiatives with which I am most familiar. Similarly, in section 4, I present some specific initiatives related to work with individual schools, or groups of schools in particular regions, with which I am familiar. Other outreach work (for instance, by the authors James Robertson and Matthew Fitt, who are keen to promote the use of Scots in creative writing and in other domains, and who work extensively with schoolchildren across Scotland) is not discussed here.

ACfE.[4] So some of the issues raised here may be superseded by on-going changes. I discuss some aspects of the current situation particularly relating to the existing Language Study option in the Advanced Higher English qualification, before addressing some of the statements concerning language in ACfE that have been made public.

KAL is recognized as important in the current curriculum for Scottish school-children, though the presentation of KAL in the relevant documentation, in terms of what children need to know, and what teachers need to teach, is sometimes not very clear. These issues, and others relating to the place of KAL in the primary and early secondary curriculum, are discussed in detail by Trousdale (2006). Language study is available as an option at more advanced levels in the Scottish system (e.g. the Higher English Critical Essay paper has a section on Language); in what follows, I primarily discuss Language Study at Advanced Higher, as this is the qualification with which I am most familiar. The Advanced Higher English qualification is structured in such a way that it allows candidates to submit work on language study for assessment either as a part of a specialist study, or in response to formal, closed-book examination questions. The Language Study examination option covers a wide range of linguistic topics, which as of the 2008 examination[5] are:

- Varieties of English or Scots
- The historical development of English or Scots
- Multilingualism in contemporary Scotland
- The use of Scots in contemporary literature
- Language and social context
- The linguistic characteristics of informal conversation
- The linguistic characteristics of political communication.

While it is very encouraging to have such an option available to students, it is fair to say that this option is not taken up by many schools presenting students for the Advanced Higher English qualification: there are occasionally some Specialist Studies on linguistic topics, and there are a couple of centres whose candidates select the Language Study option, but the overall number is extremely low. This is in stark contrast to the situation in England and Wales, where increasing numbers of students are opting for the English Language A-level qualification.[6]

---

[4] This is based on the Scottish Executive's timetable as provided at: http://www.curriculumfor excellencescotland.gov.uk/about/timescales/current.asp

[5] An academic linguist was involved in producing a set of proposed revisions to the Arrangements for the Advanced Higher English (Language Study) module, which were accepted by the English panel of the Scottish Qualification Authority.

[6] For further information on the numbers of candidates for the English Language A-level in 2006, see Goddard and Beard (2007: 13). The A-level in English Language has become increasingly popular over the years, and was "the eleventh most popular A-level subject (out of a list of eighty subjects)" (Hudson, Chapter 3 in this volume) offered by one board in 2005.

This has led to some discussion as to the best way to support teachers keen to promote KAL in Scotland's schools: should the emphasis be on supporting work at Advanced Higher level (with the downside that there is less support at the 'foundation' level, so that all significant study of linguistics takes place at the senior end of the school), or should the emphasis be on developing foundation work (where the problem is that there is no lower level qualification in linguistics to aim at; given the already crowded curriculum, teachers may be cautious about devoting time to a subject which may be perceived as only tangentially related to the main traditional subjects of study)? To a certain extent, this is a false dichotomy, and all involved in such discussions have attempted to promote KAL at all levels (including work at primary level, i.e. from ages 5 to 11). But it nonetheless raises the important issue of support for teachers by academic linguists as and when requested, and the potential need for greater collaboration between teachers and linguists when it comes to developing resources, as detailed in sections 3 and 4.

The general statements of intent regarding the place of language in the new curriculum in ACfE seem to reflect existing practices. For instance, there is an emphasis on the value of the community languages of Scotland, and the benefits for education of such a diverse linguistic situation: teachers are especially encouraged to use the varieties of language that children bring to the classroom in order to develop an enthusiasm for language, to explore issues of identity and community, as is currently the case (on which see further McGonigal 2003 and Donovan and Niven 2003). Similarly, there is some mention of not only the learning of languages, but also the learning of language, and reference to register and audience: again, this currently exists in the 5–14 Guidelines (SOED 1991), where there is a proposed 'line of development' on the issue of KAL, including advice on expected outcomes relating to competence in grammar and spelling.

3   Some recent and current university-led initiatives to promote the teaching of KAL in Scottish schools

This section provides a discussion of some of the ways in which university linguists have tried to engage with the Scottish school curriculum in order to promote the teaching of linguistics at pre-university levels. The projects listed here are either recent (i.e. initiated or published since 2000) and now completed, or are on-going. They are provided in order to give a sense of what practical 'top-down' involvement has been possible in this particular educational context. Where possible, the particular advantages and shortcomings of the various initiatives have been outlined.

3.1   CLASS

CLASS was established at the University of Edinburgh in order to facilitate further discussion between the following groups on the subject of KAL in the school system in Scotland:

- academic linguists (those involved in teaching and research in the fields of English Language, general linguistics, and modern languages at the level of higher education);
- educationalists (those involved in teaching and research in the fields of educational policy and teacher training in Scottish higher education institutions);
- Scottish writers who have a particular interest in the place of Scots in the curriculum; and most importantly:
- teachers, mostly of English, and mostly at the secondary level (roughly from ages 11 to 18), who are keen to be involved in discussions surrounding the promotion of KAL in the Scottish curriculum.

CLASS has been involved in a number of particular events aimed at raising the profile of KAL in Scotland's schools, including a one-day event in September 2005 which brought together English and modern foreign language teachers from across Scotland, to discuss: the teaching of the Scots language and literature in Scots; developing a Higher in Language; the success of the A-level in English Language in England and Wales; the relevance of KAL to modern languages, classics and English. More recently, in March 2007, as part of a workshop on Northern Englishes, a special session on language in schools was organized, and included presentations from: the Principal Assessor for the Advanced Higher English qualification, on the importance of KAL at the senior secondary level; a teacher from Aberdeenshire on personal experiences of teaching KAL in Scotland; a member of CLASS, on the committee's work to date; and two colleagues from England (one of whom had been Chief Examiner for one of the A-level English Language specifications) discussing the situation in England. One of the many benefits of this session was that it encouraged more teachers to join the committee, who could then steer the work of the group on more practical issues which would be of more direct relevance and use in the classroom. One suggestion which emerged from CLASS meetings was the production of a website (on which see further section 4.2 below) containing downloadable resources for teachers; in some cases, these resources are tailored specifically to topics listed in the arrangements for public examinations such as the Language Study section of the Advanced Higher English qualification. Thus, while the committee is still in its infancy, it has been able to bring together two distinct groups: academics who have worked for some time on language in education in Scotland, as well as those new to the field; and teachers, some of whom again have been working in the classroom for some time, as well as those who have just qualified. In other words, it has been possible to initiate the formation of a network, the aim of which is ultimately to support teachers working on a particular range of topics for which there are limited resources appropriate to the Scottish context. It is clear that, on some levels, direct contact will necessarily be with only a few teachers, at least in the initial stages; but the website should enable some of the work of CLASS to reach a wider audience. A further suggestion made by one of the CLASS teachers is to have a teachers' blog where a network of teachers working on KAL in Scotland can share experiences and materials, and we are hoping to incorporate this into the new website; we have already set up an associated Google Group, with the intention that this will function as a web-based forum for discussion, and for the uploading and sharing of resources, some of which will be profiled on the CLASS website.

3.2   Association for Scottish Literary Studies

The Association for Scottish Literary Studies (ASLS) is an organization based at the University of Glasgow whose aim is to promote teaching, learning and research into the literature and languages of Scotland. The Language Committee of ASLS (often in collaboration with other ASLS committees, such as the Education and Schools Committee) has in recent years been active in promoting the teaching of KAL in Scotland's schools, largely by running day-long conferences aimed primarily at teachers. These conferences contribute a specific number of hours (usually eight) to a teacher's CPD, a system designed to encourage teachers to engage in a range of learning experiences during their careers.[7] CPD was defined in a Scottish Executive's booklet on the subject as 'anything that has been undertaken to progress, assist or enhance a teacher's professionalism' (Scottish Executive 2003: 3), and is a mandatory part of a Scottish teacher's employment, to the extent that a CPD plan must be agreed between a teacher and his or her manager, and the teacher must also provide a record of the 35 hours of CPD activities undertaken in any given year (Scottish Executive 2003: 7, 10, 12 and 14).

The Language Conferences in 2005 and 2006 included specific sessions on the following topics: KAL in the Scottish curriculum; developing resources for teachers (including the use of the SCOTS corpus (www.scottishcorpus.ac.uk), a web-based resource which provides a four million word database of written and spoken texts in the languages of Scotland); a report on developments with ACfE in relation to KAL in the English and foreign language classrooms; and Gaelic-medium education in Scotland. Such conferences serve to raise the profile of

---

[7] Further CPD work on KAL at the University of Edinburgh is discussed in section 3.4.

KAL among the delegates attending the event, and to draw attention to the range of materials that members of ASLS have provided and/or collated to promote the teaching of language in Scotland's schools.[8]

3.3   The LILT project

The LILT (Language Into Languages Teaching) project was the result of a combined effort from academics in English Language, Modern Languages and Language Education at the Universities of Glasgow and Strathclyde, with primary publication of the materials in 2001. The materials consist of a CD and three booklets, which were intended to be distributed to every secondary school in the country.[9]

A notable feature of the LILT materials is that they are designed to be of use in both the English classroom and in the modern foreign language classroom: for instance, many of the discussions of grammatical concepts (such as modality or gender) are illustrated, where relevant, from languages such as French, Spanish and German. This allows for cross-curricular reinforcement of particular linguistic terms and concepts relevant to the study of the first, second and other languages of many of Scotland's schoolchildren (McGonigal, Corbett, Kay, Templeton and Tierney 2001: 2). The support materials provided as part of the LILT "package" are provided to encourage teachers as they develop or reinforce their own KAL, and reflect the general practices involved in teaching KAL, from the direct teaching of grammatical concepts when teachers observe non-standard features in a student's writing, to the introduction of more general issues of register and formality. It is clear how such an approach is of direct relevance to work undertaken in both the English and Modern Language classroom; and it is also clear to see how such collaboration might be taken further, with additional linguistic concepts introduced. Consider, for example, the well-known difference in formality associated with preposition stranding in English:

(1) You don't know the boy of whom I am talking.

(2) You don't know the boy I'm talking of.

A similar difference exists in the French examples (3) and (4):

(3) Tu ne connais pas le garçon dont je te parle.

(4) Tu connais pas le gars que je te parle de.

But the difference in the French examples is perhaps more striking, since many French speakers would consider (4) not informal, but ungrammatical, perhaps

---

[8] A list of such materials, some of which are available online, can be found at www.arts.gla.ac.uk/ScotLit/ASLS/Language_Resources.html

[9] Many of the materials are now available via the University of Glasgow website at www.arts.gla.ac.uk/SESLL/EngLang/LILT/frameset.htm

because the development of preposition stranding in French seems to be highly localized (to a set of varieties of Canadian French, see King 2000) and the product (perhaps indirectly) of sustained contact with English. Such examples therefore open up the possibility of further discussion, with the most advanced students, of the effects of English as a world language on other languages both within Europe and beyond, which could be tied in to work on some of the other themes and topics at Advanced Higher in modern languages (such as work on globalization and the economy, or on identity). The LILT materials therefore offer teachers the opportunity for a range of different kinds of work on language, and for a synthesis of the teaching of linguistic concepts in both the English and modern language classrooms.

3.4   Other CPD developments

At the University of Edinburgh academics from the subject area of Linguistics and English Language have developed a CPD course (entitled *Language in Textual Analysis*) which covers a range of linguistic topics, including work on grammar, stylistics, Scots, and language variation and change. One of the particular aims of the course is to provide teachers with a range of materials that will either be of direct use in the classroom, or can be tailored by teachers to suit their particular purposes. Like the LILT project, it aims to provide teachers with an opportunity to extend and consolidate their own KAL, by making available some of the recent research on linguistic topics that have a bearing on language in schools, and by raising the profile of new resources produced with students in mind. An example of this is the recent project at the British Library, *Sounds Familiar*.[10] This website charts some of the variation and change in the accents and dialects of England. It is predominantly concerned with recent changes in the phonology, syntax and lexis of English, but does make reference to earlier stages of the language. It is clearly designed as a resource for schools, with interactive maps, texts and sound recordings; the team who have produced this resource are also keen to have students make their own recordings which will then be uploaded on to the website. The site also has a number of specific activities on phonological, grammatical and lexical varia-tion and change, designed to encourage students to collect and analyse their own data. Such activities can easily be tailored to suit the social and ethnic make-up of particular communities: for example, an activity designed to estab-lish the extent to which traditional English dialect words are dying out could be adapted to establish the extent to which words from community languages in the United Kingdom, such as Bengali and Polish, are being used by different generations. Furthermore, the current website has focussed almost exclusively

---

[10] The *Sounds Familiar* website is available at: www.bl.uk/learning/langlit/sounds/index.html

on English English, since one of the main points of comparison for establishing the extent of change was the *Survey of English Dialects* (Orton 1961), which dealt with data from communities in England; but given the existence of a Scottish survey (*The Linguistic Survey of Scotland*, on which see further McIntosh 1952), it would be quite feasible for students to use the model adopted in the *Sounds Familiar* website to create a 'Scots' version, tracking some of the changes that have happened to local varieties of Scots in the recent past; one of the aims of the CPD course has been to encourage teachers to consider how to incorporate such media and data into the English classroom.

Another feature of the course has been to consolidate, and where relevant develop, a linguistic approach to the close reading of written texts, and extending this to an analysis of specific kinds of spoken language. For example, the classes on figurative language considered the extent to which figurativeness is common in 'everyday' language, or whether it is restricted to literary texts, by examining the pervasiveness of metaphor in casual, conversational English; and discussions of rhetorical patterns in a range of texts (from Martin Luther King, Jr's 'I have a dream' speech, via an extract from Dickens' *Bleak House*, to the ballad of Sir Robin in *Monty Python and the Holy Grail*) illustrated how helpful a detailed knowledge of basic grammatical terminology can be for uncovering, analysing and discussing syntactic patterns which emerge across very different genres. Such textual analysis is central to current practice in the English classroom, and the feedback from teachers suggests that a securer knowledge of grammar prompted an analysis that was both more concise and more precise. It was also the case that teachers felt that this kind of activity was directly applicable in the classroom, and in terms of the teachers' own KAL, allowed for a direct application of linguistic terminology and concepts to material and types of activity with which they were already familiar.

At present, the CPD course is also offered as an elective to trainee teachers taking their postgraduate teacher training qualification in English. Those involved in the course at Edinburgh have found such a practice to be conducive to an enhanced learning experience for all concerned: for instance, the experienced teachers have been able to advise on which aspects of the subject material in any given session will be of direct relevance to a particular age range; the trainee teachers have been able to suggest ways in which the subject material relates to specific aspects of the educational policy and practice that they are exposed to in other courses for their postgraduate qualification; and the linguists are able to tailor the material more effectively for subsequent cohorts taking the course. One of the more striking things to emerge from the first run of the course was again the need for more resources on KAL, and particularly online resources. This experience has been one of the main motivations for the development of resources on the CLASS website, as described in section 4.2 below.

4   Establishing relationships with specific schools

One of the outcomes of some of the events outlined in section 3.1 above has been an increase in specific, targeted associations between university academics and particular schools, or sets of schools from a particular area. This has led to a number of potentially exciting initiatives, all of which are currently in their infancy, but which, it is hoped, will allow for the establishment of firmer links between those involved in academic research in linguistics, and those involved in teaching KAL.

4.1   *Examples of particular events involving schools in Scotland*

A conference was organized at the University of Edinburgh for students and teachers at schools in the Borders region; specifically, the event was aimed at those involved in teaching and learning at S5 and above, where the students are typically at least 16 years of age. The conference involved a series of presentations by academic linguists on topics ranging from stylistics to language change. The topics were chosen deliberately to be of relevance either to the students' curriculum (by providing a linguistic analysis of the kinds of texts that they would be exposed to in the classroom while studying for the Higher or Advanced Higher English qualifications) or to aspects of their extra-curricular activities: one presentation, on attitudes towards language change, began with a discussion of the language of text messaging (or SMS as it is also known), and considered the nature and appropriateness of this style of writing in formal and non-formal contexts.[11] This presentation provoked a great deal of debate from all of the conference delegates (academics, teachers and students) not just on general issues of texting, but of specific issues which resonate with many linguists: discourse structure, prescriptivism, phoneme–grapheme correspondences, the social context of language change, and so on. The discussion – led largely by the students themselves – nicely illustrated how engaging certain aspects of linguistics can be at a pre-university level; more importantly, the conference as a whole engendered further and on-going collaboration between teachers of English in a series of Borders schools, and academics at the University of Edinburgh.

An alternative method is to have the linguist visit the school, rather than having the students visit the university. One such collaborative venture of this kind has involved an academic linguist visiting a particular high school in Scotland to discuss relevant issues with the English department of that school, and also to set

---

[11] By coincidence, this proved to be a timely discussion. A couple of weeks after the conference, there were a number of reports in the British media about the use of text messaging in responses to literature examination questions set by the Scottish Qualification Authority (see, for instance, the discussion in the Education *Guardian* on Wednesday 1 November, 2006: 'Exam board attacked for approving text message answers').

up a particular project for younger secondary school students. The project involved a discussion of the language of names, and was structured as follows. Before the visit, the linguist produced a presentation and exercises on the grammar and sociolinguistics of names in English, and naming practices in the world's languages. The presentation and set of exercises were discussed with the teacher in advance, for comment and revision, to ensure things were 'workable' in the classroom, and in the time available; and the exercises were then used when the linguist attended the school to work with the children. The exercises drew on the students' individual experiences of language, and on a variety of media sources. For example, the students looked at a scene from the film *Spiderman*, where various well-known power and solidarity relations are clearly marked by the use of family name only (*Parker*); given name only (*Peter*); and title plus family name (*Mr Jameson*). This was then extended to a discussion of an extract and themes from the Harry Potter novels, where the students were asked to think about when – and by whom – one of the characters was referred to as *Snape*, *Severus*, and *Professor Snape*, and how variation in naming practices was used as a means of characterizing aspects of the relationships between various protagonists of the novels. The students were also asked to reflect on their own naming practices, by considering the various ways they were addressed, and the ways they addressed others. This was then followed up by a discussion of cross-linguistic naming practices, and allowed the teacher to introduce further resources on names (including an article on names which had recently appeared in a national newspaper), and work on language and identity. This project as a whole was designed to enable students to work on the language of names as part of the coursework folio for the Standard Grade in English: as part of this folio, students have to submit an extended piece of discursive and analytic writing, and the teacher involved believed that a project on names would be appropriate for this task. It was noteworthy that the teacher involved, who was keen to promote the study of language in her school, believed that this might be one of the more effective ways of incorporating the study of an aspect of linguistics into the current English curriculum in Scotland; it provided a good example of how linguistic study can be incorporated into the existing curricular arrangements.

Many of these endeavours may seem obvious to academic linguist and teacher alike, and the materials used may also seem standard. But experience has suggested that one of the major anxieties that many teachers have about teaching KAL is a lack of resources and a lack of support, and we have tried to downplay that anxiety by providing resources and support in the following ways.

4.2   Developing resources

One of the aims of the CLASS website is to develop free, downloadable resources that can be of use to teachers. Examples of such resources include:

- An activity based on Liz Lochhead's translation of Molière's *Tartuffe*. Lochhead translated the play into Scots in 1985, and the activity involves work on the history of Scots, encouraging students to discover the history and use of words such as *dominie, crabbit, stramash,* and *smeddum* using the online *Dictionary of the Scots Language* (www.dsl.ac.uk). Students are then encouraged to discover more about other languages which have been influential in the development of Scots, using the *Scottish Language Dictionaries* website for more information (www.scotsdictionaries.org.uk). The issue of translation into Scots is also addressed, encouraging both classroom discussion (e.g. 'What does the fact that Scots is considered as an appropriate medium for translation suggest about the status of Scots?') and specific individual or group activities (e.g. 'Choose a short passage from any play by Shakespeare and translate it into Scots. What changes did you make to the original? Why did you make the changes you did? What problems did you encounter in your translation attempt?').

- An activity based on dialect grammar. Students are given a series of phrases and clauses (taken from a Google search) which include the forms *sortae* and *kindae*, such as: *A sortae contrast tae the movie o life; Ye jist cannae reason wi Voldie when he's in that kindae mood; It's kindae based oan an amalgam o incidents an observations; Morally he's probably right, but I do kindae think that dozens of strikers in the league would have done precisely what I suggested.* The students are then asked about the grammar of these words, including: details of the fusion involved; the lexical category of the forms before and after fusion, and how to establish membership of a category based on standard substitution tests; and a final question on the relevance of knowing such things about grammar. Suggested answers to these questions are also provided. One of the primary aims of the CLASS website will be to show that grammar can be taught using the non-standard dialects many of the Scottish schoolchildren will be familiar with, illustrating points of comparison with Standard English where relevant.

- An activity based on a sound file of a recording of a conversation between speakers who use an English English regional dialect. This activity is designed to encourage children to be aware of the patterns of interaction associated with informal conversation, including interruptions, pauses and false starts, and to familiarize them with non-standard varieties of English outside Scotland. The sound file is available on the website, along with a transcription of the first part of the conversation. In addition to being asked about transcription conventions and the functions of various interruptions, students are also encouraged to provide a transcription of the rest of the sound file (and a transcribed version is also available for download in order that students can check their understanding), and then to record and transcribe other conversations that they have with classmates.

These resources represent some of the activities being developed by the CLASS committee, and they are aimed at more senior students. Some of the activities are designed particularly with the Advanced Higher Language Study module in mind: as noted in section 2, one of the topics in the Advanced Higher exam is 'The linguistic characteristics of informal conversation', for instance, so students could use these activities in preparing for that formal assessment. Particularly, the aim of the CLASS resources is not to provide a list of reading or a summary of the research literature on a specific topic, but to encourage students to get their hands dirty with some linguistic data, to become linguistic detectives themselves, discovering what patterns emerge, and what problems arise, when the linguist is confronted with new data.

5   Conclusions

The aim of this chapter has been to give an account of recent developments in the increasingly collaborative work carried out between those teachers and university academics who are keen to promote the teaching of KAL in Scotland. Many of the schemes outlined here are in their infancy, and the success of the projects is not yet known. However, those involved have considered the initial reactions to be positive and encouraging. Perhaps the greatest challenge – but clearly the one which is seen as the most important from the teachers' perspective – has been the provision of functional, realistic and cheap resources. It is also clear that such resources must be the product of genuinely collaborative work: the academics can provide some guidance and training on issues concerning linguistic terminology, and recent research in a particular area, but it is the teachers who are the classroom experts, who know what is or is not serviceable in a particular lesson for a particular age group, and who are the ones most familiar with the changing curricula. One aspect of the collaboration which seems to have worked particularly well has been the balance between contact with individual schools, and the provision of more general resources via the internet, which are mutually supportive endeavours. Materials created for the website can be trialled in individual schools when an academic visits, and modifications to the resources based on the classroom experience can then be reposted on the website; or materials which have emerged through class-based work at an individual institution can be uploaded to the website for widespread dissemination. To a certain extent then, the success of any schemes relating to the teaching of KAL in Scotland's schools will rest on both a top-down and bottom-up approach.

Acknowledgement

I am grateful to Dick Hudson for comments on an earlier version of this chapter.

5   Envisioning linguistics in secondary education: an Australian exemplar

Jean Mulder

1   Introduction

A fundamental issue in successfully integrating linguistics into the school curriculum is developing a vision of language and linguistics which is relevant to the needs of school learning. While suitably packaging linguistics for study in primary and secondary education may sound simple, it is far from easy and by tradition academic linguists have not been particularly concerned about engaging with the challenge. However, with the relatively recent emergence and recognition within the discipline of 'educational linguistics' and a growing acknowledgement within education and society generally in the US, the UK and Australia of the need for knowledge about language to be an integral part of the school curriculum, it is timely to reflect on what linguistics has to offer of value to education and explore ways in which we as linguists can get the study of language and linguistics into schools. For these reasons, this chapter identifies some of the legacies and considerations in elaborating a viable vision of linguistics and describes one example of such a vision that was collaboratively developed and translated into a senior secondary subject with accompanying textbooks in Victoria, Australia.

The subject VCE (Victorian Certificate of Education) English Language (henceforth EL) is the result of university-based linguists and secondary English teachers working from the 'top down' to introduce a new subject into the state of Victoria's curriculum. As discussed in Mulder (2007), the two most important factors in getting EL off the ground were the effective collaboration that evolved between academic linguists and English teachers and the long-term commitment to establishing the subject demonstrated by members of both groups. Matching this initial top-down approach has been the continuing 'bottom-up' enthusiastic support of the subject by teachers and their students. In Chapter 19 in this volume, Caroline Thomas and Sara Wawer, both experienced in teaching, designing curriculum resources and providing professional development for EL, discuss the subject from the perspective of teachers, examining some of the reasons why EL is so appealing and some factors that have contributed to the uptake of the subject by many schools.

The focus of this chapter is on articulating the vision of the study of language and linguistics that emerged out of the initial partnership of linguists and teachers and which provides the orientation for EL. The next section outlines ways in which teaching practices, educational frameworks and traditional conceptualizations of grammar have informed the resulting vision of linguistics, while the subsequent section gives an overview of how the subject EL encodes this vision of linguistics. This is followed by a discussion of how the vision was further developed through writing textbooks and how a linguistically informed model of language can be used for teaching grammar in context. The chapter ends by highlighting the broader themes that may be useful to other linguists who are addressing how to integrate linguistics into education in a viable way.

2 Developing a vision of linguistics

In 1995 the Board of Studies[1] made an extensive review of the English area of the Victorian Certificate of Education (VCE), which is an accredited qualification recognizing the successful completion of the final two years (or equivalent) of senior secondary school. One of the recommendations from the review was that the study of grammar and knowledge about language be 'reintroduced' into the curriculum and that possibilities for developing a new subject focusing on the explicit study of language structure and variation be explored. The following year a working party composed of secondary English teachers from the state, independent and Catholic sectors and four linguists, including myself, representing the three major universities in Victoria with linguistics departments was appointed and the work of developing the vision of language and linguistics that turned into the two-year subject EL began. It was through the regular meetings of this group over a three-year period that an effective partnership developed and the new subject was defined.[2] Central to the partnership was the shared understanding that the members of each group were both experts and learners. In this section I muse on some of what I learned from listening to the teachers in the working party and how that shaped the way we came to view the study of language and linguistics.

2.1 The legacy of traditional grammar

While throughout the US, the UK and Australia, the 1960s saw the widespread abandonment of 'traditional' grammar from the English curriculum, it is this concept of grammar that has become entrenched as what might be called the

---

[1] At this time responsibility for the development, provision and assessment of school curriculum in Victoria came under the auspices of the Board of Studies. In 2001 the Board of Studies became the Victorian Curriculum and Assessment Authority (henceforth VCAA).
[2] See Mulder (2007) for a detailed discussion of the many issues and challenges in getting EL established.

dominant 'folk' conceptualization of grammar. That these traditional under-standings of grammar have survived in the folk psyche is evidenced by letters to the editor and articles by grammar pundits. More importantly, though, as studies by Huddleston (1989), Collins *et al.* (1997) and Horan (2003) have found, and my experiences with teachers in the working party have corroborated, it is this traditional conception of grammar that is almost universally held by teachers and is the main inspiration for the metalanguage used in describing English, including, for example, parts of speech.

At the same time, the last fifty years of linguistic scholarship have produced many advances in our understanding of language and of the grammar of English in particular. Yet for the most part a linguistically informed model of language does not seem to have found its way into school education (see Denham and Lobeck, 'Introduction' to this volume).

The message to linguists is three-fold: First, the abandonment of teaching of traditional school grammar has left a void that modern descriptive linguistics could insightfully fill.[3] Second, in doing so, if we are to 'meet teachers where they are with what they need' (Denham and Lobeck, 'Introduction' to this volume), then wherever appropriate we need to build upon rather than replace the meta-language of traditional school grammar. Third, this is our chance to show that the study of language is so much more than just 'correct usage' of grammar: there is a diverse range of metalinguistic awareness which can support the acquisition of skilled language use. Indeed, one of the strongest arguments for including the study of language and linguistics in the curriculum is the diversity of functions it can serve, including its value in preparing students for a wide variety of life roles and for further learning in other areas of study. To consider just a few examples: the study of the linguistics of English could help prepare students for LOTE learning; it could help prepare Australian students to grow in their understandings of Aboriginal languages and cultures; it could help prepare people for parenthood by introducing them to the fascinating area of child language acquisition.

In the working party, we were united from the start about the need for more metalinguistic awareness for talking about language and communication than appears in traditional school grammar. In considering, for example, the role of parts of speech in the types of understandings and skills we decided students should be able to demonstrate, we chose to build on traditional terminology by including noun, verb, adjective, adverb, preposition, pronoun, but then added auxiliary, conjunction and determiner for a total of nine parts of speech. The general guideline that we came to use in determining whether or not to include a particular metalanguage term was to decide if the term was necessary or useful

---

[3] While systemic functional grammar has made some inroads into the education system in a few places such as in New South Wales, Australia, Horn (2003) found that even here "traditional grammar continues to hold an entrenched, profoundly influential position" (p. 2).

in helping students understand and discuss the chosen language content. The message from teachers underlying this guideline was that metalanguage needs to have direct value.

In considering what a more linguistically informed model of language for teaching grammar might look like, we ended up scrapping any mention of the term 'grammar', given the range of attitudes and understandings within the general populace about what the study of grammar encompasses. Instead, the teachers introduced two terms that proved very useful in conceptualizing a relevant image of language: knowledge about language and language awareness.[4] Knowledge about language came to be taken to be explicit knowledge about the structure of language and a metalanguage for talking about it, while language awareness was understood to be the explicit study of the nature of language in human thought and communication. Thus, in the model of language that evolved, language is conceptualized as a system made up of the subsystems of phonetics and phonology, morphology and lexicology, syntax, semantics and discourse, with metalanguage defined as a rich set of distinctions for describing and classifying language and its use.

2.2   Situating the study of linguistics within English

The fact that the subject which the working party was set up to potentially develop was to be situated within the English area had a significant impact on the conceptualization of the vision of the study of language and linguistics that evolved.

As a fundamental aim of English generally in school curricula is that students learn how to use English more effectively and creatively, particularly its more standard written and spoken varieties, any linguistics subject situated in the English area will need to combine the development of linguistic knowledge with the development of language literacy. In best practice, these two outcomes are treated as complementary. What is worrisome is when increased written and spoken competence is taken as the primary motivation for the study of language and linguistics. For however appealing this may be, the assumption that the study of language will improve language use has not been established in the research literature and in some cases the lack of hard evidence to support this assumption has led to the demise of linguistics in schools (see, for example, Denham and Lobeck, 'Introduction' to this volume, and O'Neil, Chapter 2 in this volume).

---

[4] In England, Hudson (e-mail message to author, 17 October 2007) notes that the use of these two terms 'started among educationalists (e.g. inspectors and teacher trainers) who knew quite a bit about linguistics' and that the ideas the terms embody 'can definitely be attributed directly to linguistics' (Hudson 2007: 233). Similarly, in Australia these terms seem to have first been bandied about in education circles, with the linguists in the working party, for example, then subsequently strongly supporting their use.

The current approach to English in Australia, at least, is to focus upon the close study of texts, with considerations of style and genre variation viewed as providing useful tools for the analysis of texts.[5] Building on this orientation, the working party's vision of the study of language came to be centred around the linguistic analysis of actually occurring texts. Texts are taken as providing the frame of reference within which the elements of linguistics and language analysis are identified and interpreted. Thus, the study of linguistics provides a range of analytic and descriptive tools for students to expand their descriptive, analytical and critical skills in dealing with texts from a variety of contexts. With the foregrounding of texts, the study of grammar, and more broadly knowledge about language, becomes meaningful as it is always set within the context of actual language use.

To see an example of this orientation, consider the following activity from the topic area of variation across different registers drawn from Mulder *et al.* (2002).

Activity

1. View the segment from the Australian film *The Wog Boy* where Steve is pulled up by the police because of the car he is driving. In this scene, the first police officer uses a formal police register, so much so that Steve requires the communication to be interpreted. The second police officer supplies the interpretation:

   Police register: *Please exit the vehicle making sure to keep yourself between the vehicle and ourselves at all times and keeping your hands in full view.*
   Interpretation: *Get out of the car.*
   Police register: *May I inquire as to your intended destination at this untimely hour?*
   Interpretation: *Where are you going so early in the morning?*
   Police register: *Your vehicle seems to be disproportionately well maintained for a person of your fiduciary capacity.*
   Interpretation: *Nice car for a dole bludger.*[6]

   a. Compare the language used by the two police officers in terms of lexical choice, sentence length, and complexity of sentence structure.
   b. Consider Steve's actions and discuss the ways he uses language to get the officers on side.
   c. Write your own sentences containing either police or some other clearly identifiable register and provide a suitable interpretation.

As this activity illustrates, the focus is not on linguistic analysis per se, which is the focus for most linguists, but on language use in a text, which is the focus students

---

[5] See Carter (1995) for a discussion of the 'personal growth' approach to English in UK schools which focuses upon the use of texts to foster personal development and imaginative growth.

[6] A 'dole bludger' is someone who is considered to be 'working the system' to fraudulently receive public assistance payments (i.e. the 'dole').

and teachers are familiar with from their previous study of English. Here linguistic analysis provides a tool for uncovering the effect of particular uses of language.

2.3   The resulting vision of linguistics

What evolved over the three years that the working party met was a shared vision of how the study of language and linguistics could be approached in the secondary English area. Important features of this vision included:

- conceptualizing the study of language as consisting of knowledge about language and language awareness, where knowledge about language includes a metalanguage for describing and classifying language and its use, a range of analytic and descriptive tools for studying language and explicit knowledge about the structure of language, while language awareness includes the understandings students are expected to develop in their study of the nature and functions of language;
- centring the subject around real-world texts and their use for identifying and interpreting linguistic understandings;
- making language use rather than language description the focal point in the study of language; and
- recognizing that for the study of knowledge about language, and grammar in particular, to be meaningful it must always be done within the context of actual language use.

The challenge to us linguists was to provide not only linguistic knowledge about the study of language, but to relate it to actual effects in language use.

3   The subject VCE English Language

3.1   Overview

In 2001, five years after the working party began its work, EL was fully accredited and up and running in schools. This subject is unique within Australia, combining a systematic exploration of the English language with the development of skills in the linguistic description and analysis of a diverse range of spoken and written English texts ranging from spontaneous informal conversation to established written literature.

Through EL the importance of the explicit study of linguistics 'in and of itself' for senior secondary students has been recognized in the state's curriculum. It is one of four subjects in the English area of the VCE and shares with English/ English as a Second Language (ESL), Literature and Foundation English a general focus on developing language literacy through a variety of contexts in which language is used, but EL has a distinctive focus on the development of knowledge about the linguistics of English. Students learn a metalanguage and a range of analytic and descriptive tools for studying language. This enables them to use their knowledge of language in a variety of contexts, such as investigating language variation, the link between language and identity, distinctive character-istics of English in Australia, and the ways in which writers and speakers adapt language and structure according to their purpose.

While EL is only in its ninth year of being fully available, there have been steady yearly increases in student enrolment (from 686 students completing Units 3 and 4 in 2001 to 2,013 students in 2008) and numbers of schools offering the subject (from 30 schools offering Units 3 and 4 in 2001 to 80 (15 per cent) of schools in 2008). The growth of the subject has also been positively influenced by the broadening of the 'English requirement' of the VCE. When the subject was initially accredited, students still has to do some units of English/ESL to satisfy the English requirement for the award of the VCE. However, as of 2006 a student can, for example, satisfy the requirement solely with EL units. This has contributed to the substantial growth of the subject.

3.2   Study design

As set out in the current *English Language Victoria Certificate of Education Study Design* (VCAA 2005),[7] EL consists of four one-semester units. Unit 1: 'Language and communication' focuses on the functions and differing nature of written and spoken language, the ways in which language encodes social and cultural understandings, convention and creativity in language, the nature and developmental stages of child language acquisition, and language prescription versus appropriateness of language use. Unit 2: 'Language change' explores the historical development of English, the nature and effects of language change, attitudes to language change, the globalization of English, the development of pidgins and creoles, and the decline and death of languages as a result of the worldwide spread of English. Unit 3: 'Language in society' investigates language variation according to both the user and its occasion of use, attitudes to different varieties, language as a means of inclusion or of exclusion and discrimination, and the use of language to reflect and construct identity. Unit 4: 'Texts in their Australian contexts' gives students a framework for describing the interrelation-ship between words, sentences and text and the distinctive stylistic features of a range of spoken and written varieties of English, including conversational max-ims and textual cohesion and coherence.[8]

Each unit, which is designed to involve a minimum of fifty hours of class-room instruction, focuses on two areas of study together with particular aspects

---

[7] The VCAA publishes a study design for each subject (or 'study' in VCE terminology) which spells out the content for the subject and how students' work is to be assessed.

[8] A more detailed summary of the linguistic content of EL is given in Mulder (2007).

Table 5.1 *Structure of VCE English Language*

Unit 1: Language and communication

Area of study 1	Outcome 1
The nature and functions of language	On completion of this outcome students will be able to: identify and describe primary aspects of the nature and functions of human language.
Area of study 2	Outcome 2
Language acquisition	On completion of this outcome students will be able to: analyze what children learn when they acquire language and explain a range of perspectives on how language is acquired.

Unit 2: Language change

Area of study 1	Outcome 1
English across time	On completion of this outcome students will be able to: describe the making of English, identify how language change takes place and analyze a range of attitudes to language change.
Area of study 2	Outcome 2
Englishes across the globe	On completion of this outcome students will be able to: investigate the effects of the globalization of English in terms of both conformity and diversity.

Unit 3: Language in society

Area of study 1	Outcome 1
Language variation according to users	On completion of this outcome students will be able to: analyze a range of attitudes to language varieties, and how language variation reflects its users and contributes to a sense of identity.
Area of study 2	Outcome 2
Language variation according to use	On completion of this outcome students will be able to: identify the ways in which language features are used in societal interaction and analyze variations in language use.

Unit 4: Texts in their Australian contexts

Area of study 1	Outcome 1
Spoken language	On completion of this outcome students will be able to: identify and analyze distinctive features of spoken English texts involving more than one speaker.
Area of study 2	Outcome 2
Written language	On completion of this outcome students will be able to: identify and analyze distinctive features of written English texts.

of 'Language description', language description being taken up in all four units. Each area of study within a unit has a corresponding outcome statement of key knowledge and key skills students will be able to demonstrate as a result of achieving the outcome. The layout of units, areas of study and outcome statements for EL is given in Table 5.1.

Each unit has a wide range of assessment tasks from which teachers can choose in order to assess each outcome. While the assessment of levels of achievement in Units 1 and 2 is a matter for school decision, in Units 3 and 4 a student's level of achievement is determined by school-assessed coursework (25% for each unit) and an external state-wide end-of-year examination (50%).

3.3   The vision of linguistics embodied in EL

In considering how the working party translated their vision of linguistics into the framework of a senior secondary English subject, what we find is that, in broad terms, the metalanguage and linguistic understandings about the structure of language (that is, the knowledge about language) are identified in the content of 'Language description', while the topics to be covered in the study of language (that is, the linguistic subject matter or language awareness content) are laid out in the areas of study of the four units. Language description was purposefully spread across all four units so that students are introduced to the elements of linguistic analysis and the relevant metalanguage within the context of the study of language. By taking texts as the frame of reference for the study of language and within which the elements of language description are identified and interpreted, the central focus is on language in use. The upshot is that students develop descriptive, analytical and critical skills in dealing with a diverse range of texts.

A good way to see how the vision of linguistics was embedded in EL is through an overview of the two-hour end-of-year examination, which contains three sections. The first two sections, which are worth 30 per cent each, are in the form of short answer questions – one section based on analyzing the transcript of a spoken text/s and the other on analyzing a written text/s – while the third section, worth 40 per cent, is an essay, or 'sustained expository response', to one of three questions. The following essay question from the 2006 examination illustrates the key features of EL:

Essay question

Why do people insist on holding private conversations in public? Intimate conversations, swearing, complaining about workmates – these are just not appropriate topics for discussion on the mobile phone on the train trip to work or school. (letter from a train traveler)

We've shampooed the camels, laid on a nice sunset, and the beer is waiting at the other end, so where the bloody hell are you? (Australian government tourism authority advertisement)

As long as you stay mindful of the existence of a whole range of equally useful adjectives and superlatives it is almost un-Australian not to throw in the occasional expletive for a bit of no-nonsense impact. (Tracee Hutchison, journalist, in *The Age*, 4 February 2006)

Discuss the use of appropriate language in one or more specific Australian contexts. Refer to at least **two** subsystems of language in your response.

Using examples from texts, in this case aided but not limited to that of the stimulus material, students are asked to demonstrate their ability to use appropriate metalanguage to describe and analyze linguistic usage along with their knowledge of the relevant topics from Unit 3: 'Language in society' and Unit 4: 'Texts in their Australian contexts'. At the same time, as the subject is situated in the English area of the VCE, which has a general focus on developing language literacy, students are required to demonstrate their 'ability to write responses that are clearly organized, using effective, accurate and fluent language' (VCAA 2006). The level of linguistic analysis that the better students are producing is commensurate with the range that I find in a first-year undergraduate class in Linguistics.

4   The role of textbooks

While the *English Language Victoria Certificate of Education Study Design* outlines the content of the subject, textbooks play an important role in fleshing out the study design and 'giving legs' to ideals such as grounding the subject in the analysis of language use in texts and teaching knowledge about language, and grammar in particular, within the context of actual language use. However, not surprisingly, writing textbooks for the senior secondary level is quite different than typical research writing and even tertiary textbook writing. In the next section I discuss some of what I have learned in co-writing two textbooks for EL and substantially revising one of these for a new edition (Mulder *et al.* 2001, 2002, forthcoming).

4.1   Some considerations in writing textbooks

In writing a textbook, some of the considerations and challenges for linguists are pedagogical and some are practical, but some are also linguistic. The first step in planning a textbook is putting together a team of authors. Again a partnership of linguists and teachers who can collaborate and learn from each other is critical as each group brings complementary skills. For example, linguists are typically good at laying out the scope and sequence of the material to be covered, while teachers are particularly good at finding engaging texts and designing activities.

From a design standpoint it is crucial that a textbook be readily accessible for teachers and students. In the case of EL, this means first of all writing to the study design. To make the textbooks as transparent as possible the chapters need to be organized to mirror the layout of the units and outcomes of the study design. For teachers it is helpful to chunk the text and accompanying activities into sections that are appropriate for a standard fifty-minute teaching period and to organize the chapters for each outcome and unit around the teaching time available in the four-term school year. As EL is taught by English teachers with varying levels of expertise in linguistics it is also important that the text be rich enough for teachers to be able to teach with a relative degree of authority and direct students to appropriate explanations when, for instance, they raise questions based on their own experiences. Likewise for teachers new to the subject it is helpful if the text and activities build on familiar teaching techniques and use resource materials that are either easily available or are supplied, for example, as audio files on an accompanying CD. Making the text accessible to students means ensuring that they are able to explore the subject content systematically through explanation, examples, and hands-on activities drawing on a range of approaches to learning and modes of presentation. As the subject is centred around actually occurring texts, it is important to ensure that activities are achievable by students and are consistent with the topic being covered. In terms of the text it means that explanations must be interwoven with examples and the writing style crafted to be engaging, for example by using first- and second-person pronouns to lessen social distance.

From a linguistic standpoint, it is sometimes necessary to make judgements about providing enough metalanguage and linguistic detail to give a linguistically sound explanation without overwhelming teachers and students. While we as linguists are generally tempted to include more rather than less, doing so can actually complicate matters for teachers and students as it is not always clear how the additional information fits in to the rest of the subject content and it can cloud being able to discern what the key content is for successfully mastering the subject. The approach we aimed to take was to tie the content of the textbooks directly to that of the study design and to strive for coherence and consistency across the textbooks.

Writing to such a tightly prescribed formula is different for most academics and is easier for some than others.

4.2   *Integrating knowledge about language with language awareness*

A major challenge in writing textbooks for EL is to overcome the legacy of negative attitudes to learning about grammar. Too often the attitude toward grammar is that of a four-letter word. This has much to do with the fact that grammar has traditionally been taught and learned in an environment that is devoid of context. Instead, the approach that has been taken in the textbooks developed for EL is to completely integrate the study of knowledge about language with the study of language awareness by not only introducing students to metalanguage terms and knowledge about the structure of language in small incremental steps, but by further introducing each metalinguistic term and linguistic concept within the context of a particular aspect of language use. It involves viewing grammar, and more broadly knowledge about language, as a means for taking language apart in order to see the ways in which we can communicate effectively in a range of situations and for a range of purposes. Thus students are not faced with having to plough through hours of grammatical study before seeing how it relates to actual language use.

To illustrate just how the study of metalanguage and knowledge about the structure of language can be integrated with the study of language, consider the following text extract from Mulder *et al.* (forthcoming) which introduces knowledge about sentence types. The extract is part of a larger discussion of the use of language to create and express solidarity and social distance, with the previous section focusing on choice of address terms.

Text Extract

Awareness of social norms is shown not only through your choice of address terms, but also through the general politeness with which you use language. Politeness itself is socially prescribed. Being linguistically polite is often a matter of selecting language forms that express the appropriate degree of social distance. One means of creating or maintaining social distance is through the use of various politeness strategies.

Courtesy expressions such as greetings and farewells are examples of linguistic politeness. When you greet someone, you expect an echo of your greeting. The failure to acknowledge your greeting in some socially acceptable way may cause a range of responses, from minor concern about what is wrong with you to feeling tense and hostile. In some cases, the omission of a courtesy expression of politeness such as *please* and *thank you* can lead to social sanctions – as children sometimes find out.

Closer together or further apart?

To see how politeness can be used to create social distance, consider the range of communicative functions that a sentence can have in discourse. For example, the meaning of the simple sentence *There's a biro[9] on the floor* seems plain enough. If this sentence was an answer to the question *Have you seen my biro?* it would be interpreted as a statement of fact. But if a teacher was pointing out the biro to a student in class, it would be interpreted as an indirect command to pick it up.

---

[9] A 'biro' is the common name for an inexpensive ballpoint pen.

There are four main sentence types in English and each type has a primary communicative function.

- **Declaratives** are the most basic sentence type and their main function is to make a statement; that is, to be informative, such as in *I saw Jillian at the careers expo*. In terms of syntactic structure, the clause contains a subject that typically precedes the verb. In casual speech, the subject is sometimes omitted as in (*I*) *don't know*.
- **Imperatives** are most frequently used to direct someone to do something. They include a range of things, such as commands (to be quiet), requests (to open the window), instructions (to cream the butter and sugar), prohibitions (to not walk on the grass), permission (to help themselves to the cake) and even advice (to put part of each week's pay into a savings account for buying a car). Syntactically, imperatives have an 'understood' subject *you* and the verb is in its base form as in *Please be quiet*.
- **Interrogatives** are used to pose questions. The most common type of interrogative is the yes–no interrogative. This name derives from the questions always seeking a positive or negative reply, as in *Did you lock the back door?* Other interrogatives are open interrogatives and seek a reply from a wide range of information; that is, the questions are open-ended. Open interrogatives typically begin with one of the interrogative words: *what, who(m), which, whose, where, when, why* and *how*, as in *What are you planning on doing about it? Where did the bus break down?* and *When do you need to be there?* Notice that all interrogatives must contain at least one auxiliary and the subject always comes after the first auxiliary.
- **Exclamatives** are used to make exclamatory remarks. They are very much like declaratives in meaning, except that they have an expressive or emotional component. The primary structural feature of exclamatives is that they begin with the adverb *how* or the determinative *what* as in *How well I remember the 'joys' of house sports!* and *What fun (it was)!* Unlike interrogatives, however, the subject comes before the verb.

If you wanted to ask someone to do something like shutting the window, the most direct way would be to use an imperative such as *Shut the window*. But this would be viewed as not polite in many everyday situations as it is too direct or abrupt. Polite attempts to direct someone to do something tend to use interrogatives or declaratives and stress such factors as the hearer's ability or desire to perform the action, or the speaker's reasons for having the action done. These more linguistically polite approaches are less direct and longer than the simple imperative:

> *Could you shut the window?* (interrogative)
> *Would you mind shutting the window?* (interrogative)
> *It'd help to have the window shut.* (declarative)
> *It's getting cold in here.* (declarative)
> *I'd be grateful if you'd shut the window.* (declarative)
> *Shall we keep out the draught?* (interrogative)
> *You'd be more comfortable with the window shut.* (declarative)

Any of these could, in the right situation, function as a request for action, despite the fact that none has the clear form of an imperative.

In general, we tend to use imperatives with people we know well or to subordinates, while we reserve interrogatives and declaratives, including hints, for those who are more socially distant or where there is some reason to feel that the task we are requesting is not routine and we are trying to be extra polite in making our request. There are many qualifications to these generalizations and, of course, it is always open to the person we are addressing to misunderstand an indirect request – either accidentally or deliberately.

5   Some general principles

In sum, this chapter has discussed one example where the study of linguistics has been successfully envisioned in a way that is relevant to secondary education. I end by highlighting some general principles that may be useful to other linguists working on integrating linguistics into education in a viable way:

- It takes time and long-term commitment by both linguists and teachers to develop a shared vision of language and linguistics which is applicable to the needs of school learning and then to establish and support a new subject. In present university climates it can be challenging for academic linguists to maintain this level of involvement.
- To develop effective collaboration between university-based linguists and secondary English teachers each group needs to be able to position themselves as both learners and experts.
- In developing a shared vision of the study of language and linguistics it is important to build where possible on what teachers already know and to fit within existing curriculum frameworks. In this instance, it has meant positioning the new subject EL within the English area of the VCE, centring it around texts and making language use rather than language description the focal point.
- Writing linguistically and pedagogically sound textbooks (and related resource materials) can be an effective means of codifying a linguistically informed model of language for teaching knowledge about language and grammar in context.
- While integrating linguistics into education can be quite challenging, the journey can be exciting and rewarding.

Acknowledgement

I would like to thank the many VCE English language teachers whose dedication to the subject has made it the success that it is. I am grateful to Mark Durie, Richard Hudson and Caroline Thomas for valuable discussion of the ideas in this paper, none of whom is responsible for what I have done with their advice.

6   Linguistics and educational standards: the California experience

Carol Lord and Sharon Klein

Why do citizens in a democracy need an understanding of the nature and functions of language? With some insight into the nature of language structures, their acquisition and their use, as well as awareness of language variation over time and across communities, the individual is more likely to be able to do the following:

- examine attitudes toward regional, social, and "standard" dialects and the people who use them;
- recognize a range of structures and registers and use them to communicate effectively at work and at home;
- understand the crucial importance of language interaction for children and its impact on language acquisition and later school success;
- take an informed position on political issues such as establishing English as a national language, or prohibiting bilingual education;
- appreciate the variety and complexity of human languages, and linguistics as a science;
- understand the nature of systematic inquiry, even as it applies to the most familiar phenomena, such as the language we develop, know, and use.

But the sustained absence of any systematic study or public awareness of language in the United States has left linguists bemused (Liberman 2007; O'Neil 1998c). Like gravity, language and its fundamental role in defining our humanness are virtually invisible. When the public does notice language, the goal typically is not inquiry and understanding, but rather a concern about usage or questions about prescription, often narrowly focused on written forms. Efforts have been made to introduce linguistics directly into the curriculum (Honda and O'Neil 1993; contributors to Denham and Lobeck 2005; and Honda, O'Neil, and Pippin 2006, to name a few). Others have sought a bridge to language awareness through a focus on usage (Malmstrom and Lee 1971; Adger, Snow, and Christian 2002; Battistella 2005; Wheeler and Swords 2006; and Adger, Wolfram, and Christian 2007, among several others). But even these successes, though important, have had limited effect.

If we agree that awareness and knowledge of language is important for citizens, and crucially important for leaders and policy makers, then it is reasonable that it should be a part of the general school curriculum. Why is this not the case? Who decides what is taught and how?

Some argue that research scholars are the best qualified to determine the content of the K-12 curriculum. This was the assumption of Jerome Bruner when he directed a gathering of thirty-five scientists, scholars, and educators at Woods Hole on Cape Cod in 1959 to discuss how education in science might be improved in primary and secondary schools. According to Bruner, the best minds in any particular discipline must be put to work on the task of designing curricula (Bruner 1960: 19). However, research scholars "often evade public opinion and common sense in their eagerness to bring research knowledge directly into the classroom," according to Symcox (2002: 20), who cites as examples the National History Standards Project and the social studies curriculum *Man: A Course of Study* in the 1960s.

Can scholars of language and linguistics influence the content of K-12 education in the US in the twenty-first century? How? To address these questions, we need to consider influences on education policy, the successes and failures of previous curriculum reform efforts, and the interrelationships of curriculum, standards,[1] textbooks, assessment, and teacher education. We begin here with a historical overview of these relationships in the United States and then narrow our focus to examine events and structures in the State of California. If we understand the mechanisms, we can be more effective in our efforts to give the study of language a wider stage.

The emergence of educational standards in the United States: an overview

Sixteen years after the first settlement in the colony of Massachusetts, America's first college was founded – Harvard College, in 1636. The early curriculum echoed that at Cambridge and Oxford, where a number of the settlers had been educated. Along with some logic, physics, rhetoric, history, ethics, politics, arithmetic, geometry, and astronomy, the curriculum was dominated by Latin and Greek, necessary for reading Scriptures. Instruction was by means of lecture, declamation, and disputation. This curriculum became the model for other colleges as well as grammar schools and preparatory academies, continuing for two centuries (Willis, Schubert, Bullough, *et al.* 1993).

In 1749, Benjamin Franklin proposed adding an alternative course of study for the youth of Pennsylvania. Those preparing to be merchants would study

---

[1] In the context of education and educational policy, the word *standard(s)* is used on the one hand for the notions of objectives and goals in terms of the actual nature of the knowledge – "students should know this, or understand that" – and, on the other, for the levels of desired performance – "our standards should be rigorous; students should be able at least to do this at this level." We try to keep these references clear.

French, German, and Spanish instead of Latin and Greek, and other topics such as drawing, mechanical arts, geography, civics, and horticulture would be introduced. He suggested new instructional approaches such as active inquiry and field trips, and relevant considerations such as social usefulness and student choice. Franklin's proposal had little immediate impact, and it was not until the nineteenth century that such approaches began to appear in local academies. In Massachusetts, a state board of education was established in 1837; state law required that all children be taught orthography, reading, writing, English grammar, geography, and arithmetic (Willis, Schubert, Bullough, *et al.* 1993).

A new professional group, the National Teachers Association, was established in 1857, with a membership of school administrators, university leaders, and teachers. It later became the National Education Association (NEA), and in 1876 it weighed in with a report containing recommendations for "A Course of Study from Primary School to University," attempting to combine both traditional, humanistic subjects and modern, practical subjects.

In 1862 the Chicago Board of Education published a detailed description of content as well as specific instructions about how it should be taught.[2] The Chicago "Graded Course of Instruction" was copied by other school systems and used as a text in teacher education ("normal") schools. A similar course of study was adopted by the St. Louis Public Schools in 1902, including practical and scientific studies and modern languages, with student choice at the secondary level (Willis, Schubert, Bullough, *et al.* 1993).

At the end of the nineteenth century, demographics emerged as an influence on school curriculum. In 1880, less than 10 percent of children age 14 to 17 were in high school; by 1930, the number was more than 70 percent. As the proportion of students who came from low-income and linguistic minority families increased, there was recognition of the need to adapt the curriculum to the changing school populations (Resnick and Resnick 1985). Another influence was a shift in the nature of work, with a greater demand for clerical, managerial, and supervisory workers. In 1870, white collar workers made up less than 10 percent of the work force; by 1980, the proportion was close to 50 percent.

A major question in the curriculum discussion has been whether there should be a common curriculum for everyone, or whether there should be different programs for students with different abilities, interests, and goals (Resnick and

---

[2] The level of detail in the Chicago instructions is comparable to some of the scripted programs used in the first decade of the twenty-first century, e.g., "Special attention should be given to syllabification, in connection with both written and oral spelling. In oral spelling, pupils should syllabicate in all cases, as in the following example: *a-m, am, p-l-i pli, ampli, f-y fy, amplify*. In written spelling, it may not be necessary to syllabicate at every recitation; but in a portion of the exercises, even in written spelling, pupils should be required to divide the syllables, and failures should be marked as errors" (Willis, Schubert, Bullough, *et al.* 1993: 57).

Resnick 1985). In 1893 the Committee of Ten, a group organized through the National Education Association including five college presidents, recommended a college preparatory curriculum as the best preparation for both college and life in general. The committee recommended a rigorous academic core curriculum for high schools; specifically, "every subject which is taught at all in a secondary school should be taught in the same way and to the same extent to every pupil so long as he pursues it, no matter what the probable destination of the pupil may be, or at what point his education is to cease" (Raubinger, Piper, Rowe, and West 1969: 39). But as the demographics shifted between 1890 and 1920, the vocational education movement established a rationale for differentiated programs responsive to students' aptitudes and interests, to prepare students for employment in agriculture, trade, and industry.

Evidence of successful implementation of a curriculum can be found in the assessment of student achievement. In the United States, the scientific measurement of educational products was developed by E. L. Thorndike and his students, who produced standardized tests in reading, language, arithmetic, spelling, and drawing in 1916 (Office of Technology Assessment 1992; Thorndike 1918). Thorndike saw potential benefits for teachers, administrators, parents, and students. The tests could provide information about individual student achievement and could determine the effectiveness of teaching and of whole school systems.

In the 1930s a system for using assessment in curriculum development and improvement was developed by Dr. Ralph Tyler of the University of Chicago. The framework called for defining appropriate objectives, organizing learning experiences, using comprehensive evaluations to determine whether the objectives were achieved, and revising ineffective aspects of learning. These evaluations would also serve to check on the effectiveness of school programs and policies, provide for guidance of individual students, and provide concrete evidence of success or failure for participants and the community. In addition, the formulation and clarification of objectives would serve to focus the efforts of teachers. Much of the goals and scope of Tyler's system reappeared seventy years later in the "No Child Left Behind" legislation of 2001.

The 1950s saw the launch of Sputnik by the Soviet Union, an achievement which raised concern about the quality of education in the US. In response, President Eisenhower asked Congress for a fivefold increase in funding for educational initiatives sponsored by the National Science Foundation. University research scholars participated in creating new K-12 curriculum materials in mathematics, physics, biology, chemistry, and later social studies. These were produced in federally funded projects, with some private sector publishers eventually disseminating the materials. However, twenty years later, these efforts showed relatively little impact on the schools, with only a small percentage of courses (10% to 35%) using project materials, though the projects did have some effect on the content of traditional texts (Resnick and Resnick 1985); a noteworthy example was the inclusion of evolution as a topic in biology textbooks. In addition to science and mathematics, some projects in English and linguistics were funded, including transformational grammar curriculum materials for seventh and eighth graders (Brown, Gallagher, and Turner 1975; Gallagher 2000).

Despite the cooperation of scholars and educators, the reform efforts of the 1960s ultimately had limited impact. According to Atkin (1985), the intent was to promote learning through inquiry, providing children with the experience of engaging in scientific argument. However, when the curriculum developers observed classrooms using the new texts, they were shocked to find teaching that was directly counter to the spirit intended by the developers; the classes were engaged in reading and lecture followed by recitation. The curricula produced by the reform projects of the 1960s were pitched at a high intellectual level. Says Gallagher (2000: 301): "In the Curriculum Reform movement we had unashamedly written materials for gifted students: we assumed that if we set high standards, many students would rise to meet the standards." According to Ravitch (1983), participating teachers were from leading secondary schools rather than from typical schools, and this may have deprived the projects of persons familiar with the wide range of abilities represented in the average public school classroom.

As Gallagher (2000: 282) reflects, "Events were to prove that it was not enough for brilliant men to be theoretically right." Among the reasons cited were the inefficiency of the discovery method and the intellectual demands it places on the teacher, along with the need for strong classroom management skills. Of the Physical Science Study Committee project, it was observed that the planning of the text, the lab, and the films had taken precedence over thinking about the training of teachers (Gallagher 2000). The funding for the projects was intended to be short-term, through the National Science Foundation, rather than through the State superintendents of education, so when the federal funding ended, the projects ended. The primary participants were scholars and scientists and local school districts; a major error was the failure to bring in State boards of education and teachers' colleges. The lack of involvement of professors of education probably slowed the adoption of the new materials by teacher trainers (Ravitch 1983). Gallagher (2000: 304) says, "We assumed that excellence would speak for itself, that it would be universally adopted, and, most important, that it would thereafter survive for the long term on its own merits." The government-sponsored materials were intended to be freely available for anyone to publish. But commercial publishers were not interested in marketing something that someone else could also sell. Furthermore, materials were copyrighted by the projects, and publishers were reluctant to commit to products that they could not revise later to maximize salability in response to shifting social and political priorities and future trends in pedagogy.

The work on the English language curriculum in the 1960s was challenged at a month-long seminar at Dartmouth in 1966, the Anglo-American Seminar on the Teaching of English. In Wayne O'Neil's assessment, "The examination of language rationally ... was put down by folks whose sympathies simply did not lie with rational inquiry, or worse, who did not even understand it" (Gallagher 2000: 302). (See also O'Neil, Chapter 2 in this volume.)

According to Ravitch (1983: 49), as the Cold War subsided, attention shifted to the racial revolution, and "the pursuit of excellence was overshadowed by concern about the needs of the disadvantaged." In 1969, periodic assessments were begun under the federally funded National Assessment of Educational Progress (NAEP). Students in Grades 4, 8, and 12 were tested in reading, mathematics, writing, science, and other areas, producing "The Nation's Report Card." Another measure was the Scholastic Aptitude Test (SAT), administered by the College Board, and used for college admissions. Trends in student performance on these measures, and on international comparisons, led to the formation of the National Commission on Excellence in Education (NCEE 1983). Its report, "A Nation at Risk," found a decline in student achievement – specifically, a "rising tide of mediocrity" (NCEE 1983: 5). It recommended that schools "adopt more rigorous and measurable standards, and higher expectations, for academic performance and student conduct" (NCEE 1983: 27). Further, the report recommended standardized tests of achievement (state and local, not Federal) to evaluate student progress and identify need for remedial intervention.

According to Fuhrman (2003: 10), in the late 1980s, "a few pioneering states, like California, began to create more coherent policies, using substantive expectations for what students should know and be able to do in different subjects – content and performance standards – as anchors to which policies on textbook adoption, student assessment, and teacher certification could be tied. So began the *standards* reform movement ..."

A number of groups formed to assess the condition of public education and make recommendations for its improvement. In 1989 the State governors met and agreed on broad goals to be reached by the year 2000 (National Education Goals Panel, NEGP 1991). One of the goals to be reached by the year 2000 was that American students become "first in the world in science and mathematics achievement" (NEGP 1991: 10). The National Council of Teachers of Mathematics and other national subject matter organizations proceeded to define standards for subject matter knowledge. The Goals 2000: Educate America Act funded group efforts to identify academic content standards, develop measures of student progress, and assist efforts to help students meet the standards.

The Improving America's Schools Act (IASA) reauthorization in 1994 required States to establish challenging content and performance standards for all students, and to develop assessments that were aligned with those standards, with the States accountable for student performance. The explicit alignment of assessments with standards was a significant development in their use in improving schools and student achievement. Earlier, scores on the NAEP and SAT tests had been regarded as indicators of (declining) school and student success; however, the content of these (predominantly multiple-choice) tests often did not correspond to what students had been taught. In their efforts to bring up student scores, some teachers had begun to teach to these tests, i.e., narrowing the range of subject matter and focusing on content at the multiple-choice item level, in effect neglecting the development of complex thinking skills (Resnick and Resnick 1992; Haertel and Herman 2005). Critics argued that if assessments could be aligned with ambitious performance standards, they could be a valuable tool for educational reform. According to this view, the problem was not with the testing, but was instead with using the wrong sorts of tests (Haertel and Herman 2005). Using performance assessment meant "having tests worth teaching to," according to Baker (2007). However, the prospect of large-scale performance assessments raised concerns about feasibility (time, expense), validity, and fairness, and in the following decade those concerns appeared to have been valid as the popularity of performance assessment waned (Baker 2007).

The accountability requirements of the 1994 IASA were strengthened in 2002 with the passage of the No Child Left Behind Act. All students were to be assessed in reading and mathematics (and later science) annually in Grades 3–8 and in high school based on academic content standards. Each State was to establish performance goals, with all students achieving proficiency by the year 2014. NCLB required schools to meet targets for adequate yearly progress for every group of children, as defined by race, language status, poverty, and disability, or face school sanctions that could lead to reconstitution or closure. NCLB called for rigorous standards coupled with multiple assessment measures. However, as Haertel and Herman (2005) point out, the cost of extensive annual testing appears to have discouraged the use of extended performance assessments; the States retreated to the predominant use of multiple choice items. According to Darling-Hammond, the "noble agenda" of the NCLB Act has been nearly lost in its problematic details (2007: 13).

For the system to work, standards, assessments, and classroom instruction must be aligned. The system breaks down when standards and State assessments are not matched. Thus, for a specific curriculum strand, such as linguistic awareness, to become firmly established and maintained over time, it must have a place in the standards statements, must be included in crucial State and national assessments, must be the focus of appropriate learning materials, and must be an integral component of teacher preparation programs and credential exams.

To summarize: nationally, the school curriculum has moved from an initial focus on classics to the inclusion of more practical subjects and differentiated programs in the 1800s. More recently, the alignment of standards and assessments has been advocated as a prerequisite to measuring school success and a means of enforcing accountability. Participation of research scholars has been limited, but was most influential in developing new curricula and materials during the 1960s in federally funded curriculum projects. Although California is a relatively young state, Californians have been actors in these movements. The next section sketches the California experience.

The California story

Trends in education in California were influenced by the national social and political movements of the nineteenth and twentieth centuries. But in California, the focus was largely on teacher preparation; major reforms grew out of legislative initiatives, most notably seeking to ensure that teachers were prepared to teach the curriculum content established by performance standards and curriculum specifications. We review some of these reforms here.

The structuring of California's educational system began in the 1860s with John Swett, an early Superintendent of Schools. Before Swett took the reins, there was neither formal teacher training nor requirements for level of educational attainment for teachers. Swett brought authority for teacher preparation and evaluation under the State Board of Education, although hiring remained a highly politicized local process (Hendrick n.d.). Swett's initiatives touched every area; he worked to reform what was taught and how, to change the manner of testing of pupils, to systematize and regulate the preparation of teachers across the state, and to develop successful and widely used textbooks that would reflect and align with curricular goals (Swett 1911; Hackett 1892; Hendrick n.d.). By 1901, although elementary teachers were locally certified, upper level teachers were required to have graduated from an "approved program" at a normal school or university in order to be eligible for a "life diploma" (Hendrick n.d.: 5–7).

During the early decades of the twentieth century, the rigor of teacher preparation programs tended to rise and fall in contrast with the student population. The 1920s and the Depression years, for example, saw a decreased need for teachers along with a critical look at their preparation and evaluation (Hendrick n.d.).

In the 1950s, the California State legislature became a player in educational reform. Rudolph Flesch published the classic *Why Johnny Can't Read*, the Russians launched Sputnik, and the legislature strengthened teacher preparation, requiring a post-baccalaureate "fifth year" for both elementary and secondary teaching candidates, and, for the first time, an undergraduate academic major. Elementary candidates needed a liberal arts major, and secondary candidates, an academic major aligned with the subject matter they would teach. This initiative, sponsored by State Senator Hugo Fisher, at once streamlined the credential process and deepened its rigor.

Efforts of California Assembly member Leo J. Ryan led to the creation of the Commission for Teacher Preparation and Licensing in the 1960s, an organ independent of the State Board of Education. This later became the Commission on Teacher Credentialing, the CTC of today. Notably, it was the first such agency in the country (Inglis n.d.c). The Ryan Act not only furthered the emphasis on subject matter preparation (academic rather than pedagogical) at the undergraduate level, it also provided for a subject matter examination for teacher candidates, a requirement that could be waived only by completing an approved subject matter degree program.

Following the Ryan Act, changes were made in teacher preparation requirements in response to the perceived needs of the growing numbers of English language learners. All programs preparing teachers for elementary school ("multiple subject") classrooms were required to include "foundational" coursework that would prepare teachers to work with pupils who were learning to speak, read, and write English, as well as learn with it. In some programs this took the form of an introductory linguistics course; in others, the requirements were addressed by coursework combining such an introduction with insights about language development and language acquisition. Some programs tried to present these notions along with an added focus on some idea of syntactic structure, combining traditional descriptive and prescriptive grammar with linguistic perspectives on sentence structure.

In the 1980s, at the national level and also in California, business leaders saw education as a key national problem and priority. The California Business Roundtable members, corporation presidents, focused on the problems of education and possible remedies (Atkin 1985). The 1980s saw a radical change in instructional practice for beginning readers: the 1987 English/Language Arts framework banished phonics instruction in favor of immersion in texts ("whole language"). The Reading Wars raged until the 1994 NAEP reading scores showed that, in just eight years, California had fallen from first among states to last, tied with Louisiana. Some suggested that the drop was attributable to large numbers of immigrants; however, nowhere else in the nation did the children of college-educated parents score lower than in California (Gordon 2003). The framework was revised to call for a balanced, comprehensive approach, including direct instruction in phonics, vocabulary, and spelling (see Lemann 1997). Unfortunately, misinterpretation and misapplication of linguistic insights contributed to the battles fought on this ground.

Near the end of the 1990s, a committee of educators developed a set of content standards for English language arts for K-12. As stated in its preface (signed by the President of the California State Board of Education and the State Superintendent of Public Instruction), "With the adoption of these English-language arts content standards in 1997, California set forth for the first time a uniform and specific vision of what students should know and be able to do in the subject area" (California Department of Education 1997: iv). As an example of the document's "specific vision," 5th-graders were expected to "know abstract, derived roots and affixes from Greek and Latin and use this knowledge to analyze the meaning of complex words (e.g., *controversial*)" (p. 28). The *Reading/Language Arts Framework for California Public Schools* of 1999 spelled out course content and classroom pedagogy recommended for achieving the goals defined by the standards document.

In parallel with the development of these standards, as well as the national Goals 2000 initiative, the California legislature passed Senate Bill 2042, providing for the alignment of teacher preparation with what teachers were now expected to be able to do. The CTC set up panels of experts to decide what knowledge and skills teachers would need in order to accomplish the goals spelled out in the standards and framework documents. These committees included teachers and education administrators, as well as linguists. The authors of this chapter had direct input in the design of the 2001 multiple subject (K-8) and the 2004 single subject (secondary school English) teacher preparation standards respectively. We also served as reviewers for university teacher preparation programs submitted in response to these standards for CTC approval, to ensure that the standards were adequately addressed.

The creation of standards for teacher preparation is one area in which academic linguists can and should play a role. In our case, close collaboration with departments of education in our universities provided us with opportunities to participate in teacher preparation. (One author has a joint appointment in both the departments of teacher education and linguistics; the other has developed and taught curriculum in collaboration with education faculty and is a member of the university's K-8 and secondary education committees charged with curricular and advisory decisions.) In turn, it is this sort of participation that can lead to positions on such panels and task forces. Helping to shape the structure of teacher preparation programs is one of the ways in which we can begin to weave linguistics into the school curriculum. Such requirements are translated into university coursework, places where students preparing to teach come into contact with focused study of language – its nature, structure, varieties, and its development, leading to new insights and questions – a platform with potential.

But even such efforts, when successful, can sometimes be frustrated. The SB 2042 multiple subject standards were approved by the CTC on September 6, 2001. Five days later, the political world changed. And on January 8, 2002, George Bush signed the No Child Left Behind Act of 2001. One direct effect in

California was the supplanting of the newly adopted 2042 program standards with a required standardized test for teacher candidates. Earlier, for students who successfully completed an undergraduate baccalaureate degree in an approved subject matter program, any requirement for a comprehensive exam was waived (whence the moniker "waiver programs" for those approved by the CTC). But with the adoption of the NCLB requirements, California's process changed. All prospective teachers were required to take and pass a new exam, the CSET (California Subject Examinations for Teachers). They were no longer required to complete one of the university programs so carefully aligned with the new content standards. Consequently, for university programs, one quality control mechanism, CTC review, became irrelevant. In principle, it was still possible for linguists to have some input regarding the teacher exam questions, but in practice the exams were created by independent contractors. For the prospective teacher, studying for and completing a set of multiple-choice items was not comparable to the experience of an undergraduate program offering not only coursework but also peer exchanges and opportunities to formulate questions in pursuit of wider understandings and applications of the material. In this context, the good intentions of NCLB had negative consequences.

This setback provides an instructive lesson, nonetheless. It shows that multiple initiatives need to be pursued. There are many ways to access opportunities for developing children's understanding and awareness of language. We conclude with a discussion of those opportunities from our perspective on the California experience.

Opportunities for developing language awareness through our schools

There are opportunities for participation by linguists at many points in the machinery of education, including standards-setting, curriculum development, assessments, textbooks and materials creation, direct contact with students and teachers, and networking with academic colleagues, educators, and policy makers.

Standards

As we have outlined, in California, classroom instruction related to language study is guided by a set of content standards, or goals for student achievement. For teacher preparation, there are three sets of standards: those for programs preparing multiple subject teachers (Grades K-8), those preparing single-subject English Studies teachers for secondary school, and those preparing teachers coming from states outside California to work particularly with English language learners, from kindergarten through 12th grade. If language awareness is to be part of the school curriculum, it must be explicitly included in all these documents. And for this to happen, language scholars need to engage in influential collaboration with the policy makers responsible for designing these pieces of the educational system, as these policy makers often may not have the disciplinary background that would help them to recognize the value of particular approaches to language and language arts study. Participation on standards-setting committees provides the most direct influence. In California, linguists have had a low profile in the development of curriculum content standards for children, as opposed to our more successful participation in the design of standards for teacher preparation programs.

The increasing numbers of English language learners in California schools may provide an opportunity. In 2006, the CTC approved program standards for the preparation of teachers who have received credentials (e.g., from another state) that did not include a focus on working with English learners. The program, named the CTEL (California Teachers of English Learners) credential, provides for both the examination protocol and waiver (university) programs. Importantly, the requirements call for explicit linguistic content in university preparation, including the fundamental nature of human language, children's language development, language acquisition, language variation, and language change. Prospective teachers of English language learners can benefit from not only applied perspectives but also primary lines of linguistic inquiry in their coursework.

Curriculum

A curriculum informed by linguistics for Grades 11 and 12 has been adopted in Victoria, Australia (see Mulder, Chapter 5 in this volume). In contrast, linguists have had little direct or significant input in curriculum development in California. We must learn from Mulder's successful example. The *Reading/ Language Arts Framework for California Public School*s of 1999 has recently been revised, after almost ten years. But there was no linguist on the panel of authors; in fact, the only consulting representative of post-secondary education was a professor of biology from a California State University campus. Nonetheless, although these content standards still include some strange goals (for example, kindergarten children are expected to speak in "complete sentences"), the focus on both early reading instruction and intervention for struggling readers in Grades 4 through 8 are noteworthy. The Department also established provisions for evaluating textbooks which are richer and more detailed than those attached to the 1999 Framework; a comparison is available on the Department of Education website (Department of Education 2007). Extending the participation of linguists in curriculum reform and textbook evaluation remains a challenge in California.

Assessment

For standards to be effective, they must be aligned with instruction and assessments. In fact, according to Stotsky (2000: 249), "A state assessment is the tail that wags the curricular dog. Ultimately, state assessments are far more important than the standards on which they are based... The penalties or rewards attached to student achievement on state assessments are the only real leverage a state has on the content of local curricula."

With the NCLB emphasis on demonstrating student improvement through test scores, teachers are under strong pressures to "teach to the test." The testing process requires oversight with respect to appropriateness and validity of test items as well as relative emphases on specific topic areas. If teacher certification is to be determined by examination rather than by completion of an approved course of study, determining and monitoring the content, appropriateness, and validity of the tests becomes crucial. Language scholars need to be participants in test design and evaluation.

School success in California is measured by examinations administered to K-8 students and by the controversial California High School Exit Examination (CAHSEE), implemented in 1999. Thus far, linguists have not been directly involved in either the design or evaluation of test items, but as students take the test, and as results emerge for both native speakers' and English learners' performance on particular items, there will be observations to be made; the forum has been created.

Textbooks and learning materials

It has been claimed that the most powerful force influencing curricula in American schools is the textbook; as much as 95 percent of classroom instruction is textbook-based (Resnick and Resnick 1985). Linguists have produced textbooks for the college level, but their contribution to K-12 texts has been limited. Again, we turn to the success of Jean Mulder and her colleagues in Australia. Mulder's textbooks (*VCE English Language*) introduce high school students to a range of linguistic concepts.

Media in the public sector present another opportunity. In public television we have seen the success of *American Tongues* (Alvarez and Kolker 1986), "The Human Language" series (Searchinger 1999), and "The Story of English" narrated and co-written by Robert MacNeil, as well as his more recent three-hour broadcast *Do You Speak American?* (MacNeil *et al.* 2005), which recognizes and publicizes the work of such linguists as Walt Wolfram, William Labov, Dennis Preston, John Baugh, and Carmen Fought, in the area of dialect awareness. Importantly, the Center for Applied Linguistics (CAL), long committed to educating the public about language, developed extensive curricular support materials for high school and university instruction. (See also Reaser, Chapter 7 in this volume.)

Newspapers provide a resource and an opportunity to increase public awareness. In the fall of 2007, for example, *The New York Times* published articles about an endangered language (Murphy 2007) and teaching languages in elementary classrooms (Berger 2007). A piece in *The Wall Street Journal* (Johnson 2007) looked at the politics of language use and language teaching in reporting the resurgence of the Basque language. Linguists should contribute to such forums.

Direct participation in schools

Linguists can work with K-12 teachers and children directly in school classrooms (see Chapters 12, 13 and 14 in this volume by Honda, O'Neil and Pippin; Denham; and Lobeck, for inspiration). Academics can collaborate with K-12 teachers; the work of Wheeler, Sweetland, and Ann and Peng, reported in this volume, is instructive. (See also Godley *et al.* 2006.)

On college campuses, linguists can collaborate in teaching classes with colleagues in departments of education. As linguists supervising graduate students, we can encourage dissertation projects such as Julie Sweetland's at Stanford University, where she developed and tested an elementary language arts curriculum module incorporating dialect awareness and contrastive analysis (Sweetland 2006). In addition, colleges can consider extending the role of faculty in arts and sciences departments to include serving as mentors and consultants for new teachers. Among the benefits: students' experience in university courses would continue into their professional lives, and both faculty and students could benefit from discussing language issues observed firsthand.

Networking

Linguists need to give priority to communication with educators at all levels, sharing information and perspectives. Each group has much to learn from the other. Linguists can participate in conferences with educators, such as the recent conference at California State University Northridge sponsored by Teachers for a New Era, whose goal is the establishment of model teacher preparation programs.

Leaders of professional organizations for linguists and for educators have established lines of communication resulting in, for example, joint symposia at conferences of the Linguistic Society of America and the National Council of Teachers of English. Durable links can be formed among other professional organizations such as the American Association for Applied Linguistics, the American Educational Research Association, and the International Reading

Association. As linguists, we are aware of our own expertise, but we need to be clear that we have much to learn from the experience of educators and classroom practitioners.

As we began this chapter, we conclude it. The value of insights about human language – and about humans – is not in question. The challenge is to share this understanding and to put it to work in the most effective ways and in the most critical environments. The California example illustrates some potential "openings." As other chapters in this volume illustrate, linguists are working to design access portals. Taking time to understand how the public education system works, and how it got that way, is fundamental to such work.

7 Developing sociolinguistic curricula that help teachers meet standards

Jeffrey Reaser

1 Introduction

Over the past half-century, advances in analyzing and understanding language – as it exists cognitively and as it is used socially – have shed light on the role language plays in perpetuating inequalities among stigmatized groups. Despite the importance of such information, sociolinguistic knowledge has not yet permeated mainstream American education even though there have been some who appealed for it roughly fifty years before modern sociolinguistic study emerged. The first president of the National Council of Teachers of English (NCTE), Fred Newton Scott, encouraged the inclusion of information about language diversity to be included as part of English studies (Carpenter, Baker, and Scott 1908). While it may be tempting to conclude that linguists have not been proactive enough in making the general public aware of the importance of their findings, the continued embrace of traditional grammar instruction is probably more attributable to revered notions of traditional grammar instruction as opposed to a failing of any specific groups, be they linguists or English teachers.

Linguists should not be overly dismayed at the apparent lack of progress in convincing teachers to incorporate sociolinguistic information in public schools. Though unquestionably from a different era, it is worth considering one such corollary of how slowly traditional views change. In 1514, Copernicus published observations that postured, contrary to conventional wisdom and theological doctrine, that the Earth revolved around the Sun and not vice versa. Galileo confirmed this in 1610, which led to his eventual imprisonment in 1633. It was not until almost 250 years after Copernicus, in 1758, that the prohibition against teaching the heliocentric model was lifted. Further, it was not until 1838 that astronomers proved that the Sun itself was not fixed in the heavens. Though modern linguistic theory may have caught up to the astronomy of 1838, it is worth pausing momentarily to consider the fact that most surveys suggest that roughly 20 percent of American high school graduates still believe the Sun revolves around a fixed Earth. Instead of being discouraged by an apparent lack of progress, linguists should be encouraged to seek new ways of making their findings relevant and important to teachers and school administrators.

In the past few years, more and more American linguists are doing just that. Currently, there are more linguists actively engaged in educational settings and there are more sociolinguistically sensitive materials being produced than at any other time.[1] These materials are appearing, however, at a slightly unfortunate time. While mainstream education has never embraced linguistic study as a significant part of the curriculum, currently, teachers are reducing the already small amount of instructional time devoted to language (Applebee 1989). One explanation for this trend may be that English language arts (henceforth, English) teachers now face increased pressure to improve students' writing abilities as (most commonly) measured on high-stakes, single-draft, timed writings. As anxieties associated with accountability escalate, teachers are pressured to dedicate increasingly disproportionate amounts of time to writing practice. While this chapter is not about the effects of increased accountability on language study, this consideration illustrates a naivety that accompanies many top-down attempts at language education in the public schools; namely, that teachers have clearly defined responsibilities that currently do not emphasize language instruction. Merely creating materials that teach about, for example, dialect awareness will not likely help teachers meet the demands imposed by their states' or districts' standard course of study (SCS), which they are required to teach. Linguists must be able to articulate clearly how their programs will help teachers meet their goals and responsibilities.

One recent example comes from Julie Sweetland's dissertation research (2006). She measured the effectiveness of a twelve-week sociolinguistic sensitivity curriculum that draws heavily from dialect literature; has students learn about dialect through comparative methodology; and has students expand their range of written registers through non-traditional writing assignments. Sweetland assessed improvements of elementary school children on standardized writing assessments, comparing classes that were taught the sociolinguistic curriculum with peer students (same grades, academic levels, and schools) who were taught for the same time-period using a prevalent method of composition instruction known as "process writing" and students who were taught with traditional pedagogical approaches. Among the many intriguing findings, Sweetland reports that the students who were taught the sociolinguistic curriculum outperformed peers on standardized writing assessments. In other words, instruction that may seem to be irrelevant or tangential to the goal of improving

---

[1] Some of the recent public outreach materials on language include documentaries on language (e.g., Hutcheson 2005; McNeal-Lehrer Productions 2005) and sociolinguistic-based curricular materials for teachers (e.g., Reaser and Wolfram 2005; Reaser, Adger, and Hoyle 2005; Wheeler and Swords 2006).

student writing scores was found to be more beneficial than direct instruction in writing and traditional grammar-focused methods. It takes a confident teacher to accept these results and abandon his or her "drill and kill" style instruction[2] – a relic from 1920s behaviorist studies of rats and characterized by a "practice makes perfect" mantra – for this more progressive approach; however, research-based findings such as this one enable teachers to make the case to a principal or department chair that teaching about language helps accomplish the goals set forth by the state and/or school.

While the sociolinguist's goal may be confronting linguistic prejudice, doing so while also demonstrating measurable student improvement on standardized writing assessment may be among the most compelling arguments a linguist could make to a teacher or principal about the need to incorporate sociolinguistics information in schools. This chapter examines another approach to encouraging teachers to include sociolinguistic materials in classrooms; namely, creating materials that help teachers meet the prescribed requirements of their SCS. Ideally, linguists would be invited to help shape educational standards (see Lord and Klein, Chapter 6 in this volume, for one such example); however, it is possible to accomplish much while working within established frameworks. This chapter examines two such efforts. The first is the high school curriculum that accompanies the PBS documentary, *Do You Speak American?* (henceforth, *DYSA*). This curriculum was developed for a national audience and therefore utilizes national standards such as those endorsed by NCTE and the National Council for the Social Studies (NCSS). The second example is the Voices of North Carolina (henceforth, VoNC) dialect awareness curriculum, which is intended for 8th-grade students in North Carolina. Being a state-based curriculum, this product was created to align with the SCS of North Carolina.

2 Standards and the DYSA curriculum

2.1 Introduction to the DYSA project and curriculum

Do You Speak American? is a three-hour sociolinguistic travelogue, starring Robert MacNeil, on language variation in the United States (MacNeil-Lehrer Productions 2005). The program first aired in January, 2005, on PBS and is distributed as a set of three web-enabled DVDs. In order to enhance the program's appeal, MacNeil-Lehrer compiled a rich set of online resources (hosted at www.pbs.org/speak). These resources include essays by linguists

---

[2] The term "drill and kill" was offered by participants in a weeklong workshop on language diversity in North Carolina. The teachers used this term to describe the sorts of exercises that can roughly be thought of as direct instruction or practice for a test including, e.g., teaching prescriptive conventions in isolation from writing or repeatedly practicing timed writings.

and others, maps, web links, vignettes from the documentary, and games related to language. MacNeil-Lehrer also contracted with the Center for Applied Linguistics (CAL), with funding from the Ford Foundation and the Carnegie Foundation of New York, to develop teaching and learning materials for middle school students, high school students, and college students.

The CAL team, led by Carolyn Temple Adger, conducted focus groups with middle and high school teachers and with high school students. The responses adamantly suggested that few parts of the program were suitable for middle school students. Moreover, some segments were deemed to be inappropriate or problematic even for high school settings. One, perhaps surprising, example that teachers noted was a segment featuring Texas humorist Kinky Friedman, who smokes a cigar throughout his time on screen. Teachers were quick to point out that depicting tobacco use is forbidden in many schools. Based on the teacher responses, the CAL team renegotiated its contract and opted to produce a set of continuing education materials for in-service teachers in lieu of the middle grades curriculum. The CAL team also assumed responsibility for marking section and chapter breaks on the DVDs so that teachers could easily skip objectionable or controversial clips.

The teachers unanimously agreed that they would not show all three hours of the documentary or even a single hour in one sitting to their classes and encouraged us to take a thematic rather than chronological approach to the documentary. We developed five curricular units around topics the teachers identified as most interesting or important: Perspectives on Written and Spoken English; Major Regional Dialects; African American English; Spanish and Chicano English; and Communicative Choices and Linguistic Style (Reaser, Adger, and Hoyle 2005). Each of these units includes between three and seven vignettes of two to ten minutes each from various parts of the documentary. The units are available for free on the *DYSA* website (www.pbs.org/speak/education) along with a teacher's manual that provides a general overview of the documentary, curriculum, and ideas for ordering and grouping the units in various settings. A set of college-level units on the same topics is also available. The professional development materials repeat some of these themes though they follow the chronology of the video more closely. The development of these materials demonstrates the importance of working closely with teachers to find out what they need or are interested in: the consulting teachers significantly improved the curriculum. This is one way to ensure that linguists' work in schools will be appreciated and accepted (see Reaser and Adger 2007, for more information about pedagogical decisions made in developing the curriculum).

Each unit of the high school curriculum is organized in the same way. A menu with hyperlinks to each section is the first thing a teacher encounters under the unit's title. Each unit contains the following sections: Overview, Key Ideas, Key Terms, NCTE Standards Addressed by this Unit, Student Objectives, Using the Unit, Video Sections Used in this Unit, Descriptions of Video Segments, Background Information, Discussion Questions, Student Activities/Assessments, and Resources. While many of these sections are self-explanatory, a few brief notes about some of them may be useful. The "Key Terms" section contains every linguistic term used in or relevant to the curricular unit and related vignettes. Also, each term is linked to an online glossary wherever it appears in the text of the unit. The "Using the Unit" section offers pre-teaching strategies including ideas for activating students' schemas or building scaffolding that will help class discussions. It also includes suggestions for teaching the unit – for example, if it is advisable to set ground rules for certain discussions – and ideas for follow-up activities. The "Background Information" section is written in a conversational tone and presented in a question–answer format. This information is intended to be accessible to teachers and provide the most crucial information since few teachers have the time to explore all the related articles in the online database. Throughout the units are links to relevant materials in the database.

2.2   DYSA *and standards*

One of the challenges of ensuring that any national curriculum will be useful to teachers is that it is up to each individual state to set its educational standards. While there are similarities among states – such as teaching prescriptive writing conventions – the sequencing and details are often quite different. Ultimately, it is the state's SCS that teachers are responsible for fulfilling. Thus, an inherent weakness of a national curriculum that is outside the norms of mainstream education such as this one is the fact that teachers who choose to use it must justify how it helps meet state-mandated standards. To facilitate this justification, the CAL team turned to the standards published by national organizations such as the NCTE and the International Reading Association (NCTE/IRA 1996) and the National Council for the Social Studies (NCSS 1994), which have shaped many states' standards. In addition to citing relevant standards, we include annotations about how the curricular materials address each standard. These annotations can help teachers develop a convincing rationale for using the curriculum to meet objectives based even very loosely on the national standards.

Information about standards is presented in two places: the teacher's manual and the units themselves. Since *DYSA* was envisioned as being used primarily in English classrooms, program standards of NCSS are only addressed in the teacher's manual. NCSS (1994) recognizes ten thematic strands that it recommends be included in all social studies programs. The *DYSA* materials are relevant to five of these. Table 7.1 summarizes these strands and quotes information from the *DYSA* teacher's manual about how the curriculum can help teachers meet them (Reaser *et al.* 2005; reproduced with permission from MacNeil-Lehrer Productions).

Table 7.1 *NCSS strands addressed in the* DYSA *curriculum*

NCSS strand	Addressed in *DYSA* curriculum by
1 Culture Social Studies programs should include experiences that provide for the study of culture and cultural diversity.	*Do You Speak American?* units draw connections between language and cultural identity. Through discussions of linguistic diversity, students become aware of differences and similarities among regions, ethnicities, age groups, genders, etc. Such discussions foster cross-cultural understanding.
2 Time, Continuity, and Change Social Studies programs should include experiences that provide for the study of the ways human beings view themselves in and over time.	Language itself is a complex time capsule, preserving, over decades and centuries, some aspects of syntax, semantics, pronunciation, and spelling, while modifying others beyond recognition. The *Perspectives on Written & Spoken English* unit highlights tension between people who deride all linguistic change and those who either study it systematically or celebrate creative additions to language. The unit on *African American English* (AAE) demonstrates the rich history of the dialect by introducing two theories about its origin, each of which date it back centuries to times of slavery. The integration of history and language will help to inform students of the ways in which human experience influences language and what that means in today's context.
4 Individual Development and Identity Social Studies programs should include experiences that provide for the study of individual development and identity.	Self-expression through language use is a reflection of personal identity. Units in *Do You Speak American?* encourage students to continue to build their language style-shifting skills by helping them recognize and appreciate their ability to do so naturally and masterfully. Additionally, acknowledgment and respect for different languages and dialects in the classroom provides marginalized linguistic minorities with self-respect and pride for his or her native tongue.
5 Individuals, Groups, and Institutions Social Studies programs should include experiences that provide for the study of interaction among individuals, groups, and institutions.	The units dispel common myths about language and language variation that help children build respect for people of different racial, ethnic, or regional background. Discussions of institutionalized discrimination and linguistic profiling inform students of hegemonic structures in society. Additionally, the series includes legal and educational responses to linguistic diversity and marginalization.

Table 7.1 (*cont.*)

NCSS strand	Addressed in *DYSA* curriculum by
6 Power, Authority, and Governance Social Studies programs should include experiences that provide for the study of how people create and change structures of power, authority, and governance.	Units provide questions surrounding language use and access to community, education, and professional development. Imbedded in these discussions are issues of institutions and the power structure within them. Legal and educational responses to linguistic diversity and marginalization are mentioned. Students are encouraged to challenge the abuse of power that lies in assumptions of linguistic homogeneity, as discussed in the *African American English* unit.

Most sociolinguists could see easily how sociolinguistic information is relevant to a number of the broad NCSS strands. Also apparent is the breadth of the strands and the fact that they are at the heart of virtually all social studies programs. Therefore, it is not unreasonable to assume that social studies teachers who wish to use *DYSA* in their classrooms could use the annotations to formulate an argument for doing so.

Given that *DYSA* is a documentary about language, the most obvious use for the curriculum would be in English classes. While the teacher's manual has a similar discussion of NCTE/IRA (1996) program standards addressed throughout the curriculum, the individual units reference standards they address. As with the NCSS strands, the standards are cited in their entirety and are followed by annotations that explain how each is relevant to the unit. Table 7.2 summarizes these standards and quotes information from the *DYSA* teacher's manual and units about how the curriculum can help teachers meet them (Reaser *et al.* 2005; reproduced with permission from MacNeil-Lehrer Productions).

Given that the *DYSA* curriculum is relevant to roughly half of the NCSS and NCTE/IRA standards, it ought to be a useful resource for helping classroom teachers meet objectives based on these national standards. At the same time, since the curriculum is relevant to only half the standards, it can only be one component of classroom instruction and not a replacement for existing curricula. Tables 7.1 and 7.2 also suggest that the curriculum is more directly applicable to some standards than others. For example, NCTE/IRA standard 9 – about developing a respect for and awareness of language diversity – is the central theme around which the documentary was created. The seeming redundancy by which all curricular units are applicable to this standard should not be thought of as a limitation of the curriculum however, as nationally there is a severe dearth of sociolinguistic-based materials when compared to materials about reading,

Table 7.2 *NCTE/IRA standards addressed in the* DYSA *curriculum*

NCTE standard	Addressed in *DYSA* curriculum by
1 Students read a wide range of print and non-print texts to build an understanding of texts, themselves, and the cultures of the United States and the world; to acquire new information; to respond to the needs and demands of society and the workplace; and for personal fulfillment. Among these texts are fiction and nonfiction, classic and contemporary work.	**Teacher's manual**: Through visual and web-based media, *Do You Speak American?* engages students with both print and non-print texts focusing on cultural diversity in America, contemporary language issues, and the social implications of language use for the individual, the group, and the society.
4 Students adjust their use of spoken, written, and visual language (e.g., conventions, style, vocabulary) to communicate effectively with a variety of audiences and for different purposes.	**Perspectives on spoken and written English**: In this unit, students are introduced to current debates surrounding perceptions of ever-changing spoken and written English. Students can assess the ways in which their own styles of written language differ from their oral language styles.
	African American English: This unit addresses style shifting in oral communication depending on audience and purpose.
	Communicative choices and personal style: In this unit, students increase their awareness of the broad range of communicative styles that speakers use. Discussing the use of different styles in different social situations fosters appreciation for individuals' communicative resources.
6 Students apply knowledge of language structure, language conventions (e.g., spelling and punctuation), media techniques, figurative language, and genre to create, critique, and discuss print and non-print texts.	**Perspectives on spoken and written English**: In this unit, students reflect on their own command of linguistic rules (in the descriptive sense).
	Spanish and Chicano English: In this unit, students can apply their knowledge of some features of Chicano English in reading and critiquing fiction that incorporates this dialect.
	Communicative choices and personal style: This unit touches on language varieties and communicative styles that depart from general conventions. In analyzing style differences, students will apply their knowledge of language structure and conventions for written English.

Table 7.2 (*cont.*)

NCTE standard	Addressed in *DYSA* curriculum by
8 Students use a variety of technological and informational resources (e.g., libraries, databases, computer networks, video) to gather and synthesize information and to create and communicate knowledge.	**Teacher's manual**: Each unit includes exercises that require students to utilize various informational resources in both print and electronic format as well as exercises that require students to scientifically investigate language use.
9 Students develop an understanding of and respect for diversity in language use, patterns, and dialects across cultures, ethnic groups, geographic regions, and social roles.	**Teacher's manual**: The primary goal of *Do You Speak American?* is to make its audience more aware of the rich geographic and social linguistic diversity and the language history of the United States. Along with discussion about variation in linguistic style, the units also emphasize that all speakers share the need to communicate with different audiences through various language styles. From a scientific perspective, all languages and dialects are equal because they are all systematic (rather than random) in structure. This finding has significant social and political implications that are important to discuss.
	Perspectives on spoken and written English: This unit presents two competing perspectives on American English, one of which respects variety, the other of which respects uniformity. Having such information will allow students to think critically about both sides of the debate and develop their own views on language variation.
	Major regional dialects: This unit supports students' learning about some of the patterns of language structure and language use that characterize major regional dialects. It encourages them to examine their own and others' attitudes toward regional dialects and their speakers.
	African American English: This unit supports students' learning about the patterns of language structure and language use that characterize AAE, as well as attitudes toward this and other dialects.
	Spanish and Chicano English: In this unit, students consider how Chicano English is structured, how it is used, and how it relates to English and to Spanish. Students extend their understanding of how language is linked to social identity as they read materials mentioned in this unit.

Table 7.2 (*cont.*)

NCTE standard	Addressed in *DYSA* curriculum by
	Communicative choices and personal style: Students are not only exposed to linguistic diversity in America but also are challenged to view language in a social, political, and historical perspective. This unit encourages them to understand and respect linguistic diversity as an aspect of cultural diversity.

writing, and literature. In this sense, *DYSA* is filling a known need. It is somewhat disheartening, perhaps, that of the NCTE/IRA standards, this is the one least commonly codified in states' SCSs. Thus, despite the enthusiasm that linguists may have with respect to a national curriculum on language diversity and the fact that it dovetails nicely with national guidelines, it is also important (or perhaps even more important) for linguists to work to create materials that fill the needs at local and state levels.

Before leaving the discussion of *DYSA*, it is worth noting that the curriculum is equally relevant for English and social studies standards, which reflects the multi-disciplinary or interdisciplinary status that sociolinguistics occupies. One of the concerns with multidisciplinary programs in compartmentalized environments such as high schools, however, is the possibility that each department assumes teaching the information is the responsibility of some other department. However unlikely, it would be ideal if teams of social studies and English teachers would collaborate on a unit such as this. In order to help whomever decides to teach the unit, we have attempted to include enough background information in each unit so that it may be taught effectively by either an English teacher or a social studies teacher. The professional development materials encourage teachers to seek ways of working collaboratively and encouraging school- or grade-wide participation to ensure all students be exposed to information about language variation.

3   Standards and the VoNC curriculum

3.1   Introduction to the VoNC curriculum

The VoNC curriculum (Reaser and Wolfram 2005; revised in 2007) is a 450-minute (equivalent to one week of block scheduled classes or two weeks of traditional classes), multimedia curriculum focused primarily on language variation in North Carolina. It is created so that public school teachers without a background in linguistics can teach the curriculum. In order to improve the usability of the curriculum, special attention was paid to the layout of the materials, the amount and accessibility of background information, and the amount of linguistics vocabulary (see Reaser 2006, for more information on these and other pedagogical choices). The curriculum itself consists of a teacher's manual, a student workbook (not a textbook), and two DVDs that contain video and audio materials that support the unit and contain two interactive maps along with a Jeopardy-style review game. This curriculum grew out of the longstanding engagement of Walt Wolfram in the public schools and still incorporates adaptations of some of the original information and exercises from *All about Dialects* (Wolfram, Adger, and Detwyler 1992) and the later *Dialects and the Ocracoke Brogue* (Wolfram, Schilling-Estes, and Hazen 1997).

The 210-page curriculum introduces several key concepts for understanding language variation such as the difference between grammatical, pronunciation, and lexical levels of language; the notion that everyone speaks a dialect; and the fact that language variation is patterned. The curriculum examines dialect patterns and sociocultural information related to Outer Banks English, Appalachian English, Lumbee English, African American English, Hispanic English, Spanish in North Carolina, and Cherokee language. It also contains short articles on these language varieties as additional information.

3.2   The rationale for situating VoNC in social studies and North Carolina's standards

The VoNC curriculum is situated in 8th-grade social studies, a decision that diverges from virtually every other language awareness initiative in the public schools (e.g., Sweetland 2006; Wheeler and Swords 2006). On the surface, English classes seem like the ideal place for students to learn about language. However, sociolinguists typically consider themselves to be social scientists and the discipline draws on studies of psychology, history, politics, and culture, key areas which are crucial for social studies.

This decision to locate VoNC in social studies was in part because the North Carolina English SCS contains no objectives requiring education about scientific workings of language variation. The dissimilarity between North Carolina's SCS and the NCTE standards is somewhat troubling, though not unexpected given the importance of prescriptive English conventions on increasingly rigorous standardized testing. Trying to dovetail the VoNC with the English SCS is exceedingly difficult and perhaps futile. The most promising connections can be made using the 9th-grade SCS, which includes competency 6.01 (2004): "[Students will] demonstrate an understanding of conventional written and spoken expression that … analyzes the place and role of dialects and standard/non-standard English" (www.ncpublicschools.org). Other foci of competency 6.01 include students' ability to use multiple sentence types, proper verb tense, identify parts of speech, and use roots and affixes properly. Despite use of the term "dialect," this competency goal is about familiarizing students with and getting students to use prescriptive conventions. In fact, within the context of other competencies, it may be reasonable to conclude that analyzing "the role of dialects" is tantamount to suggesting dialects have no role in formal education. This conclusion is supported by the way the term "dialect" is used elsewhere in the English SCS. At any rate, dialect awareness has no obvious fit within North Carolina's English SCS.

There are still other reasons to look for a home outside English classes. When teachers face anxiety resulting from high-stakes testing, they are likely to resort to "drill-and-kill" instruction in things overtly related to the test itself. For example, teachers may gravitate toward direct teaching of "grammar skills," test-taking strategies, and practice tests as a means of improving students' writing scores. Such an approach ignores research findings suggesting that a focus on rigid writing instruction at the expense of reading and creative writing results in poorer writing skills (Macauly 1947; Elley, Barham, Lamb, and Wyllie 1976; McQuade 1980; Weaver 1996). It takes a leap of faith (and administrative support) for a teacher to embrace dialect awareness as a means of improving writing (though Sweetland 2006 demonstrates this very finding). Further, teachers may believe that if they teach about the social roles of dialects, some students will resist learning standard English. Though there is no evidence supporting this, it is possible that examining complex rules of dialect grammar could create a tension between non-standard and prescriptive norms that English teachers would prefer to avoid. Situating the curriculum in the social studies classroom avoids all these issues.

Another advantage of situating the curriculum in social studies is that, currently, social studies is typically subjected to less standardized testing than English. Thus, social studies teachers have more flexibility to incorporate a unit on dialects. Also, there are fewer resources readily available to social studies teachers than to English teachers, so they may be more enthusiastic about new materials. This is especially true of 8th-grade social studies in North Carolina, where students learn about the history and culture of the state. Needless to say, there is not an excess of textbooks and materials supporting this rather narrow subject.

Despite our efforts to create a product tailored to North Carolina social studies, a brief anecdote from our work in the public schools illustrates the strong inclination to include it as part of the English curriculum. Walt Wolfram and I have taught some form of the curriculum every year on Ocracoke Island, NC, since 2000. With one exception, we have been placed in the English class instead of social studies despite the fact that we always offer to teach in either class.

3.3   *VoNC and North Carolina's standards*

The VoNC curriculum was created so that it dovetailed with a number of objectives of the North Carolina SCS for 8th-grade social studies (www.ncpublicschools.org

2003). These are summarized in Table 7.3, along with information about how the curriculum helps teachers meet these objectives.

Table 7.3 *North Carolina SCS objectives addressed in the VoNC curriculum*

NC 8th-grade SCS objective	VoNC curriculum
1.01 Assess the impact of geography on the settlement and developing economy of the Carolina colony.	The curriculum examines how isolation caused by ocean, swamps, and mountains shaped dialects. Further, geography explains the Great Wagon Road, which has had a lasting impact on NC dialects.
1.02 Identify and describe American Indians who inhabited the regions that became Carolina and assess their impact on the colony.	The history, culture, and language of the Cherokee and Lumbee American Indians are examined.
1.07 Describe the roles and contributions of diverse groups, such as American Indians, African Americans, European immigrants, landed gentry, tradesmen, and small farmers to everyday life in colonial North Carolina, and compare them to the other colonies.	American Indians, African Americans, diverse groups of European Americans, and the more recent Hispanic population are examined in urban and rural contexts.
3.04 Describe the development of the institution of slavery in the State and nation, and assess its impact on the economic, social, and political conditions.	Slavery had an effect on the language of many African Americans, which continues to impact the economic, social, and political status of African Americans.
3.05 Compare and contrast different perspectives among North Carolinians on the national policy of Removal and Resettlement of American Indian populations.	The historical contexts of the Lumbee and Cherokee are contrasted, including the early integration and loss of native tongue for the Lumbee and the forced removal and resettlement of the Cherokee.
5.01 Identify the role played by the agriculture, textile, tobacco, and furniture industries in North Carolina, and analyze their importance in the economic development of the state.	The curriculum explores the role of agricultural and fishing industries on the dialects, people, and places of North Carolina.
5.02 Examine the changing role of educational, religious, and social institutions in the state and analyze their impact.	These changing systems are examined in part by describing how they correlate with language changes in urban and rural settings.
5.03 Describe the social, economic, and political impact of migration on North Carolina.	Historical migration of British and Scots-Irish populations are examined, as is the current immigration of Hispanics in NC.
7.02 Evaluate the importance of social changes to different groups in North Carolina.	The effect of social changes on language changes are examined.

Table 7.3 (*cont.*)

NC 8th-grade SCS objective	VoNC curriculum
8.01 Describe the changing demographics in North Carolina and analyze their significance for North Carolina's society and economy.	One of the fastest growing populations in North Carolina is Hispanics. This causes people to make assumptions about the effects of this group. The linguistic and social effects are examined.
8.04 Assess the importance of regional diversity on the development of economic, social, and political institutions in North Carolina.	Understanding regional diversity can be enhanced by examining regional linguistic diversity, which is reflective of social and economic institutions.
9.01 Describe contemporary political, economic, and social issues at the state and local levels and evaluate their impact on the community.	Many of the most pressing issues the state faces today are based on language prejudice, which is examined in detail.

As part of making the VoNC curriculum appealing to teachers, we strove to make it consonant with goals and objectives of the North Carolina SCS for 8th-grade social studies. Though the SCS objectives do not explicitly require examining language, the curriculum demonstrates that language is inseparable from culture and reflective of history. We maintain that it is actually *impossible* to fulfill these objectives without some discussion of language. To further underscore these connections between language and culture, the video vignettes incorporated into the curriculum include as much discussion about local history, culture, and music as they do about language. Thus, the vignettes and some of the curricular resources (e.g., the interactive maps) could benefit teachers even if they did not wish to teach about language variation explicitly. An innovative teacher could likely utilize the resources of and integrate the information contained in the VoNC curriculum at various points throughout the grade as opposed to teaching a separate unit on language. In other words, the curriculum can help teachers teach what the state mandates whether they ever explicitly discuss language or not.

4   Conclusion

Among the barriers to introducing linguistic perspectives into schools is the paucity of learning materials that reflect and promote a sociolinguistic view of language. This is further exacerbated by the fact that even teachers who have a stronger than usual interest in language may not feel competent developing curricular units and learning materials for their students. Teacher preparation in the language arts, the discipline in which learning about English is vested, has not kept up with developments in linguistics. At the same time, many English teachers are overwhelmed by an increase in the amount of material they are required to teach and by the high-stakes standardized tests by which they are held accountable for their students' performance despite the fact that these tests do not necessarily measure accurately students' knowledge, academic growth, or writing abilities.

Introducing scientific perspectives and materials into K-12 education requires linguists to work closely with educators and within the goals, policies, and expectations of school frameworks: something linguists may find difficult because it lies outside their area of expertise. This arrangement can be time-consuming, onerous, and expensive, but it is the most promising route to introducing sociolinguistic perspectives in the classroom. Linguists can be most effective by seeking ways to help teachers meet the demands already placed upon them instead of pressuring them to take on new challenges. Linguists should be able to demonstrate how including sociolinguistic information benefits teachers and students in ways that are tangible and easily measurable. Sweetland (2006) demonstrates one means of this; namely, how such information can help lead to better student performance on standardized writing tests. Another means, the one described in this chapter, is creating materials that help teachers meet the demands of existing educational frameworks, be they national, state, or local frameworks. Sociolinguistic programs will only be embraced when teachers view materials as beneficial to their students and useful to their jobs.

8   Linguistic development in children's writing: changing classroom pedagogies

Debra Myhill

Introduction

The role of linguistics in writing instruction is a contentious issue. Both in the classroom and at policy level, the subject of 'grammar teaching' almost inevitably raises professional or political hackles. As a writer, my choice of the noun 'linguistics' in the opening sentence is deliberate, a way of positioning myself as author with a stance of academic respectability. 'Linguistics' confers a different status on the topic and would allow me, if I chose, to neatly side-step the negative associations which frequently attend the word 'grammar'. In the UK in the 1980s, the phrase 'knowledge about language' was used as a lexical choice to mediate between political efforts to re-introduce grammar teaching and professional resistance to the idea. Right-wing politicians saw the demise of grammar teaching during the 1960s and 1970s as indicative of a decline in standards; and, at its most extreme, politicians made a link between educational standards and moral standards. Conservative politician Norman Tebbitt, in a BBC radio interview in 1985, argued that allowing standards to slip to a position where "good English is no better than bad English" invidiously eroded the nation's moral standards to the point where there was "no imperative to stay out of crime" (BBC Radio 4, 1985, quoted in Cameron 1995: 94). Perhaps not surprisingly, teachers rejected spurious connections between grammar and moral turpitude, and saw efforts to re-introduce grammar as a return to sterile, ineffective modes of teaching. From Kolln and Hancock's (2005) outline of the story of English grammar in the US, it would appear that these attitudes are transatlantic. Describing the profession's rejection of grammar teaching in the 1970s and 1980s, Kolln and Hancock note that 'When grammar finds its way into NCTE [National Council of Teachers of English] journals today, it is presented not as a topic for discussion but rather as an issue to be debated' (2005: 12). This would appear to be endorsed by the Minutes of the Meeting of the Committee on Language in the School Curriculum which record that following discussions between NCTE and LSA (Linguistic Society of America) on "how to better integrate linguistics into the curriculum," NCTE had indicated that they were "not eager to step in as partners in such a project [initiated by linguists]" (LSA 2006: 1).

The grammar debate in the twenty-first century is further fueled by the raising standards agenda and international concerns about standards in writing. In Australia, a survey of children's literacy standards came to the conclusion that too many children were not achieving "a minimum acceptable standard in literacy" (Masters and Forster 1997: Preface), which led to the implementation of a National Plan to assess systematically children's literacy needs and the use of early intervention strategies for children who were struggling to achieve expected standards. In England, similar concerns led to the introduction of the National Literacy Strategy (DfEE 1998), now the Primary National Strategy (DfES 2006), which specifies teaching objectives in reading and writing for each school year from age 5 to age 11. In the US, the National Commission on Writing reported in 2003 that, although most children reach basic levels in writing in NAEP (National Assessment of Educational Progress) assessments, "by grade 12, most students are producing relatively immature and unsophisticated writing" (NCW 2003: 17), and the report was followed by the major policy change legislated in No Child Left Behind (US Department of Education 2002). Concern about writing standards is repeatedly represented as a critical situation for the nation: Graham and Perin, for example, argue that "poor writing proficiency should be recognized as an intrinsic part of this national literacy crisis" (2007: 3). In both the US and England, grammar has been reintroduced as part of this 'raising standards' agenda. In England, a publication, *The National Literacy Strategy: Grammar for Writing* (DfEE 2001b), and an associated training program specifically address what grammar should be taught in the context of writing instruction and the new Standard Assessment Task in the US explicitly tests children's use of grammatical structures in writing.

Unfortunately, robust research into the role and impact of grammar teaching on children's development in writing is, at best, inconclusive and, at worst, tendentious. Several reviews in the past fifty years have come to the conclusion that grammar teaching has no proven useful role in writing instruction (Braddock *et al.* 1963; Hillocks 1984; Wyse 2001; Andrews 2005), reviews which have been significant in strengthening professional resistance to advocacy of the benefits of grammar teaching in writing. Braddock's review argued that not only was grammar teaching not beneficial, it was actually detrimental: "the teaching of formal grammar has a negligible or, because it usually displaces some instruction and practice in actual composition, even a harmful effect on the improvement of writing" (Braddock *et al.* 1963: 37). Hillocks states categorically that traditional school grammar "has had no effect on raising the quality of student writing" (Hillocks 1984: 160), and Wyse, critiquing policy implemented without research evidence, notes that grammar teaching has a "negative impact on pupils' motivation" (Wyse 2001: 421). The most recent study in England, a systematic literature review of the impact of teaching grammar on writing, concluded that "there is still a dearth of evidence for the effective use of grammar teaching of any kind in the development of writing" (Andrews 2005: 75). Yet all of these reviews are undermined by a significant methodological flaw: they do not distinguish between studies which analyze the impact of formal grammar teaching in which children are given a separate course in grammar (including, as Hillocks noted, "the definition of parts of speech and the parsing of sentences" Hillocks 1984: 160) and studies which consider how writing instruction which draws attention to grammatical concepts impacts upon writing. The overwhelming majority of studies fall into the former category, and one can only wonder why anyone would think that labeling adjectives or underlining subordinate clauses on Tuesday would have any transferable effect on a child's writing on Thursday!

Because integrating a focus on linguistic constructions into writing instruction is not a common pedagogical practice, there are very few studies which explore this. Fearn and Farnan (2007: 2) note that in the US, the nature of grammar instruction is descriptive, based on identification and terminology, and is tested in high-stakes tests. It is not integrated pedagogically into teaching about how to write. However, Fogel and Ehri's (2000) study sought to examine whether explicit teaching about the differences between Black Vernacular English (BVE) and Standard English (SE) would help them combat difficulties ethnic minority students faced in writing in SE. The link between the grammar focus and writing instruction is explicit: the purpose of the study was "to examine how to structure dialect instruction so that it is effective in teaching SE forms to students who use BEV in their writing" (Fogel and Ehri 2000: 215). They found statistically different positive effects for the group who were given strategies and guided practice in transforming BEV to SE, and as a consequence they maintained that the guided practice "clarified for students the link between features in their own nonstandard writing and features in SE" (2000: 231). In other words, when teaching attention to linguistics responded to an identified learning need, and when writing instruction helped writers to make links between grammatical constructions and their own writing, there was a positive impact on development. More recently, Fearn and Farnan (2007) found strong positive effects on students' writing when teaching made connections between the grammar being taught and children's writing: "grammar instruction influences writing performance when grammar and writing share one instructional context" (Fearn and Farnan 2007: 16).

This chapter, then, will argue that the place of linguistics in the writing instruction classroom is twofold: firstly, to provide learners with the meta-linguistic understanding to enable them to become confident crafters and designers of written texts; and secondly, to provide teachers with an understanding of how to assess children's development in writing and their instructional needs.

Insights from linguistics into writing development

Historically, the principal accounts of writing development have articulated growth in writing from rather differing perspectives. Cognitive models of development (Bereiter and Scardamalia 1987; Kellogg 1994; Hayes 1996; Alamargot and Chanquoy 2001) have focused on identifying and describing the components of the writing process and have framed development largely in terms of increasing automatization of sub-processes and an increasing repertoire of structures and schemas to draw upon. In contrast, process models of development have adopted a stronger socio-cultural stance, seeing writing development as a social and collaborative learning process, and these models have frequently placed high emphasis on personal growth and development of voice (Emig 1971; Graves 1983). Linguistic accounts of development are sparse: Kress (1994) argued specifically that he was attempting "to provide a linguistically – rather than psychologically or literary – or textually or anthropologically-based account of writing" (1994: xv), though his own work eventually developed from sociolinguistic analysis into conceptualizing writing as a multimodal enterprise. However, those studies which do exist provide important insights into children's development of linguistic mastery in written form.

One more thoroughly researched aspect of development is the acquisition of the ability to differentiate, albeit implicitly, between the linguistic demands of speech and writing. Perera reminds us that "writing is not simply the language of speech written down" (Perera 1987: 17) and understanding of the linguistic differences between speech and writing are well-rehearsed. Writing involves more complex syntactical structures, including higher levels of subordination, premodification and embedded clauses (Czerniewska 1992: 24); it has higher lexical density (Perera 1984); it uses fronting and thematic variety differently from speech (Leech and Svartvik 1975: 174); and it makes less use of repetition and clausal chaining (Kress 1994). Very young writers tend towards writing which has very strong echoes of speech patterns, including the tendency to chaining ideas together through coordination.

Perera (1986) maintained that children do learn fairly quickly to discriminate between oral and written structures. She found that children's use of constructions which are only found in speech increased dramatically between the ages of 8 and 10, indicating continuing linguistic development in spoken language. But at the same time, she found that there was a virtual absence of these oral constructions present in their writing, suggesting that "as young as eight ... children are differentiating the written from the spoken language and are not simply writing down what they would say" (Perera 1986: 96). However, a more recent study of 16-year-olds writing in examinations (Massey *et al.* 2006) revealed that there had been an increase in the use of nonstandard forms or colloquial usages in formal writing and they suggest that for some writers this indicates "poor judgment or simply failure to appreciate the distinction [between speech and writing]" (2006: 64). This touches on an issue which I will develop in more detail later: that linguistic development in writing is not solely related to age, but also to ability.

Other linguistic studies provide further insights about development, particularly at the level of the sentence. At word level, Tolchinsky and Cintas (2001) show how emergent writers have to learn about the word as a unit and the orthographic conventions of marking word boundaries with spaces. Initially, many early attempts at writing are in scriptio continua where all the words run into each other. Understanding of lexical separation, however, does not precede initial attempts at the sentence: rather they develop in conjunction with each other. Indeed, Kress (1994) argues that early grasp of the sentence is more as a textual unit than as a syntactical unit, and some complete pieces of writing are composed of a single sentence. He suggests that acquiring understanding of the sentence as a syntactical unit is a significant developmental stage, as it is essentially a written form, not mirrored in speech. Young writers have to learn about sentence boundaries, internal syntactical cohesion, and cross-sentence cohesion.

A small number of studies have undertaken detailed analysis of linguistic constructions at sentence level. Hunt's (1965) small-scale study of 4th-, 8th-, and 12th-grade writers found little evidence of linguistic structures which appear only in older writers and he argued that his study provided "no justification for teaching some structures early and others late" (1965: 155). But other studies have revealed developmental differences. Loban (1976), looking at children from Kindergarten to Grade 12, found that factors that characterized language development included the use of longer sentences, greater elaboration of subject and predicate, more embedded clauses and adjectival dependent clauses, and greater variety and depth of vocabulary. From his analyses of 7–11-year-old writers, Harpin (1986) argued that sentences and clauses lengthened with age; the use of subordination increased; and there was a decrease in the use of personal pronouns. Perera's (1987) detailed study of writing in children aged 8–12 found that immature writing was characterized by the predominance of coordination, the use of simple noun phrases, the use of active lexical verbs rather than of passives and modals, difficulties using causal and adversative connectives, and limited thematic variety. There is quite a high degree of consistency in many of the studies about the pattern of development at sentence level, despite the different time frames, national contexts, and methodologies used and Applebee summarizes these, maintaining that "what seems to develop during the school years is students' ability to manage an increasing degree of structural complexity – that is, to include more structures effectively within a single sentence" (2000: 97).

Common to all these enquiries is the use of age as the key variable in development, but as children grow older they do not all develop writing maturity at similar rates. Because more empirical work has focused on young writers, it may be that these differences have been less evident and Perera acknowledges that "knowledge about the later stages of acquisition is slight in comparison with the considerable amount of information that has been accumulated about the first three years" (1984: 12). The Massey study (Massey *et al.* 2006) referred to earlier is unusual in looking at writers of the same age but of differing levels of achievement. Their analysis indicates some parallels between age-related patterns and achievement-related patterns: sentence length increased with grade; lower graded writers used more compound than complex sentences and made more limited use of simple sentences. The increase in sentence length was also apparent in Haswell's research into college students' composition, and he emphasizes that from a writing development point of view, it is not merely a numerical issue of more words in a sentence, but one of increased ability to shape a sentence for better communicative effect. These more mature writers were able to compose sentences "serving specific rhetorical motives, opting for syntactic and tonal choices that heighten register, generate rhetorical emphasis, and increase readability of thought units of a certain logical complexity" (Haswell 2000: 338).

Investigating linguistic development in high school writers

The empirical findings which are at the heart of this chapter are drawn from a subset of data from a larger study funded by the Economic and Social Research Council. This was a two-year study which investigated writing from three perspectives: the perspective of the text, the writer, and the implied reader. The first phase involved a detailed linguistic analysis of 718 complete texts from a sample of 359 students aged 13 and 15, stratified by gender and writing quality. The second phase involved an observation of a sub-sample of students as they undertook a writing task in the classroom, followed by interviews in which their reflections on their writing processes and writers' decisions were explored. The linguistic analysis looked firstly at word and sentence level features and at whole text features: full details of the study's methodology and findings can be found on www.people.ex.ac.uk/damyhill/patterns_and_processes.htm but this chapter will look at the findings relating to linguistic development at word and sentence level.

Developmental trajectories in adolescent writing

The detailed analysis of 13- and 15-year-olds' writing provided a valuable insight into patterns of development in older writers, and the decision to investigate not just differences in development at two chronological points but also to compare differences between writers of differing ability proved judicious. In general, the most significant differences in linguistic structures used were between writers of differing ability, rather than writers of different ages, suggesting that, by adolescence, age is no longer the principal factor in development. The analysis also indicated that there were very few gender differences (for more detail, see Jones and Myhill 2007). In the section which follows, therefore, I will concentrate on illustrating the principal developmental differences by ability, but I will draw attention to chronological differences where these were important.

Lexical choice

At word level, the analysis indicated that word length increased with both age and ability, confirming what might be called the common-sense professional view that vocabulary choice and deployment is a developmental indicator. Word length, however, can only be used as a generalized proxy for lexical sophistication as, in English, there is no direct correlation between length and lexical complexity. The qualitative analysis explored the characteristics and quality of lexical choices made and found that there were three categories of usage which related to development: the use of 'writerly' vocabulary; the use of appropriately formal vocabulary; and the use of adjectives and adverbs. More able writers appeared to enact their understanding of some of the differences between speech and writing by using lexical items which are more strongly characteristic of writing than of speech. In argument writing, these were often the adverbs which helped to manage the logic of the argument such as *nonetheless*, *contrary* [to], or *alternatively*. This category also included the use of more sophisticated vocabulary which seemed to represent the writer's choices about how to position himself or herself in relation to the reader – examples of this included words such as *traumatized*, *outmoded*, *mutilate*, *malicious*, and *lured*. In some cases, the lexical choices seemed to be specifically about achieving a higher degree of formality in writing where formality was required by the form or implied by the reader. Here there may be a more direct connection between word length and sophistication as one way of achieving greater formality in English is to shift from using words of Anglo-Saxon origin to words of Latin origin which are often longer (Sharples 1999: 94). Below are some examples of formal word choices made by able writers, compared with the parallel, more typical choices of weaker writers:

Less able	Able
lots	*majority*
place	*environment*
give up	*sacrifice*
stories	*narratives*
saying	*proposing*
nose	*nostrils*

The third category relating to lexical choice related to the differences in the use of adjectives and adverbs. In general, the weakest writing made minimal use of adjectives or adverbs, meaning absence was a more significant factor than presence. However, writers of average ability made greater use of adjectives and adverbs than either weak or strong writers and there was a tendency in some of these writers towards a redundant use of adjectives and adverbs. Particularly in the premodifying position, adjectives were used by some children in ways which did not contribute to the communicative effect. The tautologies in *a cold chilly breeze, a wet tear*, and *spiders lurked in every corner, waiting to catch their poor unfortunate prey* are typical of these usages. Developmentally, this may represent the beginnings of ambitious vocabulary choices and an emerging awareness of how choices can impact upon the reader and as such should be viewed as an encouraging sign of growing lexical maturity. On the other hand, there is little doubt that, in England at least, adjectives and adverbs are frequently taught as the key components of good description with the possibility that these writers may have assimilated a hidden message that adjectives and adverbs are intrinsically good and writing should be liberally sprinkled with them.

Sentence structures

At sentence level, the analysis revealed a significant number of differences in the linguistic constructions and patterns present at different age and ability levels (summarized in Table 8.1).

As several of the previous studies had found, sentence length increased with age, and also with ability. Perhaps more significantly, however, was the finding that the able writers used variety in sentence length as a meaning-making device, juxtaposing long and short sentences, using a sequence of short sentences to create pace or tension, or using short sentences for emphasis, as in the example below.

She smiled sheepishly at the absurdity of what she was doing and wondered at what this surprise was going to be. He took his hand away and told her to open her eyes. She gasped.

Both Harpin (1986) and Perera (1987) found that subordination increased with age in writers aged 7–11; here the finding is subtly different. On the one hand, weaker writers did indeed use less subordination than coordination, but the use of subordination did not increase with either age or ability. Instead, the most able writers used fewer sentences of multiple clauses because they also used simple sentences. In some cases, the simple sentences were short sentences used for effect, as in the previous example; in other instances, able writers used simple sentences which showed evidence of descriptive or elaborative expansion, as in: "A layer of grass enveloped the bank, wet from the rainfall that morning."

Table 8.1 *Differences in linguistic constructions according to writing ability*

Weak	Average	Strong
Length and Management		
shorter sentences		longer sentences
similar sentence lengths		contrasting sentence lengths
		sentence patterning for effect
some coherence lapses	fewer coherence lapses	coherence lapses when expressing complex arguments
Clauses		
more multiply-claused sentences	similar numbers of compound and complex sentences	some simple sentences
more compound sentences than complex		fewer compound than complex sentences
use of common temporal and causal subordinators (*when; if; because*); use of non-standard '*like*'		use of wider repertoire of subordinators (e.g. *as; how; before; although; while; therefore*)
Sentence Expansion		
heavy use of finite verbs	more use of adjectives and adverbs for expansion	fewer finite verbs
		more present participle clauses and more non-finite clauses
Thematic Variety		
reliance on subject to open sentence	greater use of adverbials to open sentences, as well as subject	greater use of non-finite clauses and adverbials to open sentences
few passive constructions		greater use of passive constructions
no subject–verb inversions		more subject–verb inversions

The greater dependence of weaker writers on finite verbs also points to more limited sentence expansion, although as writers become more able they appear to use adjectives and adverbs initially as the mode of expansion, later developing a broader repertoire including non-finite clauses and post-modification of nouns. The study suggests that in older writers the developmental trajectory is not a straightforward linear transition to greater use of subordination; instead, least assured writers develop from over-use of coordination to greater use of subordination, while more able writers develop the facility to intersperse effectively controlled subordination with some simple sentences, and to use appropriate sentence expansion, achieved through a variety of linguistic constructions.

A further significant developmental pattern identified was the increase in thematic variety in more able writers. The theme of the sentence naturally tends towards being the subject in English, and most sentences tend towards being Subject–Verb–Object sentences. But the writer's choice of what is positioned as the theme is important as it is one way to signal emphasis or to draw attention to information in the sentence; "what the writer puts first will influence the interpretation of everything else that follows" (Brown and Yule 1983: 133). The strong tendency to start with the subject in weak writers develops into greater use of adverbials as theme in average writers, and greater thematic variety, not just through adverbials, but through non-finite clauses, and subject–verb inversion is evident in able writers, as is exemplified in the brief extract below:

After an hour or so of hard shopping, we were laden with bags so we decided to take a break. Café Metzzo was very classy and quite posh but we were soon lured inside when we noticed the delicious milkshakes available. Dripping wet, we walked in and took the window seat near the door. We sat on the comfy white leather sofas and picked up the menu …

Hunt (1965) argued that there was no evidence of linguistic structures appearing in the writing of older writers, but our study suggests that in adolescent writers while some structures simply increase in use, such as premodifying adjectives, the use of the passive, and subordination, there are other structures which are rarely present in the writing of many weaker writers. These would include non-finite clauses in thematic position and subject–verb inversions. There is evidence to support Applebee's (2000) contention that development is marked by greater structural complexity; but our analysis also indicates that the most able writers also understand how to use simplicity and brevity for effect, through, for example, short and simple sentences.

Conceptualizing the place of linguistics in writing instruction

Our research, analyzing the linguistic structures and patterns in young people's writing, complements earlier work on linguistic development in younger writers, and points to the potential value of linguistic perspectives in the writing classroom. But what is needed is a fully conceptualized view of the role of linguistics within a pedagogy for writing. Firstly, we need to eschew a view of grammar which positions it exclusively as the arbiter of correctness in the context of writing. On both sides of the Atlantic, there has long been a dominant tendency to conceptualize grammar as a means of error correction, or a way of ensuring 'verbal hygiene', as the satirical title of Cameron's book (1995) suggests. Kolln and Hancock (2005) cite Gleason's (1965) observation that grammar in English lessons was concerned wholly with error correction and error avoidance, and the Bullock Report (DES 1975), a major review of the teaching of English, also noticed the prescriptiveness of language teaching which "identified a set of correct forms and prescribed that these should be taught" (1975: 169). This represents an impoverished view of the potentialities of linguistic understanding in the context of writing, a view reflected in the NCW report (2003):

> Writing extends far beyond mastering grammar and punctuation. The ability to diagram a sentence does not make a good writer … writing is best understood as a complex intellectual activity that requires students to stretch their minds, sharpen their analytical capabilities and make valid and accurate distinctions. (2003: 13)

Here grammar is dismissed, along with punctuation, as something merely to be mastered, before one gets down to the real business of writing. It is a perspective which fails to grasp that grammar is "a dynamic description of language in use," not "a rigid prescriptive code" (DES [Kingman Report] 1988: 3), and which fails to acknowledge the role that grammatical understanding might play in developing young writers' "analytical capabilities" or in supporting their ability to make "valid and accurate distinctions." Instead, we need a more contemporary, post-modern conceptualization of 'grammar for writing', which is concerned with describing, investigating and analyzing how language works in specific contexts, for specific purposes: grammar for effectiveness, rather than grammar for accuracy.

At the heart of such a re-conceptualization would be a pedagogical approach to writing which drew on linguistics to develop writers' explicit understanding of choices, effects, and possibilities in their writing. Perera noted the fundamental linguistic differences in prosody between speech and writing, and that where talk can draw on rhythm, intonation, modulation, and so on to direct the listener's attention to the key points of the utterance, in writing these "paralinguistic and prosodic features are absent, so monotony of grammatical structure is thrown into prominence" (1987: 187). In our study, it was evident that able writers were more adept at thematic variety and using varied sentence lengths for effect, but their less assured peers might benefit from understanding both the prosodic differences between speech and writing, and being introduced to possible linguistic strategies for creating less repetitive and monotonous sentence structures which are better aligned to their communicative intent. In a similar vein, our study showed that average writing was characterized by greater use of adjectives and adverbs than either weak writing (which used few) or good writing (which used a greater range of descriptive elaborations). Writing instruction could well draw attention to the repertoire of possibilities for creating description and expansion, and avoid what I have called elsewhere (Myhill 2006) Rottweiler syndrome – the tendency to think that good descriptive writing uses an abundance of adjectives ('a fierce brown, slobbering dog') but not to appreciate that a well-chosen noun ('a Rottweiler') can be equally descriptive. Czerniewska argues that if we want children "to have freedom and power over language," then we need to ensure they are given "guidance about how meanings can be shaped through language" (1992: 146). Supporting developing writers in acquiring metalinguistic understanding of how different linguistic constructions can create different effects is central to pedagogically appropriate teaching of grammar in the writing classroom. Not only would such teaching offer writers more understanding of choices to be made at the creating and generating stage of writing a text, but it would also enhance revision processes, opening up a lens through which to look at what has been written. Many writers find evaluating their writing and putting right the problems they identify very difficult, and some of this difficulty stems from a lack of metalinguistic understanding. As Bateman and Zidonis (1966: 2) suggested, "a pupil who has only a vague notion of sentencehood is doubtless at a disadvantage in evaluating the quality of the sentences he has produced or in understanding the constructive criticisms of them offered by his teacher."

Informed assessment: using linguistics to identify writers' needs

A second, and equally important, element of a conceptualization of the place of linguistics in writing instruction is in strengthening and enhancing teacher assessment of writing and the quality of feedback provided to writers. Teachers' holistic judgments of writing in terms of formal grades or scores are reasonably accurate, but it is not always easy to deconstruct what aspects of the writing determined the judgment, or to be specific about how writers might improve. In England, the government's inspectorate of schools (Ofsted) noted that "the use of assessment to define the problems in pupils' work that need to be addressed remained a weakness in most schools" (Ofsted 2002: 11), and children's reflections on their writing frequently reveal that they lack confidence in understanding what was successful in their writing or how to make changes. From an assessment point of view, there is "a difference between what teachers need to know about language and what they need to teach" (Perera 1987: 3). Linguistic understanding can often provide the flesh on the bones of holistic judgment and can make visible what was previously unseen. Gordon observes that linguistic knowledge enabled teachers in her study to see beyond superficial error in children's writing to evidence of growing syntactical maturity. Previously, for these teachers "the 'writing virtues' of their pupils often went unseen and unacknowledged because of their own lack of knowledge about language" (Gordon 2005: 63). Likewise, Perera argues that "teachers need to be aware of some of the linguistic difficulties that pupils encounter as they attempt to master a formal written style" (1987: 22). Knowing typical patterns of linguistic development in writing can also help provide feedback which is related to the writer's immediate need. Table 8.2 takes an extract from three pieces of writing of differing quality and highlights, through annotation, some of the linguistic characteristics of each which would permit a valuable dialogue about the achievements and the possible areas of development. This dialogue should avoid formulaic interpretations of development (e.g. "you need to use fewer finite verbs to make your writing better") but should embed discussion about the communicative goals of the writer and how the varying linguistic structures might have different impacts on the way an implied reader engages with the text.

Teachers' linguistic subject knowledge

Conceptualizing a role for linguistics in writing pedagogy in terms of how linguistics can support young writers' access to a repertoire of choices for meaning-making in their writing, and how linguistics can support teachers' assessment of writing, has implications for teachers' linguistic subject knowledge. In England, explicit grammar has not been taught in schools for at least two generations, but the recent policy initiatives for both primary and secondary literacy (DfEE 1998; DfES 2001a and b) reintroduce explicit grammar into the curriculum. There is considerable danger in policy implementation which does not pay sufficient attention to academic and pedagogic teacher education needs. A Qualifications and Curriculum Authority (QCA 1998) survey of teachers in the period immediately following the introduction of the National Literacy Strategy indicated considerable lack of confidence in linguistic knowledge, particularly with sentence grammar. The report concluded that there was a "significant gap ... in teachers' knowledge and confidence in sentence grammar and this has implications for ... the teaching of language and style in texts and pupils' own writing" (QCA 1998: 35). More recently, Cajkler and Hislam (2002; 2004) have shown how pre-service teachers struggle with linguistic subject knowledge and its appropriate use in the classroom. Hudson argues that without adequate linguistic knowledge teachers cannot make the analysis of texts explicit, nor can they structure the teaching context effectively (Hudson 2004).

Table 8.2 *Annotated writing samples*

Writing samples	Commentary
Good writing	
*I suppose when someone close to us **dies**, it **is** only human nature to question life and mortality.* [a] *On the sixteenth of June, 2003, when my Grandpa John **died** I **felt**, of course, deeply saddened.* [b] *But I also **felt** a little bit strange. I **think** young people always **rely** on elder relatives to keep on standing; maybe taking them for granted, but also believing them to be as solid as a rock physically and emotionally. When it **happened**, when John **died** so recently, I **began** to contemplate my life, and the billion to one chance of how I **came** into this world, fourteen years ago…* The one particular second when I **was** born really **was** a momentous occasion of extreme proportions. [c] [d] *Thrust into a cruel and cold world, free for just a few moments before being taken and manhandled by some unknown pair of hands and operated on.*	• Thematic variety: 7 sentences but only 3 begin with the subject • Expansion around finite verb: 14 finite verbs in 148 words (9%) • Several well-managed long sentences • 'writerly' vocabulary choices [a] Elaborated sentence: two finite verbs and detail provided through additional adverbials [b] Simple sentence for emphasis [c] Non-finite clause to start a sentence [d] Minor sentence – emphasis
Average writing	
*I **stepped** out onto the pitch, the opposition **were** colossal, and I **was** merely a shrub in a forest. I **looked** around at my new team-mates. They all **looked** confident, but I **didn't** have a clue about what **was** ahead of me.* [a] *We **huddled** into a tight circle. We all **got** told what position we **were** about to play. I **was** put at inside centre, and this **was** a role that I **had** no knowledge to.* The refee **approached** our team and **told** us the basic rules and **checked** all of our studs with great care. [b] *At this point I **was** very nervous but I **knew** that I **had** to get rid of these feelings if I **was** to survive the match.* We **got** told to line up in our positions for kick off; it **was** there kick to us. They **kicked** it straight to our forwards; they **chased** it down like a pack of savage dogs. Josh **took** the ball into the tackle. There **was** a smash and Josh **fell** to ground like a sack of patatoes. [c] *Their forwards **drove** our pack back towards our try line and then with one quick burst of pace one of their players **burst** through and **placed** down the ball over our try line.*	• Less thematic variety: 12 sentences, 11 beginning with the subject • Some 'writerly' vocabulary choices • Frequent use of co-ordination • High finite verb use: 30 in 211 words (14%), though partly reflecting action of match [a] Simple sentence for emphasis [b] Adverbial: thematic variation [c] Elaborated sentence

Table 8.2 (*cont.*)

Writing samples	Commentary
Weaker writing *My oldest brother and i **were** playing hide and seek in the hallway and upstairs. **I was** standing on the electric meter hiding. he **came** in and **pulled** my leg and **I slipped** and **cracked** my head right open. **I had** to go to the hospital again and **get** it stitched. When **I got** home **I did'nt** go school for 2 weeks because **I had** pains at the back of my head. When it first **happened I had** felt the back of my head and it **was** literally covered in blood and I almost fainted.* [a] *Later i **had** an appointment at the hospital and **had** the stiches taken out. **I was** unlucky enough to have another accident where I also **hit** my head. This **happened** at school when **I was** playing around with some of my mates in the Sand pit. **I had** made up a game where we **had** to jump onto a bench and then into the Sandpit. It **went** wrong and **I fell** over and **hit** my head on the concrete. [b] my teacher **took** me to the nurse. [c] my head **was** porring out of blood.*	• Limited thematic variety: 13 sentences, 12 beginning with subject • Heavy use of co-ordination • Generally everyday vocabulary • Limited sentence expansion • High finite verb use: 28 in 188 words (15%) – narrative driven by events [a] Adverbial start: thematic variety [b] [c] Simple sentences but no evident reason for their use

From a pedagogical perspective, linguistic subject knowledge is far more than the ability to use appropriate terminology: crucially, it involves the ability to explain grammatical concepts clearly, and the possession of a good understanding of stylistic aspects of linguistics, so that judicious decisions can be made in the classroom context about which features to draw attention to. Andrews suggests that it is "likely to be the case that a teacher with a rich knowledge of grammatical constructions and a more general awareness of the forms and varieties of the language will be in a better position to help young writers" (Andrews 2005: 75). In contrast, weak linguistic knowledge can lead to an over-emphasis upon identification of grammatical structures without fully acknowledging the conceptual or cognitive implications of that teaching (Myhill 2003). Changing classroom pedagogies requires an acknowledgment of the significance of assured linguistic subject knowledge and strategic action to address it.

Conclusion

Teaching children to write is essentially a social process, one in which developing writers learn how to actively create meaning through written language, and in which they develop an ever-increasing understanding of the needs of the reader and the social conventions of the genre they are writing. It is not a passive or reproductive process, "not one where you learn the shapes of existing kinds of texts alone in order to reproduce them, but where you learn the generative rules of the constitution of generic forms within the power structures of a society" (Kress 2003: 186). I have argued elsewhere (Maun and Myhill 2005) for a broadening of the theorizing of writing instruction to embrace the notion of writing as design, building on Sharples' (1999) framing of the cognitive processes of writing as a design activity. This means that we need to develop writers as designers (Myhill 2006), who actively construct the process of writing as a creative, meaning-making endeavor in which they have a repertoire of choices at their disposal, and who can craft and shape language, like putty, to make it match their design intentions. Linguistic knowledge is not the only component of this design repertoire, but it is the component which is repeatedly overlooked, and whose creative, generative potential is underestimated. If we wish to change classroom pedagogies in relation to writing and linguistics, then, as Micciche contests, we need a discourse about grammar which "takes seriously the connection between writing and thinking, the interwoven relationship between what we say and how we say it" (Micciche 2004: 718).

Part II

Linguistics from the bottom up: encouraging classroom change

Introduction to Part II

Kristin Denham and Anne Lobeck

The contributions in Part II concern successful "bottom-up" projects involving linguists working in primary and secondary schools in partnership with K-12 teachers. As in Part I, the projects discussed here are diverse, but several themes emerge. One is the necessity for linguists doing such work to transition from "expert" to "learner," in order to truly understand not only which language issues are of concern to teachers, but also why teachers teach what they do and how they do so. Of primary concern to K-12 teachers are lessons that help meet existing educational goals in effective ways. Linguists must therefore often leave their own agendas at the door, and realize that the linguistic knowledge we hope to integrate into the curriculum can emerge in other, sometimes unexpected ways, building a strong bridge between theory and practice. A companion theme in this section is that linguist–teacher partnerships not only change K-12 education in positive ways, but also have a positive impact on linguistics. Linguists learning how teachers teach, how students learn, and how linguistics fits into K-12 education are "doing linguistics" in ways that have not always been respected within the academy. The authors demonstrate the importance and effectiveness of bringing linguistics out of the academy and into the public eye and mind.

Rebecca Wheeler's chapter traces her personal journey from rejection to acceptance in the schools, and some of the difficult lessons she learned in her attempts to help teachers teach their students, speakers of African American Vernacular English, to write in Standard English. Wheeler's experiences under-score the need to connect lessons and materials to teachers' immediate needs and goals (to teach students to write in Standard English), rather than to her own goals as a linguist (to raise awareness and tolerance of dialect diversity). Wheeler outlines her successful model of teaching writing in Standard English through contrastive analysis which avoids the pitfalls of her earlier approach, and shows how this model, intimately connected to teachers' goals, raises awareness of linguistic diversity through teaching, rather than through "expert intervention."

Long Peng and Jean Ann's chapter, like Wheeler's, focuses on their own rather bumpy road toward developing successful relationships with teachers and administrators, and their move from position of expert to position of learner. They discuss how an initially chilly and unproductive reception in the schools developed into a constructive partnership, and how this collaboration arose unexpectedly, from informal discussions with teachers about language issues important to them. Peng and Ann also reflect on their own attitudes and preconceptions about teachers, and how, by learning more about teachers' methods, strategies, and needs, Peng and Ann, like Wheeler, were able to put their expertise to work constructing a professional development program for teachers, in this case, for teachers of English to speakers of other languages (TESOL). Peng and Ann show that the most important thing linguistics can offer teachers is not necessarily specific content, but the ability to analyze language data, because it is this skill that most clearly connects to practice, and is the most useful tool we can offer teachers who grapple with a range of language issues on a daily basis. Peng and Ann also make the point that while they worried at first that working in the schools would take them away from "doing linguistics," their collaborations with teachers and students are what have reinvigorated linguistics for them, and made them researchers in the truest sense of the word.

Julie Sweetland's chapter brings together some of the themes discussed by both Wheeler and Peng and Ann; namely that in order to be successful in the schools, linguists must shift their focus from what teachers need to know about linguistics to what linguists need to know about teaching. Sweetland proposes that one way to do this is to focus sociolinguistic research on K-12 teaching. Her own research project is designed to investigate teachers' language attitudes, and how those attitudes impact their teaching. The results of Sweetland's socio-linguistic experiments show that changing teachers' negative attitudes about AAVE, for example (attitudes also noted by Wheeler), can lead to a change in practice, in the form of lessons that promote tolerance of and respect for dialect diversity. As Sweetland remarks, "ask teachers to teach what you want them to learn." Like others in this volume, Sweetland advocates for materials for teachers that they can immediately use and which are connected to their existing curriculum.

Linguists Maya Honda and Wayne O'Neil discuss their longtime collabora-tion with teacher David Pippin, and how they as a team promote "linguistics literacy" in the schools. The goal of their work is to improve education about language, but more specifically to introduce students to the science of language, an area of study as important as the study of any other natural phenomenon. They present a model of linguist–teacher collaboration that is unique in that lessons are not explicitly connected to existing curriculum; rather, students are encouraged to "do linguistics" in the same way as linguists proceed in their research. They outline their step by step method of encouraging students to collaboratively examine language data, form hypotheses about the data, and examine more data to come up with a parsimonious hypothesis and choose among competing hypotheses. They emphasize how students learn by doing, and advocate for linguistics literacy as a way of contributing to students' knowledge of the world and science-forming capacity.

Kristin Denham's chapter provides an overview of her work teaching linguistics lessons in a multi-grade primary classroom, work supported by a grant awarded to both Denham and Anne Lobeck (whose chapter follows) by the National Science Foundation. Denham demonstrates how the lessons she developed and taught, in partnership with teacher Deidre Carlson, connected with the school curriculum, and how this work contributed to her own teaching of undergraduates in linguistics classes. Denham's work provides important insights into teaching linguistics lessons to younger students, particularly students perceived as "struggling readers" who excelled in her linguistics lessons, suggesting a rethinking of the notion that struggling readers have "poor language skills." Denham's work shows that linguistics lessons in the schools tell us much about how children think, what they know, and how they learn, and that it is such hands-on work that, together with teachers who may already be doing work that is linguistically informed, leads to creating useful materials and teacher education courses that go beyond content to provide a guide to practice.

Anne Lobeck's chapter complements Denham's, and concerns how their collaborative work, with each other and with K-12 partner teachers, contributes not only to education, but to the field of linguistics itself. Lobeck describes ways in which teaching partnerships such as those discussed in this volume provide linguists and linguistics with a gateway to the community outside of the academy, and help dispel the perception that linguistics is arcane, irrelevant, and too academic and technical to be of use beyond university borders (see Battistella's chapter in Part I). Lobeck also discusses a number of ways to move from the "linguist in every classroom" model to a more sustainable model that maintains and expands partnerships with teachers, through a website (constructed by Kristin Denham) as the beginning of a central repository of linguistically informed materials, and an annual workshop that brings together teachers and linguists to maintain community and share ideas. She also discusses the importance of involving undergraduates in teaching partnerships in order to bring this work full circle. These activities all contribute to professional linguists' teaching, research, and service, and therefore are not only valuable for education, but for the expanding field of linguistics itself.

Ivan Derzhanski and Thomas Payne's chapter gives an overview of the Linguistic Olympiad competitions both in the US and in Europe, and discusses how the LO provides an extracurricular activity that allows secondary students who have never studied linguistics at all to analyze language data. The chapter tells the story of the pilot Linguistic Olympiad held between 1998 and 2000 in Eugene, Oregon, which involved university faculty, graduate and undergraduate students, community volunteers, corporate sponsors (Cambridge University Press), local bookstores, and news media. Secondary school students participated in this first local competition, and others have sprung up around the country. Derzhanski and Payne also discuss the first North American Computational Linguistics Olympiad (NACLO) held in the US in 2007, with funding from the National Science Foundation (to Carnegie Mellon University). The LO, which requires collaboration on a number of levels, has the promise of being an important educational tool, introducing students to linguistics, doing linguistics, and to another way of looking at "grammar."

9 From cold shoulder to funded welcome: lessons from the trenches of dialectally diverse classrooms

Rebecca S. Wheeler

Spring, 2000: During the fall of 2000, I initiated exploratory research in a "majority minority" school division, where a majority of the system's students were African American. My intent had been to ascertain (1) whether student vernacular language patterns transferred to student writing and (2) how teachers conceived of and responded to student vernacular. My hypothesis was that student vernacular language did occur in student writing and that teachers would take a traditional, correctionist approach to student vernacular. If so, my next step would be to initiate professional development for teachers in sociolinguistic approaches to language varieties and research-based approaches for teaching Standard English, in order to improve students' performance on year-end, state-wide tests of writing. The grant writer for the district had organized this meeting; I was one item on a much larger agenda.

With dozens of school principals in the audience, I was to share the results of my linguistic analysis of urban 3rd-grade writing. Analysis of approximately 100 essays from five, 3rd-grade classrooms had revealed nearly three dozen, African American English syntactic patterns (subject–verb agreement; *be* understood; past time shown by context; possessive shown by adjacency; plurality shown by context; *a* v. *an*, and so on) occurring in the writing of local Tidewater, Virginia students (see Figure 9.1 for an example of one of these essays). As expected, teachers saw student writing as error-filled, with missing endings, and they saw students as confused and stumbling with English. The room was packed.

I tried to report on how African American English grammar patterns transferred into the writing of local schoolchildren, and the implications of this language transfer. I gave tallies, showed examples of year-end NCLB (No Child Left Behind) tests that penalized exactly the patterns I was finding (e.g. possession, plurality, subject–verb agreement, showing past time). I had thought that the principals would welcome data regarding student performance, data which could help teachers respond to African American student writing needs. I had thought that the "data would speak for themselves." Yet, I should have known better. A Chicago Linguistic Society tee-shirt from the 1980s comes to mind: "I've been in a room with data. They never spoke a word." Data do not speak for themselves. The data needed a proper introduction.

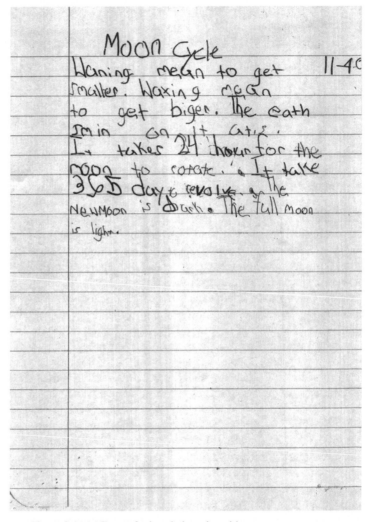

Figure 9.1 AAE transfer into 3rd-grade writing

Part way through my ten minutes, I suspected something had gone seriously wrong. By the end of my presentation, I knew it. None of the principals would talk to me, and were clearly offended by my presentation. I had failed to build a bridge between linguistics and the schools. Time to fundamentally retool. Time to analyze the error of my ways.

Summer, 2007: Our project is a go. With a rural, low SES (socio-economic status, i.e. "poor") school system on Virginia's Eastern Shore, I and my two collaborators, Dr. Raj Chaudhury, educational physicist, and Ms. Diane Gladstone, Director of Curriculum and Instruction for the division, are leading TELES: Technology Enhanced Learning of English and Science in Middle School, a Teacher Quality Grant from the State Council of Higher Education of Virginia (SCHEV). Funded under the federal Title II, Part A – Improving Teacher Quality State Grants, we are integrating reading and writing across the curriculum, enhancing writing and vocabulary learning in science, and boosting Standard English skills. We are building vertical and horizontal learning communities among teachers, reading specialists, and special education teachers, Grades 6–8, across the English and science classrooms. At each grade level, science teachers will be running TELS modules (Technology Enhanced Learning of Science), from the Berkeley platform (www.wise.berkeley.edu) funded through the National Science Foundation, to promote science inquiry. In collaboration with a web-designer, I have adapted the WISE science education platform (Web-based Inquiry Science Environment) to teach contrastive analysis and code-switching (a method I discuss below). English teachers will be running four code-switching modules (plural, possessive, past time, subject–verb agreement) to teach Standard English among vernacular speaking students as we employ technology to enhance learning of English and science in a low SES, high minority middle school. How did I get my foot through the schoolhouse door?

Lessons learned along the way. Or how *not* to prompt another Ebonics firestorm

Over an often very uncomfortable ten years, I've learned a lot about what does and does not work in responding to African American English (AAE) in the schools. This chapter shares lessons learned and rhetorical stances adopted on my path of teaching Standard English to African American English speaking students. I share five principles, and respond to FAQs and FAAs (frequently asserted assertions). I outline key curricular barriers to linguistic work in the public schools, survey the horizon, and muse on next steps. Now for the principles guiding my work in the schools.

Principle 1: If you're working with African American English, never ever name the language variety

At the 2001 LSA, upon first attempting to work with AAE in the schools, I bumped into Walt Wolfram. Naturally, I asked what advice he might offer, what tips he might share. He replied, "Whatever you do, do NOT name the variety.

Never, *ever* call it African American English." He was right. On those occasions when I have attempted to test the limits, push the boundaries, and use this technically accurate term, the consequences have been starkly unpleasant and damaging to my work. Thus, in 2005, I tried using the term AAE in an article written for general, lay audiences ("My Goldfish Name is Scaley," *DoubleTake/ Points of Entry*). I had enjoyed a friendly, warm relationship with an African American colleague. We had talked at some length about my work on language in the schools helping children transition from "informal" to "formal" English (terms I use to characterize the difference between AAE and SE in schools). Then I gave her a copy of my *DoubleTake* article. That friendship ended. She came to my office visibly angry. She, a highly educated woman, told me she resented my suggestion that African American people use some dialect other than the prestige standard.

Of course, I had couched my reference to AAE with all the usual caveats (not all African Americans, not only African Americans, those African Americans who do speak the dialect do not always do so, and so on). Of course, I referred to and cited decades of research in linguistics detailing and naming the dialect.

None of the scholarship mattered. She never spoke to me again. Lesson learned. While my interactions with this colleague may seem extreme, they are actually characteristic of what happens when I have referred to African American English in any audience of non-linguists.

Even recently, I have failed to heed my own advice, with equally rocky outcomes. In June 2007, I spoke at the Achievement Gap Initiative Conference at Harvard University. Surely, there, I reasoned, I could use the technically accurate term – African American English. I reasoned that audiences *should* be able to connect with the technical literature if they are interested, and AAE is the hook. But still no. Nonetheless and yet again, in the garden party after the conference's first day, an African American man approached me, seething. "What do you mean, African American English? Listen to me," he says, "I speak PROPER English and everybody I work with does too." And again, the usual caveats of "not all, not only, not always" held no truck. I stood and for fifteen minutes attempted to respond to the stone wall of his anger, to no avail.

Principle 2: Leave race out of it

Putting aside what we call the dialect, referring to African Americans as a group can similarly land one in a world of trouble. Leave race out of it. Never mind that the national news media is filled with concern over the Black/White achievement gap. Never mind that closing the Black/White test score gap (Jencks and Phillips 1998) is a national mandate under US federal legislation (No Child Left Behind Act 2001). Referring to the achievement gap or to the disparate performance of Black and White students entails referring to racial groups, and is likely to derail any professional development moment.

For example, at one workshop for elementary teachers, Grades 1–5, in attempt to outline a problem needing a solution, I spoke about the achievement gap between Black and White students' performance on the 3rd and 5th-grade Standards of Learning, Virginia's NCLB year-end test. An African American teacher raised her hand, "Why are you singling out Black people?" In attempted answer, I referred to the No Child Left Behind Act with its requirements that we disaggregate student performance, so that we could track the performance of Black, White, Hispanic, Asian, and other groups. I pointed out that NCLB required that schools succeed in teaching all students, and that all ethnic groups were expected to pass the NCLB tests; indeed, Annual Yearly Progress (AYP) on these objectives, and school accreditation, rested upon schools' successfully assuring that all groups passed the year-end tests, etc. I pointed out that the data provided by our local school system revealed that, as across the country and across decades, Black students scored considerably below White students on the tests, and that the school would lose its accreditation if they did not reverse this trend.

All true. And all irrelevant to this and several other workshop participants. In attempting to answer her questions, we spent twenty-five minutes of a fifty minute workshop. In the end, I had all the facts straight but had lost my audience. Now, I leave race out of it.

Principle 3: Anchor in teachers' needs: "What do we do about all those missing –ed's and –s's?"

If it is unproductive to talk about the achievement gap, or African American students or African American English, how *does* one broach the topic of linguistic understanding of and response to vernacular dialects in the classroom? I start with a no-name approach, anchoring directly in student writing, and teachers' needs in the writing classroom. I begin with an example of a representative student essay (see Figure 9.2).

I then lay out that we're going to talk about grammar, and focus on what the teachers identify as errors in student work. I acknowledge the time and effort that they put into correcting students' errors, and ask them if they are seeing improvement as a result, and acknowledge their frustration at the lack of student progress. I share with them that that is also what research shows us, namely that correcting errors doesn't really make them go away, and that I hope to offer them a strategy that I have found to be very successful for teaching Standard English. This approach builds on teacher knowledge and experience, and provides them with an alternative to achieve their goals. Here are the steps:
• Anchor in student data – written essays
• Home in on problem (grammar)

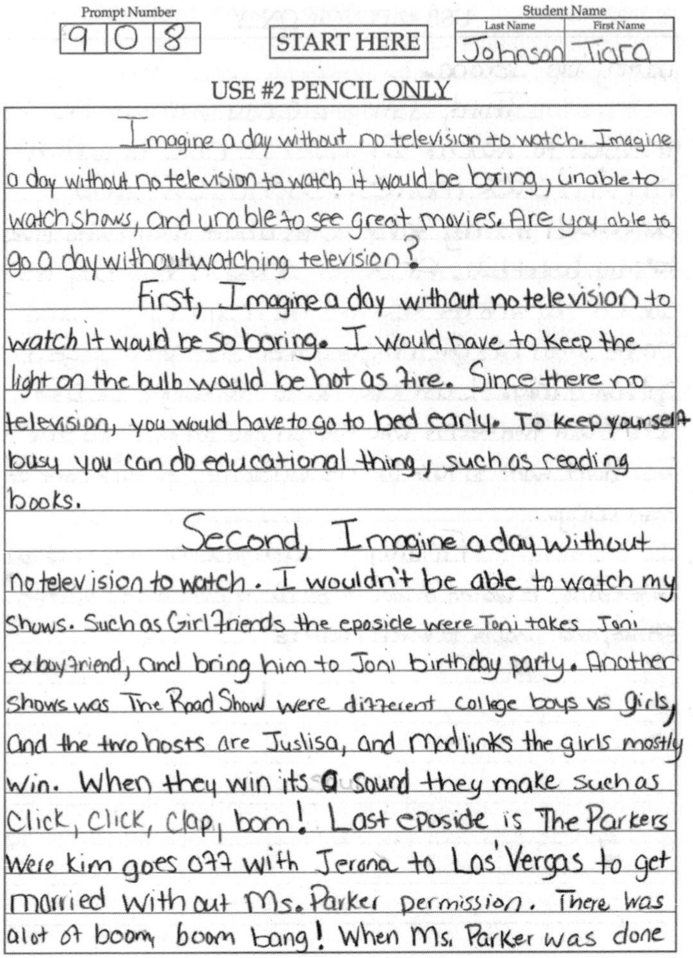

Prompt Number 9 0 8

START HERE

Student Name: Last Name Johnson, First Name Tiara

USE #2 PENCIL ONLY

Imagine a day without no television to watch. Imagine a day without no television to watch it would be boring, unable to watch shows, and unable to see great movies. Are you able to go a day without watching television?

First, Imagine a day without no television to watch it would be so boring. I would have to keep the light on the bulb would be hot as fire. Since there no television, you would have to go to bed early. To keep yourself busy you can do educational thing, such as reading books.

Second, Imagine a day without no television to watch. I wouldn't be able to watch my shows. Such as Girlfriends the eposide were Toni takes Joni exboyfriend, and bring him to Joni birthday party. Another shows was The Road Show were differrent college boys vs girls, and the two hosts are Juslisa, and Madlinks the girls mostly win. When they win its a sound they make such as Click, Click, Clap, bom! Last eposide is The Parkers Were Kim goes off with Jerona to Los Vergas to get married without Ms. Parker permission. There was alot of boom boom bang! When Ms. Parker was done

3

Figure 9.2 8th-grade NCLB essay illustrating student vernacular grammar transferring into school writing

- Evoke recognition
- Give space for teachers to voice frustration
- Affirm frustration. Note how much effort they expend, to little outcome
- Offer insight/explanation (students not making mistakes; following distinct pattern)
- Offer strategy that works.

Not only do I not name the variety African American English, I do not even suggest that any particular variety exists. Many teachers believe that the writing of vernacular-speaking students is rampantly riddled with mistakes, and focusing on how such features actually constitute a system, a distinct language variety, is at this point unproductive. For the moment, I look for teacher recognition of student grammar issues – how to respond to a student's vernacular grammar and how to help vernacular-speaking students learn the Standard dialect.

Principle 4: Induce theory from practice

Excerpted from my article in *Educational Leadership*, the Journal of the Association for Supervision and Curriculum Development (ASCD) (Wheeler 2008), Principle 4 illustrates how I lead with issues of practice on the way to linguistic insights and strategies for an audience of curriculum designers, principals, and superintendents. My purpose is both to illustrate the approach I offer the schools, and to illustrate the terms, tone, and depth in which I present these linguistic insights and strategies to school officials.

The framework: insights and strategies From culturally relevant pedagogy, we know that today's world "demands a new way of looking at teaching that is grounded in an understanding of the role of culture and language in learning" (Villegas and Lucas 2007: 29). To succeed in teaching any student, the teacher must be able to (a) accurately assess students' performance, and (b) build upon students' existing knowledge. This is particularly true as teachers work with students from dialectally diverse backgrounds to scaffold new knowledge, Standard English. Yet, we don't offer teachers the kind of linguistic training and classroom strategies required to build upon the language skills children bring to school. Wheeler and Swords' work in teaching Standard English in urban classrooms fills this gap. One linguistic insight and three strategies can serve as a framework for teacher education and professional development programs seeking to respond to the grammar needs of African American students throughout the US (Wheeler and Swords 2006).

One linguistic insight When African American students write *I have two sister and two brother*, or *My Dad car is a Ford*, teachers traditionally diagnose "poor English," finding that the students are "having problems," or making "errors" with plurality, possession, or verb agreement. In response, the teacher "corrects" the child's writing, showing them the "right" way to convey these grammatical points. Yet, scholarship has amply demonstrated strong connections between teachers' negative attitudes about stigmatized dialects, lower teacher expectations for students who speak them, and lower academic achievement on the part of students (Nieto 2000). Furthermore, traditional correction methods fail to teach speakers of non-standard varieties the Standard English skills our society demands (Adger *et al*. 2007).

Insights and strategies from linguistics offer a way out of this dark labyrinth (Godley *et al*. 2006; Wheeler and Swords 2006). When traditional approaches assess student language as "error-filled," they misdiagnose student writing performance. Linguistics reveals that students using vernacular language (*My goldfish name is Scaley*, etc.) are not making errors in Standard English, but instead, are writing correctly in the patterns of the community language variety (Adger *et al*. 2007; Green 2002; Sweetland 2006). With this insight, teachers can transform classroom practice and student learning in dialectally diverse schools.

Three strategies   Equipped with the insight that students are following grammar patterns of the community language variety, a teacher leads her students in critical thinking to foster discovery learning of Standard English grammar using three strategies: Scientific method, Comparison and contrast, and Code-switching as meta-cognition.

Scientific method   As the teacher grades a set of papers, she will likely notice the same "error" cropping up repeatedly in her students' writing. My work with K-14 public schools over the past decade has revealed over thirty Everyday English (informal English) grammar patterns transferring into student writing. Among these, a consistent top ten emerges (including subject–verb agreement, *Mama walk the dog every day*; showing past time, *Mama walk the dog yesterday*; past time (2), *I seen the movie*; possessive, *My sister boyfriend came over*; showing plurality, *It take 24 hour to rotate*; and *a* vs. *an*, *a elephant*). The linguistically informed teacher understands these represent grammar patterns from the community dialect transferring into student writing, not errors in Standard English. A linguistically informed teacher sees such examples as data (Wheeler 2005).

To begin, the teacher will assemble a set of sentences, all drawn from student writing, all showing the same grammar pattern, and build a code-switching chart, our core graphic organizer (see Figure 9.3).

She provides the Standard English equivalent in the right-hand column. The teacher then leads students in the scientific method:
- **Examine sentences**: She starts by reading the informal sentences aloud.
- **Seek pattern**: Then the teacher leads the students to seek the grammar pattern these sentences follow. She might say, "*Taylor cat is black*. Let's see how this sentence shows ownership. Who does the cat belong to?" Once students answer that the cat belongs to Taylor, the teacher will then ask "How do you know?" Students will most likely answer that it says *Taylor cat*. Or that the word *Taylor* sits next to the word *cat*.

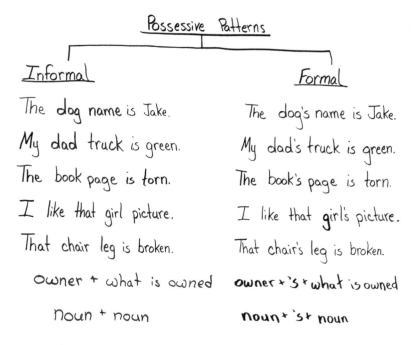

Figure 9.3 Code-switching chart for possessive patterns

- **Define pattern**: Now the teacher turns to helping students define the pattern by repeating their response, putting it in context. "Oh, *Taylor* is next to *cat*. So, you're saying that the owner, *Taylor*, is right next to what is owned, *cat*. Maybe this is the pattern for informal possessives – [owner + what is owned]?" Students have thus formulated a hypothesis for how Informal English shows possession.
- **Test pattern**: True to the scientific method, next she will test the hypothesis. After the teacher reads the next sentence aloud, she will have the students determine if the pattern holds true. So, after reading *The boy coat is torn*, the teacher might ask, "Who is the owner?" The students will respond that *the boy* is the owner. The teacher will probe further, "What does he own?" The students will say that he owns *the coat*. The teacher will then summarize student discovery: "So *the boy* is the owner and *the coat* is what he owns. That follows our pattern of [owner + what is owned]." It will be important to test each sentence in this manner.
- **Write informal English pattern**: Finally, the teacher will write the pattern, *owner + what is owned*, under the last informal sentence. (Wheeler and Swords 2006; Wheeler 2008.)

Comparison and contrast   Next, the teacher applies the most effective teaching strategy, comparison and contrast (Marzano *et al.* 2001), to discovery learning of grammar. Building upon existing knowledge, she leads students to contrast the grammatical patterns of Everyday English to the grammatical patterns of Formal/Standard English, and so make the language contrasts explicit and conscious to the child. The teacher leads students to explore "what changed" between the Informal English sentence (*Taylor cat is black*, etc.) and the Formal English sentence (*Taylor's cat is black*, etc.). Through detailed comparison and contrast, students discover that Formal English has an apostrophe –*s*. In particular, the pattern for Formal English possessive is [owner + 's + what is owned]. This linguistic technique is called contrastive analysis.

Code-switching as meta-cognition   Having used the scientific method and comparison and contrast to identify the grammar patterns of Informal and Formal English, the teacher then leads students in putting their knowledge to work through metacognition. Metacognition is knowledge about one's own knowledge and thinking processes, especially knowledge of strategies and the situations in which strategies might be used to boost performance (Flavell 1979). Children who are aware of their own thinking processes, especially the strategies they might use for successful reading or writing, perform significantly better on these tasks (Block and Pressley 2001; Israel, Block, Kinnucan-Welsch, and Bauserman 2005). In the case of learning about the differences between Formal and Informal English, children must learn to actively code-switch – to assess the needs of the setting (the time, place, audience, and communicative purpose) and to intentionally choose the style of language appropriate to that setting. When Swords asks, "So, in your school writing, which one of these patterns do you think you need to use – [Owner + what is owned] or [owner + 's + what is owned]?" students readily learn to choose the formal pattern.

Code-switching also requires cognitive flexibility, the ability to think about a task or situation in multiple ways, as it requires that children think about their own language in both formal and informal forms. Such cognitive flexibility plays a significant role in successful literacy learning and teaching (Cartwright 2008). Teaching children to consciously reflect on their linguistic varieties and to choose the appropriate language variety for a particular situation provides them with metacognitive strategies and the cognitive flexibility to apply those strategies in daily practice. With friends and family in the community, the child will choose the language characteristic of the community, often Informal English. In school, on NCLB tests, in analytic essays and beyond school, in the world of work, the child learns to choose the expected Formal, Standard English. In this way, we add another linguistic code, Standard English, to the child's linguistic toolbox. (Reprinted from Wheeler 2008.)

Principle 5: The method is the message: Let teachers discover respect for African American language and culture as a natural consequence of contrastive analysis and code-switching

I used to speak of honoring the students' home language and building a bridge from home speech to school speech. The floor fell through. In 2002, the director of one educational organization retorted: "We're not having any of broken English in OUR schools. Zero tolerance!" And I lost the consulting job. Learning from that early experience, I had long since dropped any explicit mention of honoring and respecting students' home dialects. That respect emerges naturally as I work with the core "graphic organizer," a contrastive analysis chart. As we work through discovery of the grammar pattern of Informal English and the grammar pattern of Formal English, teachers spontaneously comment on how respectful they find this approach – They say it's a relief to both respect the language of the family and community and teach Standard English at the same time.

However, I had not forewarned my collaborator, urban elementary educator Rachel Swords, that we needed to steer clear of issues of respect in our presentations. When the *Virginia Pilot* interviewed us upon release of our 2006 book, *Code-switching: Teaching Standard English in Urban Classrooms*, Rachel talked of respecting the children, saying "I'm still teaching standard English, but I'm going about it in a way that respects the language of every child in the classroom" (http://hamptonroads.com/node/110341). Oh, the fallout (see comments on the website). Readers lamented our political correctness, our dumbing down of the curriculum, hobbling "correct" English in deference to children's feelings, and so on – the usual knee-jerk reactions. Now, Rachel leaves respect out of it. Focus ONLY on test results, on success of the method in teaching Standard English.

Going one step further, in summer 2007 when I spoke to the Arkansas Urban Renewal Zone, after one table of teachers commented on how respectful the approach was, another group lamented that educators were giving up standards in favor of a "kinder, gentler, nurturing grammar," "gutting our expectations." As speaker, I redirected, "While this approach may be respectful, that is *not* why I practice or teach it. I teach a linguistically informed approach because it *correctly assesses* vernacular speaking students' grammar needs, and because it offers *successful* tools for assuring our students master Standard English." Of course my reality is more nuanced. Yes, I use contrastive analysis with vernacular dialects because the approach is accurate and effective in Teaching Standard English as a Second Dialect (SESD). However, I also, and even more fundamentally, use contrastive analysis and code-switching because it honors the integrity and structure of all dialects and their speakers. I'm just not going to volunteer that.

FAQs (Frequently Asked Questions)

A range of questions consistently crop up in this work. Here they are, along with answers I've developed across the years.

Q: Aren't you just encouraging that bad language in the schools?

A: No, we are teaching Standard English using highly successful techniques to do so. As in every other subject, we anchor in students' existing knowledge (Everyday English) to add new knowledge (Standard English). That's just sound educational practice!

Q: Why are you catering to the feelings of these kids? They should just buckle down and learn proper grammar.

A: I do not take a code-switching approach because it is gentle with feelings. I use these insights and strategies because they are *accurate and successful* in teaching Standard English with kids who speak a style of English different from the Standard.

Q: Does this have to do with that Ebonics stuff?

A: Absolutely not. This work has nothing to do with Ebonics. Next question?

Comment: How can this answer be true? A story helps respond:

Jerry Sadock once observed that linguistics is so young a field that it had not settled on the lies to tell beginning students. The answer "this has nothing to do with Ebonics," is one of the lies on which I've settled. Why? Any connection with the Oakland Ebonics Debacle is the iceberg to the Titanic of dialect diversity work in the schools. Any attempt to draw distinctions between what Oakland was or was not doing in comparison with what I am or am not doing is to starkly evoke the Ebonics proving ground. Mere entrance there is guilt by association. So my response is always a categorical, "This work has nothing to do with Ebonics, absolutely nothing at all." Here's the truth in that statement: by Ebonics, the lay public means "dumbing down the curriculum, saying anything goes, teaching Black English in the schools, seeking ESL funding for African American students, saying that students do not need to learn Standard English." Under all those connotative misunderstandings, my answer is fully true – CA/ CS has nothing to do with Ebonics.

FAAs (Frequently Asserted Assertions)

Aside from FAQs, here are some frequent assertions which need response.

Assertion: We should eradicate that bad language from the home.

Response: We should be very careful before we presume to go into someone's living room and tell the child how she or he will talk with grandma and grandpa …

Assertion: This language is just flat out wrong, incorrect, and we ought to just SAY SO! Enough of this political correctness. I don't have time for it.

Response: Well, English teachers have been saying that for DECADES, and look where it's got them. Students are still making the same "mistakes." Clearly, the traditional approach is NOT working. Don't you think it's high time for an approach that works?

Assertion: We should have zero tolerance for this kind of bad grammar.

Response: I completely agree with you. We should have zero tolerance for students not being able to choose the language to fit the setting.

Curricular/ideological barriers

Once in the schools, the next task is collaborating with teachers to bring linguistic insights and strategies to the classroom. Here, curricular and ideological barriers present a high hurdle.

Terrible tenacity of the traditional: Prescriptive grammar in the hearts and minds of teachers

Sponsored by the school district, I was offering professional development to middle school teachers on the rural Eastern shore of Virginia. In a series of after-school workshops, I shared student work. I had provided templates, overheads, and examples. We had worked through tokens of many grammatical types treating a top-ten pattern of vernacular grammar (AAE) transferring into Standard English writing. Teachers had explored how to use contrastive analysis charts (see Figure 9.4) to lead student grammar discovery as students induced the grammar patterns of "informal English" and the grammar patterns of "formal English."

Showing possession

INFORMAL ENGLISH

I played on Derrick team
You were going to say that boy name
You step on someone foot by accident
… in some old people neighborhood
All of us went to see my grandpa aunt
Ellen Goodman essay said it all

FORMAL ENGLISH

I played on Derrick's team
You were going to say that boy's name
You step on someone's foot by accident
… in some old people's neighborhood
All of us went to see my grandpa's aunt
Ellen Goodman's essay said it all

The Pattern

owner + owned

The Pattern

owner + 's + owned

Figure 9.4 Sample code-switching chart provided for teachers in professional development

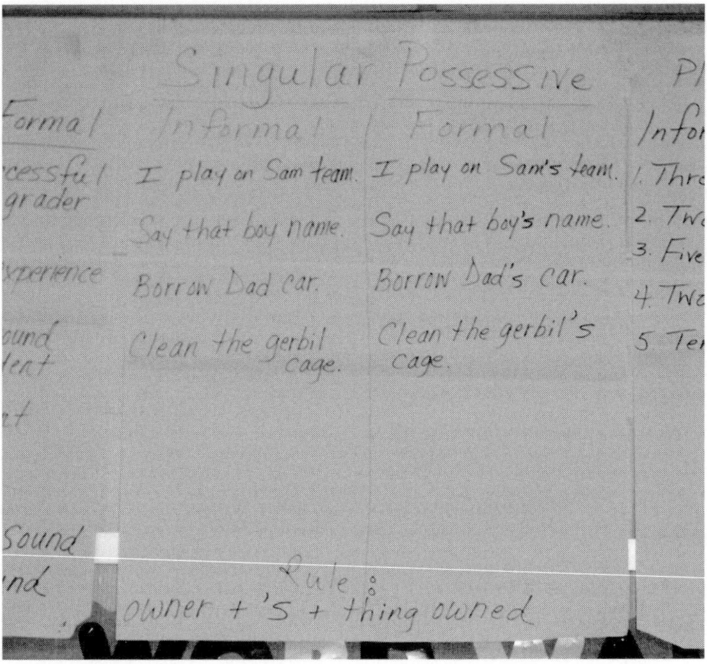

Figure 9.5 Teacher believes only SE exhibits grammatical pattern:
Possessives

And yet, the tyranny of the traditional emerged in teachers' work product (see
Figures 9.5–9.7). Even with a teacher who self-described as fully "buying-in" to
a "code-switching approach," we see stern sway of traditional assumptions; in
particular, that only Standard English is structured, and rule-governed. Other
varieties have no rules or grammar.

In Figures 9.5–9.7, the teacher creates formal/informal English columns, but
identifies only one rule, the rule of Standard English grammar, thus re-enacting
dominant language ideology. While Figures 9.5–9.7 represent only one teacher's work, they are illustrative of very common teacher reaction and implementation. Thus, other teachers in that same rural school built essentially parallel
CA charts, as have teachers in other schools in Norfolk, Virginia and in
Chicago. Common to all these teachers' work is, of course, my training/
instruction. In response, I have changed the structure of my code-switching
charts. Where previously (Wheeler and Swords 2006), I centered "The Pattern"
between the two columns, and then noted the informal grammar pattern under
the informal column, and the formal grammar pattern under the formal column,
I've made the fact of contrasting grammar patterns explicit in the structure of the

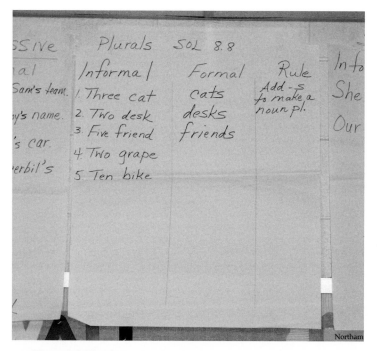

Figure 9.6 Plurals

chart. Current and future publication follows the format of Figure 9.4 where we write "The pattern" under each column, thus overtly prompting teachers to list grammar rules for each variety analyzed. But the more profound common element is traditional dominant language ideology, which holds that only Standard English is grammar, structured, and so on. Professional development must linger on and speak to these points.

The dearth of grammar knowledge

An even more profound impediment to working with vernacular dialects is that schools largely stopped teaching even traditional grammar in the 1970s (Kolln and Hancock 2005). Teachers have no specific training that would prepare them for this task.

In working with a "top five" vernacular pattern transferring into student writing (possessive, plural, *a* v. *an*, past time, s–v agreement…), I often suggest that teachers build code-switching charts based upon examples from their own students' writing. Yet, lack of background coursework in the Structure of

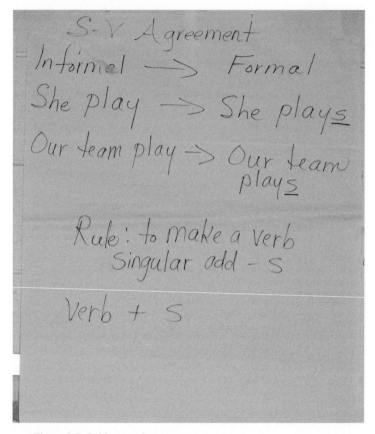

Figure 9.7 Subject–verb agreement

English interferes strongly. For example, in one of my graduate education classes, after working through the CS chart for showing regular past time across AAE and SE (see Figure 9.8), I handed out a set of sample student writing Grades 3–8.

The directions were for my education students to build their own code-switching chart for regular past time, paralleling the chart we had worked with in class (Figure 9.8). From a sample of eight student essays, my teacher education students collected examples, shown in Figure 9.9.

Despite having tracked the regular past time forms as in Figure 9.8, students were unable to independently recognize and act on their new knowledge. In Figure 9.9, while example 1 and perhaps 2 are clear examples of an AAE contrast with SE in regular past inflection, examples 3–8 were stern distractors.

Showing past time

INFORMAL	FORMAL
When he said, "I have a dream" everything change	When he said, "I have a dream," everything changed
I already finish my paper	I already finished my paper
Nat Turner change the world	Nat Turner changed the world
Yesterday, I went home and turn on the TV	Yesterday, I went home and turned on the TV

The Pattern	The Pattern
Other words show past time Common knowledge	V-*ed*

Figure 9.8 CS chart illustrating correspondence between AAE and regular SE past tense (Wheeler and Swords 2006)

Showing past time

INFORMAL	FORMAL

1. *One day she went and walk to her school*
2. *Aaliyah die in a plane crash.*
3. *Aaliyah should be acknowledge ...*
4. *He was discover as an undercover rapper*
5. *The reason I had enter was to see Jay-z*
6. *She ask and ask can she go?*
7. *My friend ask me was I going to join the contest.*
8. *I looked up and seen my aunt with bags in her hands.*

Figure 9.9 Education students' attempt to build past time chart

Class discussion revealed that students chose examples 3–5 as contenders for the chart because of -*ed* "absence" for the passive and perfect. They also chose example 4 because *was* exhibited past tense. Examples 6–7 were somewhat less transparent. While *ask* is a clear and appropriate token of regular past time, one student further elaborated that the sentences deserved to be on the chart because of the *can/could* contrast: "It says, *She ask and ask can she go*. That's present tense. It should say, ... *if she could go*, past tense." Students selected example 8 because "past tense for *see* was 'wrong'." Many of the students who responded in these ways had previously done very well in a Structure of English class. One class in grammar is not enough, and learning a task in isolation suffers in the contentful transfer.

Clearly, time to profoundly re-tool my lessons. For starters, in my graduate education class, I have begun teaching the Standard English auxiliary string (tense, aspect, mood), followed by discovery and description of the AAE patterns where such parallels exist. From that base, students are able to build CA charts, correctly sorting data by type, thus intimately linking learning to analysis and practice.

Such re-tooling is just the tip of the linguist-in-the-schools iceberg. There's the time when I modeled third-person singular subject–verb agreement (*She walk v. she walks)* for teachers in a series of in-service trainings, only later to find that a teacher had built her own CA chart including examples like *I likes my job, they walks to the store* and *I be playing basketball.*

Or there's the time when, after modeling full sentence analysis of possessive patterns a teacher built a classroom lesson for her students as in Figure 9.10.

Singular	Possessive	Plural	Plural possessive
stove	's	stoves	stoves's
puppy	's	puppies	puppies's
donkey	's	donkeys	donkies'
mouse	's		
calf			
potato	's		
elephant			
tooth			
school			
valley			
child			
man			

Figure 9.10   Teacher attempts to develop possessive lesson

The teacher is to be commended for her enterprise in collecting examples and building a student activity, even though we may be concerned with errors in plural possessives. And yet, the Tyranny of the Traditional is manifest as the AAE possessive pattern is silenced off the chart. Never mind that all the modeling I had done showed possessive forms in a full sentence context of a contrastive analysis chart, and that we attended to the noun + noun pattern for both AAE and SE. In Figure 9.10, the possessive construction is deracinated. Presumably we are seeing the first of the two-noun possessive construction, but who would know. More fodder for me to analyze the errors of my ways. Error analysis instructs my future teaching and professional development for teachers.

Conclusion

We had just finished our three-hour seminar for the American Federation of Teachers' QuEST conference (Quality Educational Standards in Teaching) in Washington, DC. A prominent representative from the New York City teachers' union approached the table where my urban elementary collaborator, Rachel Swords, and I sat. She stood silently for a moment, surveying the scene. And then she shared her impressions: "The *years* of work you have put into this approach! I watched as people who *always* react with *porcupine quills up* slowly dropped their guard. They lowered their quills! You tamed this audience!" And an AFT leader noted that the way we had anchored grammar instruction in the scientific method was pivotal – "*How* can anybody argue with the scientific

Figure 9.11 David and Spy Mouse

method? They can't. It's unassailable. And it brings deep credibility to this work." Similarly successful is our reference to Robert Marzano's work, *Classroom Instruction that Works: Research-based Strategies for Increasing Student Achievement* (Marzano *et al.* 2001). In a workshop one day, a teacher and I role-played how to respond to hard core traditional grammarians from a CA/CS approach. Back and forth we went, her in traditional robes and me in linguistic hat, illustrating for the rest of the group. One turn, two turns, and three. Then I played the Marzano card: "Why, this approach isn't really new – we're just applying Marzano's number 1 most successful strategy – comparison and contrast – to grammar!" The teacher stopped short in her adversarial tracks: "OK! Uncle! I give up. Marzano is God to me. If you're following him, then I'm *with* you!"

I close with a favorite story from the code-switching classroom: David and Spy Mouse. It was the first year my collaborator, Rachel Swords, was teaching code-switching in her urban 3rd-grade classroom. One of Swords' students, David, delighted in writing stories for her. David's most recent episode in his series, *Spy Mouse – The School Detective*, sat open on his desk.

As Mrs. Swords circulated around the classroom, she paused and read David's "Spy Mouse and the Broken Globe." Swords was surprised. "David," she said, "we've studied formal and informal English. Don't you remember?" David replied, "Yes, Mrs. Swords." Rachel continued, "Well, did you understand the differences between the two?" Again, David nodded. "Then why,"

Rachel pursued, "is your book *filled* with informal English?" David was patient with his teacher … "Mrs. Swords, *I* understand the difference between formal and informal English, but *Spy Mouse* doesn't." Indeed, David had written his author's note in full Standard English. He had chosen vernacular features to create a voice for the character of his mouse detective. That's powerful agency for a student of any age, let alone an 8-year-old.

Contrastive analysis and code-switching are tools to turn the tide of dialect disdain and disregard, tools to heal the collateral damage to African American students' identity and performance in schools nationwide. Rachel Swords has completely closed the achievement gap in her classroom. Before contrastive analysis, Swords' students exhibited a thirty-point gap in all subjects. The first year she implemented CA/CS in 2001, the gap disappeared. These results have held constant each successive year, and in 2006, 100 percent of Rachel's African American students passed 100 percent of the NCLB tests.

Not simply or even primarily a matter of grammar learning, code-switching and contrastive analysis positively transform the dialectally diverse classroom. Teachers' negative expectations for vernacular speaking students reverse, becoming positive expectations for student ability and success; disengaged, disenfranchised students turn around.

For a linguist to gain traction in the public schools can be challenging indeed. But the stakes, sky high, are compelling. Are we going to lose yet another generation of African American children? We have long had linguistic tools to reach the children of urban America. Isn't it time we did?

10   Positioning linguists as learners in K-12 schools

Long Peng and Jean Ann

Introduction

In a nutshell, this chapter is about two linguists setting out to learn from teachers and elementary school students about how linguistics education might fit into a particular elementary school. We sometimes describe our experiences as having taken a journey. Looking back, we can say that our journey had a beginning, during which we made various kinds of preparations, checking them again and again. It had a middle, during which we met and interacted with individuals and institutions with unfamiliar ways of operating, and almost incomprehensible ways of explaining and understanding things. During this time, we experienced positive but also uncomfortable thoughts and feelings. Finally, our journey came to an end of sorts: a time when we had the luxury of a period of reflection. It was then that we came to appreciate that we had done nothing less than traverse "cultures" (largely unknowingly) between the university and the kindergarten to 12th-grade (henceforth, K-12) schools. We tell our yet unfinished story here, focusing on its beginnings, in hopes of encouraging other linguists to embark on similar journeys.

Preliminaries and preparations

The state of New York requires that public school teachers be certified. The requirements for permanent certification include both a baccalaureate degree and a master's degree. Hence the connection between the university and the schools: every teacher has to have a master's degree. As for university education for teachers, pre-service teachers (that is, university students who are education majors and have not yet served as teachers) attend classes offered by a "school of education" (henceforth SOE), and a "college of arts and sciences" (henceforth CAS). In an SOE, classes are offered in the cultural and social foundations of teaching, and in general as well as discipline-specific methods of teaching. In addition, field placements and student teaching experiences are provided for students. In a CAS, pre-service teachers take classes in what is unfortunately known as their "content": that is, physics for physics teachers, biology for biology teachers, linguistics, anthropology, and English for teachers of English to Speakers of Other Languages (ESOL) and the like.

We are two linguists whose tenure homes are in the SOE at the State University of New York at Oswego. Our teaching loads include both education courses for the SOE and undergraduate linguistics courses for the CAS. Our students are Teaching English to Speakers of Other Languages (TESOL) majors who plan to teach in K-12 settings in the public schools of New York state, and linguistics majors. Given our setting, we had a strong interest in connecting our largely arts and sciences backgrounds and expertise to the concerns of our SOE. This seemed an obvious thing to do to ensure our effectiveness with our university students. But, in addition, we realized quickly that making linguistics relevant to teachers in public schools and pre-service teachers made linguistics come alive for us in ways that neither of us had anticipated.

SOEs in New York state have an enormous stake in creating lasting and meaningful connections with public schools. The many advantages of doing so are reflected in the availability of grant money for this purpose. Around 2000, we were invited by our colleagues to do professional development (henceforth PD) work with ESOL and bilingual education teachers in a nearby urban elementary school. The student population consisted roughly of 49 percent Latinos, 39 percent African Americans, 10 percent whites, and 1–2 percent Native Americans. Most of the students were from low socio-economic backgrounds with over 95 percent of the students on reduced or free lunch programs.[1] This school is unique because it is the only one in the area that offers a bilingual (English–Spanish) program. Its bilingual program is labeled as a late-exit transitional program. In it, students are taught first in Spanish with some ESOL and are then gradually transitioned (in 3rd grade) to instruction in English. Our project in that school would be under the umbrella of Project SMART, a project funded by a federal grant at our university. The grant was to provide each of us with released time for one course each semester to work with teachers and students in the school. It was something new for both of us and we carefully considered it.

Go into the schools – or don't?

When we were approached about working in the school, we had a fair amount of enthusiasm along with a small set of misgivings. We had some sense of the reasons that it might be worth going into the schools. Our colleagues had made

---

[1] This is a measure used by the US Department of Education to express the economic condition of children in school (students from wealthy or middle-class families do not receive free lunch or lunch at a reduced cost during the school day).

the argument slowly over a period of years that despite our best efforts to make the university courses we teach excellent, if our TESOL majors were not able to make sense of all they'd learned in their program, we would still run the risk of failing to produce ESOL teachers who were knowledgeable about English and second language acquisition and who could connect with their elementary school students. This presented the problem of possibly having to live with the fact that our hard work and good intentions had not produced quite what we had hoped. Previously, our work in the CAS at various universities had not presented this dilemma: what undergraduate linguistics majors had actually understood about linguistics and how they might use linguistics after graduation was almost always unknown, certainly not scrutinized. But assuming a position of relatively blissful ignorance of how our students ended up in the real world was impossible in our SOE jobs. Upon their graduation, our TESOL majors would assume highly visible jobs in which their work and their knowledge of language, specifically, would be scrutinized by politicians, district superintendents, principals, and colleagues. What they knew, what they believed, and what they would do about what they knew would have tangible effects on real human beings who were young learners of English as a second language, many of them immigrants to the US, and some of them vulnerable in the society. Thinking of things this way presented us with a great deal of added pressure, but it helped us start to think about what we wanted to teach them in linguistics and education courses. We wanted to push the students in their ability to think in general, to think about language issues, and to think about young learners of English as a second language in public school settings. If we did a superior job in helping our students become great teachers, we could feel satisfied, confident, and proud of what we were doing. To go into the schools and learn about young ESL students and their teachers seemed an obvious way to help reach this goal. Still, we hesitated.

We wondered if our PD work (which was not, after all, direct teaching of linguistics – something we were very used to) would present enough questions germane to linguistics to make it worth dealing with the complicated logistics of our being both in the school and in the university located an hour away. Conversely, we wondered if there would be so much need for and interest in linguistics that our PD work would threaten to take over our academic lives. If we turned out to be good at PD, would we ever do linguistics again? At some point, we finally consented to try PD work in the school, reasoning that, if nothing else, we would gain experience which would help us continue to clarify what to teach in our university classes. If we managed to accomplish anything else, so much the better.

An honest description of our early thinking about our PD work would have to focus on both positive and negative. Since we both had significant experience (and sometimes learned things the hard way) negotiating other cultures in university settings, but were both novices in K-12 settings, we knew that we had to "gain entry." Two bits of wisdom permeated our early thoughts about this. First, both of us assumed that within organizations, even organizations that don't function particularly well, there are people who understand the problems and are trying hard to fix them. If only from a practical perspective, we knew it would be risky to take the stance that we were there to help save the school. Second, despite the fact that we saw our jobs as to help the teachers improve their practice, we knew that we had to proceed carefully. Professors assume that they know more about the theories, history, and background of educational dilemmas, while they assume that teachers know more about the children, classroom management, the school, and the community. Perhaps these assumptions are true. But that our knowledge (which we saw as highly valuable and trustworthy) should not be worth more than that of the teachers seemed clear to both of us. We knew that if the situation were reversed and we had a team of elementary school teachers visit our university setting to examine our teaching and interactions with students with an eye to doing PD work with us, we would function best if one main understanding was clear at the outset. We would insist that before making judgments, such visitors must at least first understand why we made the pedagogical choices we made. And insofar as actually changing our practice is concerned, it was fairly clear that we ourselves could change our teaching practice only under the right circumstances. Our sense was that these circumstances were the following: (i) that we ourselves came to understand that there was a problem that we could do something about, (ii) that we would be supported to find an appropriate solution, and (iii) that we could ask for help (and get it) from colleagues who could be respectful of our efforts to implement changes. If these were not the circumstances, it would not be easy to change or even see a reason to change. It was completely understandable if teachers felt the same way about us. Though we did not think that we would or could be experts about issues such as how to improve grades in the school, we did carry the residual feeling that teachers do not know enough. This missing "knowledge," we thought, would make a big difference. In this sense, we saw ourselves as experts with something to give the teachers, although, to be fair, as experts go, we were not particularly arrogant ones. And when we began our work in Spring 2002, many teachers wanted to work with us.

An evolving partnership

Sometimes our panic at what to do with the teachers who joined the project surfaced. Our SOE colleagues suggested in response that our basic responsibility was to avoid getting thrown out of the school, and while we were there, to learn what we could about the school, everything it did, and everyone in it. Though these were our marching orders, we were, of course, tacitly expected to adhere to three key principles of PD. First, following research on professional development schools (Levine and Trachtman 1997; Teidel 1997; Trachtman 1997; and Abdal-Haqq 1998), the goal of our SOE has been to develop a long-term, sustained partnership that benefits both the university and the school. The two parties share responsibility, with both parties contributing to and benefiting from the partnership. Second, professional development work is grounded in research conducted at and about the school. The university faculty is not presumed to have the sole expertise (Allen and Hermann-Wilmarth 2004). An effective partnership taps into what Cochran-Smith and Lytle (1993, 1999) call teachers' "knowledge in practice," valuing the local, context-dependent knowledge and exploring it to design professional development activities. In this project, the stance had to be to not subscribe to the deficit view that classroom teachers are knowledge-deficient and that the deficiency can be remedied by expertise provided by the university-based personnel. Teachers are valued for their knowledge of the students and school (Cochran-Smith and Lytle 1993, 1999) and encouraged to exploit this knowledge for the benefit of their students. While most professional development projects focus on increasing teacher knowledge (i.e. Foster 2004; Lawrence and Tatum 2004), this partnership is concerned directly with student learning and centers its activities around the students, a point that over time has been repeatedly emphasized by the school principal and embraced by the participants. As we look back, we realize that there were three phases of our early PD work, which we describe next.

The learning and research phase: January 2002–May 2002

During this time, we visited bilingual and ESL classes at various grade levels, talked with teachers, asked a lot of questions, wrote extensive field notes, and tried to learn as much as we could about the school, its academic programs, its curricula, its students and teachers. In the course of listening to everyday talk in the classroom between students and teachers we discovered lots of language issues. Here are a few examples. First, teachers would illustrate what they called "the 'th' sound in English" by listing words such as 'the' and 'think,' conflating θ and ð. Second, a bilingual student suggested one day in class that it was incorrect in English to say sentences such as *Mary had had a birthday before she went to Puerto Rico*. The teacher said it was correct. The bilingual student was clearly worried about the sequence of two of the "same" verb (*had had*), and the teacher's answer clearly did not satisfy the child, but the teacher had no more to say about the issue. Third, we noticed that teachers might describe the same child simultaneously as having language delays and having highly fluent language when able to talk about topics of high interest (Ann and Peng 2005). When we tried to talk about matters such as these with teachers, it was clear that although they were pleasant enough about it, they saw what we were saying as pedantic and irrelevant. We had to think about the reasons for this and ways to deal with it if we were going to have a meaningful partnership.

The problem-identifying phase: September 2002–May 2003

On the basis of what we learned in the first phase and in consultations with the school administrators and the teachers themselves, we proposed forming a study group. We hoped to meet and talk with teachers about more global matters and take the focus off specifics. We thought we could discuss issues such as how they think about teaching, and how they approach situations in which speakers of different languages and cultures come in contact with each other (such as in educational systems). We carefully selected the readings listed below. We knew that they would bring up linguistic (ESOL/bilingual and multicultural) issues.

(1) *Hunger of Memory: The Education of Richard Rodriguez* by Richard Rodriguez
(2) *When I Was Puerto Rican* by Esmeralda Santiago
(3) *Holler If You Hear Me: The Education of a Teacher and His Students* by Gregory Michie
(4) *A Place to be Navajo: Rough Rock and the Struggle for Self-Determination in Indigenous Schooling* by Teresa McCarty
(5) *The Spirit Catches You and You Fall Down: A Hmong Child, Her American Doctors, and the Collision of Two Cultures* by Anne Fadiman
(6) *The Tipping Point: How Little Things Can Make a Big Difference* by Malcolm Gladwell
(7) *Fluency Through TPR (Total Physical Response) Story Telling* by Blaine Ray and Contee Seely
(8) Selected articles

For example, *Hunger of Memory: The Education of Richard Rodriguez* makes the point that Rodriguez's home language, Spanish, was supplanted by English once he got to school. When we asked questions trying to get at whether the teachers saw this as acceptable, we again found that "direct instruction" about language rights, bilingual education, code-switching, and how to approach the teaching of ESOL was met with skepticism and, in some cases, anger.

By this point in our foray into the public schools, when we took stock, we concluded that we had managed to stir up some misunderstanding, and we had not been able to talk much about linguistics. All our expertise was going to waste: what we said was irrelevant to the teachers, despite our attempt to hook what we said to their world. Somehow, we did manage to meet about twelve times throughout the school year, ostensibly to talk about the readings. What often happened is that the teachers talked about their concerns, the issues they faced, the problems they had, and their hopes for their students and themselves.

We realized that if nothing else, we had created a forum for them to air their thoughts about their work. As we listened, we began to see this as an accomplishment, especially since we had come to the realization (which we would have had no way of knowing unless we had seen it for ourselves) that teachers' days are so busy that they do not often have the time or mental energy to reflect upon their teaching, or the material they are teaching, or how their students respond to any of it. To have offered them this period of reflection taught us that *they* had so many ideas about their situation that we finally realized we had to give up trying to direct things. We asked them to define the issues that they saw as important to solve. When we did this, everything changed. They identified, along with other things, many of the very same linguistic issues we had wanted to talk to them about, and this time, they had a burning desire to know. In the time that we have been connecting with teachers on their terms, we have been able to share information about allophones versus phonemes, about word order in the Spanish and English noun phrase, about the tense system in English, about language rights, about bilingual education, and about the influence of L1 on L2. By the end of this phase, we were ready to consider taking actions that would solidify our relationship with each other, and give us chances to benefit from the knowledge that we all had.

The action phase: September 2003–present

In consultation with school administrators and teachers, we (the teachers who joined the project, and both authors) divided ourselves into essentially two teams and worked on projects proposed by the teachers or by us. These projects included first, the "College Experience" for the elementary school students, in which we arrange for each bilingual/ESL student in a particular grade or class to be paired with a(n often monolingual English-speaking) partner from SUNY Oswego who is a pre-service teacher. They meet and talk weekly, and write with each other over the course of the semester. The semester culminates in a field trip in which the elementary students visit the college for a day and attend classes and visit campus locations of interest with their SUNY Oswego college partner. Second, we set up a program for the SUNY Oswego pre-service teachers who have field placements at the school. They receive an enthusiastic welcome and orientation to the school and its issues with poverty, racism, language, test scores, and the like. These two groups have remained mostly stable through the semesters. In addition, other groups of interested participants spring up and disband as necessary. One time, a group familiarized itself with a professional development endeavor called Generating Expectations for Student Achievement (GESA), through Graymill Training Programs (www.graymill. com) in which teachers are invited to evaluate their own practice in a non-threatening way, and, as a result, decide on their own if they should make changes, and if so, how. Another time, a group looked at problems associated with curriculum for the children who are transitioning from Spanish with some ESOL during the school day to English only. And another time, a group looked at a questionnaire administered by the school district to determine children's home languages. Our revisions to that questionnaire were adopted by the school although not by the district, as far as we know. In all our work in these projects, linguistic issues presented themselves, and we had opportunities to talk with both teachers and pre-service teachers about them.

As our relationship with the school has deepened and changed, we have realized the complexity and tenuous nature of effective PD work in general and getting linguistics into this particular school. And now we know that urban schools are characterized by rapid, significant changes: teacher and administrator turnover makes continuity of successful programs difficult, children leave the school during the school year bound for their homelands (if they are relatively close) or other US locations, pre-service teachers who are effective in their field placements in the school one day graduate and move on, professors go on leave or their research interests shift. But despite the difficulties, our long-term study of and relationship with the school is necessary if we are to understand how and where linguistics could fit.

Reflections on what we've learned

Surely the point of getting linguistics into the schools revolves around the complicated questions of how to help children invest in school and to learn more so that they can avail themselves of more opportunities in later life. With this in mind, here we try to express the major lessons we learned from our intense learning experience in the schools so far. We classify what we learned into three categories: (a) dispositions; (b) the school's actual needs as related to linguistics; and (c) the ways to address these needs through expertise in linguistics.

Dispositions

First and foremost, we learned to examine our own assumptions and perceptions about public schools and the teachers, students, and administrators who inhabit them, and about linguists as a group and ourselves as linguists. More specifically, although neither of us can pinpoint exactly how and when, somewhere in our educations, we internalized, to some extent, the disturbing idea that "those who can't do, teach." This created unfortunate ramifications, for example the not-necessarily articulated but covertly held idea that professors in the SOE are not as knowledgeable as professors in the CAS, and, related to this, that teachers in schools (who at one point were pre-service teachers, that is, education majors) are not knowledgeable. These understandings contributed to our early belief that we were experts going into the schools to provide the missing knowledge. Although we quickly intuited that it would not be helpful for us to take this stance when we worked with school personnel, and then later read the PD research that says in no uncertain terms that such a stance is unwarranted, we still believed to some extent that knowledge is what separated effective teachers from ineffective ones. In fact, research suggests that the differences between expert versus novice teachers does not lie in their knowledge base (Ericsson 2002; Walls *et al.* 2002; and Hogan and Rabinowitz 2003). The difference lies in the following areas. First, expert teachers look at the learner and student achievement while novice teachers focus on their own instruction. The difference can be illustrated by the questions each ask themselves:

EXPERT: Did I get through to the kids?
NOVICE: Did I cover the material?

Next, expert teachers know how to use information they get from the learner to inform instruction, while novice teachers do not know how to access this information for instructional purposes. This is partially because they do not see the relevance of the information for instruction and student learning. Finally, expert teachers look at the knowledge of a discipline as a coherent system and they attempt to present it to students as such. Novice teachers look at knowledge of a discipline in a piecemeal fashion and present it to students as disconnected pieces of knowledge. The same research suggests that expert teachers have stronger analytical skills than novice teachers do. In other words, expert teachers are able to make sense of the data they are dealing with, while novice teachers lack the analytical abilities to do so. This confirmed an observation we had presented elsewhere (Ann and Peng 2005). Our own experience tells us that teachers' observations about their students, their schools, and their problems are often quite astute and on-target. We always thought that the problem lies in the interpretations and conclusions regarding those observations. Based on these assumptions, we've concluded that what teachers need more than anything else is to develop the ability to figure out *how* particular knowledge is connected to a problem they are facing. Isolated pieces of knowledge are not what is needed. In other words, what teachers need more than anything else is to develop the ability to analyze the data, namely, linguistic data. Thus in Ann and Peng (2005), we argued that although linguistic content can be very helpful to teachers, knowledge of how to do linguistic analysis could potentially be more helpful. For example, learning to make sense of language data by doing all of the things that linguists do (making observations, describing data, finding patterns in data, finding explanations for the patterns) would be very beneficial for teachers.

We don't deny that sometimes teachers do need more information, but of course, so do linguists. A part of the reality here is that children who are dealing with some of the thorniest problems that anyone can face are delivered by our society to the public schools each day. Their teachers are faced with meeting all of the children's educational needs in increasingly linguistically, culturally, and cognitively diverse classrooms. No teacher can be an expert on all of the issues necessary to accomplish that.

The actual need for linguistics in the school

How can linguistics fit into schools in general or our school in particular? We realized quickly that no one could tell us. We had to learn for ourselves what the issues were and think for ourselves about what the solutions might be. To do this we realized that unless we were willing to examine and challenge our own assumptions about public schools along the lines described above, we were not going to be able to see what was really going on there. When we positioned ourselves as learners, we got some insight into the needs of the particular school we were working with and its actual needs as related to linguistics. We learned that there is good news and bad news.

The good news is that linguistics is definitely needed in the sense that language issues abound in schools in general and certainly in this particular school. These issues require knowledge that ranges from knowledge of grammar to knowledge of sociolinguistics and applied linguistics to knowledge of language acquisition to linguistic analysis. We provided a few examples earlier of the need for knowledge of grammar and the need for a knowledge of linguistic analysis. Knowledge of sociolinguistics and applied linguistics would be very helpful for questions about bilingual education, such as effective models of bilingual education or the importance of input for language acquisition. Knowledge of first and second language acquisition is crucial to understand what "normal" language development looks like. Knowledge of how sound and spelling interact in bilinguals would help explain why children who are Spanish-dominant and just acquiring English without a thorough knowledge of Spanish literacy might write "caso" for "castle."

The bad news is that linguistics is not perceived to be relevant to the problems the school faces. Schools such as ours are fraught with overwhelming difficulties stemming from racism and poverty. Questions of language, language analysis, and acquisition are, in comparison, seen as peripheral, no matter how important they are to linguists. Beyond this, there are rigidities that make it hard to find time to introduce anything besides the accepted curriculum. In the US, the accountability movement creates a great deal of pressure for students to perform well on standardized high stakes tests. The strategy that our school and the district uses to deal with this pressure is to adopt scripted programs for literacy and math. The use of a scripted program introduces rigidities because children are tested often as they are learning the curriculum. The curriculum and testing take all the available time, and little wiggle room is left for guest speakers, field trips, or innovations such as exploration of linguistics. And we must admit that even if we could get schools to see the relevance of linguistics and buy into it completely, linguistics alone cannot solve everything.

Ways to address the needs with linguistic expertise

In spite of this, for anyone who wants to keep trying, there is much to be done. What can linguists do to make linguistics relevant to K-12 teachers? We can summarize our advice in a few sentences. First, we certainly advise adopting the PD stance of not being the expert assumed to have the solutions to all the problems in PD work. It is crucial to find out what *they* know. Second, in your work, encourage teachers to initiate projects that *they* deem important. Linguistic issues are very likely to come up. Third, there is no way to do this work from afar. The linguist must involve him or herself directly in these projects. Finally, through participation in these projects, linguists can identify issues of relevance to linguistics and bring linguistics to bear on these issues. Only in so doing can linguists and K-12 teachers see the relevance of linguistics to the issues they face and, if we can get this far, students get a chance to learn more about language.

Our final thoughts are that the biggest barrier to "getting linguistics into the schools" is that, at best, linguists have a hazy understanding of the issues that confront classroom teachers in K-12 settings. If we linguists don't know what teachers and school administrators think the issues are, we can't identify situations in which an understanding of linguistics and languages would come into play. If we can't identify such situations, we can't bring linguistic analysis or critical thinking about language to bear on these situations. As a consequence, linguistics has been and continues to remain irrelevant: teachers have little access to or interest in what we know, and we don't know what they might need. No understanding is gained on either side. This is obviously a problem, because it is clear, at least through our observations, that much of what teachers are dealing with *does* connect with language. Therefore, we believe that linguists have to (we had to) position ourselves as learners in order to perceive for ourselves what a school actually needs.

It is now obvious to us that as long as we saw ourselves as experts who had something to deliver to the teachers, we couldn't get the teachers' attention. We had to become researchers in the true sense of the word. We had to learn a great deal about the people to whom we wanted to offer insights from linguistics (the teachers) and their context before we could be of any use to them at all, and share what we know about language. The benefits of shifting our perspective have helped the teachers, and their students, for sure. But we ourselves have benefited too, as we have taken steps outside of our comfort zone, and learned about compromise and change.

Acknowledgments

This chapter is based on a paper originally presented at the 79th Annual Meeting of the Linguistic Society of America in Oakland, California on January 6–9, 2005 with the title of "If the Mountain Can't Come to You …" at the symposium titled "Forging Connections between Linguists and Educators." We thank our audience at that talk and our editors, Kristin Denham and Anne Lobeck, for their comments and helpful suggestions. Finally, we acknowledge assistance from Bonita Hampton, Barbara Beyerbach, Tania Ramalho, Bobbi Schnorr, Sharon Kane, Mary Harrell, and Chris Walsh.

11   Fostering teacher change: effective professional development for sociolinguistic diversity

Julie Sweetland

For nearly four decades, linguists concerned with educational inequity have argued that teacher change is a crucial element in the quest for educational justice around issues of language (Baugh 1999; Delpit 1995; Labov 1970; Le Page 1968; Seligman, Tucker, and Lambert 1972; Shuy 1969; Smitherman and Scott 1984; Winford 1976). Yet teacher education for sociolinguistic diversity remains an issue on which there is much discussion and some scattered efforts toward change, but little influence in the schools as a whole. By and large the field still does what it has always done to try to influence teacher attitudes and practices. Concerned linguists write journal articles, design and teach courses aimed at pre-service teachers, and offer the occasional in-service workshop for practicing educators. While such efforts undoubtedly prepare the soil of change, they have not yet borne the fruit we seek – the widespread adoption of linguistically sound teaching practices in K-12 classrooms. Nor have these efforts led to an adequate, research-based understanding of how and if negative language attitudes might be ameliorated. Effective models are sorely needed. In the absence of learning opportunities that expose them to research on language variation and its application to the classroom, teachers work with the same language ideologies at play in the wider society. Too often, this means that teachers believe that the language used in the African American community is a deficient, 'broken' form of English. In language attitude data collected for the study I will describe in this chapter, for example, only one of nine participating elementary teachers initially agreed with the statement, 'Black English is a clear and expressive language.' The impact of teacher beliefs on students' success in school and in life is not as well studied as it ought to be, but evidence from educational research on the role of teacher beliefs has led many linguists to take the position that "attitudes shape teacher expectations, which crucially affect student performance, and negative attitudes rooted in ignorance of the rule-governed nature of vernaculars are likely to exacerbate the academic problems faced by their speakers" (Rickford 1999a: 11).

To the extent that language differences are related to academic failure, teacher attitudes are part of the problem. This chapter outlines evidence that engaging teachers in learning through teaching is one way that teachers can become part of the solution. I describe a promising model of influencing teachers' attitudes by supporting them in changing their classroom practice. I argue for three alternative strategies for change: connecting to existing practices and concerns; treating negative attitudes as a baseline, not a barrier; and capitalizing on the influence of classroom experiences. In the pages that follow, while describing the project in greater detail, I argue that by rethinking assumptions about teachers' language attitudes and how they might be changed, linguists improve the chances of affecting teachers' beliefs and practice.

My argument is based on research that I conducted in a small public school district on the urban fringe of Cincinnati, Ohio. The majority of the student population (68 percent) is African American and half are eligible for free or reduced-price lunch. At the time of the study, the district had been designated 'Academic Watch' under federal accountability guidelines (Ohio Department of Education 2004). Mirroring the situation in many school systems nationwide, the teaching staff of the district is largely (87 percent) white while the student population is largely (68 percent) nonwhite. As part of a larger research project investigating the impact of dialect-sensitive instructional approaches on African American students' writing achievement (Sweetland 2006), I provided training on sociolinguistic diversity for nine elementary teachers. Subsequently, I observed six of these teachers as they implemented a ten-week language arts unit I designed to integrate several promising approaches to addressing African American Vernacular English (AAVE) in the classroom. The curriculum incorporated dialect awareness (Wolfram, Adger, and Christian 1999), the use of children's literature to teach about sociolinguistic diversity (Le Moine 2001), and the use of contrastive analysis to teach Standard English (Rickford 1999b; Wheeler and Swords 2006). A language attitude survey given to the teachers before the initial workshop and again at the close of the research showed that while exposure to ideas about sociolinguistic diversity made some difference, actually using those ideas in the classroom had an even greater impact. I conclude that these results are evidence for a different approach to teacher change. Instead of working from the assumption that negative beliefs have to be unseated before new ways of teaching can take root, change agents may find that they achieve greater impact by making the innovation easy to adopt, and relying on the new *experience* take on some of the hard work of changing what people think.

Strategy for change: link desired innovations to existing concerns and practices

A solid body of research demonstrates that professional development activities for teachers have the greatest impact when they are clearly and closely related to the teaching context (Borko and Putnam 1996; Darling-Hammond and McLaughlin 1995; Kagan 1992). If teachers (like the rest of us) are presented with information that doesn't seem to apply to them, they are likely to disregard it. Ideas that teachers can use 'on Monday' are more likely to be retained and seriously considered than information that seems of less immediate use. Even relevant information is unlikely to lead to a change in practice unless it comes along with specific strategies for its use. For example, one study of what teachers learned in a course designed to prepare them to teach in racially and linguistically diverse classrooms suggests that because the course lacked a practical component, "teachers seemed to think that their responsibility for language diversity ended when they heeded the warning not to put students down for the way they spoke" (Cross 2003: 206). Such findings are especially important to keep in mind when seeking to introduce a linguistically informed approach to language, since such an approach necessarily goes against the grain of existing practice in many schools. Although scholars of language are sensitized to the fact that language permeates the school day and mediates almost every learning activity, teachers are more likely to think of language as what gets taught, say, from 9:00 to 10:30, when students open their reading textbooks, complete a vocabulary exercise, and revise a draft of a paragraph. That is, schools approach language as a subject to teach rather than as an object of study. There are plenty of creative options that might be fruitful in changing this orientation; for example, Wolfram, Adger, and Christian (1999) have considered incorporating dialect awareness into the social studies curriculum, and it strikes me that a unit on human communication might also be developed for elementary science classes. The *Do You Speak American* project provides another interesting means of bringing a metalinguistic conversation into the K-12 classroom (see Reaser, Chapter 7 in this volume). But perhaps the most obvious place to try to cultivate an awareness of language is in the language arts curriculum. The largest existing dialect-sensitive programs currently operating in public schools – the Academic English Mastery Program in Los Angeles Unified School District (Hollie 2001; Le Moine 2001) and the Bidialectal Communication Program in DeKalb County, Georgia (Harris-Wright 1999) – integrate language awareness and linguistically informed teaching techniques with literature study, writing, and public speaking. Taking a cue from these successful programs, my own approach incorporated linguistic awareness activities for both students and teachers into language arts instruction. After developing a curriculum that integrated dialect awareness activities and contrastive analysis exercises into a ten-week writing unit, I set out to recruit 4th-, 5th-, and 6th-grade teachers through short informational sessions. The stated goal of the project was to improve student writing, a concern shared by many teachers in an era of high-stakes standardized tests that include essay tasks. Many of the proposed teaching techniques were likely to be familiar to most upper-elementary teachers: using children's literature to introduce grade-level content or as a springboard for writing and discussion; small group 'jigsaw' tasks; use of the process approach to writing instruction; and journaling. Thus, although the material and underlying linguistic concepts were often new to teachers, the goals and methods of the classroom intervention were not.

Teachers' initial responses to the curriculum highlight the importance of 'taking the mountain to Mohammed' in promoting an educational innovation. In introducing the project to administrators and teachers, I typically highlighted the fact that studying language-in-use is likely to improve outcomes in writing and speaking, but also discussed the ways in which this approach differs from existing practice in language arts instruction. Information sessions focused on language-related lesson plans, giving examples of children's literature selections that would be used to stimulate class discussions about social context and language, as well as describing writing activities that would provide the context for contrastive analysis of the differences between Standard English and AAVE. I mentioned specific features of AAVE that would be targeted for instruction and made some reference to the change in perspective a contrastive approach would require. Despite this emphasis on the linguistic aspects of the curriculum, at the outset educators invariably latched onto the part about writing and all but ignored the part about linguistics. School district officials, principals, and teachers all articulated their reasons for interest in terms that were more familiar in the classroom context, including the desire to find new ideas for instruction, the emphasis on writing, and the use of children's literature. Such responses are concrete examples of the ways in which educators filter new information through their existing frame of reference – a worldview that differs significantly from that of a researcher/observer. As teachers, their job is not to maintain objectivity or merely analyze – but rather to achieve certain goals for and with students.

The form of linguists' message to teachers, then, is critical in gaining an audience. The first step in planning for professional development (and eventually, change) around a complex topic such as sociolinguistic diversity should be to find ways to make the new and potentially threatening seem familiar and helpful. During my research intervention, I made efforts to (a) arrive prepared with something of value to offer – in this case, a ready-to-teach curriculum, (b) link dialect awareness and contrastive analysis to concerns about students' writing achievement, and (c) rely primarily on familiar teaching techniques and materials. Teachers appreciated this approach. At the end of the study, each participant volunteered the adjective 'teacher-friendly' to describe the curriculum, and most singled out the children's books as one of their favorite elements of the project. My efforts at being teacher-friendly probably did little, in and of themselves, to influence deep-seated beliefs about race, language, and pedagogy. But they most certainly opened the doors to school buildings and classrooms, disposed teachers to listen with attentiveness and curiosity, and made it attractive to try something new and different.

Strategy for change: treat negative language attitudes as a baseline, not a barrier

Although the major emphasis of the study was student outcomes in writing and Standard English usage, teacher attitudes were also of interest because of the critical role they play in the school experience of students who speak non-standard language varieties. Shortly after agreeing to participate in the project, partner teachers completed an adapted version of the Language Attitude Scale (LAS), a Likert-type survey (Taylor 1973). When Taylor initially implemented the LAS in 1973 with over 400 teachers nationwide, respondents generally reported positive or neutral attitudes toward the language variety. The pre-intervention results for the present study, however, were slightly less encouraging. For example, six of the nine teachers initially agreed with the statement, "Black English sounds sloppy and imprecise." The overall scores indicated that, as a group, these teachers held a mildly negative to neutral attitude toward the language variety spoken by the majority of their students. The highest score was obtained by the single teacher who had been previously exposed to linguistics coursework, an observation that is in line with previous research finding that even a minimal amount of exposure to scholarly research on AAVE reduces the most gross stereotypes about language variation (Bowie and Bond 1994). While the quantifiable results of the language attitude survey clearly indicated that this group of teachers held some negative and/or uninformed attitudes about language variation, their comments and questions throughout the training workshop painted a more complex, more hopeful picture of their dispositions toward language, language teaching, and language learning. The most notable quality of teachers' metalinguistic discourse was a palpable curiosity – these teachers were not only willing but eager to learn more about spoken language and how it affected student writing. The workshop was characterized by constant questions, from the amusingly trivial ("Is it true that Dolly Parton could change her accent if she wanted to?") to exactly the sort of questions linguists believe teachers should grapple with as a part of regular reflection on their daily practice ("What should I do when kids spell words phonetically?" "How do I respond to the fact that my students will be penalized for using nonstandard English on standardized tests?" "How can a white teacher bring up issues of language and race in a way that won't offend her Black students?"). To some extent, the teachers' curiosity was not surprising, since the workshop participants were self-selected by virtue of volunteering for a project on 'dialect and writing.' Yet their curiosity also revealed the extent to which linguists have failed to influence policies and practices in teacher education.

One consequence of these teachers' lack of exposure to linguistic training was that they seemed to have never considered language as a potential site for discrimination. For example, one teacher was astonished and moved by a scene from *American Tongues* (Alvarez and Kolker 1987) in which a young woman from one of the New York boroughs admits that she felt "horrible" every time she opened her mouth because she knew she sounded "stupid." "That was so sad," commented a 4th-grade teacher when I brought up the vignette. "I never realized people could feel bad about the way they talk. That must be awful!" I asked the group how they thought the woman in the film had developed such a damaging belief about her own speech. "Teachers!" replied the teachers. In a separate conversation, another 4th-grade teacher who described herself as "the daughter of an English teacher with very good grammar" wondered aloud if it was possible that she had hurt or alienated her students by correcting their speech. Comments such as these illustrate that these teachers were initially unfamiliar with the idea of linguistic prejudice, but were willing and able to recognize its relationship to classroom practice and its potentially harmful consequences for students. They also illustrate teachers' habit and skill in immediately connecting new information to their teaching context.

Yet some participants displayed an urge to minimize the problem of linguistic prejudice. Two of the teachers, who had each experienced a certain amount of language discrimination themselves, seemed to feel that to the extent that the problem existed, it was a purely personal issue best dealt with through individual grit. A white 5th-grade teacher noted that his strong southwestern Indiana accent had attracted a lot of teasing from friends and acquaintances when he moved to Cincinnati:

Everyone made fun of the way I said 'friend.' I don't know how I said it that made it so funny, but people talked about it all the time. I tried to change it, but I guess I couldn't. But you know what I did? I just started using the word 'buddy' instead.

The teacher's narrative communicates a belief that experiences of language-related prejudice are not exclusive to any one race, and moreover, that such incidents don't have any serious consequences. The latter assertion was echoed a bit later when another 5th-grade teacher (the only African American participant) related that, on occasion, she had been teased by her Black peers for "sounding white." When the teacher from Indiana asked her how that felt, and how she had dealt with it, she responded, "Personally, I didn't let it bother me. I asked them why they said it, sometimes, just to see what they were thinking. And sometimes I would talk to them about it. But it's not like I cried over it." Her white colleagues nodded their approval of her thick-skinned response, and one teacher voiced her wish that students were able to react to teasing so sensibly. Notably absent from these discussions is a sense of the institutionalized power relations inherent in issues of language subordination; also missing is an understanding of how difficult it can be, on both practical and emotional levels, to change one's speech habits (cf. Lippi-Green 1997).

Teachers' comments also revealed many misconceptions about the primary language spoken by the majority of their students. One teacher expressed her belief that AAVE "doesn't exist." Several equated the variety with "slang," further suggesting that it was nothing more than a collection of lexical items and verbal posturing acquired from "rap videos on BET." All agreed that the children in their classes tended to "write exactly the way they talk" and that this hampered their facility with written expression. And the majority felt that the appropriate response to students' home language was to insist that it be kept at home: eight of the nine teachers spontaneously volunteered descriptions of their approach to AAVE as involving some form of a short lecture that informed students that "talking that way is fine for home, or with your friends, but at school, you need to speak proper English." (The ninth teacher, when asked, said she didn't broach the topic at all.)

Overall, the partner teachers' initial language attitudes could be characterized as hovering on a thin line between an eradicationist (Smitherman 1974), deficit perspective and a pragmatic, bi-dialectal perspective. When introduced to the idea that all languages deserved equal respect, these teachers expressed some sympathy for this egalitarian perspective, and in discussions they willingly entertained the possibility that traditional responses to language could have negative and unintended consequences. There were no reactionary responses expressing fears that acknowledging the vernacular would only encourage 'bad habits.' Yet the habit of discussing language in terms of 'right' and 'wrong' was ingrained and hard to break; the vocabulary of 'mistakes,' 'errors,' and 'good' or 'bad' grammar pervaded their discourse. Their self-reported existing responses to nonstandard language consisted only of correction and censure, and whether or not individual teachers viewed language difference as a major 'problem,' none looked at the vernacular as a potential source of strength.

Clearly, a good deal of professional growth was necessary for these teachers to effectively implement lessons based on a descriptive perspective toward language. But I didn't want to wait until I had "fixed" their attitudes before I asked them to try out new ideas – quite the opposite. Contemporary approaches to in-service teacher professional development challenge the traditional view that practice can change only after attitudes have been ameliorated, a challenge based on the mounting evidence that "it is not professional development *per se*, but the experience of successful implementation that changes teachers' attitudes and beliefs. They believe it works because they have seen it work, and that experience shapes their attitudes and beliefs" (Guskey 2002: 383). The reverse, of course, is also true: Teachers are unlikely to believe that a new idea will work until they have seen it in practice. Such a 'wait-and-see' attitude was evident in a 4th-grade partner teacher's written reaction at the close of the training

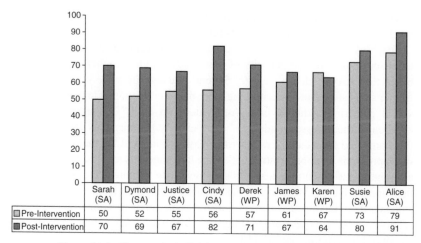

	Sarah (SA)	Dymond (SA)	Justice (SA)	Cindy (SA)	Derek (WP)	James (WP)	Karen (WP)	Susie (SA)	Alice (SA)
☐ Pre-Intervention	50	52	55	56	57	61	67	73	79
■ Post-Intervention	70	69	67	82	71	67	64	80	91

Figure 11.1 Changes in individual partner teachers' self-reported language attitude scores over the course of research. Writing Process (WP) teachers only participated in a workshop on sociolinguistic diversity. Sociolinguistic Approach (SA) teachers participated in the same workshop but also implemented an innovative dialect awareness curriculum in their classrooms.

workshop: "Not sure quite yet what I think. I will have more insight as I take and absorb information into my teaching."

In the end, it did indeed turn out that participants' initial negative attitudes were a starting point, not an ending point. Each teacher in the study completed LAS a second time during an exit interview held during the final week of the intervention, allowing for a six-month interval between the first and second round of the survey. The results indicate that with one exception, teachers' self-reported attitudes toward AAVE became more positive during the course of their participation in the study, with individuals gaining as much as 22 points (see Figure 11.1). The mean score rose from 61 points to 73 points, a statistically significant difference.[1] The average gain on the survey score was 11.8 points.

While all methods involving self-reporting carry inherent limitations, the survey data was complemented and corroborated by classroom observations, informal conversations, and semi-structured interviews. Taken together with the survey results, these data showed that noticeable, positive changes in teachers' language attitudes occurred over a relatively short period of time. The best

---

[1] A pair-wise t-test indicated that the change in the group mean was statistically significant at a level of $p < .002$ (t-stat -4.37).

example is the case of 'Cindy,' who had held a quite negative attitude toward AAVE at the outset of the project but described her experience in terms of dramatic change:

The one I think I really changed on was accepting Everyday Language, Black dialect, as a part of something that's okay to use in school, and in writing. Where before, I wanted the kids to use Standard English, you know, proper grammar, this is the way it should be done, there's no other way to do it. Well, that's not true. I've changed my mind on that ... it's one way to express, and it's part of a culture. And it needs to be part – you know, it's part of their culture, so why should it not be okay to use it? (Pause). Now, they need to learn that's there's a time for Standard, if they're going to do a résumé, or write an article, or something like that, that there are certain times they must use their Standard English. But other times, with a lot of the writing they do – why not? Where before, I would have said no, it has to be done "the right way."

Cindy's statement suggests that, for her, learning and teaching about language variation allowed her to revise her previous 'zero tolerance' approach to vernacular language and to do so in good conscience. This latter consideration is, I suggest, especially important for teacher educators to keep in mind when faced with seemingly intractable, clearly negative views. The teachers I worked with desperately wanted to do a 'good job' with their students. As an outsider, I could also see that the language- and race-related biases they carried were obstacles to reaching that goal, but I found it more productive to focus on the goal rather than the barrier. Maintaining a commitment to providing a strength-based intervention allows change agents to meet teachers where they are and build on whatever foundation exists without losing hope or losing sight of a higher standard.

Strategy for change: capitalize on the influence of classroom practice

An important theme emerging from the research on teacher change is that the most common form of learning opportunity provided for in-service teachers – a single-day workshop or lecture – generally does not lead to observable changes in teaching practice unless it is reinforced in some way at a later date. To increase the likelihood of making a significant impact, then, a professional development program must present its material multiple times in multiple ways. One of the most powerful methods of initiating and sustaining change is to provide the opportunity for teachers to try new ideas in the classroom.

My data suggest that the most important factor in influencing teachers' attitudes toward sociolinguistic diversity is the opportunity to teach about it. Returning to the results of the LAS given before the workshop and again after a

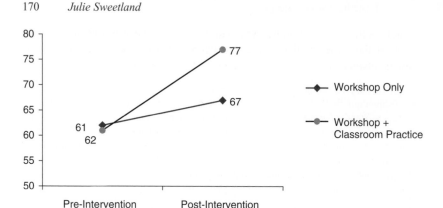

Figure 11.2 Comparison of changes in mean scores on language attitude surveys, pre- and post-intervention, for teachers who received a partial intervention (workshop only) versus a full intervention (workshop plus classroom practice).

full quarter of teaching, it appears that teachers who were asked to put what they learned into practice more fully internalized the new information about language. Recall that while nine teachers attended the training workshop, three of those teachers did not teach the dialect awareness curriculum to their classes. These teachers constituted a partial-intervention group: Students in their classes could be expected to benefit from their teachers' heightened awareness of sociolinguistic concepts, but would not engage directly in learning activities on those themes. Although both groups of teachers had virtually identical attitude scores before the workshop,[2] and both groups of teachers participated in the same training, the teachers who implemented the version of the curriculum that incorporated lessons on dialect diversity into the writing classroom reported much more positive attitudes toward AAVE at the end of twelve weeks. Figure 11.2 provides this data, documenting a 15-point average gain for teachers who actively engaged in the sociolinguistic approach with their students, compared with a 6-point gain for teachers who merely heard about it.

This suggests that while exposure to new information can somewhat ameliorate negative attitudes, hands-on experience in a classroom context has an even greater impact. The results here are in line with contemporary research on teacher change, which stresses that successful professional development

---

[2] Prior to the training workshop, I assigned the partner teachers to either the full-intervention or partial-intervention condition in a semi-random manner which ensured that the two teams of teachers at each school were balanced in terms of years of experience, professional qualifications, self-reported teaching strengths, and language attitudes.

engages teachers actively rather than simply providing them with information and expecting them to figure out a way to use it. And, perhaps because they are wary and weary of professional development experiences that leave them with nothing more than underdeveloped ideas, some teachers may actively resist internalizing new ideas presented as 'expert information.'

In describing their own learning, teachers were more likely to point to information and understanding gained during the intervention itself than they were to refer to information covered during the official teacher training. This tendency could be explained by the fact that at the time of the exit interviews, teachers' classroom experiences were fresher in their minds than the summer workshop held months earlier. It seems at least equally likely, however, that teachers did not truly internalize linguistic concepts until they were raised in the context of their teaching.

The clearest example of learning from teaching comes from a lesson on Appalachian English and language prejudice. The lesson relied on two primary teaching texts: a recording of Ray Hicks, a noted Appalachian storyteller, giving his rendition of *Jack and the Beanstalk*; and a short informational article describing Appalachian English and the widespread prejudice against the language variety. When teachers were first exposed to the recording during the summer workshop, their responses were what one might expect from a group of urban non-Appalachians: They laughed when they heard him, characterized his accent as "country," and "slow," and two made mildly offensive jokes at the expense of the speaker. But by the end of the intervention, teachers who had used the same texts in their classrooms showed no sign of having ever held such attitudes. Consider the similarity of these three full-intervention teachers' positioning with respect to the Hicks recording:

I was always going back to one, 'cause it always stuck in my head, the Jack and the Beanstalk. Just, you know, he just talks differently. It doesn't mean it's right or it's wrong, it's just different. (4th-grade partner teacher)

Well, they kind of had to think about that [using criminal stereotypes when writing about urban characters]. And we brought back the Jack and the Beanstalk thing. You guys thought he was kind of dumb, but when you found out it's just a different way of talking, well then, it's fine. (4th-grade partner teacher)

The kids got it. It wasn't hard to teach. They made fun of the guy, and then I had them talk about why, and then we read the sheet. And we had to ask ourselves, is it okay to judge people by the way they talk? Of course it isn't. (6th-grade partner teacher)

In each of these interview quotes, the teachers demonstrate ownership of the idea that making judgments based on language is a form of prejudice. They seemed to have been changed by the very act of teaching the material – the responsibility of guiding their students in discussion had led them to relate to the ideas as an expert rather than as a novice.

Goodman (2003) highlights 'critical teaching moments' as opportunities to make students more aware of how language operates in spontaneously arising situations. It seems useful to also consider critical teaching moments from the perspective of teacher learning: Both theory and observation suggest that teachers deepen their understanding of new concepts and materials as they respond to the unpredictable flow of interaction that characterizes the classroom setting. In my study, children's questions often served as opportunities for teachers to solidify their own emergent understanding of unfamiliar concepts. In the process of translating the teaching materials into terms more readily grasped by a 9-year-old, teachers improvised wonderfully rich and creative ways of presenting new language-related ideas. "Dialects are like different kinds of ice cream," explained one teacher to a 4th-grader who was confused about the difference between languages and dialects. "So, dialects of English might all be chocolate, but some might be chocolate chocolate-chip, some might be chocolate mint chip, and some might be rocky road. And other languages, they're still ice cream, but they're totally different flavors, vanilla or strawberry or something." After the lesson, the teacher asked me, "Was that right? I'm still not sure about all the linguistic stuff – like what's the difference between an accent and a dialect?" (Accents are like chocolate chips or bits of marshmallow, I answered – an ingredient of dialects, but not the only ingredient.) Another 4th-grade teacher hit upon a wonderful way of eliciting children's language-related stereotypes during the lesson on Appalachian English and language prejudice. After playing the abovementioned Appalachian version of *Jack and the Beanstalk*, the teacher asked, "What do you think the storyteller looks like?" The children collectively came up with a description of an old, ignorant, bald white man with no teeth, wearing overalls but no shoes, who lived in a log cabin on a mountain. The teacher's facial expression clearly showed that she was taken aback by their spontaneous production of such specific and negative stereotypes. "The way people talk really gives us lots of ideas about them, doesn't it?" she wondered aloud to the class. And since this same teacher had previously confided that the storyteller's accent reminded her of her grandfather in Tennessee, it is likely that she simultaneously realized that such associations with language varieties are full of prejudices and prejudgments.

These instances of learning-from-teaching highlight the critical role that hands-on practice can play in teacher change. Until an individual teacher has the opportunity to field-test a suggestion, see kids' reactions, and formulate a response to children's reactions, even concrete lesson ideas remain abstract and remote. And as long as ideas remain merely theoretical possibilities, they have no chance of gaining a serious following, for the gold standard in teachers' circles is the assurance that a given idea will "work with real kids." Once a teacher implements an idea for the first time, however, it takes on the quality of lived experience, a transubstantiation of sorts that transforms it from the theoretical to the practical – perhaps the only alchemy that will lead to any sort of change in actual school contexts.

Conclusion

To the extent that language differences are related to academic failure, teacher attitudes are part of the problem. This chapter outlines evidence that allowing teachers to learn through teaching is one way that teachers can become part of the solution. As the model of professional development embodied in this research diverges from most previous efforts by linguists to influence teachers' language-related attitudes and practices, the work presented here contributes to our knowledge of relevant theoretical and practical considerations in effecting teacher change. This work also, I hope, makes some progress toward answering Rickford and Rickford's (1995) call to reopening empirical research on pedagogical responses to vernacular dialects such as AAVE.

I hope to have also illustrated the importance of engaging more deeply with the larger literature on teacher change and effective professional development. In particular, it is vital for linguists to recognize that teachers are not only engaged in learning when they are listening to presentations by an expert outsider: they are also learning as they plan for lessons, as they teach their classes, and as they reflect on the day's work. There are inimitable sources of power in hands-on classroom experience: the influence of curricular materials; the opportunity to engage repeatedly with new ideas; influential learning that happens during those critical 'teachable moments' that can arise only in the context of an actual classroom; and perhaps most importantly, the pleasure that comes from witnessing first-hand student engagement, learning, and success. It is therefore essential to conceive of the professional development aspect of any school-based intervention in the broadest possible terms. A related point is that in addition to learning from the research on teacher change, sociolinguists should be actively adding to it. In an era where the importance of multicultural education is increasingly taken for granted, the relative paucity of research on language sensitivity training for teachers indicates the failure of our field to effectively influence the agenda of teacher education and the research on it.

The central finding presented in this chapter – that teachers who implemented dialect-based instruction internalized pluralist attitudes to a much greater degree than did teachers who only passively engaged with the descriptive perspective on language – offers a challenge to scholars concerned with issues of sociolinguistic diversity and educational equity. We must not only do more, we must do different. The most important strategy for supporting teacher change is simple: Ask teachers to teach what you want them to learn. Yet this simple strategy is far from easy. It will require concerned sociolinguists to develop a solid understanding of the conditions in which teachers work and of the craft they ply. It will be most effective when the asking is also an offering – of new insights into persistent problems, of great books to read to eager children, of questions that spark the curiosity of a nine-year-old, of ways to reconcile pre-existing demands with our new suggestions. All of this will require a good deal more respect for teachers and teaching, and an added measure of empathy and humility in the face of their supposed "ignorance," than has typically charac-terized sociolinguists' discourse on teacher attitudes. But it will be worth it. Engaging teachers as partners in thinking and doing can and will bring forth desperately needed changes in teachers' thinking and doing.

Acknowledgments

This material is based upon work supported by the National Science Foundation through Dissertation Improvement Grant No. 0424135 (John R. Rickford, Principal Investigator). Any opinions, findings, and conclusions or recommen-dations expressed in this material are those of the author and do not necessarily reflect the views of the National Science Foundation. I also wish to gratefully acknowledge the financial support of the Stanford University Department of Linguistics and the Stanford University Graduate Research Opportunity fund, as well as the cooperation and collaboration of Mt. Healthy Public Schools and the partner teachers who generously gave of their time and insight. Finally, I am grateful for the advice and assistance of those who reviewed earlier drafts of this work, including John Rickford, Penny Eckert, Arnetha Ball, Mary Rose, and the editors of this volume.

12   On promoting linguistics literacy: bringing language science to the English classroom

Maya Honda, Wayne O'Neil, and David Pippin

In schools in the United States as well as in teacher education programs, knowledge about language, when it is considered seriously at all, is generally pursued only insofar as it is believed to be a tool for achieving some other curricular goal – better language use in, say, reading or writing. However, from another perspective, one that we hold, the formal study of language is self-justified. Given this view, there is intrinsic value in attempting to understand something as intriguing and difficult to explain and as central to human nature as one's tacit knowledge of language, in developing **linguistics literacy**: scientific literacy about the faculty of mind referred to by linguists as "mental grammar."

We realize that it is unusual to talk about promoting linguistics literacy in American schools, for the United States is close to unique among the world's nations in neglecting the study of its dominant languages, not to mention the study of other languages and language in general. In Iceland, by way of contrast, the national language is not only studied extensively in schools, but also celebrated on November 16th, *Dagur íslenzkrar tungu* (Icelandic Language Day), a day on which there are nationwide conferences on the language and an award given to the person or people who have served the language in a special way during the previous year.

The pursuit of knowledge about language for its own sake, however, need not be only an end in itself in schools: The goals of linguistics in education can be more broadly conceived.

Background

Over the years, we (a *we* which began as an *I*, became dual, and later trial) have developed a rationale for the study of mental grammar (see Honda and O'Neil 1993 and Honda 1994, for example), focused on triggering the 'science-forming faculty', the human need to inquire and create and explain (see Chomsky 2000: 82–83 and 2003: *passim* for more discussion). Toward this end, we have designed a series of problem sets that enable a teacher and a class of students to construct a connected story about language through the close investigation of English and other languages. These problem sets motivate students to approach language descriptively and analytically, with the primary goal being not to make them better readers or writers, but to give them a scientific way to think about language – a means of expression that some students require and that all students should be exposed to in their schooling.

Our work proceeds on the belief and from the evidence that the study of mental grammar can develop in students an understanding of the nature of scientific inquiry (Honda 1994), as well as an appreciation of the complexity, diversity, and universal features of human languages. Working in English classrooms and science classrooms, in public schools and independent schools, with 4th-graders through adults, we have observed time and again that this domain of inquiry is captivating and that the phenomena are conceptually accessible to investigation and explanation of some depth.

Often in American schools, students are introduced to science in domains where they lack domain-specific knowledge and/or where the problems of science seem quite unproblematic from a common-sense point of view. In such situations, very little inquiry can be conceptually motivated in an accessible or meaningful way. In contrast, by examining their own (and others') knowledge of language, students from the upper-elementary grades on can very quickly uncover some intriguing problems, not to mention surprises, about why, for example, regular nouns in English have three slightly different sounding but rule-related plural endings or why you can't contract *want to* to *wanna* whenever you wanna.

From our perspective then, the English classroom is an underused laboratory for the pursuit of serious scientific inquiry, where students can enjoy the challenge of formulating and testing hypotheses about language, and in turn pose questions that ask teachers to learn more about theories of language and about how children think and learn. While teachers of mathematics and science are often asked to support the goals of reading and writing classes, the goals of math and science classes rarely find their way into the English or language arts classroom. The study of English, and of language in general, is not traditionally associated with the investigation and explanation of data, but we believe that the scientific study of language has an important place in the schools, be it in science, social studies, or language arts classes. That we focus our attention in this paper on the latter type of class is because of our current work with Pippin's students.

Linguistics literacy as science literacy

Promoting linguistics literacy in schools and in teacher education can be viewed in the context of the goals of the American Association for the Advancement of Science's (AAAS) Project 2061, a long-term initiative to advance literacy in science, mathematics, and technology before the next appearance of Halley's comet. Consider the following remarks taken from the Project 2061 *Benchmarks*

On-line (AAAS 1993), in which we selectively substitute *linguistics, linguists,* and *linguistic* for *science, scientists,* and *scientific:*

- The study of [linguistics] as an intellectual and social endeavor – the application of human intelligence to figuring out how the world works – should have a prominent place in any curriculum that has science literacy as one of its aims.
- When people know how [linguists] go about their work and reach scientific conclusions, and what the limitations of such conclusions are, they are more likely to react thoughtfully to scientific claims [about language] and less likely to reject them out of hand or accept them uncritically.
- Once people gain a good sense of how [linguistics] operates – along with a basic inventory of key [linguistic] concepts as a basis for learning more later – they can follow the [linguistics] story as it plays out during their lifetimes.
- The images that many people have of science and how it works are often distorted. The myths and stereotypes that young people have about science are not dispelled when … teaching focuses narrowly on the laws, concepts, and theories of science. Hence, the study of [linguistics] as a way of knowing needs to be made explicit in the curriculum.

We turn now to explicating some of these points, drawing on our work with primary and secondary students, as well as with teachers. We then provide a detailed account of 5th-graders tackling a problem of English morphophonology and pursuing related phenomena and issues in Pippin's classroom.

Linguistics as an intellectual and social endeavor

Begin with the notion that linguistics is "an intellectual and social endeavor … [of] figuring out how the world works." That it is an intellectual endeavor is clear enough, but what does it mean to say that linguistics is a social endeavor?

In our work with students, we emphasize the collaborative nature of linguistic inquiry, understanding that collective work on a phenomenon generally results in a better explanation than working alone.

Take, as an example of this emphasis, a class of 5th-graders working in small groups on a phonology problem set, attempting to explain New England /r/-lessness and intrusive /r/. Why do speakers of this variety of English pronounce the words *water* and *law* differently in phrases such as the following?

(1)   *a puddle of watah next to the rug ~ a puddle of water on the rug*
(2)   *the lawr of the land ~ the law from above*

On first exposure to the data, there are competing explanations of the phenomenon – some parsimonious, others not; some covering all the data, others only partially covering the data; and so on. Discussion of the alternatives within and among groups of students generally narrows the set of hypotheses to the best of them and from there, perhaps, to the best hypothesis. Discussion of the problem set also reveals a range of ideas about language that students bring to class, like the odd notion that skill in trilling /r/'s might not permit one to understand the rules of /r/-dropping, or the suggestion that the phenomenon might have something to do with a similar pattern in British English. Taking all ideas seriously and examining them with care is an important part of the group endeavor.

With classes of students who come from diverse language backgrounds, linguistic inquiry is often social in another way – through the cooperation between native speakers of a language or dialect and those who are not native speakers. For example, examining the constraint on the contraction in English of *want to* to *wanna* in normal speech requires rather subtle judgments about the well-formedness of sentences like the following (* indicating that a sentence is not well-formed; *[?] indicating ambiguity about the well-formedness of a sentence):

(3)   *Who do you wanna talk to?*
(4)   **Who do you wanna go?*
(5)   **[?]Who do you wanna visit?*

Judgments such as these may not be available to someone whose first language is a language other than English. But by working together, combining their strengths, and using what they have learned from earlier problem sets (about the movement of *wh*-question words in the formation of English *wh*-questions, for example), all students, regardless of what their first language is, have the opportunity to construct and evaluate an explanation of the phenomenon.

Linguistics as a way of figuring out how the world works

"Figuring out how the world works" is usually taken to refer to the world outside the body and if inside the body, then below the neck, thus restricting discussion to what is often considered to be the physical world. However, as Chomsky never tires of pointing out (Chomsky 1993: 45, for example), unless we are angels, we are part of the physical world – our minds and brains included. Thus mental grammar should be investigated as a part of nature, using the methods of scientific inquiry.

In our experience, we have found that younger students (4th-graders through 7th-graders) are far less infected than older students and adults by the strictures of prescriptive grammar or by mind–body dualism (but see Bloom and Weisberg 2007 on the latter). They do not resist the notion that there is a linguistics, a science of language and of mind, and they are open to engaging in the "[s]erious inquiry [that] begins when we are willing to be surprised by simple phenomena of nature, such as the fact that an apple falls from a tree, or a phrase means what it does" (Chomsky 1993: 25). In Pippin's classroom, for example, 5th-graders express wonder and delight when they discover that they somehow know that *wanna* is well-formed in sentence (3) above but not in sentence (4) and that there can be disagreement over the well-formedness of sentence (5).

Older students (and parents) are often wary of *wanna*-contraction and other linguistic phenomena, not only because they seem out of bounds for scientific investigation but also because some phenomena violate prescriptive rules of language use. Thus, the very different meanings and goals of mental grammar and of prescriptive grammar must be discussed from the outset, and in age-appropriate ways, for linguistic inquiry to proceed and succeed in any classroom.

Knowing how linguists work

Turn now to "know[ing] how [linguists] go about their work and reach scientific conclusions." It seems obvious, but in fact the only way to know how linguists work is to learn that by doing linguistics.

In our experience, we have found that students (even the older ones) are quickly engaged in linguistic inquiry, turning their surprises about language phenomena into problems to be investigated and solved. And they are masters at coming up with novel explanations that are consistent with the data contained in even the most carefully crafted problem set.

Take the *wanna*-contraction phenomenon as an example. Consistent with the data presented above in sentences (3–5), as well as in the more extensive set of data presented in the problem set that we developed and that students can add to, is a hypothesis that nearly always comes up, one that ignores the thrust of our curriculum (which emphasizes *wh*-question word movement and its consequences). On this alternative view, *want to* can only be contracted to *wanna* if the subject of *want* (the 'want-er') is in some sense the same as the subject of infinitive (the infinitival 'do-er'). This is opposed to the hypothesis that *want to* cannot be contracted when the *wh*-copy that marks the underlying position from which the *wh*-question word has been moved – the point where it is interpreted and where the answer is placed – falls between *want* and *to* as in:

(6) **Who do you wanna go?* **Who** *do you want* **who-copy** *to go?*
  I want **Emma** *to go.*

versus:
(7) *Who do you wanna talk to?* **Who** *do you want to talk to* **who-copy***?*
  I want to talk to **Emma***.*

Having two (or more) hypotheses consistent with the data can then lead to a stalemate or to a search for counterexamples as a test of each hypothesis – searching for counterexamples being something that we encourage even when there are no opposing hypotheses. Here, we note that among the specific goals that *Benchmarks On-line* set for 5th-grade students are both the acceptance of a stalemate and the search for counterexamples that might lead to resolving it: "[I]t is legitimate to offer different explanations for the same set of observations, although this notion is apparently difficult for many youngsters to comprehend"; however, "having different explanations for the same set of observations … usually leads to … making more observations to resolve the differences" (AAAS 1993). The 5th-graders we have worked with certainly are drawn toward resolving the differences rather than accepting a stalemate. For example, a problem set on Armenian noun pluralization prompted one student to ask, "Could both theories be right?" (that is, one that attributes the *-ner* ~ *-er* alternation of the plural morpheme to the number of syllables preceding the suffix; the other to whether there is a vowel or consonant preceding the suffix) – as the following data suggest:

(8)	*gadou*	'cat'	*gadou-ner*	'cats'
(9)	*tas*	'lesson'	*tas-er*	'lessons'
(10)	*kirk*	'book'	*kirk-er*	'books'
(11)	*shovga*	'market'	*shovga-ner*	'markets'

To which another student responded, "From the data so far … yes." Not content with such a conclusion, the students cried out, "More data! More data!" And then, "More analysis! More analysis!"

To this end, we emphasize that it is important to carefully work out the forms of possible counterexamples to every hypothesis. For example, counterexamples to the alternative hypothesis in explanation of *wanna*-contraction would be sentences in which contraction is possible despite the fact that the 'want-er' and the 'do-er' are not the same, and sentences in which contraction is not possible although the 'want-er' and the 'do-er' are the same. Are these examples of the latter sort?

(12)	*They want themselves to win.*
(13)	*Who do you want not to win?*

Do sentences (12) and (13) require that the hypothesis be reformulated? And if so, is the reformulated hypothesis parsimonious vis-à-vis the competing hypothesis (that *wanna*-contraction is blocked by a *wh*-copy)? Furthermore, does the competing *wh*-copy hypothesis still hold in the light of these data? If not, can it be generalized to account for (12) and (13)?

Addressing misconceptions about language

Consider further this *Benchmarks On-line* statement: "When people know how [linguists] go about their work and reach scientific conclusions, and what the limitations of such conclusions are, they are more likely to react thoughtfully to scientific claims [about language] and less likely to reject them out of hand or accept them uncritically." We proceed in our work with this fervent hope, for current public discussion about language is particularly vulnerable to uninformed opinion and this extends to discussion of language in schools. For example, the latest press release or sound bite reporting that a dog or a chimpanzee or a parrot has the language ability of a three-year-old is often accepted uncritically. Even a passing understanding of the depth and extent of the linguistic capacities of infants and young children would quickly dispel many common misconceptions about knowledge of language and its growth in the individual. As work in other areas of science education demonstrates, students are not blank slates upon which teachers impress new concepts (Bloom and Weisberg 2007). In promoting linguistics literacy, we anticipate common misconceptions and try to develop in students far more than a passing understanding of the nature of language and its acquisition.

Although much of our work with students comes in the form of problem sets about language, examining language acquisition does not lend itself very easily to this approach. Thus we turn to video clips of acquisition studies of perception, comprehension, and elicited production in order to illustrate different research methods and research results. Through the videos and discussion of them, students can "meet" some of the linguists who study children's language acquisition, as well as learn something about current research – part of "the [linguistics] story as it plays out during their lifetimes," to quote the third bulleted remark above from *Benchmarks On-line*.

There are, of course, more serious and more harmful misconceptions about language than believing that an animal's response to words demonstrates knowledge of language. The level of linguistics illiteracy revealed in the discussion of the Oakland, California Ebonics controversy that arose at the end of 1996 showed how far short of its goal of erasing language prejudice linguistics education had fallen. We should add, however, that much of the reaction was barely disguised racism based in willful misunderstanding. (See O'Neil 1998b for a discussion.)

The battle against language prejudice is a constant and ongoing struggle; thus confronting it remains a central goal of our work – particularly in teacher education, a goal that we try to reach in part by examining varieties of English, such as New England English (previously mentioned). To many educated people, and even to native speakers of the dialect, New England /r/-less-ness and intrusive /r/ seem uneducated or arbitrary, even willful errors (the result of a "lazy" tongue or a "rough" attitude) – something to be ridiculed. For example, in a recent *New York Times* article, a person is said to speak "in a Boston working-class accent thicker than the sludge at the bottom of a can of baked beans" (Newman 2004: D1, 5). However, as the rule-governed nature of the phenomenon is uncovered, language prejudice is revealed as the ignorance it is. Then the embarrassment about speaking this variety of English can disappear and self-confidence replace it. As Gina, an education student, exclaimed in Honda and O'Neil's linguistics class one day, "So that's why I say *Ginar and Petah*, but not *Gina and Peter*!"

Images of science and scientists

Now move to "the [distorted] images that many people have of science and how it works" and to "the myths and stereotypes that young people have about science." To this we add the stereotypes that most people have about who does science and under what conditions. By studying the achievements of linguistics, students can learn that scientific work is not limited to laboratories and to men in white coats. By actually **doing** linguistics, rather than "focus[ing] narrowly on the laws, concepts, and theories of [linguistics]," students can come to understand that linguistics is not static, but an evolving endeavor.

Science is "a way of knowing," something not exhausted by the standard topics in primary or secondary science textbooks or by the names of departments in a college's faculty of science. In our work, we try to show that linguistics involves forming questions about the languages we know and seeking their answers, though it is not simply that; nor is it simply problem solving. For it is only insofar as a measure of progress is made in accounting for mental grammar – in depth of understanding as opposed to breadth of description – that the pursuit of answers to coherent questions about language becomes linguistics.

Since language is a uniquely human endowment, one that is rich and complex, we fully acknowledge that the study of language can be approached in many different ways, all of them interesting and valid. However, in our collaborative work in schools and with teachers, we choose to focus on mental grammar, on the knowledge of the structure of language that a person has when she or he knows a particular language – the approach to language least represented in American education.

Linguistic inquiry enables students to understand the wonder and the complexity of things that they didn't know they knew, both about language and about their ability to appreciate and engage in scientific work. The study of language can also, we hope, bring about a better public understanding of language in order to combat the language prejudices that prevail in the United States about language variation.

We turn now to Pippin's 5th-grade English classroom to demonstrate how linguistics literacy can grow in the course of doing a linguistics problem set, one of a series of problem sets that students do across the year. Here we present an example of the work that we have been doing for the past ten years in independent and public school settings in Seattle.

The pleasures of morphophonology

An ideal educational environment is one in which the teacher and student are equally engaged in the topic at hand. In many English classrooms, this can happen through shared inquiry into a text and in the process of writing. While literature study and rhetoric (writing) are important parts of the English curriculum, we repeat here the idea that an overlooked area is the study of language itself – a satisfying inquiry in its own right.

The linguistics problem sets that we have developed are presented to students in two thematic blocks: morphophonology and syntax. In this account, we focus on a morphophonological problem set, that of noun pluralization in English, and we discuss how students' investigation of this phenomenon motivates further problem sets about related phenomena.

Listening to students

Students respond to the linguistics problem sets in predictable ways, to be sure, but each class also extends the conversation in its own way. We listen carefully to their ideas and help students build their theories with the knowledge they have – linguistics from the bottom up. The problems are introduced as conversations, and in keeping with the notion that inquiry is a social endeavor, everyone's ideas are included in the class's note-taking efforts and preserved by both teacher and student. Importantly, when students see everyone's ideas written on an overhead or on the chalkboard or hear their comments on a digital recording, they can use this information to build on one another's theories. (The teacher too can use this information to write meaningful assessments of students.)

We encourage cooperation in each class and across the grade. In small groups, some students are more likely to wrestle aloud with their ideas. Partners help each other come to some sort of workable solution, and then present it to their peers – very much like the way most science is done. In one independent school we worked at, 5th-graders traveled to specialist teachers for all of their classes, so we saw three different groups of 5th-graders in the course of the day. We shared the discoveries of each class across the grade, and students learned that there are multiple paths to take in the inquiry process.

Problem set: Plural noun formation in English

We begin by asking the class for a rule governing the formation of plural nouns in English, and the first response is always the basic spelling rule, "Add *s*." At this point, the notion of inflection in general is introduced. Contrasting English with other, more inflection-rich, languages is another direction in which to take this conversation. At some point, however, someone will mention that the add-*s* rule does not work for all words, and so a discussion of regular and irregular plurals follows. We talk briefly about language change and other sources of irregularity, but explain that scientists often set recalcitrant data aside, returning to it later, in order not to miss the more general point: in this case, the default rule for plurals. Of course, students also bring up spelling differences, but we direct them to the **sounds** of the plurals and generally they discover the three different regular plural endings (/s/, /z/, and /iz/) on their own. But if they don't, we help them along. For example, when students have difficulty distinguishing word-final /s/~/z/, as in *rocks* and *bugs*, we put the plurals in a phrase or a sentence with a vowel following; as one student discovered in Honda and O'Neil's earlier work in schools (1993), this brings out the voicing contrast:

(14)   ***rocks*** *on the floor* ~ ***bugs*** *on the floor*
(15)   *There are* ***goats*** *and* ***horses*** *and* ***cows*** *on the farm.*

We elicit more plurals from the class for a categorization exercise, and add to it with a list of our own if necessary in order to get a full array of data:

(16)   *graph*   *myth*   *wish*   *lunch*
         shape   *rib*   *room*   *star*
         tree   *dove*   *cloud*   *law*
         etc.

Phonology 101

Solving this problem requires that students think about the sounds of language. The categorization of words into plural forms proceeds easily enough, but arriving at a hypothesis that governs this distribution requires a vocabulary for discussing speech sounds. So, early in the school year, the class gets a primer in phonology. We challenge the students to find all of the phonemes in English, talk about how speech sounds are produced, and then we introduce distinctive-feature analysis. It is easy for students to see how switches like [voice] and [strident] can be turned on and off, but they remain blissfully ignorant of less intuitively accessible articulator names like [Tongue blade]. Of course, many forget the terms used to describe sounds by the time we encounter this problem set, but they have no difficulty coming up with their own names for the features, a fact also noted by Fabb (1985). Whooshies [strident], teeth blowing sounds [strident], ongoing sounds [continuant], and vibrating sounds [voice] are just some of the terms devised in this phonology-from-the-bottom-up approach.

Hypothesis formation

Most students build an initial hypothesis that looks something like this:

(17)   /z/ – follows a [+ voice] sound
         /s/ – follows a [– voice] sound
         /iz/ – follows some sort of sound that they define using a whole host of terms.

Others represent their ideas in a decision tree, such as the one in Figure 12.1. The order in which rules or decisions fall is important, and if they haven't come

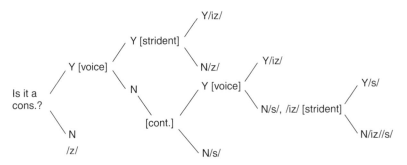

Figure 12.1 A redrawn version of a student-created decision tree for English noun pluralization

to it on their own, we prompt students to put them into a parsimonious order so that, for example, /z/ is not assigned as the form of the plural morpheme for a word such as *fuse*, which ends in the [+ voice] sound which happens to be /z/, a member of the category "some sort of sound."

To simplify matters and give them a label for the category, we tell the class that the final sound of the singular form that they have assigned /iz/ to is informally called by linguists a sibilant and is articulated by the [Tongue blade] in a manner that is [+ strident]. In this way, students realize that a revised hypothesis requires that we first pick out the way the words associated with /iz/ end and then move on to [± voice] elements. Students then define the conditions that counterexamples to the hypothesis would have to meet, and, finding none, everyone feels good about their work – until we remind them that in the beginning we said that forming the plural in English meant adding /s/, a matter to which we return later in this paper.

Presenting students with the following set of hypotheses (adapted from Halle and Clements 1983: 69) also helps them return to their initial view of the matter and to think about it in a different way:

(18)   Which of the following statements best matches your hypothesis about the unconscious knowledge English speakers have about plural noun formation? Why?
Hypothesis A: Speakers of English memorize the plural form for every noun they come across.
Hypothesis B: Speakers of English learn the plural forms on the basis of spelling. For example, they learn that nouns that end with the letter *b* are pluralized by suffixing /z/.
Hypothesis C: Speakers of English know that the final sound (not the letter) of the singular noun determines the pronunciation of the plural suffix.
Hypothesis D: Speakers of English know that some feature or characteristic of the final sound of the singular noun determines the pronunciation of the plural suffix.

Student versus expert

Inquiry science in the schools can be plagued by one of two problems. On one hand, there are classrooms where all ideas are accepted, but students sometimes end up with ideas that are at odds with an informed perspective. They never get to see the expert view of things. On the other hand, there is also a tendency to disregard the work of students because it doesn't come close enough to the expert view, leaving many students dissatisfied when their work doesn't match teacher expectations. Rather than erring on the side of student or scholar, it is possible to fuse both views (Zahorik 1997). Working on the plural problem, students feel good about achieving some sort of satisfactory conclusion, later getting exposed to an expert hypothesis, in which (it turns out) the default form of the plural noun morpheme **is** /s/:

(19)   A morphological rule first:

1. Add /s/ to form a plural noun.	*bus*/s/	*cat*/s/	*dog*/s/
Then two **ordered** phonological rules:			
2.a Insert /i/ between sibilants.	*bus*/is/	*cat*/s/	*dog*/s/
2.b Voice /s/ after voiced sounds.	*bus*/iz/	*cat*/s/	*dog*/z/

The connected story about language

As mentioned above, while working through the plural noun problem, some students are likely to discover that there are categories of irregulars. It is useful at that point to initiate an investigation into these patterns. They learn that some plural forms, like *deer, children,* and *oxen* are absolute exceptions, but find that we can generalize about the morphophonology of partial irregulars like *life, knife,* and *house* (in which, for the plural form, the final consonant of the singular is changed from a voiceless to a voiced sound, but then the form follows the rules given above). Language change, which left these forms behind as 'fossils', reminders of when the language was different from what it is now, can also be brought up in discussion of the irregular forms.

Moreover, later, when students discover that English past-tense formation is also governed by an underlying morpheme that undergoes similar phonological adjustments, they feel a great deal of pride in working at the edge of the frontier of 'morphophonology' and use the term with abandon.

From English, we proceed to other plural problem sets: Nicaraguan English offers noun pluralization with a dose of syntax and semantics; Spanish gives students access to a language with a set of phonemes that overlaps that of English; and languages like Armenian and Mandarin Chinese offer even more opportunities for cross-linguistic connections. Examining how nouns are pluralized in other languages gives students a sense of the range of the typological possibilities as well as the limits on these possibilities. Comparing English to other languages is especially rewarding when students have another language at home, for it piques their interest in these languages. Students have even on occasion asked to create problem sets on their own and have done so with the help of family members.

Learning general principles of language like voicing assimilation is refreshing to students and often leads naturally to questions about the acquisition of language. In fact connecting these problems with language acquisition is a major goal of this work (Honda and O'Neil 2007). Often 5th-graders have younger siblings who overgeneralize rules like those for plural formation or adhere to familiar patterns of phonological development like dropping the /s/ in consonant clusters. At this point, we introduce them to the research that has been conducted on these phenomena (such as the seminal work of Jean Berko-Gleason), test them with the famous wug test (Berko 1958), and even have them take the wug test home to try out with younger siblings.

Student comments

The 5th-graders' written (and sometimes misspelled) comments about the problem sets offer some insight into how they view their work and what they have learned from the experience:

- "The linguistics problem sets taught me to look more closely at the way people talk, and not just take it for granted."
- "In all honesty linguistics problem sets aren't top on my list but I did learn that the way we speak is based on sound and not spelling."
- "I have learned very interesting stuff about the unwritten rules of speaking English from the Linguestics problem sets. I find this extremely interesting because I never noticed any pattern of when I say "wanna" or /s/ instead of /z/ [in plural nouns]."
- "From the linguistics problems sets I learned that every day things in life that we say can turn into a great problem to solve. I think it is usefull to learn it even if you won't use it. I also learned the right way to write a hypothesis."
- "I also learned how to write a good, parsimonious hypothisis but most of all how to try and understand something that is comonly used in my daily life."
- "The linguistics problem sets are great for not only getting a solution in whatever you are studying in the problem, but also the hypothesis … are unpredictable. These problems … will help me in my life as a linguist."

Conclusion

In English classes, we think of students as writers and readers. Why not as linguists? By promoting linguistics literacy, we can. Through linguistic inquiry, students come to discover how very difficult it is to make explicit their unconscious knowledge of language, and also, how very satisfying it can be to do this. Explaining the nature of linguistic knowledge requires students to develop and hone methods of scientific inquiry: posing questions, collecting and analyzing data, formulating testable hypotheses, testing hypotheses by searching for confirming and disconfirming evidence, and revising or rejecting hypotheses.

Meredith Olson, a science teacher at one of the schools where we've worked, had this to say about her teaching philosophy:

Inquiry science, by its very nature, breeds a tolerance for divergent views and just treatment for all. Inquiry discussion requires that we not simply wait our turn for others to finish their reporting, but it requires that we listen with care and graft their findings on ours until a rational and considered theory emerges. Inquiry instruction inculcates the humane, rational, thoughtful, considerate mindset we hope to nurture in all citizens.

Though these remarks reflect her experience in the science classroom, incorporating this spirit of discovery into the English classroom is possible and can yield the same positive attributes, something larger than linguistics literacy.

Acknowledgments

We thank the students and staff of Billings Middle School, John Hay Elementary School, and Seattle Country Day School for their cooperation with and support of our work in their schools.

13   Linguistics in a primary school

Kristin Denham

1   Introduction

In this chapter, I discuss a linguistics course that I taught for about three years in a multi-age primary school classroom and how what started as a simple "guest spot" in a school evolved into a bigger project with broader applications. I demonstrate ways in which I, along with the primary teachers, integrated linguistics into the curriculum (into language arts, social studies, science, and even a bit into math).

It has long been recognized that K-12 teachers can benefit from linguistic knowledge. Linguists in the US began to recognize the importance of some of the findings of their field to K-12 education in the 1960s and 1970s, which led to several projects designed to determine which aspects of linguistics might be best incorporated into K-12 curriculum and how to undertake that incorporation. O'Neil (Chapter 2 in this volume) describes a 1962 US Office of Education project, strongly supported by the National Council of Teachers, called Project English. Keyser (1970) offers lesson plans that were part of a Massachusetts Department of Education project to integrate linguistics into K-12 curricula. Though these projects came to an end for various reasons, discussed elsewhere in this volume, a handful of linguists have continued to work at incorporating linguistics into K-12 classrooms.

More recently, Chomsky *et al.* (1985), Fabb (1985), Goodluck (1991), Honda (1994), Wolfram (1997), and Reaser and Wolfram (2005) have all demonstrated that linguistics activities are successful and beneficial in K-12 education. David Pippin, a teacher in Seattle, frequently uses linguistics problem-solving with his 6th–8th graders and has successfully done so with 3rd–5th graders as well, using materials from Honda (1994) and others. (See Pippin, Chapter 21 in this volume.)

However, these projects have remained only small-scale ones because the lesson plans and activities either require a linguist in the classroom or assume a great deal of linguistic knowledge and expertise. Also, the activities, materials, or curricula are not typically set up to meet other existing goals of the teachers and students. A few linguists (Reaser and Wolfram 2005; Sweetland

189

2006; Sweetland, Chapter 11 in this volume) have been developing dialect awareness curricula, and these have been successfully used by teachers with no linguistics training.

Research that examines more precisely which aspects of linguistics would be most beneficial and how that knowledge can be put to good use in the K-12 classroom has come out in the last few years. (See, for example, Adger, Snow, and Christian 2002; Denham and Lobeck 2005; Wheeler 1999a; Wheeler 1999b; among others.) But despite these steps forward, many states in the US do not require linguistics courses for pre-service teachers. Even in the states which require linguistics for teachers, such courses are not typically targeted at teachers directly; rather, they are general introductions to linguistics in which information and material that is relevant and important for teachers is not highlighted. One reason for this lack of focused instruction is that linguists are not even certain of which aspects of linguistics *are* most important for teachers to know, precisely because of the relative lack of collaboration between linguists and educators. (Another important reason that there are not always separate linguistics courses or topics for future teachers is that many fields and subject areas are competing for the few spots available in teacher preparation curricula.) Even if the teachers are able to make connections for themselves when they get into their own classrooms, the materials and curricula do not typically reflect the insights about language that they were taught in their university classrooms, and most teachers do not have the time or experience to develop their own linguistics materials.

It should be noted that some linguistically informed instructional materials do exist for the early grades, though they relate almost exclusively to reading, writing, and spelling. (See, for example, "word study" curriculum such as the following: Morris 1982; Abouzeid, Invernizzi, and Ganske 1995; Invernizzi, Abouzeid, and Bloodgood 1997; Ganske, 2000; Bear, Invernizzi, Templeton, and Johnston 2004; among others.) Beyond these, there are simply very few materials, lesson plans, or curriculum programs for K-12 education that incorporate linguistics and knowledge about language.

My work reaches beyond the one primary school classroom I have been working in since I take what I learn in the primary classroom back into the university classroom in which I am preparing pre-service teachers (among others). Also, a National Science Foundation grant, discussed further below in section 6, allows me and my colleague Anne Lobeck to expand our work into other K-12 classrooms. What we learn from the K-12 students and teachers is directly affecting the ways in which we teach introductory linguistics to future teachers. A secondary, but equally important aspect of this work is that it is resulting in a collection of materials and curricula for use by teachers in K-12 schools. I have begun to compile these (at http://teachling.wwu.edu), making them easily accessible by teachers, and I hope that others (linguists and K-12 teachers) will contribute their own materials.

Although I believe it is important to get linguistic knowledge in at every level of schooling, I also believe it is especially important to integrate linguistics at the primary school level for several reasons. One is that since most primary school teachers teach all subjects, working with primary school teachers and children allows for integration of linguistics across the entire curriculum. Also, linguistics is so well-suited to introduce to primary school-age children because there are fewer effects of literacy, the children's natural aptitude for language makes instruction rewarding as they are such eager and able participants, and there is not a great deal of language prejudice or prescriptive attitudes about language at this point. Also, language is an easy and accessible way to introduce the scientific method of analysis (as shown by Honda, O'Neil, and Pippin 2004, Honda, O'Neil, and Pippin, Chapter 12 in this volume; and Honda 1994 [for secondary students]).

I offer below some examples of the kinds of linguistic investigation I have introduced in the primary school. It is my hope that, by sharing my experiences, we can continue to effect real change in the way in which knowledge about language is taught and the ways in which it can be best integrated into K-12 education in the US.

2   At the school

The school at which I taught linguistics for almost three years is a small, private, K-5 school of about eighteen students between the ages of 5 and 11. There are two teachers who both teach all of the students. All students are native speakers of English. This school provided a unique opportunity for me to work with a wide age range of students. Typically, I worked in a multi-grade class with the older students (ages 8–11), while the teachers worked with the younger students on separate activities. For some linguistics activities though, I included the younger students as well.

When I first started teaching in the school, I had no long-term plans for the class. The school had lost their Spanish teacher, so I volunteered to teach them "some things about language" once a week.[1] I tried to formalize my own goals for this class, and made the following list.

---

[1] I have found that there are actually quite a few linguists who do similar visits to schools, giving presentations, workshops, or short lectures (often in the classrooms of their own children). It is also often the case that they then discover the dearth of linguistic knowledge in schools, prompting many to get more involved in incorporating more knowledge of the workings of language into education. Also, many linguists (it would be nice to have figures on this) teach future teachers. These linguists also must confront what teachers should know about language and how that knowledge should be transferred into K-12 classrooms.

Goals for primary school linguistics class:
- To introduce students to language as an object of study.
- To allow students to discover the unconscious knowledge they already possess with respect to language and language rules.
- To maintain and foster children's natural love of language and language play.
- To allow students to discover the patterns and systematicity of language.
- To reduce linguistic discrimination.
- To engage in scientific investigation.

The young students were so good at our language exploration and so enthusiastic that I soon began to do more: I began to collaborate more with the teachers; I began to integrate linguistics into other aspects of the curriculum; and I began to develop more materials and lesson plans. In the following three sections I describe some of the activities that I conducted with the students, noting in particular which of these require linguistic background and which could be taught by any teacher, given the proper materials and lesson plans.

3   Morphology lessons

With the students aged 8–11, I introduced morphology problems (using Hungarian, Michoacan Aztec, Turkish, Quiche, Samoan, Nahuatl, Lushootseed, and others) in which students compare partially similar words to discover patterns of the language. They were really good at these, though there seemed to be a natural split, with the older students (ages 9–11) being the ones who could do the more challenging ones, and the younger students (ages 5–8) struggling a bit more with this kind of pattern recognition. However, the youngest were not fully literate, so I found it challenging to do these kinds of morphology problems with the emergent readers since I was so accustomed to using handouts and written language data. When we investigated English morphology (the meanings and patterns of prefixes and suffixes) and there was less of a need to rely on printed data, all ages were able to participate equally well.

The benefits that these morphology problems offer – categorizing, analyzing, and simply conducting basic scientific investigation – seem obvious. Such activities can be used to meet goals and skills standards of social studies, language arts, and science. Teachers interested in seeing these kinds of morphological analysis problems can find them in most introductory linguistics textbooks, though linguists could be working to make them more accessible for those with no background in linguistics.

Below is a small sample of a larger activity the students did, based on the word-building process reduplication, common in the Salish language Lushootseed, a native language spoken in Washington state. The study of the language became part of a larger thematic historical, cultural, and linguistic study.

A		B	
ʔáʔlal	house	ʔáʔaʔlal	hut
ʔúqʷud	pull out	ʔúʔúqʷud	pull part way out
híwil	go ahead	híhiwil	go on ahead a bit
q'íxʷ	upstream	q'íq'íxʷ	a little bit upstream

*Note:*ʔ is a glottal stop, a consonant of Lushootseed (and many other languages)

We also did traditional phonology problems, including the allomorphic variation of English plural. I did not introduce any phonetic transcription at first, but just used s/z/ez and emphasized that we were talking about sound and not spelling. They were so much faster at this problem than my university students, being less influenced by literacy. The younger ones, being preliterate, were not affected by English spelling patterns so they tuned in quickly to the differences in sound. They got the voiceless/voiced distinction immediately and even the sibilants. They were the ones who made the connection to spelling, realizing why they had spelled some words incorrectly. "So that's why *dogs* sounds like it ends in a /z/?" Yes![2] They came to understand the mismatch between sound and spelling themselves.

This sort of linguistics problem-solving activity develops analytical skills, introduces the scientific method, allows for exposure to other languages and their diversity, and is, quite simply, fun. Working with other languages also allows for insight into English and its structure, which can be difficult to reflect on without the comparison of a different kind of system. However, teachers may not be able to teach such lessons without some knowledge of linguistics, and they might not see the benefits of teaching them unless those benefits are clearly laid out and it is shown how such lessons could help accomplish other goals and standards that they need to be satisfying.

The English plural ending lesson is also an excellent example of how linguistic knowledge – in this case, knowledge of phonetics and phonology – is so important for teachers. In order to understand how to teach spelling, how to recognize why students are making errors, and how to properly respond to misspellings, knowledge of phonetics and phonology is crucial. This isn't new news; ever since linguist Charles Read (1971) first discussed preschoolers' spelling inventions, some curriculum programs and teacher preparation

---

[2] This phonology problem allows students to discover that it is the final sound that a word ends in that determines which of the sounds /s/, /z/, or /ez/ is added to the word as a plural ending. So words that end in "voiced" sounds (with vocal cord vibration) take /z/ as a plural ending, words that end in "voiceless" sounds (no vocal cord vibration) take /s/ as a plural ending, and words that end in what are called sibilants (hissing or hushing noises) take /ez/ as a plural ending. Thus, *dog* takes /z/: *dogz*, *cat* takes /s/: *cats*, and *dish* takes /ez/: *dishez*.

materials emphasize the importance of an understanding of phonetics and phonology. (See, for example, Bear *et al.* 2004; Ganske 2000.) But many do not, and many teachers for whom linguistics was not a required course still seem unaware of the importance of phonetics and phonology, among other areas of linguistic study.

4   Morphosyntax lessons

As further illustration of lessons I conducted with the students, I offer below two lesson plans on syntactic categories – parts of speech, showing how a linguistically informed approach may differ from traditional approaches to teaching grammar. The student comments included below illustrate some of their insights – and the success of this approach. These two lessons emphasize what the students already know about parts of speech as speakers of a language. I think they show too that there may be some real results from this approach for "struggling readers." These lesson plans also illustrate the importance of having linguists work on developing materials for use in primary school classrooms, but then how such materials can be "freestanding" after that, allowing all teachers, regardless of their training, to make use of the lesson plans.

4.1   Be a word in a sentence

Goals:
- To introduce parts of speech.
- To see that there is a difference between content words and function words.
- To discover how parts of speech have to do with meaning and that we can describe content words by their meaning and function in the sentence.

I handed out words on individual pieces of paper to seven students.

I asked the students to put themselves in order to make a sentence, then they acted out the words for the rest of the students and those students tried to guess what the words were. As expected, those with the words *rabbit, hopped, tall,* and *grass* all could act out their words fairly easily (though *grass* was kind of tough); *the* and *in* were harder.

We did it with different students and a second set of words.

| A | | cat | | is | | eating | | a | | bird |

Here *cat, eating,* and *bird* were easy to act out, but not *a* and *is*.

Then we talked about which words were harder to act out. I put the words into groups on the board (using different colors for each group too):

rabbit	the
hopped	in
tall	a
grass	is
cat	
eating	
bird	

What follows is the dialogue between me (KD) and the students.

KD: What makes the words in the first column easier to act out?
STUDENTS: They mean something. They're things and actions. They also describe.
KD: What about the other ones?
STUDENTS: They don't mean anything. You need them, but they're hard to act out because they don't mean anything.

We discussed the fact that the function words do, in fact, have meaning, but that they are indeed harder to act out. (They tackled describing the difference, for example, between *a* and *the* – not an easy task – and ended up with quite an accurate description of the definite/indefinite distinction.)

KD: What can we call the kind of words in the first column?
STUDENTS: Nouns. Verbs. Adjectives.[3]
KD: Are nouns, verbs, and adjectives more meaningful than the other words?
STUDENTS: Yes. But the others still mean something.
KD: OK, so one way we can identify nouns, verbs, and adjectives – parts of speech – is by their meaning. How can we describe nouns?
STUDENTS: Things, people, places, stuff you can touch.
KD: How can we describe verbs?
STUDENTS: Actions, doing-words.
KD: How can we describe adjectives?
STUDENTS: They describe.

4.2   Follow-up and extensions

The students really like doing this charades-like activity and want to play it all the time. They have developed a system for representing some of the functional category words: one student made her body into an *A*-shape for the determiner *a*. The students guessed the word so now they use that body position not only for *a*, but for other determiners – if it is not *a*, they go through

---

[3] They were already familiar with the terms *noun*, *verb*, and *adjective* from other games we had played (Mad Libs, Parts of Speech Bingo).

a list, guessing *the*, *that*, *this*, *each*, *some*, etc., showing excellent command of the category determiner. Also, I have used different verb forms to see what they do with these (*ate, is eating, have eaten*, etc.). It is obviously difficult to get at these distinctions via charades, but again, the students started going through lists of verb forms: *is eating, ate, have eaten, will eat*, illustrating their unconscious knowledge of the verbal system. It is important for teachers to do the following activity too, however, to make it clear that our understanding of syntactic categories goes much deeper than just meaning.

4.3   Jabberwocky

Goals:

- To see that meaning is not the only way we understand parts of speech – we also use our syntactic and morphological knowledge.
- To understand that we already have all of this knowledge simply by being speakers of the language.

I wrote on the board this nonsense sentence:

The froobling greebies snarfed the granflons with great libidity.

We circled the words that are English words: *the, with, great*.

I then asked if there were pieces of the other words that they recognized from other English words: *–ing, –(e)s, –ed, –s, –ity*. We talked a little about what these suffixes mean.

KD: What part of speech is *greebies*?
STUDENTS: Noun.
KD: How do you know it's a noun?
STUDENTS: Because it has an *–s*.
KD: How else? What other word nearby gives you a clue that it's a noun?
STUDENTS: The word *the*.
KD: So you know that if you have a *the* that there will be noun nearby?
STUDENTS: Yes.
KD: So what part of speech is *froobling*?
STUDENTS: Verb. Adjective.
KD: Yes, you're both right. Do verbs sometimes have *–ing*?
STUDENTS: Yes.
KD: Is this a verb here?
STUDENTS: No, it's describing *greebies*.
KD: Can you think of other words that describe nouns that have *–ing*?
STUDENTS: The running horse, the drinking cat, the spitting boy.
KD: So sometimes *–ing* words are verbs and sometimes they are adjectives?
STUDENTS: Yes, it depends on where they are in the sentence.

We did this for the other nonsense words in the sentence. *–ity* was interesting since most of the suffixed *–ity* words they thought of were "big" words –

probability, fluidity – that some of the students didn't know the meanings of. When we put several of these words into sentences with more context, such as the following, the students instantly used morphology to understand the category noun:

The probability of rain is low.

STUDENTS: Oh, it occurs with *the* so it's a noun!

They also mentioned *city* and *kitty* and said that these are nouns too.

KD: They are, but how are they different?
STUDENTS: They don't mean anything when you take off the *–ity*.
KD: Exactly. So we have two *–ity*s. One can attach to an adjective and make a noun, the other can't be separated from the noun.
STUDENTS: There's also *itty bitty*!

Then we go back to the nonsense sentence.

KD: How do we know the parts of speech of these words when we don't even know what the words mean?
STUDENTS: We have the other words and parts of words as clues.

They also wanted to know the names for the function words which they didn't want to call the "little" words. They were quite pleased with the word *determiner*. I have found that instead of shying away from "hard words," the young students are proud of being privy to special vocabulary and remember it quite well too.

An additional benefit of many linguistics lessons such as these is that they appear to be very appealing to some "struggling readers." In the school I worked in, there were a handful of 4th and 5th graders who self-identified as "math and science" types and didn't like "reading and writing." However, they really loved linguistics and were very good at these analytical problem-solving language activities. As Honda, O'Neil, and Pippin (2004) also found, reluctant or struggling English language arts students excel at linguistics problem-solving. My bet is that introducing linguistics problem sets will perhaps turn students who struggle with "language" in a broad sense into students who can be successful with language-related activities.

5   Other language study activities

The following activities illustrate other ways in which I incorporated language study into the curriculum, especially as it relates to geographic and cultural study. These support the idea that language itself, not just reading and writing and spelling, should be studied, and that there are a myriad of ways to integrate it across the primary school curriculum.

5.1   Languages of the world

I began to integrate linguistics into the school's thematic studies. For example, when the students were doing a study of continents, spending about a week on each one, I discussed languages of those regions. When studying the African continent, I introduced languages of Africa and we investigated five of them more closely (Swahili, Arabic, French, Fly Taal, and Tswana), leading to discussion of language change and language contact. We learned greetings in these languages and made decorated signs with these greetings to use throughout the month. We made an illustrated Swahili–English alphabet book. We talked about Swahili words they knew (from *The Lion King*) – *rafiki, samba, pumbaa, hakuna matata* – and their meanings. For languages of Asia, we also talked about five of them in depth, and two of them, Japanese and Mandarin, even more. This led to discussion of writing systems, comparing alphabetic to ideographic, and the students practiced writing the Chinese characters for some words, and created a Japanese counting book with the numbers and their characters 1–10. They also used greetings from the five languages we discussed throughout the month. We did an excellent exercise (found at www.askasia.org) on Chinese dialects, in which the students looked at characters and translations, but made up (in groups) their own pronunciations. Each group was able to understand only their own group's sentences. This again led to discussion of writing systems, dialects, and the arbitrariness of the sign, among other topics. Later, they studied Hawaii and so I discussed Hawaiian and Hawaiian Creole English. This offered a great opportunity to talk about Creoles in general and language genesis.

5.2   Language change

The broad area of "language change" is one in which linguistic training plays an important role, though the amount of knowledge a teacher might acquire in an introductory linguistics class would be sufficient to conduct this sort of study. With the students, I introduced the notion of language change frequently and in various contexts. We looked at Old English and listened to recordings of it (along with discussion of other aspects of the people and their culture, geography, immigration, and settlement patterns). We frequently discussed spelling and the historical reasons for many of the spelling idiosyncrasies of modern English. We talked about the distinction between spoken and written language and discussed the effects of standardization and the influence of dictionaries and grammar books. For a specific exercise, we researched the etymology of each of the students' names. This activity led to discussion of cultural, historical, and social influences on naming (and related conversations about capitalization and spelling conventions).

5.3   Language variation

We studied language variation by comparison of British and American dialects. We first discussed vocabulary differences that the students came up with (*lift/elevator, torch/flashlight*) and used the experience of several children in the class who had British connections (Scottish father, English grandmother). Then we turned to *Harry Potter*, which offered a good opportunity not only for discussion of British and American dialect differences and how these are represented in print, but also offered an opportunity to discuss Latin. (There is a great deal of superb information online on language in Harry Potter. The students really had fun with Latin spells, which led to more exploration of Latin and Greek roots later in the year, requested by the students.) Another way in which I have discussed variation came out of discussions I had heard the students having about variation in games and rhymes (jumprope rhymes, game calls, such as *Come out! Come out! Wherever you are!, Ollie Ollie Oxen/All Come Free*, and the students' own ludlings [language games], called Obbish and Ubby Dubby). (See Denham 2005 for further discussion of these ludlings.)

5.4   Writing systems

We have also discussed writing systems: alphabetic (Roman, Cyrillic, Greek, etc.), syllabic (Japanese, Cherokee), and pictographic and logographic systems more generally (which had been introduced when we studied Chinese and Japanese). We also talked about runes used in the writing of Old English and they "carved" (with permanent black ink) their names and/or a saying into stones.

5.5   Written word games

We have played lots of written word games, such as the following:
- Anagrams. These explore knowledge of sound and spelling and illustrate how we use our unconscious knowledge of possible letter/sound combinations. For example, *ngisre* is easily unscrambled to *singer* since many of the letter combinations are not possible in English.
- Pink Stinks. This game explores knowledge of rhyme and synonyms (and is good to do with even the very youngest students). For example, the clues *iguana snowstorm* result in the rhyming answer *lizard blizzard*.
- Word Chains. This game explores sequencing, spelling, and the sound/ symbol mismatch. Here are two types of word chains: *a, an, and, sand*; *metal, almost, stone, nest, stare, reverse, seat*. These were integrated into a math unit on sequencing.

The teachers I worked with used these kinds of language games already in their classrooms, and primary school curricula and lesson plans often incorporate similar examples of written word exploration.

6   Reflections

There are, of course, so many more ways in which linguistics – broadly defined – can be incorporated into primary school classrooms; I have merely given a sampling here of the kinds of activities I have conducted in one primary school. What will make these activities more broadly useful is developing them into free-standing lesson plans and the broad dissemination of linguistics materials and curriculum that can help meet K-12 students' and teachers' needs. The multi-age classroom I worked in provided a unique opportunity to test out lessons on a diverse age range. By and large, the students excelled at all of the linguistic activities. And having been given free rein by the teachers, I was able to integrate linguistics across the entire curriculum.

When I first started teaching university-level linguistics to pre-service teachers, I was somewhat resentful that they asked me what this information had to do with what they would be doing with their 1st graders, 5th graders, or 10th graders. I didn't know; my job was to teach them linguistics, their job was to figure out how to apply that knowledge. But as I have come to appreciate the lack of basic knowledge about language that exists in schools, in curricula, and in primary school textbooks, and as I have become a better, more experienced teacher who wants K-12 teachers to incorporate their knowledge of linguistics into their classrooms successfully, I have realized the importance of both being in schools and also becoming much more involved with teacher preparation in order to effect change.

I am now working directly with primary school teachers and students, and I believe such partnership is very important to the work of integrating knowledge about language into K-12 classrooms. Anne Lobeck and I received a National Science Foundation grant (The Western Washington University Teaching Partnership Project: Improving teacher education in linguistics through partner teaching and curriculum design) which helped support partnerships with teachers. (See Lobeck, Chapter 14 in this volume.) We identified language issues of most importance to teachers, and then determined how linguistics can be most effectively integrated into K-12 curriculum to meet teachers' and students' goals. (Lobeck worked primarily with middle and high school teachers and students. I worked primarily with elementary and middle school teachers and students.) We are now working to identify ways to expand linguistic knowledge beyond the border of current pedagogy, and together with teachers are creating effective ways to bring linguistic knowledge into classrooms. The next stage of the project is the development of a new teacher education course, informed by our fieldwork in schools.

The "partnering" aspect of our work is very important. In the field of education, teachers have always had to endure people from many fields telling them what they should be teaching. But until more linguists get into classrooms and become educated about how schools and school systems work, what takes place in classrooms, and what teachers need, little progress will be made. As I noted in section 1, there is, in fact, linguistically informed instruction already taking place, especially in the areas of reading, writing, and spelling. Also, many reading teachers know a lot about linguistics, whether they know it by that name or not. (See Carlson, Chapter 18 in this volume.) It is important to acknowledge what is already in use and then expand on that base knowledge and the existing materials.

Also, in this era of increased accountability for educators and their students in the US, it is even more important that curriculum on language and linguistics be justified. Because there is a limit to what can be taught in schools and because standardized testing and standards-based curricula are the driving forces behind what is taught, it is crucial that linguists working on integrating linguistics into K-12 education consider these factors and work within the educational framework, seeking ways that linguistics can meet existing standards.

And finally, it is important to explore ways in which linguistics and knowledge of language can be integrated into curricula other than in the traditional areas of reading or grammar, as has been done by Reaser and Wolfram (2005) in the North Carolina social studies curriculum, for example, and by Honda (1994) in the science curriculum.

The opportunity to work directly in a primary school has allowed me to begin to develop materials for teachers to use in the primary grades (but many of these could be easily adapted for use in secondary school classrooms), to explore ways to integrate more linguistic material into existing curricula, and to learn how to adapt my own linguistics course for teachers.

7   Charge to others

Although we have begun to see a shift in linguists' attitudes toward the role of linguistics in education (for example, more sessions at the Linguistic Society of America meetings on linguistics in education, more books on linguistics and education), we can do more. The following suggestions, some of which overlap with each other, will enable us to move forward more rapidly, accomplishing our goal of incorporating linguistics into K-12 education, and, therefore, moving into the public sphere.

- We need to change the way we teach introductory linguistics for teachers by finding out more about the applications of linguistics in K-12 education.
- We need to work with teachers to develop more linguistics materials for use at all grade levels and across all disciplines.
- We must connect the activities and materials to national, state, and local standards of education and assessment measures.
- We need to develop more materials that are able to stand alone, materials that can be used effectively by teachers who are not experts in linguistics.
- We need to share and disseminate the materials we have developed.
- We need to respect linguists' work on linguistics and education as legitimate and "scholarly," worthy of tenure and promotion.
- We need to have more sessions devoted to linguistics and education at local and national conferences.
- We need to collaborate more with schools of education and educational professional organizations.
- We need to require linguistics for teachers – all teachers in all states in all disciplines.
- We need to sit on state/national standards boards, both for teacher education requirements and for K-12 student standards and benchmarks.

8   Conclusion

As our field continues to grow, an area of particular interest to many linguists is how the scientific study of language can be productively integrated into K-12 education. K-12 teachers are also aware of the need for scientific study of language, particularly in order to the meet the goals articulated in state or national accountability requirements. In spite of primary and secondary teachers' and linguists' joint commitment to the importance of the study of language in the K-12 curriculum, research in linguistics has had a minimal impact in schools. Key to integrating linguistics into the schools is improving teacher preparation, and though some teacher education programs offer courses in linguistics, linguists who teach such courses typically know little about K-12 teaching. Improving teacher preparation thus depends on improving teacher education faculty expertise: linguists who teach future teachers must better understand which areas of linguistics are of most importance to K-12 teachers, and also how that material can be taught most effectively in the K-12 classroom. More linguists need to get into K-12 classrooms and work with teachers and education faculty to develop excellent resources for all of our students. My work in a primary school has fully convinced me of the importance of such partnering and of the need for other linguists to undertake similar projects.

Acknowledgments

First and foremost, I want to thank teachers Cari Duffy and Deidre Carlson and all of the students of Willowwood Schoolhouse in Bellingham, Washington for allowing me to work with them. I also thank Anne Lobeck for reading a draft of this, and for the many insights that have come out of our numerous collaborations. David Pippin also deserves special mention for being an inspiration, as do Maya Honda and Wayne O'Neil for their encouragement. Portions of this paper were presented at the 2006 Linguistic Society of America meeting in Albuquerque and at the Tufts Linguistics and Education Workshop in June 2006. Portions of this work were supported by NSF grant 0536821 awarded to Kristin Denham and Anne Lobeck. Thanks too to two anonymous *Language and Linguistics Compass* reviewers and to LNCO editor Maya Honda for very helpful feedback on a draft of this article. All errors are, of course, my own. This chapter is a slightly modified version of one that appeared in *Language and Linguistics Compass* 1 (4), 2007, 243–259. Thanks to Blackwell for allowing us to reprint in this volume.

14   Educating linguists: how partner teaching enriches linguistics

Anne Lobeck

Why grammar school is grammarless

As Mark Liberman pointed out in his 2007 Linguistic Society of America address "The Future of Linguistics," the influence of the scientific study of language has had a profound effect on other intellectual areas of endeavor. The analysis of language, long a topic of study, was a key part of medieval education, and historical linguistics was, in Liberman's words, "a model of success in rational inquiry." Linguistic anthropology, with its foundation in structuralism, put linguistic analysis at the center of the social sciences. Linguistics has also had an enormous influence on philosophy, and Chomsky's generative grammar has had a great impact on psychology. Nevertheless, as we find reiterated throughout the chapters in this book, the advances of modern linguistics have not spread very far from the academy, and, as Liberman puts it, today's "grammar school is grammarless."

Liberman cites a number of reasons for this, including the narrow definition of the field, emphasis on research over teaching, and the lack of effective efforts to help the public understand what linguistics is about (Battistella, Chapter 1 in this volume). As a result of this isolation, public policy and discourse about language are shaped not by language experts, but by those uninformed by the study of language, and perhaps even more troublesome, but not surprising, is that this state of affairs is largely accepted by those outside the borders of the discipline. (The Ebonics Controversy is one celebrated case in point of the effects of misunderstandings about language, but there are many more.)

To change the face of linguistics, linguists need to, as Liberman puts it, reclaim "the territory of language," in research, pedagogy, clinical applications, technology, and public discourse. One way to accomplish this is to broaden the "disciplinary tent" of the field, taking a more inclusive view of what constitutes linguistics, and welcoming non-linguists as collaborators.

One example of how linguists in the academy might enact this broadening of the field could be to teach introductory linguistics with an emphasis on intellectual, historical, and social issues, rather than with a more narrow focus on linguistic theory alone. Another might be to work together with colleagues in other disciplines, developing courses that integrate linguistics into other fields, such as rhetoric and composition, foreign language teaching/learning, communications, education, etc. Many of these options involve collaboration, and possible partner teaching, across disciplines at the university level, making linguistics a more visible and vibrant part of a larger, interdisciplinary curriculum.

Liberman focuses on collaboration between linguists and non-linguists as a means of revitalizing the role that the scientific study of language plays across the board, inside and outside of the academy. Linguists therefore need to proactively engage in cross-disciplinary collaboration with other scholars and teachers, if we are to change the face of our field.

Partnerships across educational levels

The kinds of collaborations Liberman proposes are possible to achieve within the academy, where linguists have the opportunity to design their own courses and team teach across disciplines. But as is evident from the chapters in this volume, a different kind of collaboration is also essential, one which reaches outside the borders of the academy, and involves K-12 teachers. The stories of such collaborations in this volume also illustrate that these partnerships take many forms, and that there is no single, right way to design them, yet they are an essential step in improving teaching and learning about language in the schools. As I show in this chapter, these collaborations also offer much more.

It is perhaps natural at this point that the growing field of linguistics and education focuses on what linguists can do to help teachers and improve teaching about language in the schools. But in order for this field to develop and grow, it can't be a one-way street; it must also enrich and inform linguistics, and energize linguists' own teaching and research. Linguist–teacher partnerships, in any incarnation, provide a way to "spread the word" about linguistics outside of the academy, into the community. As I show below, they also provide us with a means to actively engage our own students in shaping the public perceptions of the field, and to enrich our own research and teaching about language. Teaching partnerships therefore do far more than improve education about language and bring grammar back into grammar school; they change the face of the field of linguistics itself, in a number of important ways.

The Western Washington University Teaching Partnership Project

My colleague Kristin Denham and I are linguists who teach in Western Washington University's English department and Linguistics Program, and our core courses are required for the English education major. (In fact, all English majors must take the introduction to linguistics course.) Over the years, we have found that even though English education majors take up to three courses in linguistics (an introduction, a course on English descriptive grammar, and a course on the history of English), these courses alone do not provide them with the tools to apply what they have learned about language in the K-12 classroom, once they are on the job. (See vignettes by Angela Roh and Athena McNulty, our former students, in Chapters 16 and 20 respectively, and Chapter 13 by Kristin Denham.) We have also found, from our own experience teaching linguistics lessons in our children's schools as parent volunteers, that although we can easily see how linguistics can benefit K-12 education, designing effective teacher education courses requires learning much more from teachers about how linguistics could help them achieve their pedagogical goals.

With the goal of doing fieldwork in the schools, we applied for a grant from the National Science Foundation to fund our project, The Western Washington University Teaching Partnership Project: Improving teacher education in linguistics through partner teaching and curriculum design. We were fortunate to receive funding from the NSF for a period of two years, from 2006 to 2008.

The focus of our project was on fieldwork, observing and interviewing teachers, and partner teaching with them in the schools in order to learn more about how linguistics could enrich the curriculum to meet teachers' needs and goals. From the knowledge gained through this fieldwork we hoped to improve our English education courses so that they would better prepare teachers to apply linguistics in the K-12 classroom. Kristin Denham worked with elementary students and teachers, and her experiences are chronicled in her chapter in this volume. I worked with teachers in both high school and middle school English classes. The overarching goal of the project was to improve science education through a non-traditional gateway, namely through the science of language. The grant period has recently concluded, and I summarize our basic findings below, many of which echo the themes of other chapters, and in the vignettes by our partner teachers, Deidre Carlson and Athena McNulty.

Educating linguists: fieldwork in the schools

Kristin and I both found that teachers are very open to linguistics, and eager to know more about how the science of language can inform their teaching. We had many productive conversations with teachers about how linguistics could enhance the curriculum, and we quickly learned that while we could offer much in the way of ideas, our partner teachers had essential insights into how to develop and focus lessons, create and deliver materials, and shape them to meet classroom goals. The more time we spent in the classroom the clearer it became that without a "methods and materials" component, our linguistics courses, though providing prospective teachers with important knowledge of language, offered little in the way of preparing them to apply what they learned in their own classrooms. One reason why our courses don't adequately prepare students to teach linguistic concepts is that they aren't designed to do so, any more than a course on the modern novel prepares students to teach elementary or secondary students how to read critically and write coherently. While there are many obvious ways in which knowledge of language is relevant to K-12 teaching, without a clear bridge between theory and practice, linguistics, and more specifically, the practice of investigating language scientifically, will remain confined to the college classroom.

We also learned that, at least in public school (private schools may have more curricular flexibility for various reasons), it is essential for lessons to be explicitly connected to established curricular goals. Classes include students with different learning styles, different cultural backgrounds, and different developmental levels, and teachers are under pressure to teach basic skills to an often very diverse student body. Though students might thoroughly enjoy (and be good at) linguistics puzzles, lessons are most effective when seamlessly integrated into the curriculum (see Athena McNulty's vignette for examples and further discussion of this point).

Linguistics lessons must not only fit into the curriculum, but they must be sequenced appropriately, in order to provide the necessary scaffolding to reach a designated learning goal. For example, teaching "parts of speech" in a linguistically informed way might involve teaching the *Jabberwocky* lesson, where students identify the syntactic categories of nonsense words using their intuitive knowledge of syntax and morphology. When I piloted this lesson in an 8th-grade English class, however, I found that though students could easily sort words into appropriate groups, they were uncertain about the grammatical labels of each group; they knew that *slithy* was in the same category as *brillig*, but unsure of the category label, *verb* or *adjective*. Students would have benefited from a follow up lesson (or an introductory lesson to provide the relevant foundation knowledge) that would allow them to practice and master identifying and labeling the syntactic categories of words. Similarly, a lesson on Greek and Latin roots (using names of Greek and Roman gods) was a fun and effective way to explore decoding meaning and expanding vocabulary, but students would have benefited from a more basic introductory lesson on identifying morphemes as a preliminary step.

K-12 curricula available to teachers are well designed and organized, and exhaustively researched, and the challenges we met in developing and sequencing lessons in the classroom are not surprising. Integrating linguistics into existing curricula will take time, research, experimentation, and will depend on educating linguists about teaching, and educating teachers about linguistics. Our fieldwork therefore naturally evolved from observation to collaboration, developing lesson plans in tandem with our partner teachers, piloting them, and revising them based on our experiences in the classroom.

Creating materials: the Teachling web site

In an attempt to make our lesson plans available to teachers in some centralized way Kristin Denham developed the web site Teachling (www.teachling.wwu. edu/), where we posted our lesson plans. We hope to develop this site (with technical support that we have yet to secure) into an accessible, teacher-friendly repository, organized in a way accessible to both linguists and K-12 teachers. At this writing, the site includes more than fifty lessons, on a wide variety of languages (Arabic, American Sign Language, Japanese, Hindi, Michoacan Aztec, Lushootseed, Turkish, Old and Middle English, among many others), on a wide range of topics in syntax (distribution of prepositions *in* and *on*, finding subjects), semantics and linguistic diversity (exploring idioms in Swedish and English), morphology and vocabulary (studying the Latin roots of spells in the *Harry Potter* book series), phonology and spelling (comparing English and German cognates with *gn/kn* spellings), as well as many lessons on language and culture, language change and language history, pragmatics, and so on. While these lessons need to be refined, organized, and sequenced, the web site is an excellent start at a well-needed resource, and provides yet another opportunity for teachers and linguists to collaborate.

Creating a space: The World Language Club

Though our teaching partnerships were very productive and useful, the "linguist in every classroom" is not a sustainable model, and we needed to find a way to maintain our connections to the schools and to our partner teachers as our grant support (which provided us with release time) came to an end. To accomplish this we created the World Language Club at a local elementary school, in an effort to maintain and support interest in language. The club meets Friday after school for an hour or so, and offers us the opportunity to experiment with linguistics lessons on a variety of different topics, which we then post on Teachling. As I discuss below, our (ongoing) experiences in the WLC have become an integral part of our teaching and research, as well as providing an essential practicum experience for our students.

Creating a community: a workshop

Throughout our fieldwork experience we were in close contact with col-leagues doing similar work (many of whom are contributors to this volume). Together with Seattle middle school teacher David Pippin, we organized a workshop to bring together teachers and linguists in order to continue our collaborative conversation and share ideas. We held the first Western Washington University Linguistics in Education workshop (WWULiE) during the summer of 2007, which brought together some of the participants of the Tufts workshop of the previous year (organized by Ray Jackendoff and Maryanne Wolf, discussed in the foreword to this volume), and also included a number of new participants. The meeting was small but very productive, and we discussed our in-class collaborations, and experimented with Skype (an internet communication system) as a way to do such collaborations online. (Our introduction to Skype was organized by Beth Keyser, an 8th-grade teacher in Superior, Montana and WWULiE participant, and her father, linguist Samuel Jay Keyser, of the Massachusetts Institute of Technology, who joined us online.)

The second meeting of WWULiE was held in the summer of 2008, and focused on developing lesson plans, and on teaching linguistics in the context of world languages courses. The workshop grew substantially from the previous year, and included a wider variety of teachers from both public and private schools, with representatives from reading recovery, speech-language pathology, Teaching English as a Second Language, foreign language instruction, and more. Teachers came from Washington and Montana and (online) from Michigan, and linguists traveled from as far away as Texas and Massachusetts to attend. WWU students participated as well, and brought with them valuable insights and another aspect of partnership. In addition to sharing ideas we used some of the time to collaboratively revise and critique lesson plans on Teachling. The third annual WWULiE took place in summer 2009, on the theme "Voices of the Pacific Northwest." A number of colleagues, both at our university and at other area institutions, participated, and in future workshops we hope to continue to draw teachers interested in exploring teaching and learning about linguistics and language in the context of regional history and culture.

Toward a sustainable model

What began as classroom observation mushroomed into a collaborative project involving a small but dedicated group of K-12 teachers and linguists from around the country. The bridge between teaching and practice materialized in the form of lesson plans on Teachling, and the World Language Club and WWULiE offered ways to continue our collaborative work beyond the unsustainable "linguist in every classroom" model. While these were certainly valuable first steps, it remained to find ways to continue our collaboration with K-12 educators, and to integrate this work into our own teaching and research.

Partnerships enrich teaching

The original goal of our fieldwork in the schools was to improve our teacher education courses to help our students bridge the gap between theory and practice, providing them with the tools to apply linguistics in their own K-12 teaching. As a result of our experiences in the schools, each of our three core courses (*Introduction to Language, The Cultural History of English, The Structure of English*) now all include components that target education. Students can choose to do research projects on linguistics in the schools, interviewing teachers, creating lessons, and even, in some cases, piloting those lessons in a local school. Lessons are then posted on Teachling. Our English education majors usually choose to do such projects, and to explore how to apply their knowledge of linguistics in practical ways.

In addition to integrating linguistics and education into our core courses, we have also focused our elective "topics" course on linguistics in the schools. This course (*Linguistics in Education*) has been very successful, and though not required of English education or Linguistics majors, it attracts students from both fields. Students do research projects on linguistics and education (exploring bilingual education, second language acquisition, among other topics), and also develop and teach linguistics lessons either in the World Language Club or in an elementary or secondary classroom, with a partner teacher. Lessons are posted on Teachling, and as a capstone experience students present their lessons and experiences in a panel, open to the university community.

It is becoming more and more common in our Linguistics Program for students to choose linguistics and education as a topic of research and study, and for them to use their work in this area to meet graduation and major requirements. Students present their work as the topic of their Linguistics Program colloquium, a graduation requirement for all Linguistics majors, and have also presented work on linguistics and education as part of the university's Scholar's Week. As a result of this interest in education the Linguistics Program has recently instituted a variable credit "internship" course, specifically designed to encourage community outreach by providing course credit for students doing work in the schools under the supervision of university faculty. This variable credit course is also available to English education majors, providing them with another opportunity for a practicum experience where they can apply what they learn in our core courses.

Below are two excerpts from recent emails to me, which illustrate how our students create a link between the university and the community:

On October 15th I'll be applying for my teacher's certificate. It would mean a lot to me if you'd write me a letter of recommendation. I thought of you because the classes I took with you made me even more passionate to be a teacher. They were insightful and made me see how linguistics plays such a vital role in the classroom.

I wanted to let you know that I am working on setting up a language club through the YMCA at an elementary school in the Bothell/Mill Creek area … I will be using the TeachLing website for ideas, and if I come up with new lesson plans [I will] send you my ideas in hope that they can make your program better. The management people at the Y are really excited about it and tonight I will be talking about the program at a PTA meeting and talking about the importance of linguistics education for their kids … If the program is successful and people really like it, it could really help get more people on board to support linguistics and foreign language education in the schools, which would be awesome.

Partnerships enrich research and service

In addition to enriching our teaching in innumerable ways, partnering with teachers in the schools has also become a key part of our professional development and research. We have published books and articles on the subject (in, for example, the new online journal *Language and Linguistics Compass*, which devotes an entire volume to Linguistics and Education), and presented papers and organized workshops at both the National Council of Teachers of English convention and the annual meetings of the Linguistic Society of America. More and more, linguistics and education is becoming a topic of study in its own right, recognized and highly valued at the university level as scholarship, teaching, and service. Linguistics and education is also becoming more and more visible in introductory textbooks on linguistics, as a topic of study for undergraduates. Anne Curzan and Michael Adam's *How English Works* (Pearson Longman, 2006) is a noteworthy example, as is our introductory text *Linguistics for Everyone* (Cengage, 2010). We have been invited to speak about linguistics and education at various regional universities (Simon Fraser University, the University of British Columbia, and the University of Washington), and if the reception we have experienced there is any indication, graduate students are very interested in linguistics and education, and we need to provide them with opportunities to become involved in this area of research and practice.

Bringing grammar back to grammar school

I began this chapter with a call to action: linguistics is not just for linguists any more, and in order to raise public awareness of language and, in Liberman's words, reclaim "the territory of language" both within and outside of the academy, we need to broaden the "disciplinary tent" not only of what it means to be a linguist, but of linguistics itself, including and valuing subfields that may not fall under more traditional descriptions. What we were able to accomplish with the support of the National Science Foundation illustrates not just the value of collaboration between linguists and K-12 teachers for enriching education, but that such partnerships establish a valuable foothold for linguistics beyond the academy, in the community. This work also changes the face of linguistics within the academy, changing how we teach our classes, changing what we think of as "doing linguistics." Our work, like other work described in this volume, demonstrates that education, but also linguistics itself, benefits from partnerships that can take many forms and that often produce unexpected results, all of which nevertheless bring us one step closer to a goal shared by both linguists and educators, to improve education about language.

Acknowledgments

This chapter is based on work supported by the National Science Foundation Course Curriculum and Laboratory Improvement Grant No. 0536821 (with Co-Principal Investigator Kristin Denham). I thank the NSF for its support. Thanks also to my colleague and collaborator Kristin Denham, and to Edwin Battistella for their very helpful comments and suggestions on this chapter. I am grateful to many linguists and teachers who have shaped and guided my work in the schools; many of you are contributors to this volume. A special thank you to Athena McNulty; it was a great pleasure to partner with such a dedicated and resourceful teacher who can work wonders with middle schoolers!

15 The Linguistic Olympiads: academic competitions in linguistics for secondary school students

Ivan Derzhanski and Thomas Payne

1 Introduction

Since the mid-1960s, problem-solving competitions in linguistics for secondary school students have been taking place at various locations around the world. In Russia, the Moscow and St. Petersburg Linguistic Olympiads are credited with inspiring hundreds of young talented scholars to choose linguistics as an academic major and profession. Presently (2009) there are national contests in Bulgaria, the Netherlands and several other European countries, and the US. There is also an International Linguistic Olympiad in which students from many countries compete, as well as dozens of local competitions held in individual towns and schools across Europe and the US.

In this chapter we will describe the basic Linguistic Olympiad (LO) concept, and will argue for its significance for linguistics and related fields on a number of levels. Following this, we will provide specific descriptions of how the LO concept has been implemented in Russia, Bulgaria, the US and internationally.

2 The genius of LO

At the heart of the LO concept is the self-sufficient linguistics problem, a unique genre of composition that presents linguistic facts and phenomena in enigmatic form. A steady supply of original, thoughtfully created and intriguing problems is absolutely necessary for the success of any ongoing LO program. In a typical "live" competition, students are given several hours to solve a set of problems, many of which involve data from languages the students have never heard of, while others may highlight little-known features of commonly known languages or formal representations of natural languages.

Good LO problems require the solver to apply a formal style of thought familiar from the hard sciences to the realm of linguistic data, including orthographies, sounds, words and sentences. The most successful problem

213

Six dates are given in Swahili, along with their translations in random order:

1. *tarehe tatu Disemba Jumamosi*   A. Monday, October 5th
2. *tarehe tano Oktoba Jumapili*   B. Tuesday, April 2nd
3. *tarehe pili Aprili Jumanne*   C. Wednesday, October 5th
4. *tarehe tano Oktoba Jumatatu*   D. Tuesday, April 4th
5. *tarehe nne Aprili Jumanne*   E. Sunday, October 5th
6. *tarehe tano Oktoba Jumatano*   F. Saturday, December 3rd

Assignment 1. Match each Swahili date with its proper translation.

Assignment 2. Translate the following additional dates into Swahili: Wednesday, April 3rd; Sunday, December 2nd.

Figure 15.1 Swahili LO problem

solvers are able to use this exposure to unfamiliar languages to discover new ways of thinking and categorizing the universe, and in so doing ultimately to develop an appreciation for both the unity of language and the diversity of languages. They come to view a language as a system built upon complex but logical and consistent principles rather than as a frustrating collection of impenetrable facts, as lessons in "grammar" so often present. This fusion of formal logic and cross-cultural logic makes the problems attractive and profitable for mathematicians and language enthusiasts alike.[1] They bridge the "techie"/"fuzzy" divide that characterizes increasingly specialized academic cultures. For everyone there is also the appeal of the ludic element – the challenge of the puzzle, the same motivation that accounts for the popularity of crosswords, cryptograms, Sūdoku, etc. Finally, LO problems offer a chance to communicate a little, as it were, with cultures located far away in space or time by getting to know something about their languages, and to gain new and sometimes startling perspectives on the languages that the solver is already familiar with.

Figure 15.1 shows a good example of a problem that exposes students to different cultural worlds, from the 16th Moscow LO (1979). We challenge the reader to attempt to solve this problem before reading further.

This is but one template for LO problems, in which words, phrases or sentences in an unfamiliar language must be paired with their proper translations. There are many other possible templates, with correspondingly many possible strategies for solution (a few more samples will be found in the following pages). The exemplary quality of this problem is that it requires the solver not simply to infer correspondences between unfamiliar and familiar words, as though the subject language were a kind of coded English, but also to

---

[1] The word "mathematics" (or "mathematical") that often appears in the full names of LOs highlights the fact that the gist of this activity is finding structures, regularities and correspondences (which is what mathematics is all about), rather than knowing languages (which is what linguistics amounts to, according to a popular misconception).

discover something about the culture of Swahili speakers. In particular, one must realize that Saturday is considered the first day of the week, which reflects the Islamic influence on the communities along the East coast of Africa. At the same time the names of the months are English borrowings, which reflects the British colonial history of the area. Many such surprising (to most teenagers in the Western world) facts are revealed, not by instruction, but by discovery in the process of solving engaging logic puzzles. Other mind-expanding details revealed in some of the traditional problems include: that in Hawai'ian, the words for siblings are distinguished by birth order (elder sibling vs. younger sibling) and relation between the genders (same-sex sibling vs. opposite-sex sibling); that in some Samoan nouns, singularity is marked and plurality is unmarked, and so on.

In every competition discussed here, conscious effort is taken to provide problems that involve a variety of interesting phenomena, such as switch reference systems, (split) ergativity, noun classifiers, complex number systems, flexible word orders, etc. Problems are also chosen so as to highlight different areas of linguistic analysis: writing systems, phonetics, morphology, syntax, semantics and historical change. Prominent researchers in all of these areas contribute problems, or at least data sets, so that the phenomena represented in the competitions reflect the issues addressed and the concepts and methods used in contemporary professional linguistics.

Another feature of LO problems makes them particularly attractive for talented students in schools in a wide range of socio-economic contexts. This is the fact that they do not depend on any specific previous educational experience. In contrast to other academic competitions and standardized tests such as the SAT (Scholastic Aptitude Test), Stanford–Binet Intelligence tests, A-levels, etc., solving LO problems is mostly a matter of innate ability to understand and analyze a problem, envision a strategy for solution, and carry out that strategy in real time. No knowledge of linguistics or of the languages represented in the problems is expected.[2] Memorization of facts is useless. And while there are some frequently used techniques and methods that can be taught or learnt through practice which help a student solve certain types of problems, no procedure guarantees success. Each problem must be viewed as a unique challenge, requiring its own strategies and approaches.

Over the years LO programs evolve strict requirements that they impose on problem selection. There is some variation, but most tend to agree with the following.

---

[2] In fact, familiarity with the language featured in the problem (and presumed unknown to the solver) would sooner be an obstacle than an advantage, because writing down an answer obtained from a source external to the problem does not normally count as a solution.

| 1. *deniz* | "sea" | 3. *denizde* | "in the sea" | 5. _____ | "pictures" |
| 2. *denizler* | "seas" | 4. *resim* | "picture" | 6. _____ | "in the picture" |

Figure 15.2 Unacceptable LO problem (Turkish)

(a) All problems must deal with real languages that are (or once were) vehicles of human communication.[3]

(b) Everything in the problem must be accurate. Simplification is very rarely acceptable.[4] Made-up data is never allowed.

(c) Care must be taken to be respectful of the language and its speakers. The problems must not treat the languages as curiosities, but rather should present each language as a unique and valuable expression of a particular culture.

(d) Problems must be self-sufficient: all the information needed to solve a problem must be present in the data or be common knowledge. Advanced linguistic terminology is avoided (if necessary, terms may be introduced in the statement of the problem).[5]

(e) Simple analogy cannot be the only strategy needed to solve a problem. "Multi-stage logic" is required (see Figure 15.2 for an example).

(f) Sheer insight should not be the only way to solve a problem either. If no progress at all can be made unless the solver happens to stumble upon a particular idea, this is considered a serious shortcoming of the problem.

(g) There can be one and only one reasonable solution, and that solution must be consistent with the facts of the language.

Figure 15.2 is an example of a problem that would *not* be acceptable, even in a much more complicated version, for any LO because it violates provision (e) above (data from Turkish).

In this data set, the plural and locative forms of the word *resim*, "picture," are directly inferred from the forms of *deniz*, "sea." An acceptable LO problem

---

[3] More precisely, there is a hierarchy of acceptability, with natural languages at the top, followed by famous auxiliary and fantasy languages such as Esperanto or J. R. R. Tolkien's languages, then by fragments of fictional languages or notational systems created expressly for the problem but featuring interesting phenomena found in natural languages (and perhaps difficult to illustrate using authentic material). Few LOs ever use problems on fictional linguistic phenomena, on ways in which languages don't actually work (though perhaps they might). Problems on sign systems other than human language, such as bar codes, computational automata and scholarly notations used in various domains, constitute a category of their own.

[4] As a rule, simplification is allowed only in the orthography or the standard transcription when it contains much distracting detail and the problem highlights something else. In such cases, the solver should be informed that simplifications have been made.

[5] What concepts count as too advanced depends on the school curriculum: in some places even "plural" or "suffix" are disallowed, in others they are expected to be known to all students from grammar classes. Terms such as "palatoalveolar" or "suppletion," however, are unlikely to be commonly known anywhere.

1. *deniz*	"sea"	4. *okul*	"school"	7. *okulda*	"_____"
2. *denize*	"to the sea"	5. *okullar*	"schools"	8._____	"seas"
3. *denizde*	"in the sea"	6. *okullara*	"_____"	9. _____	"in the seas"

Figure 15.3 Acceptable LO problem (Turkish)

would require solvers to make at least one intermediate logical step, as shown in Figure 15.3.

In addition to recognizing the several noun suffixes, the solver must notice that they have different forms for the different roots and that the correspondences cut across the various suffixal categories (plural, locative and dative). Furthermore, there is no direct analogical model for the last translation – "in the ‹PLURAL NOUN›." The solver must notice that plurality comes before case, and then infer the order -*ler* +*de* for the noun meaning "sea," based on the order -*lar* +*a* in example (5). Crucially, no knowledge of suffixation, plurality or case, much less vowel harmony, is necessary to solve this problem. Rather, these features are "discovered" by the solver.

Predictably, the great educational potential of LO problems has been appreciated by university lecturers and school teachers, and in several countries problems from past contests have been used in classrooms. Many people outside the educational system also enjoy them as a tool for personal enrichment and entertainment.

We will conclude this description with an example, shown in Figure 15.4, of a writing system problem derived from one that the orientalist Svetlana Burlak wrote for the 26th Moscow LO (1995).

While self-sufficient linguistic problems are the centerpiece of any LO, another feature that has characterized the events since the beginning is a unique and invigorating social atmosphere cultivated in the community of scholars involved in the program. The following quote from Vladimir Plungian, internationally known specialist in linguistic typology and African linguistics, speaking of his experience as a high school student in the Soviet Union in the 1970s, captures a sense of this profound quality of the Moscow LO:

… what pleased me most about the Olympiad was not the problems, but the people. Perhaps for the first time in my life I met people who were enthusiastic about what they were doing. This was in contrast to the dominant spirit of the times in the Soviet Union, the importance of which cannot be overestimated. (Personal communication)

Such an open spirit of collegiality is a central feature of any successful LO program. Part of this may be due to the voluntary nature of LO staff. In most LO programs, none of the staff are paid a salary. Those who participate do so voluntarily, as part of their service to the discipline, motivated by intellectual stimulation involved in creating, testing and scoring problems, and satisfaction

Below are some words of Tocharian A, an ancient language that was spoken in the Chinese province of Xinjiang in the 6th–8th centuries CE.[6] Each word is presented in the traditional script and in phonetic transcription and accompanied by an English translation.

script	transcription	translation	script	transcription	translation
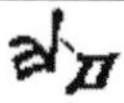 〔script〕	*lap*	"head"		*pkäl*	"bring!"
 〔script〕	*spaltäk*	"intention"		*täm*	"that"
 〔script〕	*maskäs*	"lives"		*sasak*	"only, alone"
 〔script〕	*pal*	"law"	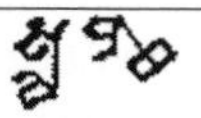 〔script〕	*slamas*	"fires"
 〔script〕	*tmäk*	"therefore"	 〔script〕	*pkal*	"he must be baked"
	säksäk	"sixty"	 〔script〕	*tamät*	"he was born"
	pat	"or"	 〔script〕		"jumping"
			 〔script〕		"sit down!"

Fill in the blanks with the correct Tocharian word or transcription.
Note: the sound *ä* is a special vowel of Tocharian, different from the vowel written as *a*.

Figure 15.4 Writing system problem from Moscow LO (Tocharian)

in seeing young people becoming enthusiastic about languages and linguistics. In contrast to the often competitive and contentious atmosphere that characterizes much academic debate, relations among LO staff tend to be very supportive, with no pressure to "outdo" one another. Careers are not on the line. Everyone's contribution is important. It is a lot of work to put on this kind of program, so anyone who can help is encouraged to do so. There are no "stars" on the staff – only dedicated scholars willing to put a great deal of time and

---

[6] Most LO problems present such background information on the languages featured (genetic affiliation, region where spoken, number of speakers if living, historical significance otherwise), usually for the sake of interest only, although sometimes such notes contain important clues for the solving of the problem.

intellectual effort into preparing and testing problems, and constructively eval-uating one another's efforts.

Students who discover they have gifts for languages and linguistics often begin to author problems themselves. These efforts draw them into the com-munity of scholars involved in ongoing LO activities.[7] Thus, as the program appeals to young scholars, it ensures its own survival by capacitating new generations of LO staff members and contributors. A great deal of that attraction stems from sheer intellectual challenge and community spirit.

3   The history of LO

The first LO for secondary school students was organized in 1965 in Moscow on the initiative of Alfred Zhurinsky (1938–1991), at the time a graduate student in linguistics under the guidance of the mathematician Vladimir Uspensky. (Zhurinsky eventually went on to become a prominent scholar of African languages.) The LO was held regularly at Moscow State University from 1965 until 1982. In 1988 it was resumed at the Moscow State Institute for History and Archives, now the Russian State University for the Humanities, and since 1989 it has been organized jointly by these two institutions. Since 1996 a mirror of the Moscow Traditional Olympiad in Linguistics and Mathematics has been held in Russia's northern capital by St. Petersburg State University.

Every year 300–500 students aged 13–17 compete in each of the two cities. There is no preliminary registration, nor any prerequisite; the contest is open to all secondary school students who can be present at the appointed place and time. The LO is held in two rounds, a fortnight apart. Each round lasts five hours, during which one has to solve four or five problems; there is a separate problem set for each class (though typically with some overlap), so that the total number of problems used each year is about twenty-five.[8] These are chosen by a committee of about a dozen professionals and university students who meet at regular intervals all year round. Submitted problems are evaluated for difficulty and clarity (by assigning them to test solvers and studying their solutions), compliance with the facts of the language (by consulting external specialists when necessary), and novelty.

---

[7] Some of the most enthusiastic contestants don't wait until they graduate. High school students have been known to organize problem-solving circles at their schools, run linguistic contests for their peers through school newspapers or over the Internet (sometimes using problems of their own composition), author problems good enough to be used in "mainstream" LOs, or design software and set up websites related to linguistics.

[8] Although participants are expected to concentrate on the problems for their own class, everyone is given the entire problem booklet, and one can get extra credit by solving more senior problems (and, in St. Petersburg, more junior ones as well: some contestants do the booklet from cover to cover).

Given are several entries from the multiplication table in Italian:

tre × tre = nove
cinque × cinque = venticinque
sette × sette = quarantanove

For how many days were ships detained by the authorities in Italian ports in the fourteenth century if they had arrived from plague-stricken regions?
(A) 9; (B) 20; (C) 25; (D) 40; (E) 49.

Figure 15.5   Problem from the Russian Bear Cub competition

A separate marking commission consisting of two members (usually college students) is set up for each problem. When the round is over, the participants' solutions are handed over to the markers, who must have agreed on a set of criteria beforehand; they process the entire pile independently of each other and then meet to compare notes under the supervision of the author of the problem or another competent person.

Traditionally the prizes for the highest scorers in each class (first, second and third, as well as honorable mention) and for the authors of the best solution to each problem are books on languages or linguistics, often donated by the organizers or the authors of the problems out of their personal libraries. Winners in their last school year receive an additional award in the form of certain advantages and benefits when applying to the philological departments of the universities that run the LO. An interesting feature of the event is the Solvers' Choice Award, a special prize given to the author of the problem liked best by the contestants.

The birthplace of LOs and the genre of the linguistic problem is also the country where the overwhelming majority of problems are composed, often as one of the products of fieldwork on Russia's numerous lesser-known languages or Russian dialects. But while most problems are based on unfamiliar linguistic material, many illustrate phenomena of the Russian language that lie outside the scope of the school program, aspects of its formal treatment by academic lexicography or computational linguistics, or various issues from pragmatics and sociolinguistics.

Apart from the Traditional Olympiad in Linguistics and Mathematics, linguistic problems (relatively easy ones) are assigned at the multidisciplinary Lomonosov Tournament, and also, reworked into multiple-choice questions, at the Russian Bear Cub, a linguistic counterpart to the well-known International Kangaroo Mathematics Contests. Figure 15.5 shows an interesting problem from the 2005 installment of the Bear Cub.[9]

In addition to the competitions, throughout the academic year lectures on various topics in linguistics are regularly delivered at the Russian State University of the

---

[9]   Since Russian uses the Cyrillic alphabet, this problem is somewhat easier for English-speaking solvers who are more familiar with the graphic form of the key word, *quarantine*.

Humanities in Moscow and the Anichkov Lyceum, a prominent high school in St. Petersburg, by members of the teaching staff of these and other institutions, postgraduate students and visiting scholars. Although these lectures are intended for secondary school students, they are open to all who are interested.

In Bulgaria the first linguistic contest was held in 1982, and since 1984 they have been taking place every year. The principal organizers are the Union of Bulgarian Mathematicians and the Ministry of Education. The early involvement of mathematicians and the fact that linguistic contests started life as an accompanying event to a popular competition in mathematics has dictated a similar format. Four hours are given for solving three problems, which are often harder and longer than the ones used in Russia, each featuring several phenomena. In the last decade most problems for the contests have been composed by the first author of this chapter, who also acts as a one-man problem selection committee. However, a few years ago several leading contestants taught themselves this art and joined the guild of active problem makers.

Ministerial support (in the form of funding, but also, no less importantly, help in spreading the word about the events) implies strict rules. Since 2003 one of the competitions has been included in the Ministry of Education's annual schedule as an Olympiad in Mathematical Linguistics, with the same status as the olympiads held in a dozen other sciences and applied domains, and takes place in three successive rounds (municipal, regional and national) on dates appointed by the Ministry, each featuring better and more challenging problems than the previous one and giving the right of passage to the next round to those who score at least 75 percent of the maximum. At the first two rounds, as well as the Winter Contest, younger students (Forms 5–7) participate as well, though of course they are assigned easier problems.

While most linguistic competitions are strictly individual, the national contest in 2001 also included an experimental team competition, which became a permanent feature of the national round of the Bulgarian LO. At the team competition a single problem set (usually one problem of exceptional length and difficulty) is assigned to three or four students, who work on it jointly for two hours, dividing the task as they choose, hand in one solution and share the laurels (or thorns).

The participants in the national round of the Olympiad and the Winter Contest usually number between sixty and one hundred. Because contestants have to travel to these events from all parts of the country, they are expected to register in advance, so that arrangements can be made for housing them at the venue for a whole weekend.[10] As a rule, students are delegated by their schools

---

[10] A weekend is actually a very short time within which everything must happen. The hardest part is the marking of the scripts, for which the jury has only a few hours immediately after the contest, so that the winners can be identified promptly, the certificates written and the awards distributed on the morrow, at the closing ceremony.

and led by an adult, often someone who trains them in problem solving between contests (an activity which some schools choose to credit as an elective in their curricula) – a school teacher (of mathematics, computer science or languages), an ex-contestant who is now at college, or simply an interested member of the public. This person also acts as a mediator between the participants and the organizers.

In both Russia and Bulgaria, summer (or occasionally autumn or winter) linguistic schools are regularly held, to which it is the general practice to invite the students who have performed best at the most recent national LOs. These events, which last from four to twenty days, strive to prepare the participants for further national and international contests, broaden and deepen their knowledge, and interest them in joining the LO staff after graduation or pursuing a career in linguistics (ideally both). They feature lectures on a wide variety of topics from linguistics and related fields, and may also include practical sessions in problem solving, mini-courses on little-known languages, more or less serious competitions and intellectual recreations (with a special emphasis on word games and puzzles).

Between 1998 and 2000 a municipal LO competition was held in Eugene, Oregon, US. These events were organized by an "advisory committee" composed of six faculty members from four departments of the University of Oregon and a "staff" of about fifteen student and community volunteers. U of O students could receive up to two units of academic credit for their participation, but no one was paid. Both graduate and undergraduate students participated.

The program was coordinated with the Eugene public school district, with preliminary contacts made in the Summer of 1997. Corporate sponsors were also sought, and support for operating expenses and prizes was provided by Cambridge University Press, local bookstores and a local photocopy shop. The events were publicized via flyers sent through the school district mail system to all language arts teachers and students, and by several newspaper columns contributed at the request of the local paper. Each column included a sample problem and promised a prize to the first reader to send in a correct solution. These columns generated much publicity and interest throughout the community. Dozens of solutions were received by e-mail and postal mail. Each week the winner of the previous week's challenge was announced and was sent a gift certificate (donated by a local bookstore).

About three weeks before the actual event, contact was made with teachers who had expressed interest in the program, and teams of two University students began visiting classrooms (mostly second language classes, but also English, literature and general social science) and making presentations about linguistics and the LO event. Some solved sample problems with the students, walking them through the analytic process, such that the classroom visits became kind of a "training session" for potential participants.

In retrospect, the informal competition via the newspaper and the classroom outreach was at least as significant, in terms of educating the public about language and linguistics, as the actual events themselves. Teachers and the general public were very receptive to these activities.

The first LO competition in Eugene was held on a Saturday in February, 1998, and only eighteen students came. In subsequent years, the event was held on a school day, so that groups of students participated, accompanied by their teachers, and this quadrupled the number of contestants. Eight problems were assigned, mostly borrowed from the Moscow LO, though some were authored by U of O faculty and graduate students. Competitors worked on the booklets for two hours. The advisory committee then met in a group to score the problems. In order to ensure consistency in scoring, each committee member was given one or two particular problems to score.

When a list of winners was available, students were notified via their teachers, and prizes were delivered to schools, not by student volunteers this time but by U of O faculty, who made the presentations themselves in the classroom in some cases. Other follow-up activities included a website that described the program and published sample problems, including those used in the competitions. Because of the educational interest of the site, it was listed high on most Internet search engines, received thousands of hits each month, and even stimulated the formation of several local competitions (we know of programs in New York City, Portland, Oregon and San José, California).

Figure 15.6 is an example of an authentic "American" problem, developed by a University of Oregon linguistics graduate student, Pilar Valenzuela, for use in the early LO events in Eugene, Oregon.

In 2007 the first ever national LO competition was held in the US – the North American Computational Linguistics Olympiad (NACLO). Plans are in process to make this an ongoing yearly event. The impetus for this program was a National Science Foundation grant to Carnegie Mellon University, Language Technologies Institute. Altogether 195 students participated in simultaneous live competitions in three cities and several "remote" locations nationwide. The live competitions closely followed the patterns of the programs described above, with students coming to a university location and sitting for a designated period of time working individually on a set of problems. In the remote locations, local adult "facilitators" supervised students working at the same time on the same problems.

Living up to its name, NACLO emphasizes specifically "computational" problems, as well as traditional problems, and those highlighting linguistic phenomena in English. Of the eight problems at the 2007 competition, only three were on other languages. Two involved nonsense English words, but relied on the students' knowledge of English. One illustrated the concept behind search engine technology, one featured error checking in English paragraphs, and one dealt with "garden path" phenomena in English.

Quechua was the official language of the *Tawantinsuyu* or Inca Empire before the Spanish invasion of 1532. For hundreds of years Cuzco, in what is now Peru, was the capital of the Empire. The sentences below represent the variety of Quechua currently spoken by thousands of people in Cuzco and in the area around Lake Titicaca.
The following are some sentences in Quechua, with their translations in random order:

1. *Antukaq chakranpiqa t'ikashanmi papa.*
2. *Siskuq chakranpiqa wiñashanmi sara.*
3. *Siskuq chakranpiqa rurushansi kiwña.*
4. *Antukaq chakranpiqa t'ikashanchá kiwña.*
5. *Siskuq chakranpiqa wiñashansi sara.*
6. *Antukaq chakranpiqa wiñashanchá papa.*
   A. Potatoes may be growing in Antuka's field.
   B. Barley may be flowering in Antuka's field.
   C. Corn is growing in Sisku's field.
   D. I've heard corn is growing in Sisku's field.
   E. I've heard barley is yielding fruit in Sisku's field.
   F. Potatoes are flowering in Antuka's field.

Assignment 1. Indicate which translation goes with each Quechua sentence.
Assignment 2. Provide English translations for the following Quechua sentences:
7. *Istuchaq chakranpiqa t'ikashansi sara.*
8. *Sawinaq chakranpiqa wiñashanchá kiwña.*
9. *Tumasaq chakranpiqa rurushanmi papa.*
10. *Kusiq chakranpiqa t'ikashanchá papa.*
11. *Inashuq chakranpiqa rurushansi kiwña.*

Figure 15.6 American LO problem (Quechua)

NACLO '07 was probably the first LO that was actively coordinated in cyberspace. "Referees" were on call during the competition to answer clarification questions by e-mail. Their answers were then immediately posted on a webpage so that all the sites where competitors were working would have access to the same clarifications. Also, scoring of the problem booklets was coordinated to ensure consistency and fairness from one site to another.

4   The international LO

In the first years of the third millennium teams of award-holders from the Moscow LO competed successfully in Bulgaria and *vice versa*, which demonstrated the potential for international co-operation in this field. Thus was born the idea of the International Olympiad in Linguistics. Albert Einstein is credited with saying that inventions nowadays can only be made by people who don't know that something can't be done. The organizers of the 1st International Olympiad in Theoretical, Mathematical and Applied Linguistics had to forget for a while that a multilingual LO is an extremely complex affair.

Everyone knew that, of course. Problems from the Russian olympiads had been used at contests in Bulgaria for two decades, as well as several times in the

Netherlands and the US. These experiences, along with the guest participation of Bulgarian students in the Moscow LO, had shown that while some problems are easy to translate, with others this is hard or even impossible, even between two closely related languages. And what complexities will arise when the languages grow in number and variety? The first Olympiad, held in 2003, had five working languages; the seventh, in 2009, had eleven. Yet it turns out that this is perfectly manageable, as long as the problems are skillfully and carefully chosen and tested in various languages well in advance.

Reflecting the fact that it was first held in Bulgaria, in the renowned mountain resort of Borovetz, the International Olympiad is largely modeled on the national round of the Bulgarian Linguistic Olympiad. It includes an individual and a team contest. At the individual contest five traditional problems are assigned (as in Russia), and participants are asked to vote for their favorites, so that a Solvers' Choice Award can be given at the end. The team contest has evolved as a domain for experimenting with novel problem templates, including projects that require special equipment (such as tape recorders or computers for work with recordings of audible speech or video clips), and has come to be seen as an excellent venue for showing secondary school students what team work is like in real linguistic research.

The problems for both contests are selected by an international committee of specialists, all of whom have the experience of doing the same thing for national contests. Naturally, here the task is harder, because translatability and fairness are added to the usual criteria, so that, for example, problems on Slavic languages cannot be used (because some participants are native speakers of one or the other, whereas the rest have probably never been exposed to any), and problems "on the solver's native language" can only be accepted if the featured phenomena are universal.[11] Unlike some olympiads of longer standing,[12] the relatively young International Olympiad in Linguistics allows teams to be formed in any way, even by four students from a hitherto unrepresented country who happen to have learnt about it; but in most countries there are more or less strict procedures that govern the selection of contestants, based on their performance at the national LO and perhaps other (con)tests or activities. The US made an impressive debut at the 5th ILO by sending two teams formed by the

---

[11] This concept can easily be carried to an extreme. In English no names of days of the week are related to numbers, whilst in Russian some are. Does this make the problem on Swahili dates easier for speakers of Russian, or perhaps harder (since the starting points are different)? Completely neutral problems are rare. But even if one problem very slightly favors some solvers, it is likely that another will have the opposite slant, and in a set of five the participants' chances will even out.

[12] The regulations of the International Biology Olympiad, for example, limit participation to students who are winners of national biology olympiads of the current school year. With linguistics, which is not part of the school curriculum in any country, an impromptu participation in the International Olympiad often predates and urges the setting up of a national LO.

top scorers of NACLO '07 and winning one of the first places at both the individual and the team contest, thus demonstrating that novices can do very well with expert help and the right attitudes.

5   Conclusion

The Linguistic Olympiads, in their various incarnations, are a proven method of exposing secondary school students to the complexity, beauty and wonder of the world's languages, and to the academic discipline of linguistics. Students who are frustrated and repelled by "grammar" because of early negative exposure, or who think they are "not good at languages," discover an exciting new world based on actual communicative systems used by real people in everyday life. The "hook" for such discovery is natural curiosity and a competitive spirit. Students thrive on challenge and competition. The LOs channel this drive into entertaining and genuinely educational directions; all the students need to have is enough natural curiosity to take up the challenge.

In Russia and Bulgaria, the national LOs have proven very effective in helping talented young people discover their natural gift and passion for languages and linguistics, and have inspired hundreds to take further courses in linguistics or to become professional linguists. Even the relatively "young" program in the US has resulted in several students deciding to select linguistics as an undergraduate major, and at least two to enter graduate degree programs in linguistics.

What will the future bring? Future and continuing LO programs will need to increase their profile among professional linguists in order to develop a steady channel of intriguing and educational linguistics problems. Perhaps journals or websites will be established that will serve as fora for those involved in linguistic problem creation and evaluation. New types of problems will be developed, illustrating under-represented areas of language-lore, and linguistic phenomena in unforeseeable forms. The development of computational linguistics and language technologies opens whole new prairies of fertile soil for problem composition. In addition, the computational element appeals to corporations, other possible sponsoring agencies and to parents and young people alike who see computational technologies as the "wave of the future."

Partnerships between university linguists and secondary school educators will deepen as more students and teachers discover the "genius" of language, linguistics and language technologies through LO programs. Perhaps more linguistics courses will be offerred in secondary schools, or linguistics components added to existing curricula.

The International Olympiad in Linguistics will grow larger and become more competitive, more creative and more exciting. National contests will be set up in more countries, and people everywhere will develop new ways of implementing the "Genius of LO."

Part III

Vignettes: voices from the classroom

Introduction to Part III

Kristin Denham and Anne Lobeck

In Parts I–II we have seen that in order for linguistics to be integrated into the K-12 curriculum, it must "fit" in some way with teachers' pedagogical goals and needs. This notion of "fit" can be narrow (specific lesson plans and strategies designed to improve reading and writing test scores) or broad (in the form of lessons and activities that improve students' critical thinking skills and knowledge of language). The choice of one approach over another depends on a number of different factors: resources available, curricular flexibility, testing and assessment pressures, administrative support, etc. One theme that emerges in Part III is that making room for linguistics in the curriculum does not require jettisoning something else; teachers need and embrace effective ways to teach about language, in particular given the ineffectiveness of traditional approaches. Indeed, as we've seen throughout this volume, the failure of traditional grammar teaching (if grammar is taught at all) has created a niche for a different, more effective approach to teaching about language.

This section contains contributions from K-12 teachers themselves, and is perhaps the most important part of this book. Here we see first hand the creative and inspiring ways that teachers have changed their teaching about language, and how these changes have affected not only student learning, but teachers' own attitudes and knowledge of language as well. Some of these contributors have had training in linguistics and some haven't, and though most have been involved in teaching partnerships with linguists, they have all had very different experiences. As we've seen in other sections, positive change in the classroom emerges from a variety of different sources, and even the smallest of shifts in thinking about language is still an important step on the road to improving education about language in the schools.

We see in these vignettes that teaching about language is as important as teaching about other natural phenomena, such as the workings of the human body or the solar system. We also see that linguistics offers teachers another *way* to teach; encouraging students to examine linguistic evidence, often based on their own intuitive knowledge of language, to find patterns in language, analyze them, and form hypotheses about them. Learning to think critically about language helps students make informed judgments about their own and others'

229

language, about what is considered "standard" and "non-standard," and to question rather than accept socially defined notions of "good grammar." By incorporating linguistics into the teaching of writing or history or the study of literature, teachers promote critical thinking across the curriculum, and scientific inquiry is no longer confined to science class.

In this section, teachers reflect on how the practice of inquiry and discovery inherent in teaching about language allows them to move away from the "teacher as authority" model, to a model which promotes exploration not answers. They also observe how discussions and analysis of "real language," based on students' intuitive knowledge, provides a way to make learning about language and grammatical patterns dynamic and relevant, connecting with students' lives and experience. Approaching language scientifically provides another way to study and learn, capturing the imagination of students who struggle with more conventional methods. And students who consider themselves (or who have been labeled) "good at math" may find that they are also "good at language." And several times in this section we find mention of how lessons and activities that address dialect diversity levels the playing field; speakers of "non-standard" dialects have as much to contribute to such discussions as speakers of "standard English."

The chapters in this section illustrate the importance of both "top-down" and "bottom-up" efforts to improve education about language. And throughout, we see that continued collaboration among teachers, linguists, and others remains the cornerstone of effecting change.

Secondary English teacher Angela Roh has an undergraduate degree in Linguistics and teaching partnership experience with Kristin Denham. Roh discusses the variety of ways in which she applies her knowledge of language in teaching English in secondary school. In her American Literature class she incorporates discussion of dialect and register through teaching the poetry of Langston Hughes, bringing in new ways to talk about literature and connect with students. Students analyze the grammatical patterns of African American Vernacular English in Hughes' work, alongside his use of AAVE as a stylistic choice, illustrating the connection between grammar and rhetoric. Roh also finds ways to incorporate discussion of Native American languages of the Puget Sound, analyzing the morphology of place names to deepen not only students' knowledge of languages of their region, but of grammatical structure and descriptive grammar. Roh also shows how she approaches questions of usage (for example, *they* as an alternative to generic *he*) in ways that allow students to critique and explore standard English rules rather than simply accepting them. Roh's work illustrates how training in linguistics, coupled with personal dedication, can effect positive change in the classroom.

Karen Mayer and Kirstin New, teachers in the Norfolk Virginia Public Schools, came to linguistics through a staff development course on Rebecca

Wheeler's code switching teaching strategy. Mayer and New's experience echoes the point we've seen made time and time again throughout this book; that teachers embrace successful strategies and materials that work better than traditional approaches, and are eager to try an approach that provides them with a tangible plan directly connected to their needs. They discuss how this strategy not only helps students achieve their writing goals, but at the same time validates students' language in ways that other strategies do not. Mayer and New also discuss how teaching CS changed their own attitudes about language and dialect, confirming that teachers learn by teaching, and that such hands-on experience in the classroom can shift attitudes and practice (noted by both Sweetland and Peng and Ann in Part II).

Deidre Carlson, a primary teacher at Willowwood School in the Pacific Northwest, reflects on her journey toward understanding the vital role of linguistics in the schools. Her journey begins with observing linguist Kristin Denham teach at Willowwood, an experience which leads to Carlson's partic-ipation in Denham and Anne Lobeck's National Science Foundation grant (Denham and Lobeck, Chapters 13 and 14 in this volume), and a commitment to integrating linguistics into her teaching. Carlson's experience provides important insights into how work in linguistics and education must be sensitive not only to teachers' needs but to teachers' knowledge; much of what teachers do is already linguistically informed. Carlson also observes that perhaps more important than knowledge about language for teachers is the *way* to teach about language, as exploration, comparing and contrasting, with teacher as facilitator rather than authority. This method of inquiry opens up new ways to reach children with different learning styles (struggling readers, for example, also discussed in Denham, Chapter 13 in this volume) and leads Carlson to examine some of her own attitudes, in particular about the importance of grammatical correctness.

Caroline Thomas and Sara Wawer have taught the VCE English Language (EL) curriculum developed by linguist Jean Mulder and others in Victoria, Australia, and offer their reflections. EL has been enthusiastically adopted in the schools, and offers students an alternative to more traditional approaches to the study of literature and language. They observe that EL appears to attract students who think analytically, and who like to "think outside the box" (also noted by Derzhanski and Payne, Chapter 15 in this volume). Thomas and Wawer suggest that EL is successful in part because it offers an approach to the study of grammar that relies on students' intuitions about their everyday language, an approach that both empowers and engages students. They also highlight (as does Deidre Carlson in her vignette) the importance of the study of language in and of itself, and how this approach, in contrast to more traditional approaches to language, is relevant, inclusive, and offers students the oppor-tunity for self-directed discovery learning. Language comes alive in EL, with activities and lessons based on TV, email, role playing, exploring ethnic varieties, and so on. Students of all backgrounds and language varieties can participate and contribute.

Athena McNulty, 8th-grade English teacher, recounts her experiences as partner teacher with Anne Lobeck, as part of the National Science Foundation grant (described in Lobeck, Chapter 14 in this volume). McNulty teaches in a rural public school struggling to raise its test scores in all areas, including reading and writing. The skill levels of McNulty's students range from far below grade level to far above it, and finding a way to meet all of their needs is a daily challenge. McNulty discusses, from this perspective, the logistical and pedagogical challenges and successes of developing and teaching linguistically informed lessons with Lobeck; what worked well and what didn't, and the need for lessons to build on each other and connect with curricular goals. As we've seen echoed in other vignettes, successful lessons provide students with a new way to look at language; grammar lessons in McNulty's class become language play, offering students the opportunity to discover and explore their own intuitive knowledge. McNulty observes that using linguistics in her teaching led to a shift in her own pedagogy, to a balance between prepping for "the next step," and helping students achieve a state of mind, one based on inquiry and discovery.

David Pippin, partner teacher with Wayne O'Neil and Maya Honda, discusses how he has integrated linguistics into the study of a unique literary work, *The Diary of Opal Whiteley*. Pippin provides an overview of Opal's extraordinary life and work and the controversy surrounding her diary (did she really write it, and when she was only 6 years old?). He discusses some very striking grammatical features of Opal's written language, and shows how he uses these features as a springboard for discussion of how authors' grammatical choices influence style and voice. Students study the grammatical patterns of Opal's language, and how these patterns are (or are not) similar to patterns in French, Breton, and Elizabethan English, languages with which Opal may have been in contact. Pippin's students come away from their study of Opal's diary understanding that analyzing literature is far more than simply deciding something "sounds good," and that dialect features, syntactic patterns, and an understanding of other languages and how languages change over time all contribute to our understanding and interpretation of "text."

Leatha Fields-Carey and Suzanne Sweat discuss their use of the Voices of North Carolina Curriculum (Reaser, Chapter 7 in this volume) in their classes, and how this experience not only opened their students' eyes to a different way of looking at language, but deepened their own understanding of linguistic diversity in important ways. They discuss how this curriculum is a particularly good fit for their area of the South, where a population increase has brought speakers of different language varieties, including a large Hispanic population, in contact with each other, and with that contact has come linguistic discrimination. The unit provides these teachers with a way to teach about linguistic tolerance (using language samples and hands-on activities on a range of local minority language varieties, including AAE and Cherokee) in a way that includes speakers of both standard and non-standard language varieties. Fields-Carey and Sweat discuss how teaching the unit changed their own language attitudes and raised their own awareness of linguistic discrimination, changing how they teach about "standard" English (Chapters 9, 10, and 11, among others, in this volume).

Dan Clayton teaches the A-Level English course (Hudson, Chapter 3 in this volume) to high school students in inner city London. His students speak a variety of different languages and dialects, and have first-hand experience of linguistic discrimination. Clayton focuses on his own students' linguistic resources, their "street" language or slang, to teach about language variation and change, a strategy that allows all students to participate and contribute. Students engage in debates relevant to their own lives and experience; what is "global" English, and how does language shape identity? Students build on what they've learned in earlier courses (code switching, register, covert and overt prestige) and do unique types of writing assignments, such as writing their own slang guide. Clayton ultimately brings the discussion back to grammar, discussing the semantics and morphology (non-standard plurals, for example) of slang, as well as sociolinguistic aspects of the language (gender differences, for example). Clayton's course shows that the study of language can be rooted in something other than literature, and that students' own language provides a rich resource for teaching about grammar, language change and variation, and connections between language and culture.

16   And you can all say *haboo*: enriching the standard language arts curriculum with linguistic analysis

Angela Roh

When I enrolled in the first of two required linguistics courses as an under-graduate secondary language arts education student, I expected to be inundated with grammatical regulations and inane exceptions that had no ostensible rhyme nor reason. As predicted, I was reintroduced to the same laws of grammar that had tormented me as a highschooler. However, contrary to my expectations, my linguistics courses provided the tools to analyze the English language both prescriptively *and* descriptively. I began to understand the study of language as an intriguing science with evidence and variables that could be found all around me in conversations and literature. Grammar finally made sense and I wanted to empower my future students with this same sense of appreciation and compre-hension of linguistic convention, practice, and history. As a result, I supple-mented my Bachelor of Arts in Education with an additional undergraduate degree in Linguistics. Now, as a secondary English teacher of seven years, I find that I often return to my linguistic studies to enhance the standard language arts curriculum within the public school system.

Linguistic enrichment has found a constant home in my 11th-grade American Literature class, especially due to its melding of history and literature. In this course, we study major literary movements in the United States in chronological order, beginning with the first inhabitants. In preparation for our first unit, I present examples of how Native American languages have influenced English in the United States. For instance, twenty-eight names of states come from native words, such as *Texas*, *Oregon*, *Arkansas*, *Nebraska*, and *Massachusetts*. Similarly, words such as *tuxedo*, *wolf*, *hurricane*, *hammock*, and *barbecue* also have their roots in Native American languages. In this manner, the students come to understand that native languages are an inherent part of their culture as Americans, and thus garner a greater appreciation for the literature and its contribution to their community.

Although most of the stories we study come from our textbook anthology, it is important to experience the stories as they were intended: orally. As a result, we listen to recorded Lushootseed stories. Lushootseed is within the Salish

234

language family and was spoken in our particular area of the Puget Sound in Washington state. On one particular occasion, we listened to stories told by Vi Hilbert, an elder of the Upper Skagit tribe. My students were fascinated by Hilbert's fluid interchange between Lushootseed and English. More than simply hearing the message of her stories, they were intrigued by the sounds of Lushootseed and its words.

"And you can all say *haboo*," Vi Hilbert's recorded voice requested at the end of each story.
"Why does she keep saying that?" one of my students questioned.
"Yeah. And what does it mean?" another asked.

And thus began our inquisition into learning about the language that is so steeped in our local culture and history. With the help of Kristin Denham, a linguist who has worked to preserve the Lushootseed language, we learned that *haboo* was an expected response from an audience to indicate that they had paid attention to the story and were still awake. Traditionally, children were told that if they failed to repeat *haboo* back to the storyteller, they would grow to be hunchbacks. Once my students realized this, they were quick to use it often in class, especially after I gave instructions! It also sparked other questions about the extent to which Salish languages had influenced our region. After some inquiry, we learned that many of the place names in our area begin with *s-*, a nominalizing prefix that is added to some verb stems to create a noun. We thus have words such as *Skagit*, *Snohomish*, *Snoqualmie*, and *Suquamish*. Other place names do not bear this prefix, but describe the area for which they are named. For example, *Puyallup* (a city in the southern region of the Puget Sound) means "where the river bends" and *Nisqually* (the name of a local Native American tribe, river, and middle school that many of my students attended) means "grassy land." Learning about a language that has contributed much to the area where we reside gives them a deeper connection to their own history as it mingles with those of the first inhabitants, and at times their own ethnic heritage.

Not only is language representative of our history, but also of our social groups. Often in literature, authors will use non-standard dialects to capture a character. This deviation from standard English will cause students to make judgments about the character or author of the text. For example, after we read "Mother to Son" by Langston Hughes, I ask the students what they imagine the author to be like based upon his poem. Invariably, they will answer that he is poor and uneducated. And when asked to provide substantiation, they will say it's because he doesn't use proper English, citing the lines, "Life for me ain't been no crystal stair" and "I'se still climbin'." At this point, I ask them to think about the way they talk to their friends and how this may be different from the way they speak to adults or write essays. The students usually generate many examples of words and constructions that are used within their community of teenagers. This line of questioning not only initiates a connection between the individual and the text, but it also provides an opportunity for students who typically lack confidence to participate in literary discussions. Once we have listed various examples, I then supply the terms *informal* and *formal* register. We apply these words to the examples we generated and discuss the occasions for their usage.

To continue this line of inquiry, I ask them to brainstorm other ways that English might vary in different groups of language users. Most of the examples they produce are dialectal variations, which they understand as accents. I tell them that the technical term for *accent* is *dialect*, which can be defined as a subset of a particular language used by members of a certain community. Although dialects have different sounds, vocabulary, and grammatical constructions, they are not different languages as they are mutually intelligible. When asked to provide examples of regional dialects in the United States, an amazing number of hands fly into the air; they all have a story to share about a friend from New York or when they visited their family in South Carolina. Most of their observations are of lexical differences such as the use of *soda* vs. *pop* or *standing in line* vs. *standing on line* or phonetic variations, such as the Bostonian 'r' deletion, in which *car* becomes *cah*. Invariably, a student will mention the word *y'all*, which they understand to be solely a lexical variation in the Southern dialect. I then ask them to deconstruct the word and examine its usage. They recognize it as a contraction of *you* + *all* and, after some analysis in pairs, they arrive at its function: *y'all* is a pronoun [+ plural + second person]. Usually a few will mention that other languages they study in school have a word that translates to *you all*. From this they understand that *y'all* fills a gap in English, and thus a word that they once dismissed as "weird" now has a new sense of import and esteem.

When asked to offer examples of their own dialect as residents of the Pacific Northwest, my students are usually stumped. To assist, I list the words *egg*, *bag*, and *wash* on the board and ask them to say them aloud. Some will pronounce *egg* with a vowel like in "pain" and *bag* with the vowel of "pet," both non-standard in many parts of the country, but quite standard in our area. To further illustrate my point, I ask students how their parents and grandparents pronounce the words *wash* and *Washington*. Some students will respond that their older relatives insert an *r* in the words so that they become *warsh* and *Warshington*. Although these are not striking deviations from Standard English, they do help students understand that not only are they members of multiple groups of language users, but they too may speak a dialect that is not considered Standard American English.

I then turn their attention back to the poem that instigated our inquiry by asking them which dialect they think the speaker is using. Someone in the class will usually suggest "Ebonics." After explaining to them that Ebonics is a term used primarily by the media, I provide the appropriate term, African American

Vernacular English. AAVE, like most dialects, has rules that dictate its variations in grammar and phonology. For example,

A. When the sounds t and d are the final sounds of a word, they are dropped if the following word begins with a consonant, e.g. *goo men.*
B. Multiple negation is permitted, e.g. *he don't know nothing.*
C. The use of habitual *be* (which is a construction that is present in other languages) to indicate an event or action that is repeated, e.g. *He be going to the store every night.*

I then ask them to find examples of these dialectal variations in the poem. After this analysis, the lines that they once cited to support their assumption that the author was uneducated now become rule-governed grammatical structures, i.e. "Life for me ain't been no crystal stair" contains multiple negation and "I'se still climbin'" is an example of an alternative use of *be* and the loss of final consonant sounds.

To further our analysis, I add a second poem written by Langston Hughes called "Theme for English B." In this text, the author addresses his teacher at Columbia University, where he is the only Black student in his class, "So will my page be colored that I write? / Being me, it will not be white. / But it will be / a part of you, instructor." After recognizing that Hughes was actually very well-educated, we begin contrasting the use of language in the poems. They come to realize that Hughes uses an informal register written in AAVE to capture the speaker's intimate tone in "Mother to Son." When Hughes, as the speaker in "Theme for English B" addresses his professor, he uses a more formal, standard register. In this manner, the author makes a conscious stylistic choice, adjusting the language for both occasion and audience.

By the conclusion of our discussion of these two poems, the students have learned a variety of lessons, all of which stem from their linguistic analysis and extend to a deeper comprehension of the texts and each student's sense of self in their own community. They understand that it is unfair and oftentimes inaccurate to judge a person based upon external traits, such as dialect. These lessons also offer a validation of their own dialect and supply the tools to make more deliberate and purposeful use of the variety in their own linguistic register when writing or speaking.

In addition to reflecting our inclusion in various social groups, language can also be an indication of our values. For example, in recent decades, those interested in creating a more egalitarian society have initiated changes in linguistic conventions to make them more inclusive. Over time, many gender-related modifications have been adopted as standard usage, e.g. *Ms.* instead of *Miss* or *Mrs., salesperson* rather than *salesman, human/s* as opposed to *man* or *mankind*. However, there are instances in which the formal register – and some prescriptive grammarians – have not kept pace with the progression of social values. In such cases, it is important for students to identify a conventional rule so that they are better equipped to make an informed decision regarding their own ethical use of language. For example, Standard English does not provide a neutral pronoun to use in situations in which the gender of the antecedent is either unknown or concealed. Prescriptivists have long dictated the use of *he* and its oblique forms (*his*, *him*, and *himself*) as gender-neutral pronouns, e.g. *Someone called for you. What did he say?* But as social perspectives have evolved, informal spoken language has responded by opening the traditionally closed class of pronouns to expand the usage of *they* from [+ third person + plural − gender] to also include [+ third person + singular − gender]. For instance, *Someone called for you. What did they say?* In this case, the second speaker does not know the gender of the anonymous caller, and therefore uses *they*. This pronoun extension has become common in daily oral language, and is used more often than its predecessor, *he*, in any of its various forms.

Although the published use of *they* in this capacity has also become more pervasive in recent years, most grammar guides still advise against its usage in formal writing. In addition to using the traditional *he*, they recommend an assortment of techniques, such as the combination *he/she* or interchanging *he* and *she*. These practices usually result in writing that sounds redundant and unclear. To further complicate the matter, the latter solution can only be applied when multiple anaphors are needed to refer to a single antecedent. Due to the various options and their implications, it is important to inform students so that they may make a conscientious stylistic choice in their own writing.

This linguistic predicament usually presents itself in my classroom when we begin learning to write thesis statements. Every year, a scenario similar to the following arises: When asked to write a thesis about the theme of a short story about the Vietnam War, one student wrote *When you are tormented by the experience of war, you must confront your memories in order to heal.* Once they were instructed to avoid addressing the reader through the use of *you* and to use *one* in its stead, they revised their sentence to *When one is tormented by the experience of war, he must confront his memories in order to heal.* At this point, I reminded the student that a theme is a generalization about humanity and posed the following questions: "Are you just referring to men? Don't women fight in wars as well?" The student responded, "Yes, but I still don't know what to write." I then asked them to simply tell me aloud what they meant. The student naturally replied, "When someone is tormented by the experience of war, they must confront their memories in order to heal."

At this point, I always draw the students into a whole class discussion. I begin by relating the prescriptivist suggestions. They are usually familiar with some, if not all, of these techniques. I then provide examples to demonstrate how the use of (a) *he/she* or (b) the transposition of *he* and *she* can become awkward in their usage:

(a) If a customer becomes irate, remind him/her that you are there to help him/her and ask what you can do to resolve his/her issues. If he/she asks to speak to a manager, promptly comply.

(b) If a customer becomes irate, remind him that you are there to help her and ask what you can do to resolve his issues. If she asks to speak to a manager, promptly comply.

In both cases, the students recognize that the resulting sentences are awkward and difficult to follow. Although *he* may make the sentence more fluid, it presents other issues. To illustrate, I relate the following puzzle:

Michael, Derek, Sandra, and Kyle are scheduled to attend a top secret conference. Before they meet, Derek sends an email to Kyle that states, "One of the other members told me that he was going to vote against the proposal." To whom is Derek referring?

Despite its intended gender neutral usage, the students will instantly answer that the antecedent of *he* is Michael. When asked how they arrived at this conclusion, they explain that Michael is the only other male that was mentioned, which instigates a conversation about language, cognition, society, and personal ethics. By the conclusion of our discussion, the students have not only used higher order thinking skills to analyze a problem, but they have also evaluated social implications and are thus empowered to make informed stylistic choices as writers.

Language is the implicit keeper of culture; it transforms to reflect our changing society with more rapidity and ease than the strictest grammar books could dictate or appreciate. Embedded within the words and sentences of a community is both its history and values. Incorporating the study of linguistics into the standard language arts curriculum allows students to obtain a richer understanding of themselves in relation to the group of language users that they are an intrinsic part, thus creating a stronger connection and sense of relevancy to the materials they study. Linguistic inquiry not only leads to the meaningful acquisition of language skills, but also deepens the appreciation for the tool of communication we often take for granted. *Haboo.*

17   Code switching: connecting written
and spoken language patterns

Karren Mayer and Kirstin New

It's the beginning of second semester, the first day back from winter break, and we can sense they are tired as they slowly shuffle into the room seeming to have cement in their shoes. Greeting them at the door, we smile and announce that today we will start our writing block with a code switching lesson. Then we see that spark, the excitement that comes with learning new material! The students begin to arrange the chairs in our typical semi-circle fashion around the chalk-board and charts. Grabbing pens, white boards, and their new code switching notebooks, they jump into their seats ready to hear about code switching. Before our winter break we had told them we would be learning a new writing strategy. They were intrigued by the words code switching and were looking forward to the new lessons. We assured them it was something they had never heard before and that they would find the new method to be a very useful tool to improve their own writing. With the state writing test right around the corner they willingly committed to the new learning adventure.

We became invested in code switching in the fall of 2006. We felt strongly about including code switching in our 2006–2007 school accountability plan that drives our instructional year. We are both literacy teachers with Norfolk Public Schools and after receiving staff development on code switching from our English Department, we decided to introduce the concept to our Larchmont teachers. We then heard Rebecca Wheeler and Rachel Swords speak at a city-wide staff development session. Hearing them explain code switching and how it was implemented in Rachel Swords' classroom made it even more relevant. From this point we guided our teachers through the code switching book and modeled lessons in the classroom. Dr. Wheeler visited our school and gave feedback and useful suggestions for continued implementation of code switch-ing at Larchmont.

We started using code switching during our writing block because we saw that many of our students needed help in mastering formal academic writing. Their writing was filled with things like the following: "We was going to the mall." "He be so silly at school." "They walks to school everyday." Because many of the characteristics of our students' speech were showing up in their writing, we believed that using code switching – teaching the students to be keenly aware of the differences between what we call "formal" and "informal" writing – would result in improvements in their writing and their knowledge of formal mechanics and usage. Code switching was the vehicle we used to accomplish the goal of embedding formal language into their writing.

Because grammar instruction has been overlooked for some time, but because of our belief in its importance, we felt the need to implement a new approach to the teaching of grammar and usage, especially as it relates to the writing process. Also, we were very concerned about our students' negative attitudes about writing. It was time to retire the red pen method.

Another motivation for adopting the new approach was state testing. Our students' grades on writing pieces were below grade level or failing. The state standards are included in the writing curriculum and, although some grammar instruction is imbedded within that, there is no plan for how rules of grammar and usage should be taught. Most teachers will acknowledge that such instruction is important, but many feel they don't have the tools and guidelines to deliver effective grammar instruction. Norfolk (Virginia) Public Schools uses a writing rubric that assesses student writing in three domains: composing, written expression, and mechanics and usage. Our students were low in all three domains; however, the mechanics and usage section consistently proved to be the greatest challenge. These students had previously been instructed using traditional grammar lessons through a variety of instructional materials. Our grammar lessons were primarily incorporated through the five-step writing process. The students followed the five steps in order to have a complete formal writing piece. The five steps are: prewriting, drafting, revising, editing, and publishing. Through these steps the teacher discovers a particular grammar lesson that needs to be taught. For example, in a 2nd-grade classroom, teacher A notices that many students seem to be having difficulty with subject–verb agreement. The teacher learns this through conferencing with students. Examples of the informal language appeared as students wrote phrases such as: *we rides, mom eat, flowers smells*. Through this informal assessment, the teacher would then develop a lesson on subject–verb agreement. Code switching appeared to be a clear logical focus for us to follow.

Nationally, we are all faced with state writing tests that must be written formally, using Standard Academic English, rather than informally. Our goal was for all of our students to pass the state tests; demonstrating that they could write in formal academic style was a mandatory piece. Code switching clearly addresses this issue in a non-threatening manner. Making use of key words and question stems like "This sentence should be written" and "The best way to write sentence 6 should be …" became an important part of code switching writing instruction.

Throughout the code switching lessons, we validated that our students' informal language was acceptable when in an informal situation, and this idea was a big part of our initial discussions of code switching. We continuously emphasized that there is no "right or wrong" way to speak and write. In today's world it is obvious that our school systems are filled with students who come to us with many different dialects and languages. We see and hear this reflected in their speech and writing. The many dialects and languages need to be acknowledged and respected, even as we help our kids add Standard English skills. Our goal was to teach these students to "code switch" from informal to formal, depending on the situation.

We introduced the students to code switching by using two simple terms: formal and informal language. We began by constructing three two-column charts labeled "formal" and "informal." From there, we began our brainstorming by sorting examples into the two columns of various places, clothing, and language. We asked, "What are examples of places where you would wear formal and informal clothing?" "When you go to the mall, what do you wear?" "When you go to the prom, what do you wear?" "If I was going to a wedding, what would I wear?" We listed their responses on the charts. Through discussions like these the students were able to come up with their own clear ideas about the difference between formal and informal. Of the three charts – places, clothing, and language – the language chart was by far their favorite. One student, Tila, just roared with laughter when asked for examples of informal language that they used in certain situations, i.e. their neighborhood, on the bus, at recess, with friends, times when they were relaxed and informal with each other. One of her informal language examples was "sweet butter biscuit home girl." She then told us the formal translation was "girlfriend." One reason that code switching is so effective is that students are allowed to bring in their own language examples like this, making it all seem so real for them.

Using children's literature in each of the code switching lessons was another key part of each session. *Flossie and the Fox, Don't Say Ain't, Pink and Say,* and Langston Hughes' poetry were some of the students' favorite code switching lessons. Examples that include the use of informal language in literature happened in *Don't Say Ain't* when Godmother says, "Chile, you got the highest grade on the city test. You gone too far to fall back." A woman in *Pink and Say* says, "Do your momma know what a beautiful baby boy she had?" In *Flossie and the Fox* both formal and informal language is evident. Both Wheeler and Swords use this text when first introducing formal and informal language. The fox in this story uses formal language when speaking while Flossie in contrast uses informal language. Students become aware of the obvious differences in language patterns. Conversations about language use in printed texts allowed teachers to look at informal language and teach grammar lessons that switch to formal language. Students were then challenged to identify the informal patterns, and lessons followed which focused on the formal way to state the text. We spent time discussing why the authors used the informal language by creating voice and what sort of effect this had on the reader. They came to recognize that these pieces came alive with the use of informal language, but that such language would not be appropriate in other circumstances or types of writing. The use of informal language in literature made a powerful impact on student learning.

Code switching is a different approach to teaching writing instruction without the use of the red pen. Instead, it empowers students and improves their writing in formal written English. Most of our students who were exposed to code switching passed the Virginia Standards of Learning Writing test. Next year, we plan to start in September with code switching lessons in all classes, kindergarten through fifth grade.

Code switching has changed the way we will deliver grammar instruction in the future. It allows us to address writing in a non-threatening fashion by accepting and validating our students' spoken language. As writing teachers, we understand that students often write as they speak. During the state writing exam one student reported that he had written FORMAL LANGUAGE in large letters all over his booklet. He said that it helped remind him to "flip the switch" and use formal written language rather than the informal language he sometimes speaks. When the writing scores were reported in late spring he was delighted and proud to find out he had passed. We believe that code switching instruction played a key role in making this happen. Code switching is now a component of grammar instruction at our school. As originally hoped, it did address both spoken and written language and served to move our writing program forward.

18 A primary teacher's linguistic journey

Deidre Carlson

Introduction

In the fall of 2005 I began teaching at Willowwood Schoolhouse where linguist Kristin Denham was teaching linguistics once a week. That marked the beginning of my journey toward understanding the vital role of linguistics in school curriculums. Being a partner teacher in Kristin Denham and Anne Lobeck's National Science Foundation grant (see Lobeck, Chapter 14 in this volume) has been an amazing opportunity. During the past two years I have had the pleasure of learning from Kristin from watching her teach and also from our many discussions about linguistic concepts. I've been pleased to find how my background in English and my good teaching instincts have been guiding me to make many linguistically sound choices when teaching kids about language. However, I've also become aware that some of the ways I was teaching language skills and concepts could be much more effective when informed with a deeper linguistic knowledge. Being exposed to linguistics as a field of study has enriched my teaching both as a topic in and of itself and also where it lends itself so frequently to being incorporated into other disciplines. I have been a teacher in Grades 1–6 for the past twenty-three years. I've been vaguely aware that some of what I taught in Language Arts would be considered linguistics. I was definitely aware that I was venturing into linguistic territory in my extra lessons on things like Greek and Latin prefixes or words the English language adopted from Native American languages. It surprised me then that during the first year of looking closely at the role of linguistics in the elementary classroom I had so much difficulty with understanding what linguistics is and does. In this vignette, I look back to the confusion of the first year and then go on to explain how I began to have a better understanding of what linguistic awareness can do for both teachers and their students. I conclude with a description of how the knowledge I have gained will help me to be a more effective teacher.

The first year

When I started teaching at Willowwood I was curious about how Kristin's linguistics lessons would differ from the language or literacy lessons I taught. I remember asking, "Is this linguistics?" about lessons I'd been teaching. During that first year I was the only teacher at the school when Kristin came, so I was usually working with a small group of younger students on reading or writing skills while Kristin worked with the older students on linguistics. In talking with Kristin and the older students later I recognized that some of the things they were doing were similar to lessons that I'd taught, but there were also lots of things that I'd never approached with kids, and the approach itself seemed different to the way I usually taught. (See Denham, Chapter 13 in this volume.) There was so much variety. I was having trouble piecing together what constituted linguistics in the elementary school.

In the summer of 2006 I attended the Linguistics in Education workshop at Tufts University at which both linguists and a handful of teachers took a look at how linguistics was, or was not, being taught in the K-12 schools, how much teachers know about linguistics and what teachers need to know (see Jackendoff, Foreword to this volume). A statement that was repeated a couple of times on the first day of the workshop was that teachers don't know much about linguistics. Being a teacher, and one with an English background, I felt a bit offended. I thought that if I could just figure out exactly what linguistics was I'd be much clearer on how much I really did know! But then, as Linguistic-ese flew around the room and the linguists engaged in discussions on some fine points of their field, I began to think that statement about teachers was true. I wondered in dismay if linguists meant the things they were discussing to become part of an elementary curriculum. I quietly decided that if they knew what I was thinking they'd realize they'd invited the wrong person to this workshop. Thankfully, that was a small part of the workshop, and most of the presentations and discussions were fascinating, eye-opening, and quite teacher friendly. It became clear to me that not all linguists know a lot about education just as not all teachers know a lot about linguistics. I left the workshop feeling intrigued but still not very sure that I had a handle on the larger picture of what linguistics was as it related to elementary school students.

The second year

During the second year of the linguistics–education partnership with Kristin at Willowwood I had more opportunity to observe her interactions with the students. I was amazed at the variety of engaging lessons, many about things I'd never included in my curriculum. As with the first year, often her lessons would provide an added dimension to something I was working on with the kids, such as when they examined the Hungarian language when we were studying Hungary, or *Beowulf* and Old English when we were studying alliteration. It was during this year that I realized it wasn't only the variety of topics that was distinctive about Kristin's lessons. There was something different about the way she approached the exploration of the topics. Students were doing a lot of comparing and contrasting, uncovering patterns and discussing why it might be that way. I learned that what she was doing was linguistic analysis. Linguistic analysis is a tool in the scientific study of language. Well, of course! Linguistics **is** the scientific study of language. Well, of course, I knew that! Sort of. I knew that, but I hadn't really thought much about guiding my students to look at language in a scientific way. I'd been more focused on the different linguistic topics, but not on how to approach them linguistically.

Looking at language in a scientific way with students was not something I did deliberately. The word "deliberately" is important here because it's not that it didn't happen. My approach to language from a literature/writing/teaching background was much more "Language Arts" focused than "Language Science" focused. I had unconsciously been scientific when I observed what was and wasn't effective about teaching the concepts and made needed adjustments, but it hadn't occurred to me to develop language lessons using the scientific techniques of inquiry, hypothesis-formation, and comparative analysis. So, what linguistics in the elementary school might look like involved a lot more than a selection of interesting topics. It needed to include a way of looking at language. Language Arts or Literacy curriculums often include elements of linguistics, but the depth and breadth of linguistics can't be pigeonholed in Language Arts. It is a field in and of itself with its own history, techniques, and proven methods for studying language in a myriad of ways; from where language comes from, how sounds are made, how the brain processes information to the social ramifications of language. This scientific way of looking at language has far reaching effects in other fields such as history, anthropology, psychology, and sociology.

The 2007 Linguistics in Education workshop took place at Western Washington University in Bellingham, Washington. The presentations and discussions were interesting and felt extremely relevant to me. My sense of confusion about the relevance of our efforts that I'd experienced during the 2006 workshop was gone. My understanding of the importance of linguistics as a field in K-12 education had evolved with my linguistic awareness. As a traveler on a linguistic journey I now felt I had a road map and a basic understanding of the lay of the land.

Third year and beyond – The effect of linguistic knowledge on my teaching

In this section I've presented my ideas on how I'll use what I've learned about linguistics to strengthen my teaching during the next school year and in years to come. I've also included some opinionated justification for some of my ideas.

Linguistics as a field of study

The first area I'd like to address has to do with promoting linguistics as a field of study as I'm teaching. When we are engaged in studying language scientifically, I will tell students that what they are doing is linguistics and that it is a field of study – just like biology or anthropology or mathematics. I'll let students know that there are people who make a career out of studying language and they are called linguists – just as there are biologists, anthropologists, and mathematicians. And, fortunately for us, these linguists can be very helpful when we need to consult an expert about a linguistics question. I'll also help students to become aware of the vast number of other resources available on linguistics. Reading from some of the entertaining best-sellers on linguistics such as *The Language Instinct* by Steven Pinker or books about related issues like punctuation (*Eats, Shoots and Leaves* by Lynne Truss, for example) would be a great way to share the fact that people actually have fun messing around with language and linguistics. I will also promote linguistics as a field by introducing students to linguistic vocabulary such as adjectives, stress, dialect, metalinguistic knowledge, and code switching. When we share common terminology, we can then go on to talk about these things in context. And, I will share with students the relevance of linguistics across the curriculum by using linguistics to enrich our studies in history, cultures, art, math, and science. In another big plug for linguistics as a field I will discuss metalinguistic knowledge with students. I want students to understand that when they become aware of how they use language, they become aware of choices, and there is power inherent in being able to make choices. (That concept of power in choices of course is one that reaches far beyond the field of linguistics.)

Using tools of linguistic analysis

The second area of my teaching I want to strengthen has to do with using tools of linguistic analysis to guide students in meaningful and practical discussions about linguistics. Over the past fifteen years, discussion-leading techniques using higher level thinking skills have also become a strong focus in math, science, and social studies programs, but language skills such as those dealing with formal linguistics are usually still presented in a traditional manner. The traditional way of teaching grammar (with a presentation of rules followed by instructions for the students to copy the sentences and the circle, underline and draw arrows to show understanding of the rules) doesn't do justice to the complexities of the topic or the fun, engaging discussions that can be had when examining the structures of language. For one thing, the traditional approach immediately places students in a position of trying to apply rules, followed by being corrected and then given a score based on what they got wrong. Another problem with the traditional approach to grammar is that many of the rules provided for students to memorize have not kept pace with linguistic knowledge. Furthermore, when students aren't given the opportunity to examine grammar with critical analysis we aren't honoring what they already know. They are all speakers of language and they arrive in our classrooms with innate, if sometimes unconscious, understandings and insights about language. Our job as teachers is to help bring that knowledge to the surface. Using only a traditional approach to grammar often isn't good for the teacher either. It puts the teacher in the role of imparter of information. Often a teacher will feel a bit shaky about that information and with good reason. The rules of grammar are complex and not always consistent from one source to the next. A teacher without a very strong linguistic background can easily be "caught out" by students' questions. In contrast, when a teacher participates in an exploratory discussion it frees him or her up to be one of the learners. I'm not suggesting the teacher shouldn't be as well-informed as possible in order to guide the discussion effectively, just that the position as guide or fellow learner is a much more pleasant place to be than in the hot seat of expert. When I played the teacher-as-expert role and explained to my students that a sentence was a complete thought, we always reached dead ends. To elementary school students, and most of the rest of us as well, many of our fragments seem like complete thoughts. My experience exactly! It was very reassuring to learn at the 2007 Linguistics in Education Workshop that linguists can't agree on what a sentence is. That doesn't mean the rest of us are off the hook and don't need to have a discussion about it. But it means that we can agree to let things remain complicated and our exploration doesn't have to end with everything tied up neatly. That, in itself, is a wonderful thing to model for students. A teacher as a model for not knowing all the answers, for living with the complexities ... That is a complete thought! An important part of being that kind of a model is also demonstrating the desire to find out and having good ideas about where to find resources.

Meeting different learning styles

I want to mention here that some students will enjoy approaching language from a series of rules and a set of written exercises to hand in for correction. That brings me to my third area for strengthening my teaching with linguistic knowledge and that has to do with meeting different learning styles. As I watched Kristin guiding students to approach language scientifically I was often struck by the high level of involvement of students who usually struggled with language concepts. These students were stronger in math and science, and a scientific approach to linguistics made language come alive for them. So, this is definitely something to keep in mind when engaging in language activities. On the other hand, even though I feel strongly about the importance of linguistic analysis in a discussion format, it's appropriate to provide additional activities to meet other learning styles. Written language play is something many love to do while for others it is pretty tedious. Language concepts can also be explored with manipulatives and moving bodies and also with computer programs to help teachers reach students with many different learning styles.

Sociolinguistics

The fourth area of my teaching that new linguistic knowledge will strengthen has to do with sociolinguistics and sensitivity to language variation. At the 2007 Linguistics in Education meeting one linguist described the problem of language discrimination as "the last acceptable prejudice." Our discussion made me aware that this prejudice also applies to me. It comes out in my penchant for "proper English." I have passed on my mother's corrections of my usage errors to my husband and my son. They've done well adjusting to order of pronouns, and correct use of *good* and *well*. My pet peeve for the last couple of years has been the correct use of *fewer* and *less*. While there's probably a place for oral corrections within the walls of one's home, it isn't at all appropriate in public. It's also not appropriate for a teacher to make oral corrections while a student is speaking. I can remember playing the age-old parent/teacher game of repeating "Excuse me?" until a student made a desired usage change. Another memory, one that makes me cringe, is of me pointing out to an African American student that if she had "axed her mother" that would be a very bad thing indeed. Now I recognize how those kinds of corrections reinforce language discrimination. In the future I will eliminate terms like "proper English." When discussing usage and grammar with my students I will point out that there is formal and informal language, or standard and nonstandard language, but not necessarily right and wrong language. When creating lists of formal and informal language for compara- tive analysis, students really have fun with listing aspects of their informal language. When comparing and contrasting formal and informal language students can see that there are logical patterns in all ways of speaking and this can remove the social stigma of right or wrong that becomes attached to students because of how they may speak. Teachers can reinforce the idea of formal and informal by asking students to share how they might dress for different occasions such as for school, camping, a dance, and a job interview. (See Wheeler, Chapter 9 in this volume; Mayer and New, Chapter 17 in this volume.) This can lead into a discussion of what kind of language might be appropriate for those different occasions. In this way students can learn to value "formal language" as one of the tools in their language toolbox. Again, the power of having the choice is important and if students understand that teachers want to provide them with choices, not rob them of their way of speaking, this will make a significant difference in how language lessons are received.

The sociolinguistic concepts discussed above are directly related to working with students who are English language learners. Comparing and contrasting the patterns in a student's native language with patterns in English not only honors a student's native tongue, but provides an opportunity for critical analysis for all students. By doing so students become aware of what they already know and their knowledge is reinforced. The concept that there are patterns in all language is reinforced as well. I attended a high school reunion this summer and was struck by a remark from a former classmate in my French class. He told me that the rules of English didn't really make sense to him until Madame Bennett compared the structures in the French language to those in English. I'm guessing that educational theorists have long known the importance of comparing and contrasting two or more languages. Latin used to be standard fare in the education of young boys, and most colleges include two years of a foreign language as entrance requirements.

Summary and conclusion

Language is a part of our everyday lives. Linguistics is concerned with major questions about who we are as human beings – our history, our culture, our communication, our language development from infancy to adulthood, how we learn and understand.

Language is fundamental to thought, ideas, and the expression of those ideas. Language reflects who we are as individuals and as a culture. This is far too important to be neglected in our schools and yet linguistics as a field of study is not well understood by many educators. Many educators are unprepared to provide any more linguistic exposure than they received themselves. Working toward requiring linguistics courses for students in college education courses throughout the country is one approach that will make a difference. It is also important to reach certified educators by developing programs that partner those educators with linguists.

At the beginning of my linguistics journey I was unsure about the role of linguistics in the schools. Now it seems to me that asking if linguistics belongs in the education curriculum is like asking if a field such as biology belongs in the curriculum. Biology is the scientific study of life. Linguistics is the scientific study of language. Leaving out either one would be leaving out the scientific study of our selves and our experience.

19   Why do VCE English Language?

Caroline Thomas and Sara Wawer

1   Introduction

VCE (Victorian Certificate of Education) English Language (henceforth EL) was introduced into senior years at Victorian schools in Australia in 2000 as described by Jean Mulder in Chapter 5 of this book. As most teachers are likely aware, it's relatively rare for a new subject to be added to the school curriculum so it is pleasing to note that schools, teachers, and students are taking on EL in ever increasing numbers. It is a mark of the perceived relevance and popularity of the subject that the number of schools offering the Year 12 subject has expanded from 9 in 2000 to 89 in 2007. This is 17 percent of the schools which offer VCE English. All types of schools offer EL including: State, Independent, Catholic, and Adult Education.

As two teachers who have been involved in the subject since its inception, we have been excited by how quickly EL has been adopted by schools. We have been part of its development and our discussion here is a compilation of our experiences and those of many other teachers of the subject.

2   Why students choose English Language

It is our experience that students who are very good at English are choosing Literature and EL in Year 12, or English and EL. On the other hand, some students take EL to "escape reading," and the dreaded "analysis of language" that is required of them in the English course. Such students are generally advised that this is not a good base from which to begin. Poetry, prose, and texts of all types are covered in the discussion of language in all its forms and varieties as well as quite a bit of "technical" reading.

English teachers in general comment that students who are more analytical in their approach and can "think outside the box" along with those who have a genuine interest in language are well suited to the subject. Students who have studied a LOTE (language other than English) seem to be slightly advantaged as they generally have a good understanding of the basics of grammar and have therefore experienced some of the obvious differences in form and function of different languages during the course of their language studies.

It is for these reasons that we, like other teachers of EL, have tried to make the subject as current as possible and to encourage students to take note of different language experiences be they listening to various conversations, seeking out relevant newspaper articles, watching TV, or listening to radio programs. Students report that they enjoy "spying" on those around them wearing their "linguistic hats." Many remark that they really "knew that," but didn't have the means or the formal knowledge to discuss what it is that they themselves were doing, seeing, or hearing when they communicated.

3   Benefits of the English Language course for students

We have found that the study of EL is a wonderful introduction to the notion of language difference and variety. Learning grammar by citing everyday examples, which students are all familiar with, has been a very successful and enjoyable experience for all concerned. Discussion about aspects of everyday language, which students would have never really thought about before, makes them think about what they are doing when they communicate as well as why and how they make certain choices about language every day. EL is also enjoyable and informative and provides future life skills for those students who do not enjoy reading or writing extensively about literature.

Most teachers report lively class discussion and better class participation in this subject than in some *English* classes as students are keen to identify with the concepts being taught at a level with which they feel comfortable. They are adept at supplying interesting and unusual responses you had never thought of which in turn lead to useful, relevant, and often heated class discussion.

Students we have taught remark that they feel that the subject has relevance to everyday life – a remark rarely heard elsewhere. Teachers have noted that their students' critical thinking and analytical skills steadily improve as they progress from simply looking at text for comprehension purposes to a point where they are able to understand the intent of the writer/speaker more clearly, and recognize, for example, the use of euphemism, why one might choose to avoid taboos and adhere to social norms of politeness. Many teachers report that the students' own writing, reading, and oral skills improve as they become more aware of the conventions of syntax and discourse.

In EL, we draw our texts from a variety of settings, so today's world of SMS, chat, and email, as well as the very popular Facebook and My Space, are part of the investigation alongside the language of Shakespeare and the canon of English and Australian literature. Students begin to bring in their own texts and are encouraged to discuss them with their class. To this end, many teachers encourage students to create a scrapbook of newspaper cuttings and to note down how each cutting is related to the course.

Through the study of the language used by various groups, we encourage students to be descriptive in their approach. Standard and non-standard varieties of Australian English are studied side by side and students enjoy looking at how some varieties are given prestige while others are stigmatized. Varieties like teenspeak, Aboriginal English, and ethnic varieties of Australian English fascinate the students, and they are given exercises where they collect data about the various varieties that they encounter themselves, analyze it, and present a report on its characteristics. This has proven to be a most rewarding part of the subject as students make their own discoveries about language variation that exists within their communities. In the process of collecting data, organizing it, and analyzing it, students see themselves as more self-directed, active participants in their learning, thus deriving an enormous amount of satisfaction and enjoyment from their findings.

4   The way the subject is taught

It is our experience that the best way to tackle the teaching of EL is to divide the method of teaching it into two sections: partly instructional and partly activity centered. We try to focus as much on discovery as on pre-digested information. No matter the topic, we always encourage students to explore and have fun with language while learning new concepts.

From our experience, we have found that some teaching techniques work better than others. Variety is certainly the key and students seem to enjoy the fact that each topic can be treated in a different manner. They have also remarked that we are not really teaching them new things *about* language, rather we are teaching them *new ways to think about* language.

It is our preference to seat the class in a circle or semicircle as this encourages more open discussion – it removes the role of sole instructor from the teacher and allows all of the students to relate well to each other. When studying Spoken Language in all its forms, role plays are an invaluable tool. Students work in groups creating scenarios that they act out in front of their peers. Much hilarity is generated, but the point being made is clear and the students have taken ownership of actually explaining the concept at hand to each other. We have also found that more formal presentations where students present prepared work add variety to the ordinary "chalk and talk" sessions.

We have noticed that this subject has shown itself to adapt well to the mixed ability and mixed language background classroom. To this end, group work is effective; students learn a lot from each other concerning language when they come from differing backgrounds. As a result a somewhat disparate class can become more cohesive as students really feel that they are gaining new knowledge from each other at the same time as learning about each other as people. Many students who might otherwise not have felt they had a lot to contribute have found themselves with plenty to say.

The subject is made all the more enjoyable once students become aware of the way we all communicate – we encourage them to look and listen on their way to school, at the dinner table, while out with friends, then to try and link their discoveries to what is being discussed in class. Some students eventually find themselves carrying around a notebook for jotting down anything unusual (or typical for that matter) that is related to what is being discussed in the classroom. Others will have drawings in these notebooks which denote the points they are trying to remember.

An interesting anecdote is of parents of twins studying the final year of EL who reported that they were surprised at how attentive their boys had become in church services. When they asked the boys why they were suddenly more alert during the sermon, the boys' response was that they were analyzing the use of language by the preacher.

It is also obvious that teachers cannot totally rely on their students to be the source of all the extra knowledge and examples required for teaching the course. Using graphics, DVD, videos, and relevant films from time to time helps. We ask students to record and listen to each other speak, especially for Unit 4 Outcome 1, which has a focus on spoken language. Once again, it's amazing what they discover they actually already know. Some excellent and popular resources include Australian films like *Kenny, The Castle, Looking for Alibrandi*, and *Aussie Rules*, episodes from TV series like *Yes Prime Minister*, and especially Australian programs like *Summer Heights High* and the very recent *The Sounds of Aus*. Such resources provide many examples of language use that are engaging to watch and relate to linguistic concepts taught in the subject. We also use talk back radio programs, interview programs, and "variety shows" like *Rove, The Panel*, or *The Footy Show* which air weekly in Australia and clearly reflect different aspects of the subject while providing less scripted examples of language use.

However, there are stumbling blocks. One of the biggest difficulties students face is learning the metalanguage. We have been told of teachers using "word of the day," "word of the week," computer generated puzzles, and wall posters around the room in order to help students learn and use the metalanguage.

Another area of real difficulty, which is clearly reflected in the exam results, is the relatively weak essay-writing skills of some students. Some teachers have reported setting an essay a week for homework and this seems to be helping to improve their students' study scores in the final exam. This is important because the essay counts for 40 percent of the final grade for the examination. It is an area that we, as teachers, will have to re-examine in order to improve results.

5 The role of linguists and educational authorities in supporting the subject

We acknowledge that there are many teachers who feel that their own knowledge and skills in the area of linguistics are insufficient. Throughout the development of the subject, teachers of EL in Victoria have been fortunate in having support from the community of linguists at the various universities, with the added organizational support supplied by the Victorian Curriculum and Assessment Authority and the Victorian Association for the Teaching of English. This has meant that teachers have been able to develop and refine their linguistic knowledge and skills through professional development provided by experts in the field under the auspices of various educational institutions. Such support and advice has been and continues to be an invaluable resource for teachers.

Nevertheless, many teachers also find that an important support is the option of networking with other teachers. Teachers from public and private schools have found common ground and cross-fertilization of ideas and teaching methods as they have collaborated in constructing assessment tasks and cross-marking student work. We have found that three or four teachers seems to be the ideal number to bounce ideas off one another, and that meeting on a regular basis at a commonly agreed place is most effective. We opted to meet at a local coffee shop which takes the school feeling away from the meeting, thus giving us a chance to be in a more relaxed environment while working. As well, we feel that cross-marking a common assessment task allows for good peer discussion as well as feedback about the design and content of the assessment tasks we have set. There are also opportunities for other discussions which center on strategies for teaching key knowledge and skills in the various outcomes as well as the sharing of resources.

6 Some challenges

One common difficulty that teachers of EL unfortunately face is the feeling of isolation, since most teachers are the only staff member in the school who teaches the subject. To this end, some schools have had an outside teacher mentor for first year teachers of the subject to ensure quality of delivery. We have found that this seems to have boosted the confidence of both mentor and teachers in question, as each takes away a different perspective on the subject from each meeting.

As well, problems related to the dictates of the final year assessment can lead to an increased focus on teaching toward assessment with its concomitant restrictions on in-depth exploration of various facets of the subject and narrowing of definitions. There is still more work to be done to address this area of concern; however, the people setting the examination have spent time addressing the format and content of the examination paper. Over the past two years, the changing style of the final examination, which now includes short answer questions, multiple choice questions, and essay writing, has endeavored to give balance and to allow all learners to find an area in which to excel.

7   Conclusion

We have found this subject, English Language, is exciting to teach. Students of varying abilities have remarked how satisfying they have found the classes to be – independent of the outcome of their assessment tasks and examination results. EL provides students and their teachers with an enjoyable and challenging subject to explore together.

20 Language lessons in an American middle school

Athena McNulty

Introduction

When my former linguistics professor, Anne Lobeck, approached me about doing some mini-lessons in one of my 8th-grade classes, I was thrilled. As a college student, I had taken three linguistics courses: *Introduction to Language*, *Syntax*, and *The Structure of English*. I enjoyed learning about language – the fascinating history behind it, the universal patterns, the physical structures in our body that enable us to use it. I learned the foundational grammatical concepts (e.g., subject, predicate, independent clause, etc.) that I missed when I was in school, became familiar with the implicit rules of our language, and developed a sense of appreciation for its complexity – an awareness that many of the rules are fluid and subject to change.

As a teacher, I used some of what I learned – primarily the terminology useful for teaching about punctuation and usage – but I neglected other important aspects of linguistics. What I'd learned in my linguistics courses in college just didn't seem immediately relevant to my everyday teaching. There had been no emphasis on how to apply the material in the courses I took. To help Dr. Lobeck understand why it was difficult for me to apply what I had learned from my coursework to the classroom, I thought it important to describe the context in which I teach.

School realities

This depiction will seem familiar to most K-12 educators, but others may be oblivious to our reality. For one, language arts teachers in Washington state are responsible for helping students meet standards in reading, writing, and communication (outlined in 152 pages of our *Grade Level Expectations* booklets). Unfortunately, however, many students are already behind by the time they reach middle school (Grades 6–8). According to fluency tests and state assessment scores, students in my classroom – mostly from white, rural, working-class families – ranged from those reading at 2nd-grade level (with books like *Clifford* on their recommended reading list) to college level readers. Fewer than half of all 130 students were reading at grade level. Needless to say, helping students become proficient readers (while not allowing my advanced readers to stagnate) was a priority.

In writing, as with reading, there was substantial variance in student performance. During the first week of school, I asked students to do their best on an essay for which they had no guidance. One student only had enough material for one paragraph, consisting of very little substance, filled with spelling mistakes, and comprised almost entirely of run-ons and fragments (the kind that impede understanding rather than adding style). Another student in the same group submitted a thoughtful, eloquently written multi-paragraph essay, complete with pithy quotations and stylistic transitions. But most students fell somewhere in the low-middle and needed some intensive writing instruction.

Knowing that the majority of students who make the decision to drop out of school do so between the 8th and the 10th grade – and that many choose to abandon the school system because they struggle as the expectations increase – it's my responsibility to give these students access to the basic skills they'll need in high school and on their state assessment so they aren't so tempted to opt out.

Since so many are so far behind – despite the good intentions of most teachers and parents – there is no time to waste. Unless I know a lesson is preparing students for high school, for the state assessment, or for the world beyond school, I won't use it. Students need to learn a definite set of skills and they need to understand some core concepts in order to succeed after middle school. So despite my interest in linguistics, little of what I learned from my college courses transferred to the classroom because I didn't see where the material would fit.

But as I showed Dr. Lobeck what, exactly, students were expected to know and be able to do, she thought of lesson after lesson that would not only "fit," but would actually help me teach certain skills and concepts more effectively, often in ways that were more engaging than what I had planned originally. For word choice, she talked about teaching word origins and the connotations usually associated with Anglo-Saxon versus Latin and Greek words; for organization, she suggested we discuss the differences between coordinate and subordinate conjunctions – and have students practice with each; for author's style, she expressed an interest in discussing dialect as it relates to preconceived notions about people who use non-standard English. The possibilities seemed endless.

And once Dr. Lobeck started teaching lessons to my first period class, it was exciting to see students so enthused about language study. Throughout the year, we made substantial progress ... but we had our share of challenges.

Making lessons "fit"

To begin with, we had some logistical challenges. Since we had little time to collaborate from week to week, the lessons we chose to start with, while being excellent starting points, weren't incorporated seamlessly within the existing curriculum. Even if the lessons addressed skills I was already planning to teach, our timing was often off. So, unfortunately, linguistics lessons were presented as separate from the rest of the curriculum. And since we only did one lesson a week, it was difficult to maintain a sense of cohesion among the topics we discussed. Consequently, we didn't take these initial lessons as far as I would have liked. Next year, many of these lessons will be used as hooks to introduce distinct units, offering students practical advice for improving their writing and helping them become more perceptive readers.

But overall, the lessons themselves were great. The more information I offered Dr. Lobeck about where, specifically, students needed guidance, the more valuable the lessons became. Students became frustrated only when they didn't see the direction in which we were going with the lessons. So we made adjustments along the way – adding structure where necessary, providing clearer goals, and infusing healthy doses of scaffolding – so they were more likely to be successful.

The lessons: A work in progress

Content and function words: Be a word

The first lesson we put into practice, "Be a word," included a popular, high-energy activity that helped students review their parts of speech. (See also Denham, Chapter 13 in this volume.) Working in small groups, each student had to act out a different word within the sentence they were assigned, and then the class tried to guess what word they were representing. Students discovered that the easiest words to perform were content words (nouns, verbs, adjectives, and adverbs), and that function words (determiners, linking verbs, etc.) were the most difficult. They were energized by the fact that they could recognize different word categories using their own intuitions about language, and learning how to label each category provided them with an important tool: a vocabulary with which to talk about language.

As an extension of this lesson, students can use their knowledge of parts of speech to improve their choice of words. For example, they can practice replacing dry verbs – the kind that were difficult to perform in the "Be a word" lesson – with more lively ones. We can also discuss overuse of adjectives and adverbs in writing and concentrate on using more specific nouns instead (*jalopy* vs. *old car*). And students can learn to eliminate unnecessary function words so their writing is more concise (*She didn't think it mattered* vs. *She didn't think that it mattered*).

Parts of speech: Jabberwocky

The "Jabberwocky" lesson was also engaging for students and a good follow-up to the "Be a word" lesson. Students were given phrases from Lewis Carroll's *The Jabberwocky* with nonsense words mixed with function words and were asked to label the parts of speech of each word based on how it "behaved." For example, in *the slithy toves*, *slithy* acts like an adjective because it ends with a *-y* like many adjectives do, and because it occurs before a noun. And *toves* seems like a noun because it follows an adjective. It was empowering for students to see that they all had knowledge of syntax and morphology – even when, semantically, their phrases didn't make sense. And they loved creating nonsense sentences of their own.

This lesson would work well as a springboard for subsequent lessons geared toward helping students identify and fix sentence fragments. With the use of nonsense words, students become less preoccupied with content so they can, instead, focus on sentence structure. So if students need practice linking subordinate clauses to independent clauses, they aren't bogged down thinking about the semantics. Traditional "grammar lessons" become "word play" when we can write sentences like *Because the friggle treptured the nujjle, the yefts nilked the nuggle.* They're irresistible!

Parts of a sentence

The "Parts of a sentence" lesson introduced students to the word order arrangements that form sentences. Students were given a sentence and had to create a *new* sentence using the same parts of speech, in the same order, as the original. As they did so, they learned about word placement in relation to other words (e.g., adjectives usually precede nouns, and nouns usually precede verbs). From this same lesson, students discovered that when some words (or groups of words) move, the sentence still maintains its original meaning (e.g., *Yesterday, the two huge dogs barked furiously* is the same as *The two huge dogs barked furiously yesterday*). They realized that adverbs and prepositions (or phrases headed by these words) are often the ones that move.

To take this knowledge to the next level, students can practice adding variance in their writing by beginning some of their own sentences with prepositional phrases (e.g., *Without realizing what he had done, he drove away with a clear conscious and never returned*), adjective clusters (e.g., *Cold and alone, he cursed his father for leaving*), or participial verb phrases (e.g., *Laughing uncontrollably, the group of teenagers paid no attention to the pain in the young boy's face*).

Plural nouns

"Plural nouns" was another empowering lesson, one where students became aware of their implicit understanding of the structure of language. Dr. Lobeck talked about different ways we pluralize in English: sometimes we simply add an -*s* (cat*s*); at other times, we add -*es* (church*es*); or we pluralize internally (geese, oxen). And with other words, we indicate quantity with adjectives (*some* water). She showed students that they have an internal mechanism that allows them to understand this complex set of principles without even having to think about it consciously.

Though students were involved in the discussion initially, they seemed disappointed to learn that we weren't doing more with it. It's easier to motivate them if they think the lesson will help them or if they consider it "fun." While it was interesting to some, others seemed indifferent. They wanted to know how learning this material would help them in the future. Perhaps an exposure to words that present "exceptions to the rules" that cause people to make common spelling mistakes would have helped.

Nicaraguan plurals

"Nicaraguan plurals" was another lesson with mixed reviews. Students were given examples of sentences from Nicaraguan English – some with -*dem* attached to the noun, and others without it. Dr. Lobeck prompted them to identify why -*dem* was used in some instances but not others. A few students were able to see that the suffix was added when there was no word indicating plural prior to the one being modified (*seven case of juice* vs. *the case of juice-dem*).

While this lesson made sense in conjunction with the previous lesson, students had difficulty seeing its relevance. Had we been reading a story where a different dialect was used so we could compare it with Nicaraguan English, or if we had tied it to a discussion on linguistic prejudice, it probably would have worked more smoothly. Another possibility is that students needed more time to process the information. An independent activity allowing them to ask any questions they had individually – without feeling embarrassed to ask in front of the whole class – may have led to a more substantive discussion.

Root words sequence

At the end of the year, students rated the next sequence of lessons on mor-phemes as being "the most useful" of all the linguistics lessons. They were also well-timed since we were already working with root words in class. Admittedly, I wasn't especially creative in my approach to teaching about word parts before this lesson. I informed students that familiarity with root words would not only help them decode new vocabulary so they'd become better readers, but it would help them improve their spelling as well. From there, students took notes (unceremoniously) on word parts (two a day) along with each word's definition, and then jotted down some derivatives, all of which they were required to study in preparation for weekly quizzes.

Words from Greek and Roman myths and legends

When Dr. Lobeck introduced the "Words from Greek and Roman myths and legends" lesson, however, where they learned about different mythological gods and brainstormed other words containing these gods' names, she was able to change the way students thought about root words. They were no longer simply memorizing word parts without context. Instead, they were exploring language and making interdisciplinary connections. Next year, I plan to use this lesson as an introductory activity before starting our root word study guide. And rather than choosing root words at random, I plan to use a meaningful sequence, incorporating creative writing and analysis of word parts within literature as well.

Pan- and re-

The Greek and Roman myths lesson evoked curiosity as several students noticed discrepancies. One student wrote "panda" as a derivative of Pan (the god of fields, forests, and wild animals who often evoked terror) but, understandably, didn't see how the two were related. In response, Dr. Lobeck created another lesson to address the confusion. The "Pan" lesson helped students see that, even if they think they know a root word's meaning, they need to be aware that the same word may have different origins and therefore different meanings (as was the case with *panda*). The "Re-" lesson reinforced this same concept. After being presented with a list of words beginning with *re-*, students derived that the prefix meant *again* (as in *re*lock), though sometimes, the rule didn't apply (as in respond … you can't *spond* again).

I was initially concerned that students would question the justification for teaching word parts since so many of them have multiple meanings with varied origins. I didn't want them to be confused. But ambiguity is part of life – part of our language – and it's something students are bound to come across on their own, if not in the classroom. I'd be doing them a disservice *not* to address this reality. If we are grappling with these ideas together, I can show them how it's usually easy enough to determine which root is used based on the context in which it is used, but if this isn't enough, they can always look up the word in a dictionary.

These lessons, taken together, deepened students' understanding of how words are put together and how language develops, evolves, morphs … yet remains the same in the most basic respects. And it made the material more meaningful. It became part of a larger picture of language arts, part of a cohesive whole.

What does your name mean?

In the final segment of this unit, Dr. Lobeck shared with students the origins of each of their names – personalizing the study of words, extending it beyond the classroom, and instilling a sense of excitement, once again, about language.

Conclusion

By the end of the year, these students – many with below average academic achievement – were exposed to an exciting new way of thinking about language that they would not have had access to otherwise. Students looked forward to Dr. Lobeck's visits because they never knew what to expect. And her expertise – her knowledge about the history of English and her awareness of language systems of other cultures – added richness to class discussions, enabling students to think critically about language.

As for my part, while working with Dr. Lobeck, I was reminded that education involves more than just prepping for "the next step": it's also a state of mind – one entailing thinking critically about the world, posing questions about our surroundings, and observing patterns that help us better understand our environment … as well as each other. Linguistics provides a rich avenue through which we can help students achieve this state of mind, without neglecting the skills they'll need to reach "the next step."

21   The diary of Opal Whiteley: a literary and linguistic mystery

David Pippin

Background

Eight years ago I turned to linguistics to help meet the needs of students in my 5th-grade English classes who identified more with math and science than they did with reading and writing. While most of my interest in linguistics centers on using a series of problem sets to give students an opportunity for scientific inquiry, I've also found that linguistic analysis interjects an important but oft-neglected topic of conversation into literature study: an author's grammatical choices. In the United States, teachers, and therefore their students, generally think of grammar as fixed and are not aware of the questions they might ask about grammatical choices. Consequently, conversations about literature focus on questions of narrative found in novels: the author's purpose, the plot, and the search for personal meaning in the themes of the story. While these are important conversations to have, there is more to explore: examining grammar is among the many ways of reading available to us (Montgomery *et al.* 2000).

One way of opening up this possibility for other ways of reading is to provide a text where students can't help talking about grammatical choices. *The Diary of Opal Whiteley* is one such text. I came across this text in 1995, and I've had the opportunity to teach it in both public and private schools and with students ranging in age between 8 and 13. Currently I teach 6th graders at an independent middle school in Seattle, and the students I work with there are fascinated by the writing and life of a girl who was a literary sensation in the 1920s, claimed to be the daughter of French nobility, aspired to be a Hollywood movie star, traveled to India as the guest of royalty under the name H. R. M. Mlle. Françoise Marie de Bourbon, and spent the last part of her life in an English mental institution – Napsbury Hospital at St. Albans.

Opal's life

By most accounts, Opal was born in the southeast corner of Washington State, in the town of Colton, on December 11, 1897, the oldest of five Whiteley children (McQuiddy 1996). Her father, Charles Edward "Ed" Whiteley, was involved in the logging industry, and when Opal was 5, the family moved to Lane County, Oregon, near her grandfather's farm. Opal's later account of her early upbringing is far more auspicious. As her diary was being published, she would claim that she was the daughter of French nobility, Henri D'Orléans, and that she had been kidnapped to Oregon.

A child prodigy who charmed the faculty of the University of Oregon at the age of 17, Opal had a mystical connection to the woods and fields of her childhood home. Opal amassed large collections of plants, rocks, and insects when she went "on explores." It is said that she could tame animals, a talent which is captured in a photo of her with butterflies perched on her hands, highlighted on a poster used to promote her nature lectures with a group called Junior Christian Endeavor (see Figure 21.1). After an attempt to break into the film business, her travels took her to Boston, where she arranged a meeting with *Atlantic Monthly* editor, Ellery Sedgwick. He serialized the first two years of her diary, and in 1920 it was published by G. P. Putnam's Sons as a book with the title, *The Story of Opal: A Journal of an Understanding Heart*. Within a year it was out of print.

People couldn't believe that the eloquent diary was written by a 6-year-old girl from the logging camps in Cottage Grove, Oregon. Some say that Opal created the diary after failing in her attempt to make it to the silver screen, but there are photos of her working at the home of Sedgwick's mother-in-law, piecing together the manuscript, an unusual collection of envelopes, wrapping paper, and anything else she could find, all covered with big block letters, written with crayon, and using no punctuation or word spacing. Whether or not the diary was torn up by her jealous sister, as Opal suggested, is unclear, but to a public weary of World War I, reflections of an innocent child strolling down country lanes with farm animals in tow was a blessed relief.

The editor of the *Cottage Grove Sentinel*, Elbert Bede, was one of the earliest skeptics (Bede 1954). More recently, Katherine Beck has argued that Opal could not have written the diary as a child (Beck 2003). But there is also a core of faithful supporters, and one of the most important is Benjamin Hoff, who rediscovered Opal's diary in the Multnomah County Library in 1983. He worked tirelessly to get it republished, and in 1986 a hardcover was released. In 1994 a new paperback version of the diary came out, *The Singing Creek Where the Willows Grow: The Mystical Nature Diary of Opal Whiteley*, and it is this edition of the diary that will be the reference for this article (Hoff 1994). Any citations will reference both chapter and paragraph number (e.g. 1, ii), for ease of use with other versions of the diary. Today there are several other editions of the diary in print, and Opal's writing has inspired a one woman show, a play, a collection of songs, a movie (forthcoming at the time of this writing), and even a Myspace page! While it might not be possible for students to resolve the question of whether she wrote the diary as a 6-year-old or as an adult, they

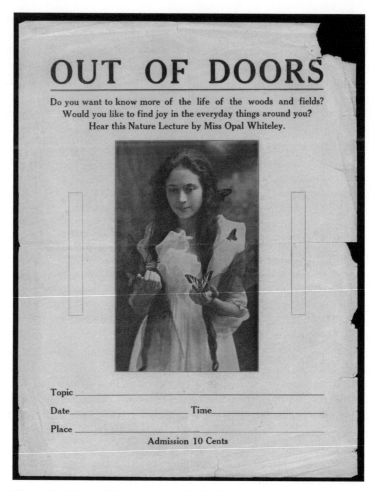

OUT OF DOORS

Do you want to know more of the life of the woods and fields?
Would you like to find joy in the everyday things around you?
Hear this Nature Lecture by Miss Opal Whiteley.

Topic _____

Date_____ Time_____

Place _____

Admission 10 Cents

Figure 21.1 Opal Whiteley, circa 1917. (Courtesy of the Massachusetts Historical Society.)

certainly do enjoy debating it. And they use some of the unusual features of the language of her writing to bolster their arguments.

Discovering linguistic patterns in Opal's writing

Opal's diary begins …

Today the folks are gone away from the house we do live in. They are gone a little way away, to the ranch-house where the grandpa does live. I sit on our steps and I do print.

I like it – this house we do live in being at the edge of the near woods. So many little people do live in the near woods. I do have conversations with them. I found the near woods first day I did go explores ... (1, i)

When students encounter Opal's writing for the first time, it is not uncommon to hear them characterize it as bad grammar. One need only read the first chapter to find, from the perspective of standard American English, excessive use of *do*, a widened use of words, overuse of determiners, overgeneralized inflections, *a*-prefixation, and invented spelling. And while some of these can be ascribed to the mistakes of a young person, students are not content with that explanation. Some of the patterns are so unusual, they want to describe them in more detail. The text can serve, then, as a springboard to grammatical analysis. Students develop an interest in acquiring the language of grammar to talk about the unusual structures they encounter.

Opal's diary has been subjected to linguistic scrutiny before, by two professors, both from the University of Washington (UW), but separated by seventy years (Beck 2003). It was first examined just after the diary was published in 1920 by Robert Max Garrett, a professor of English, who specialized in medieval literature. Dr. Garrett wrote:

All readers of language and composition will agree with me that participial forms and gerunds are not innate in the child – that they must be taught carefully and laboriously. It will take a great deal of persuasion to believe that it is humanly possible for a six year old to make use of the following expressions [see 2, ii]: "There I found the mama's thimble, *but she said the pet crow*['*]s having taken it was as though I had taken it*, because [he] was my property ..." [his italics] (Beck 2003: 257)

His remarks were directed to the question of authenticity, but it is just as fascinating to delve into the patterns of Opal's unusual style of writing and compare it with other languages and dialects.

Use of do – There are a lot of odd constructions found in Opalese, but the pattern that opens up the most interesting line of inquiry is the overabundance of *do*. Indeed, it is one of the features that make some think that Opal's writing has grammatical traces of French. In his introduction to the diary, Benjamin Hoff speaks of her use of a "wordy approximation of French syntax," using as examples, "I do have thinks" and "I did wait waits" (Hoff 1994: 74). He suggests Opal's father's French-Canadian ancestry as a possible source for this "imitative 'French'" (Hoff 1994: 53–54). But is this really French diction? In French, *faire* is used in situations when someone does something to you, as in *J'ai fait couper mes cheveux*, "I got a haircut." It is also used in combination with sporty verbs, as in *Je fais du ski*, though not always. So, one can say, *Je fais du marcher* or *Je marche*. But *faire* is always a performative; Opal's *do* is clearly the empty *do*. Professor Julia Herschensohn, a linguist at UW with a specialty in Romance languages, adds that the sample text she looked at "does not at all look like it contains mistakes 'typical' of French speakers ... There is nothing like *do*-support in French" (Beck 2003: 259). English is unusual in its use of *do* to carry tense, but the use of *do* in English has been used for different purposes over time.

It would seem that Opal's extra sprinkling of *do* is perhaps more Elizabethan English than French. Today we use *do*-support for negated statements (*I do not like green eggs and ham*), yes–no question formation without auxiliaries (*Do you like my hat?*), non-subject WH-questions (*What did you do for breakfast?*), negative imperatives (*Do not pass go. Do not collect $200*), and for emphasis (*I do like your hat*). This empty auxiliary derives historically from the productive *do* (*I do polka dancing*), meaning "to cause" or "to make." Whereas the inflected forms of verbs in Old English required no use of an auxiliary like *do*, Elizabethan authors started employing it for that purpose. They did so more frequently than today, and also for other purposes apart from carrying tense. In *A Shakespearean Grammar*, Edward Abbott, author of the satire, *Flatland*, speaks of Shakespearean use and omission of *do* as an auxiliary verb (see Abbott 1870). In this excerpt from *Hamlet* (i, 2), Abbott provides an example where Shakespeare uses *do* with the second verb, but not with the first, for metrical purposes:

It *lifted* up it [so Folio] head, and *did* address
Itself to motion

Like us moderns, the Bard may have also used *do* for emphasis. In the example below Abbott gives us a line from Shakespeare (*Hamlet* i, 1) where, he suggests, *do* is used emphatically. But as the unstressed, tense-carrying *do*, it would be part of a nice line of iambic pentameter.

The sheeted dead
Did squeak and gibber in the Roman streets.

Likewise, it is often unclear in Opal's writing if *do* is being used for emphasis or to carry tense. In the following example, which relates to her dear friend, Sadie McKibben, she might have used *do* for emphasis.

One way, the road *does* go to the house of Sadie McKibben. (1, vi)

But if that were the case, then another verb might have been necessary here.

One way, the road does go *is* to the house of Sadie McKibben.

In sentences with two clauses, it seems that Opal has a preference for adding *do* to the second.

When the *mowers* cut down the grain, they also do cut down the cornflowers that grow in the fields. I follow along after and I *do* pick them up. (1, vii)

Whether she is using *do* for emphasis, or just optionally employing *do* as a tense carrier, is not certain, but it would seem that the latter is more likely.

Issues of language change are fascinating for students, but older texts are often a bit dense. Combining an accessible text like Opal's diary and samples of older works makes the process more engaging.

In discussing the evolution of language, it is hard to prevent the conversation from moving to comparisons with other languages, which is, of course, a good thing when the teacher is prepared for extensions like this. Students reading Opal are motivated to learn something about French and ask questions that bring in other languages as well. English is unusual in its use of *do* as a dummy word to carry the tense, and that itself is a revelation for students. Breton is another language where a *do*-like verb operates in this way, but though it's spoken in the Brittany region of France, it is a Celtic language (Wojcik 1993).

Widening the use of words – Opal challenges students to reflect on parts of speech. In some cases Opal uses *have* to create a place for a nominalized form of a word that is not generally regarded as such:

I *have not knowing* of the people that do dwell in them; I do know some of their cows and horses and pigs. (1, vii)

This happens with other verbs as well, and sometimes with the verb and related noun having the same root:

I did not like *to bring disturbs* to her calm. (12, iv)

I too did feel *glad feels*, from my toes to my curls. (28, i)

It's hard for students (and teachers!) to parse out the components of sentences, and sometimes it takes glaring examples of odd word usage to create a reason to try. While it's not a good goal to go a-parsing everything one reads, it is important at times to bring to the discussion of literature an analysis of grammatical structure, an activity that is sometimes set aside in more gripping narratives.

Overuse of determiners – Opal refers to individual members of her family as "the Momma" and "the Papa" and "the grandpa," a behavior that is impersonal to be sure, not at all like The Mamas and the Papas of the sixties. This pattern is easy for students to pick up on, and discussion of the role of determiners follows from this. We talk about the difference between indefinite and definite articles, make comparisons to other languages that require the use of gender with their determiners, and connect this to common and proper nouns.

Opal also turns an indefinite quantifier into an adverbial when she says the raindrops make the quilts on the beds "some damp" (1, ii); cf. *somewhat*. I've learned from linguists I work with that many languages use *definite* determiners in this way and with proper nouns as well. Tohono O'odham, a language spoken in the

Southwest United States, uses its definite article *g* with 'titles' and names: *g je'e*, 'Mother'; *g Klistiina,* 'Cristina'; etc. Spanish uses the definite article before 'titles' like *el General de Gaulle,* names of languages, parts of the body, and personal possession ('inalienable possession'). Again, examples like these from the diary give students a need to use the teacher's language for talking about language (adverb, noun, modification, etc.) and to make comparisons to other languages.

Overgeneralized inflections – In the first entry of the diary, Opal refers to "the house that wasn't all builded yet" (1, ii) and later on she gives "advices" to Minerva, the new mother hen, about how to raise her children (22, xx). In the former example we have a case in which Opal is overgeneralizing the regular form. In the latter, she is using advice as a count noun instead of a mass noun. Students see such constructions as immature and may recognize the patterns in the speech of younger siblings. Working through a problem set on past tense formation and the related phenomenon of plural noun formation reveals just what those rules are. See Honda, O'Neil, and Pippin (Chapter 12 in this volume) for more.

A-prefixation – *A*-prefixation is a feature of Appalachian English, but in Opal's writing it seems that it is used stylistically to create a more folksy feel, as in "I go a-walking on the rails" (1, x) and "… I did go a-piping" (28, iii). The *a*-prefix is constrained by a number of rules, and attaching to a present participle is one of them. Opal's use of *a*-prefix follows the rules of traditional a-prefixation, with one exception. Just after she mentions going a-piping, she says, "Somedays I like to walk *adown* the river" (28, iv). Working through a problem set on Appalachian *a*-prefixation and comparing it to Opal's use of the *a*-prefix in her writing can be connected nicely to a larger study of dialect awareness. (See Reaser and Wolfram 2005, for more.)

Other topics for class discussion

Invented spelling – Facsimiles of the original diary reveal invented spellings along the lines of TODA THE FOAKS R GON AWA FRUM THE HOWS WE DO LIV IN. In the published diaries some of these are retained: "egg sam pull" (5, xii), "in tent shuns" (15, viii), and "screwtineyes" (4, v). Certainly students like to talk about spelling reform, and such a discussion becomes an opportunity to issue a defense of our orthography for the purposes of revealing the important histories of our lexicon. A teacher can also extend this activity in a more practical way by asking students to monitor their own patterns of misspelling.

Poetry vs. prose – In her version of the diary, Jane Boulton arranged the text as a poem (Boulton 1995). Comparing two versions of the diary raises the intriguing question, What is a poem? – a question that one can return to in encounters with red wheelbarrows in the rain and other such prosey poems. (See William Carlos Williams' "The Red Wheelbarrow.")

Conclusion

Opal was a wonder, and her diary inspires many who would like to nurture a close relationship with the natural world. Students who enjoy her writing are often left with even more interest in her incredible life story. When they can also explore some of the linguistic features of her writing, it seems likely that they might also look to other texts and their own writing in the same analytical way. "It sounds good" is not a particularly inspiring analysis of literature, but it is a common response in the classroom. A more complete answer might reference metrics, dialect features, and sentence structure, and linguists can help teachers learn how these patterns have changed over time and from place to place. Opal Whiteley's diary, as opposed to her biography, is not a great narrative. But using this book, full of wonderful reminiscences, written in such an unusual style, communicates to students that there is more to reading than following a great story. As Opal would say ... Now we go. We go on explores.

Leatha Fields-Carey and Suzanne Sweat

Ms. Fields-Carey:

Before I taught the Voices of North Carolina curriculum for the first time, I worried that my students would not be interested in the study of linguistics. Sure, as a Language Arts teacher, the subject was fascinating to me, but I had no idea if my 9th graders would be able to comprehend the subtleties that studying linguistics entails, or be interested in such minutiae as which words in Southern United States dialects can adopt an "a-" prefix and which cannot. As the unit progressed, I realized that not only had I underestimated the students' ability to understand the material, I also had no idea how fascinated they would become with the study of dialects.

The region of the Southern United States in which my students and I live is growing rapidly. Over the last several decades, as technology industry growth has expanded, the area has seen a tremendous influx of people from many other parts of the country. Consequently, the character of the South is changing: what used to be small, insular communities into which people were born and which they rarely left are now becoming far more multicultural and fluid. Media such as the Internet and cable television are making many communities in the South much less isolated and traditional. Additionally, the enormous increase in the Hispanic population in our area in recent years has wrought great changes in the community. For many students who have grown up in the South, these changes are at times painful and can feel threatening. It is often difficult for my students to accept people "from somewhere else," and they often label those who speak or behave differently as "weird." "If it's not like me, it's strange," seems to pervade their thinking.

I have found the study of language variations to be a wonderful way to address differences between people, and this aspect of the Voices of North Carolina curriculum has been the most valuable part to me and my students. Since the way we speak reflects our culture, linguistic bias is oftentimes an indicator of bias for or against other aspects of the speaker, such as his or her ethnic group, area of the country, or other factors. Discussing bias in relation to language is a non-threatening way to begin thinking and talking about biases in general. In the Voices curriculum, students are asked to analyze their personal beliefs about language, including their opinions about the degree to which our language reflects our intelligence. They take a pre-test that asks them to rate their level of agreement with various statements that address their feelings about language. One student commented on the pre-test last fall, when asked about his views on language, "I think they [dialects] are all the same." Another stated, "[I think that] there aren't many ways of talking, just city and country accents." A third stated, "People who have accents or speak incorrectly aren't educated." The students and I are then able to discuss our perceptions of the way language reflects who we are, what part of the country we come from, our culture, and our level of education. Most of the students, when the unit is first introduced, have very strong beliefs that people who speak with a certain accent or with a strong dialect may not be very intelligent or educated. Once the unit is concluded, post-test data reveals that the majority of students have come to realize that the variety present in our language is something to be cherished and that no way of speaking is "better" or "worse" than another. They understand that previously held biases are inaccurate and have a greater respect for those who are different from them. Brodie, the student who stated on the pre-test that speaking "incorrectly" denotes lack of education, indicated that "accents just come from your environment." Another student, Ryan, commented, "I love to listen to them [dialects]. It is so interesting just to catch that little change in the speech." Walker remarked, "They [dialects] are special and hold customs of how people live." Olivia summed up an important lesson from the unit: "I realize that even if people can't speak English well because of an accent, they are still intellectual."

Many of the students who have studied this unit in my classroom are minorities. Too often, these students find themselves marginalized in the study of language arts as they are told, both subtly and explicitly, that the language variation they speak is "broken," incongruent with Standard English language patterns. They are often teased by their white peers for such language patterns as the habitual *be* form ("He always be late to class") or *s*-dropping ("He sing in the choir") and are told by teachers that these speech patterns are "mistakes," when in fact they are consistent language patterns present in Black Vernacular English/African-American English. The Voices of North Carolina unit has a segment that focuses on African-American English (AAE) and its inherent patterns. The unit stresses that not all African-Americans speak AAE and that many non-blacks speak AAE. The video segment that accompanies this portion of the unit features hip-hop artists and producers from the North Carolina Triangle area, both white and black, and emphasizes the deeply rooted link between AAE and African-American heritage. The overwhelming message in this portion of the unit is that AAE is not substandard, but is instead a richly varied dialect pattern that has its roots in creoles spoken hundreds of years ago by slaves from various parts of Africa. Such a message has proven to be empowering for my minority students. For many of them, this is the first time they have been told in a school setting that their dialect is valid and not "broken." They become more engaged in class discussion as they realize that they have a unique viewpoint to offer the class about how their dialect works and how it reflects who they are as individuals. Ayeshinaye, a gifted African-American student, commented on her post-unit survey, "You can't judge someone because of the way they talk. People often judge others by what they say. When people are of a certain group, they often are presented with a bias of being the same because of dialect." George, another African-American student, who is normally reticent in class, became extremely animated during this part of the dialect unit and had a lot to offer the class regarding his viewpoints and understanding of his own language pattern.

The study of dialects has drastically changed my views of language arts teaching. When I first started teaching fifteen years ago, my emphasis, like that of many teachers, fell on the teaching of grammatical conventions and "correctness." Student expression in writing and speaking should focus, I felt, on aiming towards grammatical correctness, precision, and order at all times. Errors in speech and writing were pounced upon with the fervor of a faith healer aiming to exorcise demons. Through the study of dialects and language differences, my views of what it means to truly teach the "art of language" has broadened significantly. I now realize that to understand language is not only to know how to speak and write "standard English" correctly, but also to value the rich tapestry of language in all its forms. Understanding language is recognizing that language and culture are inherently connected and that not all people from the same region, from the same state, or even from the same county speak alike. Understanding language is realizing that differences in our language are things to cherish, not ridicule in others or squelch in ourselves in favor of some perceived "norm." I now am able to approach language teaching from a more holistic point of view and am better equipped to help my students appreciate not only differences in dialects, but in each other as well.

Ms. Sweat:

When I first told my freshman English class we were going to study linguistics, no one in the room knew what that word meant. There is no other curriculum in elementary, middle, or high school in our area that focuses on the nature, structure, and variation of language. That is what makes the Voices of North Carolina curriculum so valuable. Many students have been raised to believe (often as a result of their teachers) that if a person speaks English following the rules that govern written language, then that person is intelligent. Likewise, if a person's language usage or dialect deviates from "standard" English, then that person must somehow be less intelligent. This belief was expressed to me by several of my honors students as I explained what linguistics was and introduced the unit. Students were very open in admitting that they had shown bias towards others based on their speech. A few even stated that they didn't believe their assumptions were wrong. It was quickly evident to me that this curriculum could help change ingrained prejudices some students held against different groups of people.

Honors students look for academic evidence in determining the validity of a subject. As we began to study the rule-governed patterns of various dialects, and students began to see the use of a rule repeated over and over again, students began to realize that the language patterns of a dialect are often just as complex as rules governing standard English. This realization helped students break the biases they felt toward certain ethnic groups who speak differently than they do. However, the biggest eye-opener for this group of students came during the study of language usage around different groups of people. After reviewing the video clip in which people of various ages were interviewed about how they change their use of language in different situations, we role-played examples of this variance in our own lives. Students acted out how they would speak to the President of the United States, a teacher at school, and a group of friends. We discussed in-depth how their accent and use of language would change and why. Several students drew the conclusion that the use of a dialect often denotes a level of comfort among the people with whom one is conversing. We discussed that if we judged others based on their use of dialect, we are in a sense asking them to give up the camaraderie they feel toward each other. Students began to make the connection that one's dialect is strongly connected to one's heritage and culture. This idea was emphasized in the study of the Cherokee Indians.

The section of the curriculum that focuses on the language of the Cherokee includes a video clip giving historical accounts of young Native Americans being forced to leave their homes and families in order to attend schools where they were taught to use only the English language. Interviews with older members of the tribe recount how the language of the Cherokee Indians and the use of the Cherokee syllabary is dying out. One student noted that the Cherokee language was a large part of the Cherokee culture, and it wasn't fair for people to be forced to give up their culture. I was able to use this comment as a transition into a common bias students admitted to having earlier in the unit.

There has been a huge influx of Hispanic students into our school system in the past several years. When we discussed personal language biases as a class, one belief that was communicated by several students was that Hispanic students should not be allowed to speak Spanish in our American schools. Students also admitted to feeling that Hispanic students who did not use standard English were unintelligent. After discussing how the culture of the Cherokee Indians was intertwined with their language, we discussed how the language of Hispanic students was also an important part of their culture. Students began to realize that forcing Hispanic students to only speak English was analogous to asking them to give up part of their culture. I began to see the beliefs and prejudices once held by some of my students slowly begin to dissipate.

The second year I taught Voices of North Carolina, I was able to incorporate the unit into both my standard and my honors class. This gave me a new viewpoint as to the value of the curriculum. My honors classes once again were open in admitting their bias towards others based on a person's dialect. However, students in my standard-level English classes shared a different perspective. They admitted to having experienced discrimination from others based on their own use of language.

As we began the unit by watching a video clip from the Ad Council on housing discrimination, students in my standard-level class began to share their own experiences with discrimination. The video clip inspired students to create their own skits showing language biases in others, such as job and college admittance interviews. Their skits provided students with a voice to share their personal frustrations and experiences with language biases.

Another interesting difference between my standard and honors classes was the students' response to the audio clips. Many of the students in my standard-level class enjoyed trying to predict the rules governing a dialect before we even looked at or listened to the examples. Their hypotheses were often correct, which empowered students in their understanding of language. This group of students had more success in identifying language patterns than many of my honors students. The recognition of language patterns and governing rules made the students feel for the first time that their varied use of "standard" English did not indicate a lack of intelligence.

I see the Voices of North Carolina linguistics curriculum as having a positive effect on varying levels of students and their teachers. I, too, must admit to judging the intelligence level of others based on their dialect. Teaching this curriculum has helped me to appreciate the connection between a person's dialect and his or her culture. The curriculum has also made me aware of the many rule-governed patterns that exist in the dialects of English that make our language rich and unique.

23 A-level English Language teaching in London

Dan Clayton

My partner teacher and I teach A-level English Language to about 60–70 students across two classes in each year at St Francis Xavier College. Sixth Form Colleges are part of the English Further Education, post-compulsory sector delivering two year A-level courses to 16–18-year-olds. The A-level since 2000 has been split into a one year AS (Advanced Subsidiary) qualification which can then be followed by an A2 year, the full A-level qualification being achieved by two years of study. We're an inner city London college, taking students from some of the poorest and most deprived areas of south London. The student body is largely black: a mix of Caribbean and West African family backgrounds being the main bulk of this, while we also have a significant intake of students from Portuguese, Pakistani, Chinese and white working class backgrounds (with all the various mixes of Irish, traditional cockney and Jewish influences which that entails).

The mixture of backgrounds and the range of different perspectives our students have is a real benefit to the teaching of the A-level in English Language. Inner city London is – I suppose like any major city – in a permanent state of linguistic flux. Young (and not so young) people are constantly adapting their language use to accommodate new trends in music, fashion and media, marking out ever-shifting boundaries between and within groups of people. Attitudes to different age groups, ethnic groups, authority figures, gender roles and issues of sexuality, religion and lifestyle reflect the disparate influences of peer groups, community, pentecostal churches, mosques and cliques, as well as the more mainstream discourses of youth culture and modern urban life. The language used around us is as diverse as these influences. So far, so good.

But what's the point of teaching an A-level in English Language when fewer and fewer people are really sure what "English" is any more, or even what "England", as a nation, a place or an idea, actually means? Well, the thread running through all of this diversity is an apparent desire to use our language – the English language – to forge an identity and speak to others, to bridge gaps, but also to mark out territory and define identity within this shifting landscape.

So the A-level we teach is well-placed to offer our students a real engagement with debates about how the language is constantly changing and how they are part of that change. But it also allows us the chance to make use of our students' linguistic resources, to draw upon the language around us in the classroom, to learn from them how language is being used in their lives, and to (perhaps unfashionably!) teach them a thing or two about how it all fits into a long history of language change. And get them great A-level exam results[1] at the end of it all. Phew, not much to ask then ...

I base this vignette on the cameo appearance of one of our lessons in Dick Hudson's chapter (see Chapter 3 in this volume) and try to offer a bit more detail as to how it all fits together and works in the classroom, before offering my own thoughts on why all this means that the English Language A-level is one of the most positive developments for English teaching in recent years.

As part of the A-level, students take the AS qualification in their first year of study. This is currently a three-unit course which serves as an introduction for 16-year-olds to the basics of language study. I say "introduction" as that is what it usually is; the literacy strategy (and now the "renewed primary strategy") which should set up a sound linguistic framework in Key Stages 1–2 are often forgotten in the rush to get good results at Key Stages 3 and 4. By the time most of our students get to us, word classes are often a distant memory and sentence types are what magistrates dish out to recalcitrant ASBO-breakers. So, we start from scratch with a back to basics approach to linguistic frameworks. Once we've done this, we can then move onto wider linguistic topics such as language and representation, male/female conversation, and child language acquisition.

The A2 year allows greater depth of study. One of the topics that is studied in more depth at A2 is Language Change. This encompasses diachronic variation in its traditional timeline sense – looking at the influence of successive invaders and immigrants – and synchronic change, which looks at accents, dialects and the emergence of new words and meanings.

The series of lessons I'll concentrate on was focused on youth slang in London, and fitted into the Language Change and Variation unit. We began by looking at a couple of stimulus texts: an article from *The Guardian* news-paper called *Slangsta Rap* (www.guardian.co.uk/values/communityprojects/story/0,1394072,00.html) and the slang dictionary referred to in that article which appears in *Live!*, a south London magazine put together by teenagers. The slang dictionary provided us with a chance to look at how recent slang terms might be defined and sparked a lively debate about the accuracy or otherwise of some of the definitions. Meanwhile, the *Guardian* article placed the debate in a slightly wider context, offering an overview of the changing

---

[1] I don't wish to create the impression that every student comes out of our course as a linguistic maestro – we have our fair share of flunk-outs, resisters and downright lazy students – but I think the English Language A-level, as it is taught around the country, is turning out a new generation of gifted linguists.

nature of slang, its typical focal points – going out, partying, the opposite sex, confrontation, and violence – and gave the students a chance to see how their own slang, and (to some extent) their own lives, are represented to a mainstream audience.

With the use of an interactive whiteboard and extracts from *Slangsta Rap* projected onto it, we added our own points and comments to what had been said. The discussion soon took in areas such as slang and youth culture, the uses of slang to identify in-group affiliations and delineate out-group boundaries, the speed of change with slang and the way in which the media often tends to stereotype teenage culture as being largely apathetic, and/or violent and uneducated.

As might be expected, with such a range of language backgrounds available to us in the classroom, many of us in the class learned a lot about others' language use: young people in the class come from different parts of the city (mostly south and east), and are made up of those deeply involved in particular genres and sub-genres of urban music (rap, grime, r'n'b) and indie music (emo kids, nu-ravers, all the other new forms that spring up month after month which I'm too old to keep up with now), those acutely aware of neighbourhood and "gang" rivalries in certain areas of the capital, through to churchgoing youngsters with a deep aversion to "bad language" and highly aspirational working-class kids who know that sounding too "street" can hold them back in the eyes of employers and educators. And that's not to mention the fact that all of these were A2 students who had a pretty solid grounding in linguistics thanks to their course so far and were (on the whole) able to keep up with ideas like overt and covert prestige, register and code switching, and various references to research.

After the initial discussions had been wound up with some note taking and reflection on key themes, we then moved on in a second lesson to look at the history of slang. Perhaps I shouldn't be surprised, but many of the students took the view that their generation was responsible for slang and that it couldn't have been around for much more than ten or twenty years. So, using extracts from Jonathon Green's *Cassell Dictionary of Slang* and a short chapter from Susie Dent's latest *Language Report*, we looked at how slang has existed ever since there's been a standard form of English. This tied in nicely with the work my teaching partner, Raj, would do with our students, later in the term, on varieties of English and the Standard English debate, as well as putting slang into a historical context. As homework we set a brief assignment which we asked students to submit as a comment to our Language blog (http://englishlangsfx.blogspot.com/). We also asked them to look at a number of different slang and dictionary websites (linked from the blog) for a bit more range, including the *Oxford English Dictionary* online, etymology online, urban dictionary, and any they could find themselves (which included Cockney rhyming slang and Italian-American gangster online dictionaries).

The next stage was to get the students to start writing their own slang guides. The thinking behind this was that it would help crystallize the students' thinking about slang and its background if they were to be set a significant assignment on it, plus one of the trickier parts of the A2 exam is a piece of writing on a language issue, designed for a non-specialist audience, so this was a good opportunity to use what we had been working on as exam preparation for a different part of the course. And to quote the late, great Tony Wilson of Factory Records, "You learn why you do something by actually doing it".

To move on to the next and final stage, we decided to shift the focus away from the sociolinguistic side of things and towards a more framework-orientated approach. Again, this is linked to the syllabus we teach, in which all the wider topics are linked back to, and rooted in, the grammatical frameworks we establish in the AS year of the course.

Back in the first year we looked at the basics of morphology (often using the topic of child language acquisition as a neat way into how words are formed from smaller units) and semantics, so now we had a good chance to explore these in relation to how new words are formed or how words change meanings over time. Taking a couple of slang terms such as *mans* (a Jamaican-influenced term for men/friends) and *gash* (a term initially used to mean a wound, but now widening to mean girls/young women) we thought about non-standard plurals and how they might signify resistance and difference, processes of semantic change and how they often end up derogating women.

To round all this off, students were asked to prepare small group presentations on three slang words or phrases of their choice which they then presented back to the class as a PowerPoint presentation. They were told to make sure origins and processes of word creation/meaning change were covered as well as offering some explanatory context to the words they had chosen.

So, why is this all a good thing? Well, I'd hope that anyone interested in linguistics would see that what we're doing on this course is giving students a grounding in language study that will help set them up for further study at university level. We're drawing on the students' own linguistic resources and focusing on language change and slang, not because it's a novel or trendy thing to do but because it works best for what we want to explore: language use as it really is today.

I think too that the English Language A-level is a huge step forward for English as a subject. Students are encouraged to think about the ways in which the language is constructed and used, and to consider where their own varieties fit into this and influence the direction language change takes. Much of the English our teenagers are taught between the ages of 11 and 16 is rooted in literature, including a compulsory focus on Shakespeare. And while I love Shakespeare as much as the next English teacher, I don't think an insistence on teaching a writer of Early Modern English to twenty-first-century teenagers is very useful, when all the reports tend to suggest that many of them can't actually grasp the basics of Modern Standard English.

References

Abbott, E. A. 1870. *A Shakespearean Grammar*, in Perseus Digital Library Project, Gregory R. Crane (ed.) Tufts University: www.perseus.tufts.edu

Abdal-Haqq, I. 1998. *Professional Development Schools: Weighing the Evidence.* Thousand Oaks, CA: Corwin Press.

Abedi, J. 2004. "The No Child Left Behind Act and English Language Learners: Assessment and Accountability Issues," *Educational Researcher* 33 (1), 4–14.

Abedi, J. and C. Lord 2001. "The Language Factor in Mathematics Tests," *Applied Measurement in Education* 14 (3), 219–234.

Abouzeid, M., M. Invernizzi, and K. Ganske 1995. "Word Sort: An Alternative to Phonics, Spelling, and Vocabulary." Paper presented at the 44th Annual National Reading Conference, San Diego, CA.

Adger, C. T., C. E. Snow, and D. Christian (eds.) 2002 *What Teachers Need to Know about Language.* Washington, DC and McHenry, IL: Center for Applied Linguistics and Delta Systems Co. Inc.

Adger, C. T., W. Wolfram, and D. Christian (eds.) 2007. *Dialects in Schools and Communities.* 2nd edition. Mahwah, NJ: Lawrence Erlbaum Associates.

Alamargot, D. and L. Chanquoy 2001. *Through the Models of Writing.* London: Kluwer Academic Publishers.

Allen, J. and J. Hermann-Wilmarth 2004. "Cultural Construction Zones," *Journal of Teacher Education* 55 (3), 214–226.

Alvarez, L. and A. Kolker 1987. *American Tongues.* Film. New York: Center for New American Media. Study guide by Walt Wolfram. www.cnam.com/downloads/amt_sg.html [accessed November 17, 2007]

American Association for the Advancement of Science (AAAS) 1993. *Benchmarks On-line* [Project 2061 Benchmarks for Science Literacy]. Chapter 1, "The Nature of Science." Online at www.project2061.org/publications/bsl/online/ch1/ch1.htm

Andrews, L. 1998. *Language Exploration and Awareness.* Mahwah, NJ: Lawrence Erlbaum Associates.

Andrews, R. 2005. "Knowledge about the Teaching of Sentence Grammar: The State of Play," *English Teaching: Practice and Critique* 4 (3), 69–76.

Ann, J. and L. Peng 2005. "The Relevance of Linguistic Analysis to the Role of Teachers as Decision Makers." In *Language in the Schools: Integrating Linguistics into K-12 Education*, K. Denham and A. Lobeck (eds.) Mahwah, NJ: Lawrence Erlbaum Associates, 71–86.

Anon. 1984. *English from 5 to 16: Curriculum Matters 1*. London: Her Majesty's Stationery Office.

Anon. 1988. *Report of the Committee of Inquiry into the Teaching of English Language (The Kingman Report)*. London: Her Majesty's Stationery Office.

Anon. 1989. *English for Ages 5 to 16 (The Cox Report)*. London: Her Majesty's Stationery Office.

Anon. 1998. *The Grammar Papers*. London: Qualifications and Curriculum Authority.

Anon. 2000. *Grammar for Writing*. London: Department for Education and Employment.

Anon. 2002. *Languages for All: Languages for Life. A Strategy for England*. London: Department for Education and Skills.

Anon. 2004. *Introducing the Grammar of Talk*. London: Qualifications and Curriculum Authority.

Applebee, A. N. 1989. *The Teaching of Literature in Programs with Reputations for Excellence in English*. Albany, NY: University of New York–Albany Center for the Learning and Teaching of Literature, Report 1.1.

Applebee, A. N. 2000. "Alternative Models of Writing Development." In *Perspectives on Writing: Research, Theory and Practice*, R. Indrisano and J. Squire (eds.) Newark, DE: IRA, 90–110.

Arts Education Partnership. www.aep-arts.org

Atkin, J. M. 1985. "Changing our Thinking about Educational Change." In Bunzel 1985: 47–60.

Atwell, N. 1998. *In the Middle: New Understanding About Writing, Reading, and Learning*. Portsmouth, NH: Boyton/Cook (Heinemann).

Ayres, L. P. 1918. "History and Present Status of Educational Measurements." In Whipple 1918: Part II, 9–15.

Baker, E. 2007. "The End(s) of Testing," *Educational Researcher* 36 (6), 309–317.

Barzun, J. 1986. "What Are Mistakes and Why." In *A Word or Two Before You Go …: Brief Essays on Language*. Middleton, CT: Wesleyan University Press, 3–9.

Bateman, D. R. and F. J. Zidonis 1966. *The Effect of a Study of Transformational Grammar on the Writing of Ninth and Tenth Graders*. Champagne, ILL: National Council of Teachers of English.

Battistella, E. 2005. *Bad Language*. New York: Oxford University Press.

Baugh, J. 1999. "Considerations in Preparing Teachers for Linguistic Diversity." In *Making the Connection*, C. Adger, D. Christian and O. Taylor (eds.). Washington, DC: CAL/Delta.

Bear, D., M. Invernizzi, S. Templeton, and F. Johnston 2004. *Words their Way: Word Study for Phonics, Vocabulary and Spelling Instruction*. 3rd edition. Upper Saddle River, NJ: Prentice Hall.

Beck, K. 2003. *Opal: A Life of Enchantment, Mystery, and Madness*. Viking: New York.

Bede, E. 1954. *Fabulous Opal Whiteley*. Portland: Binfords and Mort.

Bereiter, C. and M. Scardamalia 1987. *The Psychology of Written Composition*. Hillsdale, NJ: Lawrence Erlbaum Associates.

Berger, J. 2007. "Building a Nation of Polyglots, Starting with the Very Young," *The New York Times*, On Education, November 14.

Berko, J. 1958. "The Child's Learning of English Morphology," *Word* 14, 150–177.

Bex, T. and R. Watts 1999. *Standard English: The Widening Debate*. London: Routledge.

Bleiman, B. and L. Webster 2006. *English at A Level: A Guide for Lecturers in Higher Education*. London: Higher Education Academy, English Subject Centre.

Block, C. C. and M. Pressley 2001. *Comprehension Instruction: Research-based Best Practices*. New York: Guilford Press.

Bloom, B. S., M. D. Englehart, E. J. Furst, W. H. Hill, and D. R. Krathwohl 1956. *Taxonomy of Educational Objectives: The Classification of Educational Goals, Handbook I: Cognitive Domain*. New York: Longmans, Green.

Bloom, P. and D. Skonick Weisberg 2007. "Childhood Origins of Adult Resistance to Science," *Science* 316, 996–997.

Board of Education 1921. *The Teaching of English in England* (The Newbolt Report). London: His Majesty's Stationery Office.

Bond, L. G. 2004. "Debating Teacher Qualifications, Focusing on Teacher Recruitment, Contending with a Budget Crisis." On California Commission on Teacher Credentialing website, History of Credentialing link. www.ctc.ca.gov/commission/cred-history.html [accessed July 19, 2007]

Borko, H. and R. T. Putnam 1996. "Learning to Teach." In *Handbook of Research in Educational Psychology*, D. Berliner and R. Calfee (eds.) New York: Macmillan.

Boulton, J. 1995. *Opal: The Journal of an Understanding Heart*. New York: Crown Trade Paperbacks.

Bowie, R. L. and C. L. Bond 1994. "Influencing Future Teachers' Attitudes toward Black English: Are We Making a Difference?" *Journal of Teacher Education* 45 (2), 112–118.

Braddock, R., R. Lloyd-Jones, and L. Schoer 1963. *Research in Written Composition*. Urbana, IL: National Council of Teachers of English.

Brown, G. and G. Yule 1983. *Discourse Analysis*. Cambridge: Cambridge University Press.

Brown, T., M. Gallagher, and R. Turner 1975. *Teaching Secondary English: Alternative Approaches*. Columbus, OH: Charles E. Merrill.

Bruner, J. 1960. *The Process of Education*. Cambridge, MA: Harvard University Press.

Bunzel, J. H. (ed.) 1985. *Challenge to American Schools: The Case for Standards and Values*. New York: Oxford University Press.

Button, H. W. and E. F. Provenzo Jr. 1989. *History of Education and Culture in America*. 2nd edition. Englewood Cliffs, NJ: Prentice Hall.

Cabell, B. 1999. "Kansas School Board's Evolution Ruling Angers Science Community." www.cnn.com/US/9908/12/kansas.evolution.flap/

Cajkler, W. and J. Hislam 2002. "Trainee Teachers' Grammatical Knowledge: The Tension between Public Expectations and Individual Competence," *Language Awareness* 11 (3), 161–177.

Cajkler, W. and J. Hislam 2004. "Teaching and Understanding Grammar: How Trainee Teachers Make Sense of a New Curriculum". In *Applied Linguistics in Language Teacher Education*, N. Bartels (ed.) Dordrecht: Kluwer Academic Publishers.

California Commission on Teacher Credentialing 2001. Standards of Program Quality and Effectiveness for the Subject Matter Requirement for the Multiple Subject Teaching Credential and Secondary Single Subject Standards Handbooks (with links to earlier Standards). www.ctc.ca.gov/educator-prep/STDS-subject-matter.html

California Commission on Teacher Credentialing. "History of Credentialing." www.ctc.ca.gov/commission/cred-history.html [accessed July 19, 2007]

California Department of Education 1993. *California Public Education: A Decade after A Nation at Risk.* Sacramento, CA.

California Department of Education 1997. *English-Language Arts Content Standards for California Public Schools: Kindergarten Through Grade Twelve.* www.cde.ca.gov/be/st/ss/

California Department of Education 1999. *Reading/Language Arts Framework for California Public Schools: Kindergarten Through Grade Twelve.* 1999 Standards (adopted in 1997) are accessible at www.cde.ca.gov/be/st/ss/index.asp

California Department of Education 2007. *Reading/Language Arts Framework for California Public Schools: Kindergarten Through Grade Twelve.* www.cde.ca.gov/ci/rl/cf/

California Department of Education: California English Language Development Test (CELDT): www.cde.ca.gov/ta/tg/el/

California Department of Education. Reading Language Arts Test Items: www.cde.ca.gov/ta/tg/sr/css05rtq.asp

California Department of Education: Testing and Accountability: Improvement Tools. www.cde.ca.gov/ta/lp/vl/improvtools.asp

California High School Exit Exam (CAHSEE). Overview on ETS site: www.ets.org/portal/site/ets/menuitem.1488512ecfd5b8849a77b13bc3921509/?vgnextoid=e7072d3631df4010VgnVCM10000022f95190RCRD&vgnextchannel=75dfe3b5f64f4010VgnVCM10000022f95190RCRD

California Subject Examinations for Teachers (CSET): www.cset.nesinc.com

Cameron, D. 1995. *Verbal Hygiene.* London: Routledge.

Carpenter, George Rice, Franklin T. Baker, and Fred Newton Scott 1908. *The Teaching of English in the Elementary and Secondary School.* New York: Longmans, Green.

Carroll, S. J. 2005. *California's K-12 Public Schools: How are They Doing?* Santa Monica, CA: The Rand Corporation.

Carter, R. 1990. *Knowledge about Language and the Curriculum: The "LINC" [Language in the Curriculum Project] Reader.* London: Hodder and Stoughton.

Carter, R. 1994a. "English Teaching in England and Wales: Key Reports." In *Encyclopedia of Language and Linguistics,* R. E. Asher (ed.) Oxford: Pergamon, 1137–1138.

Carter, R. 1994b. "Language Awareness for Language Teachers." In *Data, Discourse and Description: Essays in Honour of Professor John Sinclair,* M. Hoey (ed.) London: Collins, 137–150.

Carter, R. 1995. *Keywords in Language and Literacy.* London: Routledge.

Cartwright, K. B. 2008. *Literacy Processes: Cognitive Flexibility in Learning and Teaching.* New York: Guilford Press.

Cawley, F. 1957. "The Difficulty of English Grammar for Pupils of Secondary School Age." Dissertation. University of Manchester.

Central Advisory Council for Education 1959. *15 to 19 (The Crowther Report).* London: Her Majesty's Stationery Office.

Chomsky, C., M. Honda, W. O'Neil, and C. Unger 1985. *Doing Science: Constructing Scientific Theories as an Introduction to Scientific Method* (Scientific Theory and Methodology Project Technical Report). Cambridge, MA: ETC, Harvard Graduate School of Education.

Chomsky, N. 1957. *Syntactic Structures.* The Hague: Mouton and Co.

Chomsky, N. 1965. *Aspects of the Theory of Syntax.* Cambridge, MA: MIT Press.

Chomsky, N. 1980. *Rules and Representations*. New York: Columbia University Press.

Chomsky, N. 1981. *Lectures on Government and Binding*. Berlin: Foris.

Chomsky, N. 1984. "Noam Chomsky Writes to Mrs. Davis about Grammar and Education," *English Education* 16, 165–166.

Chomsky, N. 1993. *Language and Thought*. Wakefield, RI: Moyer Bell.

Chomsky, N. 1995. *The Minimalist Program*. Cambridge, MA: MIT Press.

Chomsky, N. 2000. *New Horizons in the Study of Language and Mind*. Cambridge: Cambridge University Press.

Chomsky, N. 2003. *Chomsky on Democracy and Education*. New York: RutledgeFalmer.

Christenbury, L. 2000. *Making the Journey: Being and Becoming a Teacher of English Language Arts*. Portsmouth, NH: Boyton/Cook (Heinemann).

Christensen, L. 1990. "Teaching Standard English: Whose Standard?" *English Journal* 79, 36–40.

Clifford, G. J. 1975. *The Shape of American Education*. Englewood Cliffs, NJ: Prentice-Hall.

Cochran-Smith, M. and S. L. Lytle 1993. *Inside/Outside: Teacher Research and Knowledge*. New York: Teachers College Press of Columbia University.

Cochran-Smith, M. and S. L. Lytle 1999. "Relationships of Knowledge and Practice: Teacher Learning in Communities," *Review of Research in Education* 24, 249–305.

Collins, P., C. Hollo, and J. Mar 1997. "English Grammar in School Textbooks: A Critical Survey," *Australian Review of Applied Linguistics* 20 (2), 33–50.

Commission on Teacher Credentialing (Canada) www.ctc.ca.gov/commission/cred-history.html [accessed July 19, 2007]

Cox, B. 1991. *Cox on Cox: An English Curriculum for the 1990s*. London: Hodder and Stoughton.

CPRE-Consortium for Policy Research in Education 1993. "Developing Content Standards: Creating a Process for Change." www.ed.gov/pubs/CPRE/rb10stan.html [accessed July 25, 2007]

Cross, B. 2003. "Learning or Unlearning Racism: Transferring Teacher Education to Classroom Practices," *Theory into Practice* 42 (3), 203–209.

Crystal, D. 1987. *Child Language, Learning, and Linguistics. An Overview for the Teaching and Therapeutic Professions*. 2nd edition. London: E. Arnold.

Crystal, D. 1988. *Rediscover Grammar*. Harlow: Pearson.

Crystal, D. 1991. *Language A to Z, Books 1 and 2 and Teacher's Book*. London: Longman.

Crystal, D. 1995. *The Cambridge Encyclopedia of the English Language*. Cambridge: Cambridge University Press.

Crystal, D. 1997. *Cambridge Encyclopedia of Language*. 2nd edition. Cambridge: Cambridge University Press.

Crystal, D. 2006. *The Fight for English. How Language Pundits Ate, shot, and Left*. Oxford: Oxford University Press.

Crystal, D. and G. Barton 1996. *Discover Grammar. An Enthusiastic and Practical Approach to Language Learning*. London: Addison Wesley Longman.

Curzon, A. and M. Adams 2006. *How English Works*. New York: Pearson/Longman.

Czerniewska, P. 1992. *Learning about Writing*. Oxford: Blackwell.

Darling-Hammond, L. 2007. "Evaluating 'No Child Left Behind.' " *The Nation*. May 21, 2007.

Darling-Hammond, L. and M. McLaughlin 1995. "Policies that Support Professional Development in an Era of Reform," *Phi Delta Kappan* 76 (8), 597–598.

Day, G. 1996. *Rereading Leavis: Culture and Literary Criticism*. New York: Palgrave Macmillan.

Dean, G. 2003. *Grammar for Improving Writing and Reading in Secondary School*. Abingdon: David Fulton.

Deily, M.-E. P. and V. Herman Bromberg (eds.) 2007. *The Last Word*. Editorial Projects in Education, Inc. San Francisco, CA: J. Wiley.

Delpit, L. 1988. "The Silenced Dialogue: Power and Pedagogy in Educating Other People's Children," *Harvard Educational Review* 58 (3), 280–298.

Delpit, L. 1995. *Other People's Children: Cultural Conflict in the Classroom*. New York: W.W. Norton.

Denham, K. 2005. "Ludlings Teach Language Diversity and Change: From Pig Latin to Ubby Dubby." Paper presented at the annual convention of the National Council of Teachers of English, Pittsburgh, PA.

Denham, K. and A. Lobeck (eds.) 2005. *Language in the Schools: Integrating Linguistic Knowledge into K-12 Teaching*. Mahwah, NJ: Lawrence Erlbaum Associates.

Denham, K. and A. Lobeck 2010. *Linguistics for Everyone: An Introduction*. Boston: Cengage.

DES 1975. *A Language for Life* (The Bullock Report). London: HMSO.

DES 1988. *Report of the Committee of Inquiry into the Teaching of English Language* (The Kingman Report). London: HMSO.

"Despite Elitist Gripes, He's America's Most Popular Artist," 2002. *Chronicle of Higher Education*, February 22, B4.

DfEE 1998. *The National Literacy Strategy: A Framework for Teaching*. London: DfEE.

DfEE 2001. *The National Literacy Strategy: Grammar for Writing*. London: DfEE.

DfES 2001. *Framework for Teaching English: Years 7, 8 and 9*. London: DfES.

DfES 2006. "Primary National Strategy." www.standards.dfes.gov.uk/primary/ [accessed 12 August 2006]

"Do You Speak American?" PBS documentary. www.pbs.org/speak/. The supporting CAL websites for teachers may be found here: www.pbs.org/speak/education/. These were developed by, among others, Karen Jaffe and Lee West at Center for Applied Linguistics.

Donelson, K. 1984. "Ten Teachers and Scholars Who Influenced the Secondary English Curriculum, 1880–1970," *The English Journal* 73 (3), 78–80.

Donlan, D. M. 1972. "Dilemma of Choice: Revolution in English Curricula." Dissertation. Palo Alto: Stanford University.

Donovan, A. and L. Niven 2003. "The Scots Language in Education." In *Scottish Education*. 2nd edition, T. Bryce and W. Humes (eds.) Edinburgh: Edinburgh University Press, 262–271.

Doughty, P., J. Pearce, and G. Thornton 1971. *Language in Use*. London: Arnold.

Downing, P., S. D. Lima, and M. Noonan 1992. *The Linguistics of Literacy*. Philadelphia, PA: John Benjamins Publishing Co.

Echevarria, J., M. E. Vogt, and D. Short 2004. *Making Content Comprehensible for English Learners: The SIOP Model*. Boston: Allyn & Bacon.

EdSource 2003. "Questions and Answers about California Schools: The California High School Exit Exam." www.edsource.org/pub_qa_hsee.cfm [accessed November 8, 2007]

Elley, W., I. Barham, H. Lamb, and M. Wyllie 1975. "The Role of Grammar in a Secondary School Curriculum." *New Zealand Council for Educational Studies* 10, 26–41.

Elley, W., I. Barham, H. Lamb, and M. Wyllie 1976. "The Role of Grammar in a Secondary English Curriculum," *Research in the Teaching of English* 10, 5–21.

Emery, K. and S. Ohanian 2004. *Why is Corporate America Bashing Our Public Schools?* Portsmouth, NH: Heinemann.

Emig, J. 1971. *The Composing Processes of Twelfth Graders*. NCTE Research Report No. 13. Urbana, IL: NCTE.

Ericsson, K. A. 2002. "Attaining Excellence Through Deliberate Practice: Insights from the Study of Expert Performance." In *The Pursuit of Excellence Through Education*, M. Ferrari (ed.) Mahwah, NJ: Lawrence Erlbaum Associates, Inc 21–55.

Fabb, N. 1985. "Linguistics for Ten-Year-Olds." In *MIT Working Papers in Linguistics* 6. Cambridge, MA: MITWPL, 45–61.

Farr, M. and H. Daniels 1986. *Language Diversity and Writing Instruction*. New York: ERIC Clearinghouse on Urban Education, and Urbana, IL: ERIC Clearinghouse on Reading and Communication Skills.

Fearn, L. and N. Farnan 2007. "When is a Verb: Using Functional Grammar to Teach Writing," *Journal of Basic Writing* 26 (1), 1–26.

Fillmore, L. and C. E. Snow 2002. "What Teachers Need to Know About Language." In C. T. Adger, C. E. Snow, and D. Christian (eds.) *What Teachers Need to Know About Language*, Washington, DC, and McHenry, IL: Center for Applied Linguistics and Delta Systems Co. Inc., 7–54.

Finegan, E. 1980. *Attitudes Toward English Usage: The History of a War of Words*. New York: Teachers College Press.

Finn, C. E. Jr. 1989 "A Nation Still at Risk," *Commentary*, May, 17–23.

Flavell, J. H. (1979). "Metacognition and Cognitive Monitoring: A New Area of Cognitive-developmental Inquiry, *American Psychologist* 34, 906–911.

Flesch, Rudolph 1955. *Why Johnny Can't Read – and What You Can Do About It*. New York: Harper.

Fogel, H and L. C. Ehri 2000. "Teaching Elementary Students who Speak Black English Vernacular to Write in Standard English: Effects of Dialect Transformation Practice," *Contemporary Educational Psychology* 25, 212–235.

Folsom, F. 1963. *The Language Book*. New York: Grossett and Dunlap.

Foster, M. 2004. "An Innovative Professional Development Program for Urban Teachers," *Phi Delta Kappan* January, 401–406.

Freeborn, D. 1987. *A Course Book in English Grammar*. London: Palgrave Macmillan.

Freeborn, D. 1998. *From Old English to Standard English: A Course Book in Language Variations Across Time*. London: Palgrave Macmillan.

Freeborn, D., P. French, and D. Langford 1993. *Varieties of English: An Introduction to the Study of Language*. London: Palgrave Macmillan.

Freeman, D. J. 1990. "California's Curriculum Reform Guidelines for Elementary Schools: 1983–1988." Center Series N. 16. Report, Center for the Learning and Teaching of Elementary Subjects. ERIC Document 321407.

Frohnmayer, J. 1993. *Leaving Town Alive: Confessions of an Arts Warrior*. New York: Houghton Mifflin.

Fuhrman, S. H. 2003. "Riding Waves, Trading Horses: The Twenty-Year Effort to Reform Education." In D. T. Gordon (ed.) 2003: 7–22.

Gallagher, M. C. 2000. "Lessons from the Sputnik-era Curriculum Reform Movement: The Institutions We Need for Educational Reform." In Stotsky (ed.) 2000: 281–312.

Ganske, K. 2000. *Word Journeys*. New York: The Guilford Press.

Geisel, T. (Dr. Seuss) and J. Prelutsky with illustrations by Lane Smith 1998. *Hooray for Diffendoofer Day!* New York: Alfred A. Knopf Books (Random House).

Genesee, F., K. Lindholm-Leary, W. Saunders, and D. Christian 2006. *Educating English Language Learners: A Synthesis of Research Evidence*. New York: Cambridge University Press.

Gifford, B. G. and M. C. O'Conner (eds.) 1992. *Changing Assessments: Alternative Views of Aptitude, Achievement, and Instruction*. Boston: Kluwer Academic Publishers.

Gleason, H. 1965. *Linguistics and English Grammar*. New York: Rinehart and Winston.

Goddard, A. and A. Beard 2007. *As Simple as ABC? Issues of Transition for Students of English Language A-level Going on to Study English Language/Linguistics in Higher Education*. Egham: English Subject Centre.

Godley, A. J., J. Sweetland, R. S. Wheeler, A. Minnici, and B. D. Carpenter 2006. "Preparing Teachers for Dialectally Diverse Classrooms," *Educational Researcher* 35 (8), 30–37.

Goodluck, H. 1991. "More Linguistics for 10-year-olds," *Innovations in Linguistic Education* 5, 35–41.

Goodman, Y. 2003. *Valuing Language Study: Inquiry into Language for Elementary and Middle Schools*. Urbana, IL: National Council of Teachers of English.

Gordon, D. T. 2003. "The Limits of Ideology: Curriculum and the Culture Wars." In D. T. Gordon (ed.) 2003: 99–113.

Gordon, D. T. (ed.) 2003. *A Nation Reformed? American Education 20 Years after A Nation at Risk*. Cambridge, MA: Harvard Education Press.

Gordon, E. 2005. "Grammar in New Zealand Schools: Two Case Studies," *English Teaching: Practice and Critique* 4 (3), 32–47, 48–68.

Graham, S. and Perin, D. 2007. *Writing Next: Effective Strategies to Improve Writing of Adolescents in Middle and High Schools – A Report to Carnegie Corporation of New York*. Washington, DC: Alliance for Excellent Education.

Graves, D. 1983. *Writing: Teachers and Children at Work*. Portsmouth, NH: Heinemann.

Grenfell, M. 2000. "Modern Languages – Beyond Nuffield and into the 21st Century," *Language Learning Journal* 22, 23–29.

Guskey, T. R. 2002. "Professional Development and Teacher Change," *Teachers and Teaching: Theory and Practice* 8 (3/4), 381–391.

Hackett, F. H. 1892. "The Schools of San Francisco," *The Californian* 2 (2), July 1892 [accessed at Google Books].

Haertel, E. and J. L. Herman (eds.) 2005. "A Historical Perspective on Validity Arguments for Accountability Testing." In Herman and Haertel (eds.) 2005.

Halle, M. and G. N. Clements 1983. *Problem Book in Phonology: A Workbook for Introductory Courses in Linguistics and in Modern Phonology*. Cambridge, MA: The MIT Press.

Halpern, M. 1997. "A War that Never Ends," *Atlantic Monthly*, March, 19–22.

Halpern, M. 2001. "The End of Linguistics," *American Scholar*, Winter, 13–26.

Harpin, W. 1986. "Writing Counts." In *The Writing of Writing*, A. Wilkinson (ed.) Milton Keynes: Open University Press, 158–176.

Harris, N. 1966. *The Artist in American Society: The Formative Years, 1790–1860*. New York: George Braziller.

Harris, R. J. 1962. "An Experimental Inquiry into the Functions and Value of Formal Grammar in the Teaching of English, with Special Reference to the Teaching of Correct Written English to Children Aged Twelve to Fourteen." Dissertation. University of London.

Harris-Wright, K. 1999. "Enhancing Bidialectalism in Urban African American Students." In *Making the Connection*, C. Adger, D. Christian, and O. Taylor (eds.) Washington, DC: CAL/Delta.

Hartwell, P. 1985. "Grammar, Grammars, and the Teaching of Grammar," *College English* 47, 105–127.

Haswell, R. H. 2000. "Documenting Improvement in College Writing," *Written Communication* 17 (3), 307–352.

Hawkins, Eric 1987. *Awareness of Language: An Introduction*. Cambridge: Cambridge University Press.

Hawkins, Eric 1994. "Language Awareness." In *Encyclopedia of Language and Linguistics*, R. E. Asher (ed.) Oxford: Pergamon, 1,933–1,938.

Hawkins, Eric 1999. "Foreign Language Study and Language Awareness," *Language Awareness* 8, 124–142.

Hawkins, Eric 2005. "Out of this Nettle, Dropout, We Pluck this Flower, Opportunity. Rethinking the School Language Apprenticeship," *Language Learning Journal* 32, 4–17.

Hayes, J. R. 1996. "A New Framework for Understanding Cognition and Affect in Writing." In *The Science of Writing*, C. M. Levy and S. Ransdell (eds.) Mahwah, NJ: Lawrence Erlbaum, 1–27.

Heath, S. B. 1983. *Ways with Words*. Cambridge: Cambridge University Press.

Hendrick, I. G. 1975. *Public Policy Toward the Education of Non-white Minority Group: Children in California, 1849–1970: Final Report Prepared for National Institute of Education, Project no. NE-G-00-3-0082*. Riverside, CA: School of Education.

Hendrick, I. G. n.d. "Establishing State Responsibility for the Quality of Teachers (1850–1952)." California Commission on Teacher Credentialing, www.ctc.ca.gov/commission/cred-history.html [accessed July 19, 2007]

Herman, J. L. and E. Haertel (eds.) 2005. *Uses and Misuses of Data for Educational Accountability and Improvement*. Chicago: NSSE and Malden, MA: Blackwell Publishers.

Hillocks, G. R. 1984. "What Works in Teaching Composition: A Meta-Analysis of Experimental Treatment Studies," *American Journal of Education* 93 (1), 133–170.

Hillocks, G. Jr. 2002. *The Testing Trap*. New York: Teachers' College Press.

Hillocks, G. and N. Mavrognes 1986. "Sentence Combining." In *Research on Written Composition: New Directions for Teaching*, G. Hillocks (ed.) Urbana, IL: National Council of Teachers of English.

Hoff, B. 1994. *The Singing Creek Where the Willows Grow: The Mystical Nature Diary of Opal Whiteley* with a biography and afterword by Benjamin Hoff. New York: Penguin Books.

Hoffman, M. J. 2003. "Grammar for Teachers: Attitudes and Aptitudes." *Academic Exchange Quarterly* 7 (4).

Hogan, T. and M. Rabinowitz 2003. "Representation in Teaching: Inferences from Research of Expert and Novice Teachers." *Educational Psychologist* 38, 235–247.

Hollie, S. 2001. "Acknowledging the Language of African American Students: Instructional Strategies," *English Journal* 90, 54–59.

Honda, M. 1994. *Linguistic Inquiry in the Science Classroom: "It is Science, but it's Not Like a Science Problem in a Book."* MIT Occasional Papers in Linguistics 6. Cambridge, MA: MITWPL.

Honda, M. and W. O'Neil 1993. "Triggering Science-forming Capacity Through Linguistic Inquiry.' In *The View from Building 2: Essays in Linguistics in Honor of Sylvain Bromberger*, K. Hale and S. J. Keyser (eds.) Cambridge, MA: The MIT Press, 229–255.

Honda, M. and W. O'Neil 2004. *Understanding First and Second Language Acquisition* (Awakening our languages: An ILI handbook series, Handbook 10). Santa Fe, NM: Indigenous Language Institute.

Honda, M. and W. O'Neil 2007. *Thinking Linguistically: A Scientific Approach to Language*. Malden, MA: Wiley Blackwell Publishers.

Honda, M., W. O'Neil, and D. Pippin 2004. "When Jell-O Meets Generative Grammar: Linguistics in the Fifth-grade English Classroom." Paper presented at the annual meeting of the Linguistic Society of America, Boston. Available at http://web.mit.edu/waoneil/www/k12

Honda, M., W. O'Neil, and D. Pippin 2006. "Problem-set Based Linguistics for Fifth Graders and Beyond." Linguistic Society of America, K-12 Workshop: Linguistics Materials.

Horn, A. 2003. "English Grammar in Schools." In *Proceedings of the 2002 Conference of the Australian Linguistic Society*, P. Collins and M. Amberber (eds.) www.latrobe.edu.au/rcit/als2002.html

Huddleston, R. 1989. "English Grammar in School Textbooks: Towards a Consistent Linguistic Alternative." *Applied Linguistics Association of Australia*. Occasional Papers Number 11.

Hudson, R. 2004. "Why Education Needs Linguistics," *Journal of Linguistics* 40 (1), 105–130.

Hudson, R. 2007. "How Linguistics Has Influenced Schools in England," *Language and Linguistic Compass* 1 (4), 227–242.

Hudson, R. A. and J. Walmsley 2005. "The English Patient: English Grammar and Teaching in the Twentieth Century," *Journal of Linguistics* 41, 593–622.

Hunt, K. 1965. *Grammatical Structures Written at Three Grade Levels*, Research Report No. 3. Urbana: NCTE.

Hutcheson, Neal 2005. *Voices of North Carolina*. Video documentary. Raleigh, NC: NCLLP.

Hymes, Dell 1972. *Reinventing Anthropology*. New York: Pantheon.

Inglis, S. A. n.d. a. *The Fisher Reformation 1953–1961*. California Commission on Teacher Credentialing: History of Credentialing. www.ctc.ca.gov

Inglis, S. A. n.d. b. *Specialized Interests Challenge the California Fisher Act 1961–1965.* California Commission on Teacher Credentialing: History of Credentialing. www.ctc. ca.gov/commission/history/1961-1965-Specialized-Int.pdf

Inglis, S. A. n.d. c. *California Develops the Ryan Reforms 1966–1970.* California Commission on Teacher Credentialing: History of Credentialing. www.cta.ca. gov/commission/history/1966-1970-Ryan-Reforms.pdf

Invernizzi, M., M. Abouzeid, and J. Bloodgood 1997. "Integrated Word Study: Spelling, Grammar, and Meaning in the Language Arts Classroom," *Language Arts* 74 (3), 185–192.

Israel, S. E., C. C. Block, K. Kinnucan-Welsch, and K. Bauserman (2005). *Metacognition in Literacy Learning: Theory, Assessment, Instruction, and Professional Development.* Mahwah, NJ: Lawrence Erlbaum Associates.

Jackendoff, R. 2007. "A Whole Lot of Challenges for Linguistics," *Journal of English Linguistics* 35(3), 253–262.

James, C. 1999. "Language Awareness: Implications for the Language Curriculum," *Language, Culture and Curriculum* 12, 94–115.

Jencks, C. and M. Phillips (eds.) 1998. *The Black–White Test Score Gap.* Washington, DC: Brookings Institution.

Johnson, K. 2007 "Basque Inquisition: How Do You Say Shepherd in Euskera?" *The Wall Street Journal.* November 6. Online. http://online.wsj.com/article_email/ article_print/SB119429568940282944-lMyQjAxMDE3OTA0NjIwOTY1Wj.html

Jones, S. M. and D. A. Myhill 2007. "Discourses of Differences: Questioning Gender Difference in Linguistic Characteristics of Writing," *Canadian Journal of Education* 30 (2), 456–482.

Kagan, D. 1992. "Implications of Research on Teacher Belief," *Educational Psychologist* 27 (1), 65–90.

Kantrowitz, B. *et al.* 1993. "A Nation Still at Risk." *Newsweek,* April 19, 1993, 46–49.

Keith, G. 1990. "Language Study at Key Stage 3: Knowledge about Language and the Curriculum." In *The "LINC" Reader,* Ronald Carter (ed.) London: Hodder and Stoughton, 69–103.

Keith, G. 1994. *Exploring Words and Meanings.* Cambridge: Cambridge University Press.

Keith, G. and J. Shuttleworth 2000. *Living Language: Exploring Advanced Level English Language.* London: Hodder Arnold.

Kellaghan, T., G. F. Madaus, and P. W. Airasian 1982. *The Effects of Standardized Testing.* Boston, MA: Kluwer-Nijhoff Publishing.

Kellogg, Ronald T. 1994. *The Psychology of Writing.* Oxford: Oxford University Press.

Kelly, M. and D. Jones 2003. *A New Landscape for Languages.* London: Nuffield Foundation.

Kerr, C. 1999. "Testimony before the Joint Committee to Develop a Master Plan for Education: Kindergarten through University. August 24, 1999." www.ucop.edu/ acadinit/mastplan/kerr082499.htm [accessed November 8, 2000]

Keyser, S. J. 1970. "The Role of Linguistics in the Elementary School Curriculum," *Elementary English* 47, 39–45.

Kidder, T. 2004. *Mountains Beyond Mountains: The Quest of Dr. Paul Farmer, a Man Who Would Cure the World.* New York: Random House.

King, R. 2000. *The Lexical Basis of Grammatical Borrowing: A Prince Edward Island French Case Study.* Amsterdam: John Benjamins.

Kingsbury, A. 2007. "Do Schools Pass the Test?" *US News and World Report*, June 10, 2007.

Kirst, M. 1984. "The Changing Balance in State and Local Power to Control Education," *Phi Delta Kappan* 66 (3), 189–191.

Kitzhaber, A. R. (ed.) 1968. *The Oregon Curriculum: A Sequential Program in English, Language/Rhetoric*. Volumes I, II. New York: Holt, Rinehart, and Winston.

Knafo, R. 2001. *Portrait of a Whipping Boy: Advertising's Grudge against Contemporary Art*. www.slate.com [Posted Tuesday, April 17, 2001]

Koerner, J. 1963. *The Miseducation of Teachers*. New York: Houghton Mifflin.

Kolln, M. and C. Hancock 2005. "The Story of English Grammar in United States Schools," *English Teaching: Practice and Critique* 4 (3), December, 11–31. Available at http://education.waikato.ac.nz/research/files/etpc/2005v4n3art1.pdf

Koretz, D., G. F. Madaus, E. Haertel, and A. E. Beaton 1992. *National Educational Standards and Testing: A Response to the National Council on Education Standards and Testing*. Document CT-100. Santa Monica, CA: RAND Corporation. www.rand.org/pubs/testimonies [accessed July 21, 2007]

Krashen, S. 1982. *Principles and Practice in Second Language Acquisition*. Oxford: Pergamon.

Kress, G. 1994. *Learning to Write*. London: Routledge.

Kress, G. 2003. "Genres and the Multimodal Production of 'Scientificness.'" In *Multimodal Literacy*, C. Jewitt and G. Kress (eds.) New York: Peter Lang, 173–186.

Labov, W. 1970. *The Study of Nonstandard English*. Champaign: NCTE.

Lambert, R. G. 1964. Review of *The Miseducation of American Teachers* (by J. D. Koerner, Wiley), *College Composition and Communication* 15 (2), 118.

Larson, E. 1997. *Summer for the Gods*. New York: Basic Books.

Lawrence, S. M. and B. D. Tatum 2004. "White Educators as Allies: Moving from Awareness to Action." In *Race, Class and Gender in the United States*, P. S. Rothenberg (ed.) New Jersey: Worth Publishers, 333–342.

Lee, O. and S. H. Fradd 1996. "Literacy Skills in Science Learning Among Linguistically Diverse Students," *Science Education*, 80 (6), 651–671.

Leech, G. N. and J. Svartvik 1975. *A Communicative Grammar of English*. London: Longman.

Lemann, N. 1997. "The Reading Wars," *The Atlantic Monthly*. New York: The Atlantic Monthly Group, Inc.

Lemann, N. 1999. *The Big Test: The Secret History of the American Meritocracy*. New York: Farrar, Straus and Giroux.

Le Moine, N. 2001. "Language Variation and Literacy Acquisition in African American Students." In *Literacy in African American Communities*, J. Harris, A. Kamhi, and K. Pollock (eds.) Mahwah, NJ: Lawrence Erlbaum Associates.

Le Page, R. 1968. "Problems to be Faced in the Use of English as the Medium of Education in Four West Indian Territories." In *Language Problems of Developing Nations*, J. A. Fishman, C. A. Ferguson, and J. D. Gupta (eds.) New York: John Wiley and Sons.

Levine, M. and R. Trachtman (eds.) 1997. *Making Professional Development Schools Work: Politics, Practice, and Policy*. New York: Teachers College Press.

Lewin, T. 2007. "States Found to Vary Widely on Education." *The New York Times*, June 8, 2007.

Liberman, M. 2007. "The Future of Linguistics." Plenary Address, Linguistic Society of America annual meeting, January 6, 2007.

Lipman, P. 2004. *High Stakes Education: Inequality, Globalization, and Urban School Reform*. New York: Routledge.

Lippi-Green, R. 1997. *English with an Accent*. New York: Routledge.

Loban, W. 1976. *Language Development: Kindergarten Through Grade Twelve* (Research Report 18). Urbana, IL: National Council of Teachers of English.

LSA 2006. Minutes of the Meeting of the Committee on Language in the School Curriculum. www.lsadc.org/info/pdf_files/2006LiSCminutes.pdf [accessed June 24, 2006]

Macauley, W. J. 1947. "The Difficulty of Grammar," *British Journal of Educational Psychology* 17, 153–162.

MacDonald, D. 1962. "The String Untuned," *New Yorker*, March 10 (reprinted in *Dictionaries and* That *Dictionary*, J. Sledd and W. R. Ebbit (eds.) Chicago: Scott, Foresman, 166–188).

MacNeil-Lehrer Productions 2005. *Do You Speak American?* Video documentary. Washington, DC.

MacNeil, R., R. McCrum, and W. Cran 1986. "The Story of English." Parts 1–9. PBS documentary, http://ling.cornell.edu/teachling/AV/story.html [accessed November 17, 2007]

Malmstrom, J. and J. Lee 1971. *Teaching English Linguistically: Principles and Practices for High School*. New York: Appleton-Century-Crofts.

Marzano, R. J. and J. S. Kendall 1996. *A Comprehensive Guide to Designing Standards-Based Districts, Schools, and Classrooms*. Alexandria, VA: ASCD (Association for Supervision and Curriculum Development) and Aurora, CO: McREL.

Marzano, R. J., D. Pickering, and J. Pollock 2001. *Classroom Instruction that Works: Research-based Strategies for Increasing Student Achievement*. Alexandria, VA: ASCD (Association for Supervision and Curriculum Development).

Massey, A. J., G. L. Elliott, and N. K. Johnson 2005. "Variations in Aspects of Writing in 16+ English Examinations Between 1980 and 2004: Vocabulary, Spelling, Punctuation, Sentence Structure, Non-Standard English." *Research Matters: Special Issue 1*. Cambridge: University of Cambridge Local Examinations Syndicate.

Master Plan (California's 1960 Master Plan for Higher Education), www.ucop.edu/acadinit/mastplan/mp.htm [accessed November 6, 2007].

Masters, G. and M. Forster 1997. *Literacy Standards in Australia*. Australian Council for Educational Research.

Matsumura, M. 2000. "Facing Challenges to Evolution Education," National Center for Science Education. www.ncseweb.org/resources/articles/8963_facing_challenges_to_evolution_12_7_2000.asp

Maun, I. and D. Myhill 2005. "Text as Design, Writers as Designers," *English in Education* 39 (2), 5–21.

McGonigal, J. 2003. "English Language Education." In *Scottish Education*. 2nd edition, T. Bryce and W. Humes (eds.) Edinburgh: Edinburgh University Press. 518–523.

McGonigal, J., J. Corbett, C. Kay, B. Templeton, and D. Tierney 2001. *The LILT Project Staff Development Booklet B (15–18)*. University of Glasgow.

McIntosh, A. 1952. *An Introduction to a Survey of Scottish Dialects*. Edinburgh: Thomas Nelson.

McKissack, P. C. 1986. *Flossie and the Fox* (R. Isadora, illus.). New York: Scholastic.

McQuade, Finlay 1980. "Examining a Grammar Course: The Rationale and the Result," *English Journal* 69, 26–30.

McQuiddy, S. 1996. "A New-Found Interest in 'Fabulous Opal Whiteley,' " *Lane County Historian* 41, 6–21 (available online as "The Fantastic Tale of Opal Whiteley." www.intangible.org/Features/Opal/OpalHome.html).

Meier, D. and G. Wood (eds.) 2004. *Many Children Left Behind.* Boston, MA: Beacon Press.

Mellon, J. 1969. *Transformational Sentence Combining. Research Report No. 10.* Urbana, IL: National Council of Teachers of English.

Merrow, J. "Learning Matters," www.pbs.org/merrow

Micciche, L. 2004. "Making a Case for Rhetorical Grammar," *College Composition and Communication* 55 (4), 716–737.

Minkoff, H. (ed.) 1971. *Teaching English Linguistically: Five Experimental Curricula.* New Rochelle, NY: The Iona College Press.

Mitchell, D. 1988. "State Education Policy in California," *Peabody Journal of Education* 63 (4), 90–99.

Mitchell, R. 2002. "Foreign Language Education in an Age of Global English." Inaugural lecture, February 27, 2002. Southampton: University of Southampton.

Montgomery, M., A. Durant, N. Fabb, T. Furniss, and S. Mills 2000. *Ways of Reading: Advanced Reading Skills for Students of English Literature*, 2nd edition. New York: Routledge.

Morris, D. 1982. "'Word Sort': A Categorization Strategy for Improving Word Recognition Ability," *Reading Psychology* 3, 247–257.

Morton, H. 1994. *The Story of Webster's Third: Phillip Gove's Controversial Dictionary and its Critics.* Cambridge: Cambridge University Press.

Moys, A. 1998. *Where are We Going with Languages?* (Consultative report of the Nuffield Languages Inquiry). London: Nuffield Foundation.

Mufwene, S. S., J. R. Rickford, G. Bailey, and J. Baugh 1998. *African-American English: Structure, History, and Use.* New York: Routledge.

Mulder, J. 2007. "Establishing Linguistics in Secondary Education in Victoria, Australia," *Language and Linguistics Compass* 1 (3), 133–154. Online journal: Blackwell. www.blackwell-compass.com/subject/linguistics/

Mulder, J., K. Burridge, and C. Thomas 2001. *Macmillan English Language: VCE Units 1 & 2* (textbook and CD-ROM). South Yarra, Victoria: Macmillan Education Australia.

Mulder, J., M. Clyne, C. Thomas, K. Burridge, and A. Isaac 2002. *Macmillan English Language: VCE Units 3 & 4* (CD-ROM). South Yarra, Victoria: Macmillan Education Australia.

Mulder, J., C. Thomas, K. Burridge, and A. Isaac (forthcoming). *English Language: VCE Units 3 & 4.* 2nd edition.

Murphy, M. J. 2007. "Vigil for the Vanishing Tongue." *The New York Times*, Week in Review, September 23.

Myhill, D. A. 2003. "Principled Understanding? Teaching the Active and Passive Voice," *Language and Education* 17 (5), 355–370.

Myhill, D. A. 2006. "Designs on Writing 1," *Secondary English Magazine* 10 (3), 25–28.

National Commission on Excellence in Education (NCEE) 1983. *A Nation at Risk: The Imperative for Educational Reform*. Washington, DC: US Government Printing Office. www.ed.gov/pubs/NatAtRisk/risk.html

National Commission on Writing in America's Schools and Colleges 2003. *The Neglected "R": The Need for a Writing Revolution*. New York: College Board.

National Council of Teachers of English 1952. *The English Language Arts*. New York: Appleton Century Crofts.

National Education Goals Panel (NEGP) 1991. *The National Education Goals Report: Building a Nation of Learners*. Washington, DC: National Education Goals Panel.

National Research Council 2000. *Grading the Nation's Report Card: Research from the Evaluation of NAEP*. Washington, DC: National Academy Press.

NCSS (National Council for the Social Studies) 1994. *Expectations of Excellence: Curriculum Standards for Social Studies*. Waldorf, MD: NCSS Publications.

NCTE/IRA (National Council of Teachers of English/International Reading Association) 1996. *Standards for the English Language Arts*. Urbana, IL: NCTE Publications.

Neal, D. and D. W. Schanzenbach 2007. "Left Behind by Design: Proficiency Counts and Test-based Accountability." NCTE Inbox. July 24, 2007. www.ncte.org/library/files/About_NCTE/Overview/inbox/7-24-07.html

Newman, A. 2004. "Outsourcing Comes to Summer Camp." *The New York Times*, D1, 5, July 9.

Nieto, S. 2000. *Affirming Diversity: The Sociopolitical Context of Multicultural Education*. 3rd edition. White Plains, NY: Longman.

North Carolina Public Schools Standard Course of Study: Eighth Grade Social Studies 2003 edition. Online document, www.ncpublicschools.org/curriculum/socialstudies/scos/

North Carolina Public Schools Standard Course of Study: Ninth Grade Language Arts 2004 edition. Online document, www.ncpublicschools.org/curriculum/languagearts/scos/2004/27english1

Nuffield Languages Inquiry 2000. *Languages: The Next Generation* (Final report and recommendations of the Nuffield Languages Inquiry). London: The Nuffield Foundation.

Office of Technology Assessment 1992. *Testing in American Schools: Asking the Right Questions* (OTA-SET-519). Washington, DC: US Government Printing Office.

Ofsted 2002. *The Key Stage 3 Strategy: Evaluation of the First Year of the Pilot*. London: Ofsted.

Ohio Department of Education 2004. *Mt. Healthy City Schools 2003–2004 School Year Report Card*. Columbus, OH: Ohio Department of Education.

O'Neil, W. 1968a. "Paul Roberts' Rules of Order: The Misuses of Linguistics in the Classroom," *Urban Review* 2 (7), 12–16.

O'Neil, W. 1968b. "The 13 Professors Project: A Report from Roxbury." Excerpted in *Thirteen Professors Project: Episodes in Creative Teaching*, W. C. Kvaraceus (ed.) Washington, DC: The NDEA National Institute for Advanced Study in Teaching Disadvantaged Youth.

O'Neil, W. 1969. "Introduction to N. R. Cattell," *The New English Grammar*. Cambridge, MA: The MIT Press, ix–xvii.

O'Neil, W. 1971. "The Politics of Bidialectalism." *Negro American Literature Forum* 5 (4), 127–131.

O'Neil, W. 1972. "The Politics of Bidialectalism." In *The Politics of Literature: Dissenting Essays on the Teaching of English*, L. Kampf and P. Lauter (eds.) New York: Pantheon, 245–258.

O'Neil, W. 1978. "An Alternative to U.S. Education: Teaching Minorities to Study Their Own Cultures." In *Equality and Social Policy*, W. Feinberg (ed.) Champaign-Urbana: The University of Illinois Press, 129–142.

O'Neil, W. 1990. "Dealing with Bad Ideas: Twice is Less," *English Journal* 79 (4), 80–88.

O'Neil, W. 1998a. "Ebonics in the Media," *Radical Teacher* 54, 13–17.

O'Neil, W. 1998b. "If Ebonics isn't a Language, Then Tell Me, What is?" (*pace* James Baldwin, 1979). In *The Real Ebonics Debate: Power, Language, and the Education of African-American Children*, T. Perry and L. Delpit (eds.) Boston: Beacon Press, 29–37.

O'Neil, W. 1998c. "Linguistics for Everyone." Plenary session paper presented at a joint meeting of the Applied Linguistics Association of Australia and the Australian Linguistics Society, www.als.asn.au.

O'Neil, W. 2007. "Project English: Lessons from Curriculum Reform Past," *Language and Linguistics Compass* 1, 612–623.

O'Neil, W. and A. Kitzhaber 1965. *Kernels and Transformations: A Modern Grammar of English, with Exercises by Annabel R. Kitzhaber*. New York: McGraw-Hill.

Orton, H. 1962. *The Survey of English Dialects: An Introduction*. Leeds: E. J. Arnold.

Papers on Linguistics in Education 2005. http://web.mit.edu/waoneil/www/k12/

PBS Frontline: "Testing Our Schools WGBH 2002." www.pbs.org/wgbh/pages/frontline/shows/schools [accessed July 22, 2007]

Pearce, J. 1994. "Schools Council (UK): English Teaching Program." In *Encyclopedia of Language and Linguistics*, R. Asher (ed.) Oxford: Pergamon, 3683–3684.

Perera, K. 1984. *Children's Writing and Reading: Analysing Classroom Language*. Oxford: B. Blackwell in association with A. Deutsch.

Perera, K. 1986. "Grammatical Differentiation Between Speech and Writing in Children aged 8–12." In *The Writing of Writing*, A. Wilkinson (ed.) Milton Keynes: Open University Press, 90–108.

Perera, K. 1987. *Understanding Language*. Sheffield: NAA.

Perera, K. 1990. "Grammatical Differentiation between Speech and Writing in Children Aged 8 to 12." In *Knowledge about Language and the Curriculum*, R. Carter (ed.) London: Hodder and Stoughton, 216–233.

Perera, K. 1994a. "Child Language Research: Building on the Past, Looking to the Future," *Journal of Child Language* 21, 1–7.

Perera, K. 1994b. "National Curriculum: English (England and Wales)." In *Encyclopedia of Language and Linguistics*, R. Asher (ed.) Oxford: Pergamon, 2701–2702.

Perkins, D. N., J. L. Schwartz, M. M. West, and M. S. Wiske (eds.) 1995. *Software Goes to School*. New York and London: Oxford University Press.

Perlstein, L. 2004. "The Issue Left Behind." *The Nation* Online. October 21, 2004. www.thenation.com/doc/20041108/perlstein

Pinker, S. 1994. *The Language Instinct*. New York: Morrow.

Polacco, P. 1994. *Pink and Say*. New York: Philomel.

QCA 1998. *The Grammar Papers*. London: QCA.

Quirk, R. 1962. *The Use of English*. London: Longman.

Quirk, R., S. Greenbaum, G. Leech, and J. Svartvik 1972. *A Grammar of Contemporary English*. London: Longman.

Quirk, R., S. Greenbaum, G. Leech, and J. Svartvik 1985. *A Comprehensive Grammar of the English Language*. London: Longman.

Quirk, R. and A. H. Smith 1959. *The Teaching of English*. London: Martin Secker and Warburg.

RAND Research Brief: "How Educators in Three states are Responding to Standards-based Accountability Under No Child Left Behind." www.rand.org/research_areas/education/ [accessed July 22, 2007]. Based on: Hamilton, L. S., B. M. Stecher, J. A. Marsh, J. S. McCombs, A. Robyn, J. L. Russell, S. Naftel, and H. Barney 2007. *Standards-based Accountability Under No Child Left Behind: Experiences of Teachers and Administrators in Three States*. Santa Monica, CA: RAND Corporation.

Raubinger, F. M., D. L. Piper, H. G. Rowe, and C. K. West 1969. *The Development of Secondary Education*. New York: Macmillan.

Ravitch, D. 1983. *The Troubled Crusade: American Education 1945–1980*. New York: Basic Books. Reprinted as "Reformers, Radicals, and Romantics." In *The Jossey-Bass Reader on School Reform*, San Francisco: Jossey-Bass, 2001, 43–88.

Read, C. 1971. "Pre-school Children's Knowledge of English Phonology," *Harvard Educational Review* 41, 1–34.

Reaser, Jeffrey 2006. "The Effect of Dialect Awareness on Adolescent Knowledge and Attitudes." Ph.D. dissertation. Durham, NC: Duke University.

Reaser, Jeffrey and Carolyn Temple Adger 2007. "Developing Language Awareness Materials for Non-linguists: Lessons Learned from the *Do You Speak American?* Curriculum Development Project," *Language and Linguistic Compass* 1, 155–67.

Reaser, Jeffrey and Walt Wolfram 2005, revised 2007. *Voices of North Carolina: Language and Life from the Atlantic to the Appalachians*. Raleigh, NC: NC State University. Teacher's manual, student workbook, and resource DVDs.

Reaser, J., C. T. Adger, and S. Hoyle 2005. *Curriculum Accompanying the Public Broadcasting Service Series "Do You Speak American?"* Washington, DC: MacNeil-Lehrer Productions. www.pbs.org/speak/education

Resnick, L. B. and D. P. Resnick 1985. "Standards, Curriculum, and Performance: A Historical and Comparative Perspective," *Educational Researcher* 14 (4), 5–20.

Resnick, L. B. and D. P. Resnick 1992. *Assessing the Thinking Curriculum: New Tools for Educational Reform*, in Gifford and O'Conner (eds.) 1992: 37–75.

Rickford, J. R. 1999a. "Language Diversity and Academic Achievement in the Education of African American Students – An Overview of the Issues. In *Making the Connection*, C. Adger, D. Christian, and O. Taylor (eds.) Washington, DC: CAL/Delta.

Rickford, J. R. 1999b. "Using the Vernacular to Teach the Standard." In *African American Vernacular English: Features, Evolution, Educational Implications*. Malden, MA: Blackwell.

Rickford, J. R. and A. E. Rickford 1995. "Dialect readers revisited," *Linguistics and Education* 7 (2), 107–128.

Rickford, J. R. and R. J. Rickford 2000. *Spoken Soul*. New York: John Wiley.

Roberts, P. 1967. *The Roberts English Series*. New York: Harcourt, Brace, and World.

Rury, J. L. 2002. *Education and Social Change: Themes in the History of American Schooling*. Mahwah, NJ: Lawrence Erlbaum Associates.

Schrag, P. 1998 and 2004. *Paradise Lost: California's Experience, America's Future*. Berkeley, CA and London: University of California Press.

Scottish Executive 2002. *National Statement for Improving Attainment of Literacy in Schools*. Edinburgh: Scottish Executive.

Scottish Executive 2003. *Continuing Professional Development: Teaching in Scotland*. Edinburgh: Scottish Executive.

Searchinger, G. (producer) 1999. *The Human Language* (three part series). New York: Equinox Films. http://equinoxfilms.home.mindspring.com/index.html

Seligman, C. R., G. R. Tucker, and W. E. Lambert 1972. "The Effects of Speech Style and Other Attributes on Teachers' Attitudes toward Pupils," *Language in Society* 1, 131–142.

Sharples, M. 1999. *How We Write: Writing as Creative Design*. London: Routledge.

Shiner, L. 2001. *The Invention of Art*. Chicago: University of Chicago Press.

Short, D. J. 1994. "The Challenge of Social Studies for Limited-English-Proficient Students," *Social Education* 581, 36–38.

Shugrue, M. F. 1968. *English in a Decade of Change*. New York: Pegasus.

Shuy, R. W. 1969. "Teacher Training and Urban Language Problems." In *Teaching Standard English in the Inner City*, R. Shuy and R. Fasold (eds.) 1973.

Shuy, R. and R. Fasold (eds.) 1973. *Language Attitudes: Current Trends and Prospects*. Washington, DC: Georgetown University Press.

Simon, John 1981. *Paradigms Lost*. New York: Penguin.

Slack, R. C. 1964. "Round Table: A Report on Project English," *College English* 26 (1), 43–47.

Smalls, I. 2004. *Don't Say Ain't* (C. Bootman, illus.). Watertown, MA: Charlesbridge.

Smitherman, G. 1974. "Soul 'n Style," *The English Journal* 63 (3), 14–15.

Smitherman, G. (ed.) 1981. *Black English and the Education of Black Children and Youth: Proceedings of the National Invitational Symposium on the King Decision*. Detroit, MI: Harlo Press.

Smitherman, G. 2000. *Talkin' That Talk: Language, Culture, and Education in African America*. London: Routledge.

Smitherman, G. and J. Scott 1984. "Language Attitudes and Self-fulfilling Prophecies in the Elementary School." In *The English Language Today*, S. Greenbaum (ed.) Oxford: Pergamon Press.

SOED 1991. *English Language National Guidelines 5–14*. Edinburgh: SOED.

STAR: Standardized Testing and Reporting Program Website: www.startest.org

Stordahl, L. 1969. "Review of the Oregon Curriculum: A Sequential Program in English Language/Rhetoric, Volumes I and II, by Albert R. Kitzhaber," *The English Journal* 58 (3), 461–463.

Stotsky, S. 2000. "The State of Literary Study in National and State English Language Arts Standards: Why it Matters and What Can be Done About it." In Stotsky (ed.) 2000: 237–257.

Stotsky, S. (ed.) 2000. *What's at Stake in the K-12 Standards Wars: A Primer for Educational Policy Makers*. New York: Peter Lang.

Sweetland, J. 2006. "Teaching Writing in the African American Classroom: A Sociolinguistic Approach." Ph.D. dissertation, Stanford University.

Swett, J. 1883. *Methods of Teaching: A Hand-book of Principles, Directions, and Working Models for Common-school Teachers.* (Part II Chapter 2, "Condensed Directions for Teaching Reading.") New York: Harper and Brothers, Franklin Square [accessed on Google books].

Swett, J. 1911. *Public Education in California: Its Origin and Development, with Personal Reminiscences of Half a Century.* New York: American Book Company.

Symcox, L. 2002. *Whose History? The Struggle for National Standards in American Classrooms.* New York: Teachers College Press.

Tanner, D. 1993. "A Nation 'Truly' at Risk," *Phi Delta Kappan*, December, 288–297.

Taylor, O. 1973. "Teachers' Attitudes Toward Black and Nonstandard English as Measured by the Language Attitude Scale." In *Language Attitudes: Current Trends and Prospects*, R. Shuy and R. Fasold (eds.) Washington, DC: Georgetown University Press.

Teidel, L. 1997. "Changing Teacher Education Through Professional Development School Partnerships: A Five Year Follow-up Study," *Teachers College Record* 99 (2), 311–334.

Thelen, H. 1968. "Review: *The Miseducation of American Teachers*, Koerner, James," *International Review of Education* 14 (4), 488–510.

Thompson, G. L. 2004. *Through Ebony Eyes.* San Francisco, CA: Jossey-Bass.

Thorndike, E. L. 1918. "The Nature, Purposes, and General Methods of Measurements of Educational Products." In Whipple (ed.) 1918: Part 2, 216–224.

Tinkel, A. 1988. *Explorations in Language.* Cambridge: Cambridge University Press.

Tolchinsky, L. and C. Cintas 2001. "The Development of Graphic Words in Written Spanish. What Can We Learn from Counterexamples?" In *Developmental Aspects in Learning to Write*, L. Tolchinsky (ed.) London: Kluwer Academic Publishers.

Trachtman, R. 1997. "The Stories of Insiders." In *Making Professional Development Schools Work: Politics, Practice, and Policy*, M. Levine and R. Trachtman (eds.) New York: Teachers College Press.

Trousdale, G. 2006. "Knowledge about Language in the English Classroom in Scotland," *English Teaching: Practice and Critique* 5, 34–43.

Tyack, D. (ed.) 1967. *Turning Points in American Educational History.* Waltham, MA: Blaisdell Publishing Co.

Tyack, D. 1974. *The One Best System: A History of American Urban Education.* Cambridge, MA: Harvard University Press.

Tyack, D. and L. Cuban 1995. *Tinkering Toward Utopia: A Century of Public School Reform.* Cambridge, MA: Harvard University Press.

United States Department of Education 2002. *No Child Left Behind (NCLB) Act of 2001.* Washington, DC: US Government Printing Office.

United States Department of Education 2007. Research and Development Report. "Mapping 2005 State Proficiency Standards onto the NAEP Scales." June 2007. www.nces.ed.gov/nationsreportcard/pdf/studies/2007482.pdf

Updike, J. 1996. "Fine Points" (review of Burchfield's *The New Fowler's Modern English Usage*), *New Yorker* December 23–30, 142–149.

Vaughn-Cooke, A. 1999. "Lessons Learned from the Ebonics Controversy – Implications for Language Assessment." In *Making the Connection: Language and Academic Achievement among African American Students*, C. T. Adger, D. Christian, and O. Taylor (eds.) Washington, DC and McHenry, IL: Center for Applied Linguistics and Delta Systems Co. Inc.

Victorian Curriculum and Assessment Authority 2005. *English Language: Victorian Certificate of Education Study Design.* East Melbourne, Victoria: VCAA. www. vcaa.vic.edu.au/vce/studies/englishlanguage/englangindex.html

Victorian Curriculum and Assessment Authority 2006. *VCE English Language Exam.* East Melbourne, Victoria: VCAA. www.vcaa.vic.edu.au/vce/studies/ englishlanguage/exams.html

Villegas, A. M. and T. Lucas 2007. "The Culturally Responsive Teacher," *Educational Leadership* 64 (6), 28–33.

Wallace, D. F. 2001. "Tense Present: Democracy, English, and the Wars over Usage of *Harper's Magazine*," Review of *A Dictionary of Modern American Usage* by Bryan A. Garner, *Harper's Magazine* April, 39–58.

Walls, R. T., A. H. Nardi, A. M. Minden, and N. von Hoffman 2002. "The Characteristics of Effective and Ineffective Teachers," *Teacher Education Quarterly* Winter, 39–48.

Weaver, C. 1996. *Teaching Grammar in Context.* Portsmouth, NH: Boynton/Cook.

Wheeler, R. S. (ed.) 1999a. *Language Alive in the Classroom.* Westport, CT: Praeger.

Wheeler, R. S. (ed.) 1999b. *Workings of Language: From Prescriptions to Perspectives.* Westport, CT: Praeger.

Wheeler, R. 2005. "Code-switch to Teach Standard English," *English Journal* May, 109–111.

Wheeler, R. 2006. "'My Goldfish Name is Scaley': There's Nothing to Correct," *Doubletake/Points of Entry*, 18–21.

Wheeler, R. 2008. "Becoming Adept at Code-switching," *Educational Leadership: The Journal of the Association for Supervision and Curriculum Development* Vol. 65 No. 7, 54–58.

Wheeler, R. and R. Swords 2006. *Code-switching: Teaching Standard English in Urban Classrooms.* A TRIP book. Urbana, IL: NCTE Press.

Wheeler, R. and R. Swords forthcoming. *Code-switching Lessons: Editing Strategies for Teaching Standard English in Urban Classrooms. A First Hand Curriculum.* Portsmouth, NH: Heinemann.

Whipple, G. M. (ed.) 1918. *The Measurement of Educational Products.* (Seventeenth yearbook of the National Society for the Study of Education.) Bloomington, IL: Public School Publishing Company.

Whiteley, O. 1920. *The Diary of Opal Whiteley.* Intersect Digital Library, University of Oregon. http://intersect.uoregon.edu/opal/, February 1, 2001. (This is a searchable text, where one can find a section on "Opalisms" with cross-references to the diary.)

Wikipedia, the free encyclopedia. "Outcome-based Education" (an article with warning tabs about potential bias). http://en.wikipedia.org/wiki/Outcome-based_education [accessed November 21, 2007].

Willis, G., W. H. Schubert, R. V. Bullough, Jr., C. Kridel, and J. T. Holton (eds.) 1993. *The American Curriculum: A Documentary History.* Westport, CT: Greenwood Press.

Winford, Donald 1976. "Teacher Attitudes Toward Language Varieties in a Creole Community," *International Journal of the Sociology of Language* 8, 45–75.

Wojcik, R. 1993. "Do-Support," *Linguist List 4.933*. November 4, 1993. Eastern Michigan University and Wayne State University. http://linguistlist.org/issues/4/4-933.html

Wolfram, W. 1997. "Dialect Awareness and the Study of Language." In *Students as Researchers of Culture and Language in their Own Communities*, A. Egan-Robertson and D. Bloome (eds.) Cresskill, NJ: Hampton Press, 167–190.

Wolfram, W., C. T. Adger, and D. Christian 1999. *Dialects in Schools and Communities*. Mahwah, NJ: Lawrence Erlbaum Associates.

Wolfram, W., C. T. Adger, and J. Detwyler 1992. *All about Dialects*. Washington, DC: Center for Applied Linguistics.

Wolfram, W. and J. Reaser 2005. *Dialects and the Ocracoke Brogue*. www.duke.edu/web/linguistics/2005OcracokeCurriculum.pdf

Wolfram, W., N. Schilling-Estes, and K. Hazen 1997. *Dialects and the Ocracoke Brogue*. Raleigh, NC: NC State University.

Worthen, B. R., W. R. Blog, and K. L. White 1993. *Measurement and Evaluation in the Schools*. White Plains, NY: Longman Publishing Group.

Wyse, D. 2001. "Grammar. For Writing? A Critical Review of the Evidence," *British Journal of Educational Studies* 49 (4), 411–427.

Zahorik, J. A. 1997. "Encouraging – and Challenging – Students' Understandings." *Educational Leadership* 54 (6), 30–32.

Index

A-level English Language 35, 36–39, 51,
    277–281
  history of 39–44
A-levels 215
a-prefixation 33, 270
Abbott, Edward 268
Aboriginal English 253
Academic English Mastery Program in Los
    Angeles Unified School District 163
accents 236
  English 56–57
  Indiana accent 166
  see also dialect
Achievement Gap Initiative Conference 132
Adam, Michael 211
Adger, Carolyn Temple 94, 163
adjectives 113
Advanced Higher English qualification
    51–52, 61
adverbs 113
African American Vernacular English (AAVE)
    101, 129–148, 236–237
  changing teacher attitudes to 161–174
  existence of 167
  language patterns 273–274
African Americans, achievement gap (problems
    of referring to) 132–133
African languages 198
Alabama, teaching of evolution in 16
All about Dialects (1992) 101
alphabetic writing systems 199
American Association for the Advancement of
    Science (AAAS) 176–177
American Association for Applied Linguistics 89
American Educational Research Association 89
American Federation of Teachers' QuEST
    conference 146
American Indian Language Development
    Institute 31
American Scholar, The 14
American Sign Language 205–206

American Tongues 88, 166
American Vision group 16
anagrams 199
Andrews, R. 120
Anglo-American Seminar on the Teaching of
    English (1966) 81
Anichkov Lyceum 221
animal languages 42
Ann Arbor Black English case 15
Ann, J. 89, 157
Appalachian English 101, 171, 172
/a/-prefixation 33, 270
Applebee, A. N. 110, 115
Arabic 198, 209
Arkansas, teaching of evolution in 16
Arkansas Urban Renewal Zone 139
Armenian 186
  noun pluralization 180
art 19–21
  evaluation of 20–21
Artist in American Society, The (1966) 19
Arts Education Partnership 22
AS Level English Language 278
Asian languages 198
assessment tests 81–82
Association for Language Awareness 42
Association for Scottish Literary Studies
    (ASLS) Language Committee 49,
    54–55
Association for Supervision and Curriculum
    Development (ASCD) 135
Atkin, J. M. 80
Atlantic Monthly, The 14, 265
attitudes, teachers' 161–174
Aussie Rules 254
Australia, literacy standards 107 *see also*
    Victorian Certificate of Education (VCE)
Australian English 253

Barzun, Jacques 19, 21
Bateman, D. R. 117

Baugh, John 88
Beck, Katherine 265
Bede, Elbert 265
Benchmarks On-line 176, 180–181
Bengali 56
Beowulf 245
Berko-Gleason, Jean 187
Biadialectal Communication Program (DeKalb County, Georgia) 163
Black Vernacular English (BVE) 108 *see also* African American Vernacular English
Braddock, R. 107
Breton 269
Brown, Gillian 43
Bruner, Jerome 26, 77
Bryan, William Jennings 17
Bulgaria
    Linguistic Olympiads 213, 221–222, 224–225, 226
    Ministry of Education 221
Bullock Report (1975) 116
Burchfield, Robert 14
Burlak, Svetlana 217
Burridge, K. 66, 73
Bush, George 85

Cajkler, W. 118
California
    assessments 88
    Board of Education 83
    curriculum 87
    education in 81, 83–86
    language study standards 86–87
California Business Roundtable 84
California High School Exit Examination (CAHSEE) 88
California State University Northridge 89
California Subject Examinations for Teachers (CSET) 86
California Teachers of English Learners (CTEL) 87
Cambridge University Press 222
Cameron, D. 116
Carey, Susan 29
Carnegie Foundation of New York 94
Carnegie Mellon University, Language Technologies Institute 223
Carpenter, Charles 15
Carroll, Lewis 260
Carter, Ron 44
Cassell Dictionary of Slang 279
Castle, The 254
Center for Applied Linguistics (CAL) 88, 94, 95
Chaudhury, Dr. Raj 131
Cherokee 101, 275

Chicago Board of Education 78
Chicago Linguistic Society 129
Chinese 186, 198
Chomsky, Carol 29, 189
Chomsky, Noam 27, 178, 204
Christian, D. 163
Chronicle of Higher Education, The 20
Cincinnati (Ohio) 162, 166
Cintas, C. 110
Clayton, Dan 38
Cochran-Smith, M. 153
Cockney rhyming slang online dictionaries 280
code-switching 131, 136–139, 140, 142–144, 147–148, 240–243
    children's literature and 242–243
Code-switching: Teaching Standard English in Urban Classrooms 139
cognitive flexibility 138
cognitive models of development 109
Collins, P. 64
Commission for Teacher Preparation and Licensing 84
Commission on Teacher Credentialing (CTC) 84
Committee for Language Awareness in Scottish Schools (CLASS) 49–50, 53–54
    website 59–60
Committee of Ten 79
Committee on Language in the School Curriculum 106
communicative competence 46
contrastive analysis 131, 138, 139, 141–143, 144–146, 148, 162, 163–164
Copernicus 91
Cottage Grove Sentinel 265
creationism 16–19, 21
creative writing 40
critical teaching moments 172
Crowther Report (1959) 40–41
Crystal, David 41, 48
culture and language 274–276
curriculum
    development of (America) 77–83
    development of (California) 87
    Do You Speak American? 93–100, 163
    K-12 13, 77, 79, 84–85, 189–191, 201–202
    language arts 163
    Voices of North Carolina dialect awareness 93, 100–104, 272–276
    see also National Curriculum
Curriculum for Excellence, A (ACfE) 49
Curzan, Anne 211
Czerniewska, P. 117

Dagur islenzkrar tungu (Icelandic Language Day) 175
Darling-Hammond, L. 82
Darrow, Clarence 17
Dartmouth 81
declarative sentences 74–75
Denham, Kristin 205, 206, 235, 244–246
Dent, Susie 279
determiners, overuse of 269–270
dialect 15, 102, 172, 235–237, 273–276
    awareness 162, 163–165, 190
    British and American comparison 199
    English 56–57, 60
    grammar 60
    prejudice 23
    Russian 220
    see also African American Vernacular English
Dialects and the Ocracoke Brogue (1997) 101
Dictionary of Modern American Usage 15
Dictionary of the Scots Language 60
Don't Say Ain't 242
do-support 267–269
Do You Speak American? 88, 93–100, 163
"drill and kill" writing instruction 93, 102

Eats, Shoots and Leaves 247
Ebonics 15, 21, 140, 181, 204, 236
Economic and Social Research Council 111
Education Technology Center 29–31
Educational Leadership 135
educational standards
    Do You Speak American? and 95–100
    Voices of North Carolina curriculum and 102–104
Ehri, L. C. 108
Einstein, Albert 224
Eisenhower, Dwight G., President 79
Elizabethan English 268
Elliott, G. L. 109–110, 111
England
    changes in the education system 35–36
    literacy standards 107
Englang 39
English
    informal/formal 136–143, 236
    use of *do* 268
    see also Standard English
English for teachers of English to Speakers of Other Languages (ESOL) 150
    professional development 150–159
English Language Arts, The (1952) 15, 21
English Language Victoria Certificate of Education Study Design (VCAA) 70, 71
English Literature 39, 40

etymology online 279
Eugene, Oregon, Linguistic Olympiad in 222–223
Everyday English 136–143
evolution, teaching of 15–19, 21
exclamative sentences 74

Fabb, N. 184, 189
Facebook 252
Fadiman, Anne 154
Farnon, N. 108
Fearn, L. 108
Fisher, Senator Hugo 84
Flatland 268
Flesch, Rudolph 83
Flossie and the Fox 242
Fluency Through TPR (Total Physical Response) Story Telling 154
Fly Taal 198
Fogel, H. 108
Folsom, Franklin 13
Footy Show, The 254
Ford Foundation 94
foreign-language teaching 40, 46–47
formal/informal language 136–143, 236, 241–243, 249–250
Fought, Carmen 88
Fowler, Henry Watson 14
Franklin, Benjamin 77–78
Freeborn, Denis 36
French 40, 46, 47, 55–56, 78, 198, 250
    syntax 267–268
Friedman, Kinky 94
Frohnmayer, John 20, 21
Fuhrman, S. H. 81
Future of Linguistics, The (2007) 204

Galileo 91
Gallagher, M. C. 80
Garner, Bryan 15
Garrett, Robert Max 267
gender, linguistic representation of 237–239
Generating Expectations for Student Achievement (GESA) 155
generative grammar 25, 204
German 40, 46, 47, 78
Gladstone, Diane 131
Gladwell, Malcolm 154
Gleason, H. 116
Goals 2000: Educate America Act 81, 85
Goodluck, H. 189
Goodman, Y. 172
Gordon, E. 118
Gove, Phillip, 14–15
Graham, S. 107

grammar 13, 41, 63–65
  dialect 60
  as error correction 116
  explicit 118
  generative 25, 204
  negative attitudes to 72
  new approach to 241
  teachers' knowledge of 43–44
Grammar for Writing 107
grammar patterns
  African American 129, 135–136
  comparison and contrasting of 138
  informal English 136–138, 141–143
"grammar skills" 102
grammar teaching 106–108, 118, 143–146
  demise of 39–40, 63–65, 143
  traditional approach to 247–248
grammatical choices 264–271
Graymill Training Programs 155
Greek 77–78, 207
  myths and word origins 262
Green, Jonathon 279
Guardian, The 38, 278–279

Haertel, E. 82
Halliday, Michael 41, 42, 48
Halpern, Mark 14
Hamlet 268
Hancock, C. 106, 116
Harpin, W. 110, 113
Harris, Neil 19
Harry Potter novels 59, 199
Harvard University 29–31, 77, 132
Haswell, R. H. 111
Hawaiian language 198, 215
Herman, J. L. 82
Herschensohn, Professor Julia
Hicks, Ray 171
Higher English Critical Essay paper 51
Hilbert, Vi 235
Hillocks, G. R. 107
Hindi 205–206
Hislam, J. 118
Hispanic English 101
Hoff, Benjamin 265, 267
*Holler If You Hear Me: The Education of a
  Teacher and His Students* 154
Hollo, C. 64
Holy Virgin Mary, The 20
Honda, Maya 29, 30–32, 181, 184, 189, 197
Horan, A. 64
How English Works (2006) 211
Huddleston, R. 64
Hughes, Langston 235–237, 242
human communication 163

"Human Language, The" 88
Hungarian 192, 245
*Hunger of Memory: The Education of Richard
  Rodriguez* 154
Hunt, K. 110, 115
Hymes, Dell 46

Iceland 175
imperative sentences 74–75
Improving America's Schools Act (IASA) 81–82
Indiana accent 166
inflections, overgeneralized 270
informal/formal register 236
"intelligent design" 16, 21
International Kangaroo Contests 220
International Olympiad in Linguistics 213,
  224–226
International Reading Association 89
  standards 95, 97–100
interrogative sentences 74–75
Invention of Art, The (2001) 19
Isaac, A. 73
is-contraction 30, 34
Italian-American gangster online dictionaries 280

Jabberwocky 196–197, 207, 260
Jackendoff, Ray 209
Japanese 198, 205–206
Johnson, N. K. 109–110, 111
Junior Christian Endeavor 265

K-12 schools 16–22
  curriculum 13, 77, 79, 84–85, 189–191,
    201–202
  relevance of linguistics in 159
Kansas Board of Education 16
Keith, George 36
Kenny 254
kernel sentences 27
*Kernels and Transformations: A Modern
  Grammar of English* 27
Keyser, Beth 209
Keyser, Samuel Jay 189, 209
King School decision 21
Kingman Committee 45
Kinkade, Thomas 20
Kitzhaber, Albert 25, 26
Kitzhaber, Annabel 27
Knafo, Robert 19
knowledge about language (KAL) 42–46, 65,
  67, 73, 106, 175, 176
  and foreign languages 47
  in Scotland 49–61
Kolln, M. 106, 116
Kress, G. 109, 110

Labov, William 88
language
  ethical use of 237–239
  knowledge about the structure of 73
language acquisition 42, 181, 187
  and explicit teaching 42–43
Language and Linguistics Compass 211
language arts curriculum, promotion of
  language awareness in 163
Language Attitude Scale (LAS) 165
language attitude survey 162, 168, 169–170
language awareness 42, 47, 65, 67, 73,
  163–165
Language Book, The (1963) 13
language change 14–15, 186, 198, 269,
  277–280
language discrimination 166–167, 249, 276
language games 199 *see also* word games
Language in Textual Analysis (CPD course) 56–57
Language Instinct, The 247
Language into Languages Teaching (LILT)
  project 55–56
language misconceptions 180–181
language patterns 276
language prejudice 171, 172, 181
Language Report 279
language systems 38
language variation 14–15, 199, 249–250,
  272–276
languages of the world 198
Larson, Edward 17
Latin 77–78, 189, 207
  teaching 40–41
Leavis, F. R. 30, 34
lexical choice 112–113
Liberman, Mark 204–205, 211
LINC (Language in the Curriculum) 44
linguistic analysis, using tools of 247–248
linguistic anthropology 204
linguistic bias 272–276
linguistic diversity 208
linguistic enrichment 234
linguistic models of development 109–111
Linguistic Olympiads 213–226
linguistic patterns, unusual 266–270
Linguistic Society of America 31, 89, 106, 201,
  204, 211
Linguistic Survey of Scotland 57
linguistics
  attitudes to 13–15
  descriptive 13–15
  historical 204
  influence in English schools 41–42
  as an intellectual and social endeavor
    177–178

need for/relevance in schools 158–159
  promoting 247
Linguistics for Everyone (2009) 211
linguistics illiteracy 181
Linguistics in Education workshop (2007) 245,
  246, 248, 249
linguistics literacy 175–188
  as science literacy 176–177
Live! 278
Loban, W. 110
Lobeck, Anne 190, 200, 244, 257, 258,
  260–263
Lochhead, Liz 60
logographic writing systems 199
Lomonosov Tournament 220
London, language use in 277
Looking for Alibrandi 254
Louisiana, creationism in 16
ludlings 199
Lumbee English 101
Lushootseed 192–193, 205–206,
  234–235
Lytle, S. L. 153

MacNeil, Robert 88, 93–94
Man: A Course of Study 77
Mandarin 186, 198
Mapplethorpe, Robert 21
Mar, J. 64
Marzano, Robert 147
Massachusetts 77–78
  Department of Education 189
Massey, A. J. 109–110, 111
Matsumura, Molleen 17–19
McCarty, Teresa 154
McKibben, Sadie 268
mental grammar 175–188
metacognition 138–139
metalanguage 73, 254
Micciche, L. 121
Michie, Gregory 154
Michigan, teaching of evolution in 16
Michoacan Aztec 192, 205–206
Middle English 205–206, 268
Moore, Andrew 39
morphemes 261–262
morphology 207, 208, 280
  problems 192–194
morphophonology 182–187
morphosyntax lessons 194–197
Moscow and St. Petersburg
  Linguistic Olympiads 213, 219,
    224–226
  16th (1979) 214
  26th (1995) 217

Moscow State Institute for History and
    Archives 219
Moscow State University 219
"Mother to Son" 235–237
Mulder, Jean 59, 62, 66, 88, 251
"My Goldfish Name is Scaley" 132
My Space 252

Nahuatl 192
names, origins of 262
naming 59
National Assessment of Educational Progress
    (NAEP) 81, 82, 84, 107
National Center for Science Education 17, 22
National Commission on Excellence in
    Education (NCEE) (1983) 81
National Commission on Writing (NCW)
    Report (2003) 107, 116
National Council for the Social Studies (NCSS)
    93, 95–97
National Council of Teachers 189
National Council of Teachers of English
    (NCTE) 15, 25, 89, 91, 93,
    106–107, 211
    standards 95, 97–100
National Council of Teachers of
    Mathematics 81
National Curriculum (English) 44–46
    knowledge about language in 50
    revised 47
National Education Association (NEA) 78, 79
National Education Goals Panel (NEGP) 81
National Endowment for the Arts 20, 21
National History Standards Project 77
National Literacy Strategy 107, 118
National Science Foundation, funding 79, 80,
    131, 200–201, 206, 211, 223, 244
National Teachers Association 78
Native American languages 234–235 see also
    Cherokee; Lushootseed
Nature of Science/Scientific Theory and
    Method Project 29
Netherlands 213
New England /r/-retention and /r/-intrusion 33,
    177–178, 181
New English 25
New Fowler's Modern English Usage 14
New York state, certification of teachers in
    149–150
    college of arts and sciences 149–150,
    151, 156
    schools of education 149–150, 152–153, 156
New York Times 89, 181
Nicaraguan English 186
Nicaraguan plurals 261

No Child Left Behind Act (2001) 79, 82, 85, 107
    tests 129, 133, 148
North American Computational Linguistics
    Olympiad (NACLO) 223
noun phrase pluralization 32, 183–187
nouns
    plural 183–187
    regular 176
Nuffield Foundation 41

Oakland Ebonics controversy 15, 21, 140,
    181, 204
Ocracoke Island (NC) 102
Ofilii, Chris 21
Ofsted 117
Old English 106, 198, 199, 205–206, 268
Olsen, Meredith 188
Olympiad in Mathematical Linguistics 221
O'Neil, Wayne 30, 81, 181, 184, 189, 197
Oregon Curriculum Study Center 26–28
Outer Banks English 101
Oxford English Dictionary (online) 279

Panel, The 254
Papers on Linguistics in Education (2005) 33
Paradigms Lost (1981) 14
parsing 269
Peng, L. 78, 157
Pennsylvania, teaching of evolution in 16
Perera, Catherine 45, 109, 110–111, 113,
    116, 118
Perin, D. 107
philosophy 204
phonetics/phonology knowledge, importance of
    193–194
phonology 208
    problems 184, 193–194
Physical Science Study Committee 80
Pink and Say 242
Pink Stinks game 199
Pinker, Steven 247
Pippin, David 31–34, 178, 182, 189, 197, 208
Piss Christ 20
Place to be Navajo, A: Rough Rock and the
    Struggle for Self-Determination in
    Indigenous Schooling 154
Plungian, Vladimir 217
plural nouns 260–261
    formation of 183–187
plurals, non-standard 280
poetry vs. prose 270
Polish 56
politeness 73
Prada Deathcamp 20
prescriptivism 41–42

Preston, Dennis 88
Primary National Strategy 107
problem set approach 29–30, 32, 175–176, 182–187
problem-solving activities 192–200
problem-solving competitions 213–226
process models of development 109
process writing 92
Programme in Linguistics and English Teaching 41
Programme of Study for Foreign Languages 47
Project 2061 176–177
Project English 25–28, 189
Project SMART 150
psychology 204
Putnam's, G. P. Sons 265

Qualifications and Curriculum Authority (QCA) 118
question formation 32
Quiche 192
Quirk, Randolph 41, 48

Ravitch, D. 80, 81
Ray, Blaine 154
Read, Charles 193
Reading/Language Arts Framework for California Public Schools (1999) 85, 87
reading proficiency 257–258
Reading Wars 84
Reaser, J. 189
regular nouns 176
Rickford, A. E. 173
Rickford, J. R. 173
Roberts English Series, The 24
Rodriguez, Richard 154
role playing 253
Rottweiler syndrome 117
Rove 254
runes 199
Russian Bear Cub 220
Russian State University for the Humanities 219, 220
Ryan, Leo J. 85

Sach, Tom 20
Sadock, Jerry 140
Salish language family 234–235
Samoan 192, 215
Santiago, Esmeralda 154
Scholastic Aptitude Test (SAT) 81, 82, 215
science 182
Scopes, John, trial of 17, 21
Scotland
    education system in 50–52
    knowledge about language teaching 49–61

Scott, Fred Newton 91
Scottish Language Dictionaries 60
Seattle Country Day School 31
Sedgwick, Ellery 265
Seely, Contee 154
semantics 208
Senate Bill 2042 85–86
sentence structures 113–115
sentences
    communicative functions 73–75
    learning to form 260
    linguistic development and 110–111, 113–115
Serrano, Andres 20
Shakespeare 252, 281
Shakespearean Grammar, A 268
Sharples, M. 121
Shiner, Larry 19
Simon, John 14
The Singing Creek Where the Willows Grow: The Mystical Nature Diary of Opal Whiteley (1994) 264, 265–271
Skype 209
slang 38–39
    African American Vernacular as 167
    London youth 278–280
Slangsta Rap 278–279
social groups, inclusion in 235–237
social studies, language studies within 101–102
sociolinguistic diversity, teacher training on 161–174
sociolinguistics 24–25, 91–105, 249–250
Sounds Familiar 56–57
Sounds of Aus, The 254
Spanish 78, 150, 154, 186, 270
    in North Carolina 101
speech/writing differences 109–110
spelling 208
    invented 270
Spiderman 59
Spirit Catches You and You Fall Down: A Hmong Child, Her American Doctors, and the Collision of Two Cultures, The 154
St. Francis Xavier College 277
St. Louis Public Schools 78
St. Petersburg State University 219
Standard Assessment Task 107
Standard English (SE) 108
    teaching to vernacular speakers 131–148, 162
Stanford–Binet Intelligence tests 215
Stanford University 89
State Council of Higher Education of Virginia (SCHEV) 131

State University of New York 150, 155
Stordahl, L. 28
"Story of English, The" 88
*The Story of Opal: A Journal of an
    Understanding Heart,* (1920) 265
Stotsky, S. 88
structure of language 73
"struggling readers" 194, 197
Stubbs, Mike 43
subordination 113–115
*Summer for the Gods: The Scopes Trial
    and America's Continuing Debate
    of Science and Religion* (1997) 17
Summer Heights High 254
Survey of English Dialects (1961) 57
Swahili 198, 215
Sweetland, Julie 89, 92, 105
Swett, John 83
Swords, Rachel 135, 138, 139, 146–148,
    240, 242
syllabic writing systems 199
Symcox, L. 77
syntax 207, 208

Tartuffe (Molière) 60
Taylor, O. 165
teachers
    attitudes 161–174
    knowledge 156–158, 255
        grammatical 43–44
        "in practice" 153
        linguistic subject 118–120, 158–159
        of phonetics/phonology, importance of
            193–194
    linguistic awareness 154
    professional development 26–27, 43–44,
        54–57, 150–159, 161–174, 206–208
Teachers as Scholars 31
Teachers for a New Era 89
Teaching English to Speakers of Other
    Languages (TESOL) 150
    professional development 150–159
Teaching Standard English as a Second
    Dialect 139
Teachit 39
Teachling 208, 209, 210
Tebbit, Norman 106
Technology Enhanced Learning of English and
    Science in Middle School (TELES) 131
Technology Enhanced Learning of Science
    (TELS) 131
teenspeak 253
text messaging (SMS) 58, 252
textbooks 71–73, 75, 88–89
texts, analysis of 38, 67

thematic variety 115
"Theme for English B" 237
Thomas, Caroline 62, 66, 73
Thorndike, E. L. 79
Tinkel, Tony 36
*Tipping Point: How Little Things Can Make a
    Big Difference, The* 154
Tohono O'odham 269–270
Tolchinsky, L. 110–111
transformational grammar 26
Trousdale, G. 51
Truss, Lynne 247
Tswana 198
Tufts University 245
    workshop (2006) 209
Turkish 192, 205–206
Tyler, Dr. Ralph 79

Unger, C. 189
Union of Bulgarian Mathematicians 221
United States, literacy standards 107
Universalteacher 39
University of Chicago 79
University of Edinburgh 49, 53, 56, 58
University of Glasgow 54, 55
University of Oregon 222, 265
    English Department 25–28
University of Strathclyde 55
University of Washington 267
Updike, John 14
Upper Skagit tribe 235
urban dictionary 279
US Office of Education 189
US Olympiad 226
usage 14–15
Uspensky, Vladimir 219

Valenzuela, Pilar 223
values, indication of 237–239
Victoria (Australia) 62
    Board of Studies 63
Victorian Association for the Teaching of
    English 255
Victorian Certificate of Education (VCE) 63,
    251–256
    English Language course 62–63, 67–68,
        75, 88
    benefits of studying 252–253
    choosing to study 251–252
    study design 70
    teaching of 253–254
    textbooks 71–73
Victorian Curriculum and Assessment
    Authority 255
Virginia Pilot 139

Virginia Standards of Learning Writing
    test 243
vocabulary 208
    development of 112–113
    see also words
Voices of North Carolina dialect curriculum 93,
    100–104, 272–276
voicing assimilation 187

Wall Street Journal 89
Wallace, David Foster 15
wanna-contraction 30, 176, 178, 179, 180
Wawer, Sara 62
Webster's Dictionary of American Usage 14
Webster's Third New International Dictionary
    (1961) 15, 21
Western Washington University 246
    Linguistics in Education workshop
        (WWULiE) 209
    Teaching Partnership Project 200–201,
        205–206
Wheeler, R. 89, 135, 240, 242
Wheelock College 31, 32
When I Was Puerto Rican 154
Whiteley, Charles Edward "Ed" 265
Whiteley, Opal 264–271
Why Johnny Can't Read 83
Widdowson, Henry 43
Wilson, Tony 280
WISE science education platform 131

Wolf, Maryanne 209
Wolfram, Walt 24, 88, 101, 102, 131,
    163, 189
Woods Hole (Cape Cod) 77
word chains 199
word games 194–197, 199–200
words 112–113
    content and function 259
    widening the use of 269
    see also vocabulary
World Language Club 208, 209, 210
writing
    adolescent 111–112
    approaches to teaching 92–93
    formal academic, help with 240–243
    teacher assessment of 117–118
writing development 109–121
writing maturity 110–111
writing proficiency 258
writing skills, essay 254
writing systems 199
written text, linguistic approach to 57
written word games 199–200
wug test 187
Wyse, D. 107

Yes Prime Minister 254

Zhurinsky, Alfred 219
Zidonis, F. J. 117